CASES IN
RETAIL MANAGEMENT

CASES IN

RETAIL MANAGEMENT

Edited by Peter J. McGoldrick

Littlewoods Professor of Retailing
in the Manchester School of Management
and the Manchester Business School

PITMAN
PUBLISHING

Pitman Publishing
128 Long Acre, London WC2E 9AN

A Division of Longman Group UK Limited

First published in 1994

© Longman Group UK Ltd 1994

Copyright © Case 8 Michael Collins 1994
Copyright © Case 10 Gerry Johnson 1994
Copyright © Case 14 Andre Tordjman 1994
Copyright © Case 16 Nigel Holden 1994

British Library Cataloguing in Publication Data
A CIP catalogue record for this book can be obtained
from the British Library.

ISBN 0 273 60198 9

Typeset by 🗡 Tek-Art, Addiscombe, Croydon, Surrey
Printed and bound in Great Britain by Bell and Bain Ltd

Contents

Preface

It is fair to say that if you complain about a problem repeatedly, then it is time to do something about it. Broadly speaking, this is a fitting description of the origin of this book. Like many other retail educators, I frequently despaired at the lack of up-to-date, relevant cases to support courses in retail management. The study of retailing having grown apace, not only has this dearth become all the more noticeable, but it has also become increasingly unacceptable to rely upon cases with which few managers or students can identify.

Two factors have worked simultaneously to accentuate the need for quality case studies. First, the growing number of retailing modules available – full degree courses in some institutions – affords more time for the use of the case study method. Secondly, there has been a shift in the style of retail management education encouraging more student participation. This has been prompted in part by new European retailing textbooks, which reduce the need to formally 'teach' the subject matter. Equally, such a 'hands-on' style of education is more appropriate to the growing number of MBA programmes and courses for students with retail experience.

The principal aim of this project was to produce a comprehensive collection of high-quality cases, sufficiently diverse to support a wide range of retailing courses. In pursuit of this, cases have been designed to be worked at several different levels and on different timescales. Additional readings, thought-provoking questions and further suggestions for case instructors help to achieve this 'multi-level' characteristic. Equally valuable in today's retail environment is the international substance of the cases and the ease with which the lessons can be transferred across national borders. Even when a case relates to just one country, its international relevance is frequently irrefutable.

The option of producing this book single handedly was rejected immediately; a case book was needed now, not in years to come! Furthermore, I would be flattering myself to suggest that I could achieve the required blend of quality and diversity. Having been fortunate enough to make the acquaintance of most of Europe's retailing specialists over the years, the second option, that of involving the leading authorities in each field, was infinitely preferable. Despite the many pressures upon their time, the vast majority generously agreed to participate. Everyone was in agreement that such a collection of cases was long overdue.

The general specification and individual challenges posed were quite demanding. How do you build a case study around a particular management issue, a particular technique or even a retailing theory? As you will see, the collective response to these challenges is a diverse set of cases, in terms of their topics, companies, countries and styles. It is hoped that this diversity will heighten interest and stimulate response. It would be invidious to thank specific contributors here; a list of their names and institutions follows this preface. My grateful thanks are extended to them all for the considerable time and trouble expended on their cases.

I would also like to acknowledge the detailed attention given to every case by my associate editor, Erica Betts. Without her careful and timely work on the drafts, this project could not have met the publishing deadlines. I would also like to thank Mary O'Mahony, who has helped me for many years and is now my full-time secretary. Bringing together all these contributions and the associated notes has been a task of major proportions. We are also indebted to the resourceful Peter Lythgoe, who converted even the most novel of computer disks to a single format. Our work on this project has benefited from the enthusiasm and professionalism of the editorial staff at Pitman Publishing, especially Jennifer Mair, Liz Rawlings, Colette Rouhier and Simon Lake.

Peter J. McGoldrick
June 1993

List of contributors

EDITOR
Professor Peter J. McGoldrick, Littlewoods Professor of Retailing in the Manchester Business School and the Manchester School of Management, PO Box 88, Manchester M60 1QD

ASSOCIATE EDITOR
Erica Betts, Manchester School of Management, UMIST, PO Box 88, Manchester M60 1QD.

Nicholas Alexander, Lecturer in Retail Management, Department of Management Studies for Tourism and Hotel Industries, University of Surrey, Guildford, Surrey GU2 5XH

Dr David Bennison, Department of Retailing and Marketing, Manchester Metropolitan University, Aytoun Street, Manchester M1 3GH

Neil Botten, Director of the Strategic Change Research Group, London Management Centre, University of Westminster, 35 Marylebone Road, London NW1 5LS

Dr Sophia Bowlby, Department of Geography, Univeristy of Reading, Whiteknights, PO Box 227, Reading RG6 2AB

Adelina Broadbridge, Lecturer, Institute for Retail Studies, University of Stirling, Stirling FK9 4LA

Professor Stephen Brown, Faculty of Business and Management, University of Ulster at Coleraine, Coleraine, Co. Londonderry BT52 1SA

Dr Steve Burt, Senior Lecturer, Institute of Retail Studies, University of Stirling, Stirling FK9 4LA

Dr Francis Buttle, Institute of Services Management, Manchester Business School, Booth Street West, Manchester M15 6PB

Dr Chris Carr, Senior Fellow in Strategic Management, Manchester Business School, Booth Street West, Manchester M15 6PB

Dr Leslie de Chernatony, Reader in Marketing, City University Business School, Frobisher Crescent, Barbican Centre, London EC2Y 8HB

Professor Martin Christopher, Cranfield School of Management, Cranfield Institute of Technology, Cranfield, Beds MK43 0AL

Dr Ian Clarke, Department of Retailing and Marketing, Manchester Metropolitan University, Aytoun Street, Manchester M1 3GH

Colin Clarke-Hill, School of Business, University of Huddersfield, Queensgate, Huddersfield HD1 3DH

Michael J. S. Collins, Associate Professor and Executive Director, Australian Centre for Retail Studies, Monash University, PO Box 197, Caulfield East, Victoria 3145, Australia

Professor Gary Davies, Post Office Counters Professor of Retailing, Manchester Business School, Booth Street West, Manchester M15 6PB

Dr Ross Davies, Director, Oxford Institute of Retail Management, Templeton College, Kennington, Oxford OX1 5NY

Stuart Eliot, Lecturer, Manchester School of Management, UMIST, PO Box 88, Manchester M60 1QD

Dr John Fernie, Senior Lecturer in Marketing, Dundee Business School, Dundee Institute of Technology, Dudhope Castle, Dundee DD3 6HF

David Foot, Department of Geography, University of Reading, Whiteknights, PO Box 227, Reading RG6 2AB

Steven Greenland, Lecturer, Manchester School of Management, UMIST, PO Box 88, Manchester M60 1QD

Dr Nigel J. Holden, Lecturer, Manchester School of Management, UMIST, PO Box 88, Manchester M60 1QD

Malcolm Hughes, Managing Consultant, Watermill Consultants, 24 Watermill Lane, Hertford SG14 3LB

Professor Gerry Johnson, Professor of Strategic Management, Cranfield School of Management, Cranfield, Bedford MK43 0AL

Professor David Kirby, Booker Professor in Entrepreneurship, Centre for Entrepreneurship in the Service Sector, Durham University Business School, Mill Hill Lane, Durham DH1 3LB

Dr Barbara Lewis, Senior Lecturer, Manchester School of Management, UMIST, PO Box 88, Manchester M60 1QD

Dr Mick Marchington, Senior Lecturer, Manchester School of Management, UMIST, PO Box 88, Manchester M60 1QD

Professor Lluís Martínez-Ribes, Department of Marketing Management, ESADE, Av. de Pedralbea, 60-62, E-08034 Barcelona, Spain

Dr Alan Mitton, Department of Business Studies, Manchester Metropolitan University, Aytoun Street, Manchester M1 3GH

Helen Peck, Cranfield School of Management, Cranfield Institute of Technology, Cranfield, Beds MK43 0AL

Professor Luca Pellegrini, CESCOM, Università Bocconi, Via Filippetti 9, 20122 Milano, Italy

Barry Quinn, Faculty of Business and Management, University of Ulster at Coleraine, Coleraine, Co. Londonderry BT52 1SA

Dr Jonathan Reynolds, Fellow in Retail Marketing, Oxford Institute of Retail Management, Templeton College, Kennington, Oxford OX1 5NY

Terry Robinson, School of Business, University of Huddersfield, Queensgate, Huddersfield HD1 3DH

Nitin Sanghavi, Director, Centre for Business Research, Senior Fellow, Manchester Business School, Booth Street West, Manchester M15 6PB

Professor Leigh Sparks, Institute for Retail Studies, University of Stirling, Stirling FK9 4LA

Professor Andre Tordjman, HEC Management, Groupe HEC, 78351 Jouy-en-Josas, Cedex, France

Catherine Woodman, Manchester School of Management, UMIST, PO Box 88, Manchester M60 1QD

Steven Worthington, Manchester Business School, Booth Street West, Manchester M15 6PB

Introduction

Peter McGoldrick

Manchester School of Management and Manchester Business School

The case study method

The objective of the case study method is to promote a greater degree of realism in management education. Each case details a specific business situation. It is your responsibility to develop solutions to the problems contained within, ideally drawing upon relevant theories and principles to enhance the quality of decisions and recommendations. Thus by bridging possible gaps between theory and 'real world' retail management decision making, the case study method addresses an all too common complaint.

The cases have been designed to be suitable for use across a broad spectrum of courses. While being accessible to relative newcomers, they still pose a challenge for those at later stages of study or with experience in retail management posts. The additional references, for example, provide the means to delve further into the underlying principles, while library 'clippings files' can give additional insight into problems. Remember, however, that decisions taken in parallel 'real' cases may have been neither the most creative nor the best possible solution.

The cases are flexible in terms of the time they require, accommodating timetables and the different emphasis placed on casework by lecturers. Thus cases can be used in single hour seminar sessions while also being suitable material for major course assessment. You should be guided by your instructor as to the level of case research, analysis or other preparation anticipated.

Those less familiar with the case study method are likely to encounter a few initial difficulties. The scope of the case study analysis may at first inspection appear limited, then appear almost infinite. The problem may not be clearly defined and rarely is there a unique or 'best solution'. One of the most frequent complaints from case study users is that the information is incomplete, irrelevant and/or ambiguous. Rather than being a flaw, this does in fact reflect the majority of real world decision-making situations! Although the information provided may be supplemented in some cases, in the final analysis it is usually necessary to develop and defend certain assumptions and extrapolations.

Frustration may also be expressed that the time taken to 'solve' a case may not appear cost effective, in terms of the facts or concepts learnt. This frustration may be deepened by the refusal of the instructor to teach the case, or even initially to point out the key issues. It cannot be denied that a whole host of facts and concepts can be 'taught' in a 90-minute lecture, whereas the analysis of a case may reach only the very earliest of stages within this time. The beneficial difference is that the case study method develops a range of skills and can also promote greater understanding and retention of the concepts utilised. If a lecturer describes a concept, you will dutifully write it down and hope to remember it for your examination. To use a concept it is implicit that you understand it; furthermore, a concept used to solve a case becomes a part of your decision-making armoury.

The skills developed through using the case study method include *analytical* skills, acquired in the classification, organisation and evaluation of information/data. Skills of *application* will also be developed, through applying various concepts, techniques and principles, for example, to a retail location problem. *Creativity* is also an essential skill in helping to identify alternative possibilities and solutions. Skills of *self-analysis* can also be developed during case discussion, in that you may come to recognise the systems and values upon which your judgements are based. Both during group discussions and presentations, skills of *communication* are clearly essential. Given that each case within this book has been prepared by an expert in the subject area, you will also acquire a great deal of knowledge about the topics while working on these cases.

The cases are grouped within nine parts to help support the various components of a typical course in retail management. This should not be taken to suggest that cases in Part Six are *only* involved with merchandise management problems. Neither of course should it be assumed that operational problems can be ignored until Part Eight, nor 'people' problems until Part Nine. To a greater or lesser degree, all the cases raise strategic problems, not only those in Parts Two and Three. Similarly, operational and human factors pervade every case. This structure simply intends to guide the selection of cases, helping to ensure diversity and a comprehensive coverage of retail management issues.

Framework for case analysis

While not wishing to stifle the creative element of case study analysis, most people find some form of systematic or sequential approach helpful and beneficial in the great majority of cases. The time allocated to each stage will vary according to the nature and complexity of the case.

In an early collection of American cases, Thompson and Dalrymple (1969) suggest a four-step framework, namely:

1. Define the problem.
2. Formulate the alternatives.
3. Analyse the alternatives.
4. Recommend a solution.

This type of approach was subsequently developed by Reynolds (1980).

One of the most detailed expositions of a seven-step approach to case analysis was provided by Easton (1992), which in outline involves the following stages.

1. Understanding the situation

It is essential to know the case thoroughly; one reading is unlikely to give the familiarity required. There is always the danger on first reading the case of leaping impulsively to some obvious, and equally misguided, solution or conclusion. Very often a full understanding of the case and the information given does not emerge until you have done some further work. You may need to collate numerical or other information from various parts of the case, and even at this early stage, you might have to extrapolate from the information provided. Prior to doing this you must, of course, critically evaluate the value, relevance and accuracy of the information given.

2. Diagnosing problem areas

In some cases the problems will be hard to identify. In others they may be plain to see – but be wary of 'red herrings'! A difficulty highlighted in the case may only be a symptom of a far more serious problem. A great deal of time can be wasted in case analysis if you fail to define the problems accurately; for this reason, you are advised not to rush this stage in your desire to reach the more constructive or creative stages. For ease of use the book has been split into nine functional areas; you should not assume that the problems will only relate to the one aspect of retail management. If a number of different problems are diagnosed, it is advisable to order them in a logical way. They may be ranked according to importance, divided into strategic problems and tactical problems, fundamental problems and symptoms, and so on.

3. Creating alternative solutions

Developing solutions should be tackled in a similar way to that used for identifying problems. A bank of possible solutions should be developed and structured according to the problems they address. This is the key creative process in the course of the analysis. All other things being equal, the greater the number of solutions produced, the better the final choice is likely to be. At this stage, solutions should be of a general nature – for example, possible solutions to a problem of poor image in one commodity area may include improved advertising or staff training. The specifics of these improvements do not need to be considered at this stage.

The alternative solutions must then be ranked in terms of their level: whether they address strategic or tactical issues. This ranking is necessary since your choice of strategic solutions will invariably have significant repercussions on your tactical plans. Thus the main strategic alternatives must be examined first, and only once a decision has been made among them can the lesser tactical alternatives be considered.

4. Predicting outcomes

The next stage in the analysis is to choose between these alternative solutions. An effective evaluation will meet the following requirements:

- Ensuring that the ramifications of a solution are predicted and understood.
- Placing a value on the predicted outcomes.

Each proposed solution will have consequences extending far beyond the problem it aspires to remedy. The solution may help or hinder the solution of other organisational problems. It may create new problems or opportunities. Solutions are primarily generated by particular problems; however, they cannot be judged solely in the light of how well they solve the particular problem. The impact of each individual solution on the total organisation should be assessed as a measure of its true merit.

Predicting outcomes involves acknowledging all the possible consequences, results or repercussions that could hypothetically arise from a particular course of action. Not all of these outcomes will happen, and some will be mutually exclusive. Some are almost certain, others highly unlikely. While no easy task, it is obviously important to make some assessment of the probability of each outcome. Percentage probabilities may provide a mite over ambitious at times, but ranking is an option in such instances. Grouping outcomes according to the likelihood of their materialising is a third possibility. You must use your discretion to arrive at a well-considered decision.

5. Choosing among alternatives

Where a case is amenable to quantitative solutions, this stage may appear relatively straightforward. However, in most instances there are many qualitative aspects which require careful value judgements. One approach is to start with a clear statement expressing the goals of the organisation, with the aim of assessing the potential of each solution to realise those goals. When comparing the alternative solutions, you should consider not only this potential, but also the likelihood of their occurrence (step 4). Thus, a highly attractive outcome with low probability of occurrence *may* be rejected in favour of a moderate outcome with high probability.

The risks associated with each solution can be evaluated in a similar way, that is, by analysing the severity of the consequence in conjunction with the probability of the outcome. Unless your analysis is focused upon a single problem and a single set of alternative solutions, you may find that a flow chart helps at this stage. You will see that each solution to each problem will have repercussions on the outcomes of your solutions to other problems.

6. The plan of action

Having decided upon the preferred solution(s) to the main problem(s) identified, the next step is to specify a detailed plan of action. The format of this will be contingent on the nature of each case, but it may include clear statements of the following factors:

- corporate/strategic objectives;
- tactical objectives;
- research requirements;
- implementation strategy;
- likely competitor reactions;
- staffing implications;
- cost/profit implications;
- contingency plans; and
- control and evaluation systems.

7. Communicating the results

The written presentation will usually be in report-style format, using a clear structure of headings and sub-headings. The first page should include your name (or group members' names), the seminar leader's name, the title of the case and a list of the primary headings. Where numerical analysis is included, this must be presented concisely but clearly, with explanations of the figures and the process used to arrive at them. Similarly, you should always cover all the key assumptions and extrapolations underpinning your solutions and action plan.

The written style should be succinct. You should not rephrase or rehash large quantities of information from the case: you may confidently assume that your tutors will have read the case themselves! So, while a brief outline of the position to 'set the scene' is perfectly laudable, beware of 'wasting words'. This can do more harm than good by detracting from the overall quality of your analysis.

Verbal presentations can take many forms, depending upon the requirements of the case and the lecturer. Groups should decide upon a presentation strategy at an early stage – for example, appoint a spokesperson or clearly establish individual tasks. Some case presentations are amenable to role play between two or more of the 'characters' within the case; done well, this can be an effective presentation mode. Always rehearse the presentation in order to check your timing, become familiar with the visual materials used (flip charts, acetates, and so forth) and to reduce your dependence upon the written script. Start by announcing the structure of your presentation and make it clear when you move from one major section to the next. Tailor the verbal presentation to your audience and the time available. Do bear in mind that different formats and structures usually work best for written and verbal presentations. Finally, try to relax – presentation skills are not built in a day. Your audience will frequently be far more concerned about their own performance than they are about yours!

References and further reading

Argyris, C. (1980), 'Some limitations of the case method: experiences in a management development program', *Academy of Management Review*, April, 199-303.

Bromley, D. B. (1986), *The Case Study Method in Psychology and Related Disciplines*, John Wiley, Chichester.

Easton, G. (1982, 1992), *Learning from Case Studies*, Prentice Hall, Hemel Hempstead.

Fulmer, W. E. (1992), 'Using cases in management development programmes', *Journal of Management Development*, **11**(3), 33–37.

Masoner, M. (1988), *An Audit of the Case Study Method*, Praeger, New York.

Osigweh, C. A. B. (1989), 'Casing the case approach in management development,' *Journal of Management Development*, **8**(2), 41–47.

Reynolds, J. I. (1980), *Case Method in Management Development*, International Labour Office, Geneva.

Thompson, D. L. and D. J. Dalrymple (1969), *Retail Management Cases*, The Free Press, New York.

Part One

THE STRUCTURE OF RETAILING

In a book in which the names of national and international retailers predominate, it is fitting to start with a case based around the winner of the 1992 Independent Grocer of the Year Award. 'A winning enterprise' by David Kirby reminds us that the rewards to be gained through effective retail management are by no means restricted to the major multiples.

In 'The Co-operative difference: asset or handicap?' Stuart Eliot focuses upon the principles, structures and strategies that have differentiated co-operatives from multiples. In that the co-operatives play a dominant role in some countries, could a revival occur in the UK and elsewhere?

For many years, a major switch towards teleshopping has been forecast, so Jonathan Reynolds asks 'Is there a market for teleshopping?'. This case cuts through the hype frequently associated with this topic, encouraging a rigorous analysis of the economic, behavioural and technological issues.

In 'Re-inventing the retailing wheel: a postmodern morality tale', Stephen Brown and Barry Quinn give an old theory a most unusual treatment! It is brought to life through the story of a self-styled guru, his rise to fame, his downfall, then his new enlightenment.

A winning enterprise

David Kirby
Durham University Business School

Context

For decades, in most western-style economies, there has been a considerable reduction in shop numbers. The reasons for this are well known and well articulated, relating to the increased scale and market share of the retail multiples, together with the declining importance of the independent small business. In Britain, for example, the number of retail outlets declined from 509,818 in 1971 to 350,016 in 1989, a 31 per cent reduction. As Table 1.1 reveals, the decline has been greatest in the independent, single-outlet sector. Clearly not all independents are small. However, whereas in 1989 the average large multiple retailer had an annual turnover of £1.134 million and 19.6 employees, the turnover of the average single-outlet retailer was £0.155 million, with only 3.9 staff. Thus the majority of single-outlet businesses are small in scale and, even after decades of rationalisation, the sector is characterised by a large number of businesses that achieve marginal profitability only because they are open long hours and, until recently, when their competitors have been closed, mainly on Sundays. Indeed, gross margins in the single-outlet sector averaged no more than £45,000 per outlet, compared with £325,000 in the large multiple sector.

This decline in the importance of the small retail business has led certain commentators to suggest that independent small business retailing is an anachronism and has no part to play in a modern distribution system. Against this, others have argued that the modern retail system is polarising and that as stores get larger, numerically less numerous and spatially less concentrated, there emerges an increased need and opportunity for small stores to develop. Essentially these stores, which trade on the concept of convenience' and offer a range

Table 1.1 Shop numbers 1971 and 1989 compared

	1971	1989	Change (%)
Single-outlet retailers	338,210	215,736	−36
Small multiple retailers	83,966	67,760	−19
Large multiple retailers	87,642	66,520	−24
Total	509,818	350,016	−31

Source: Business Statistics Office *Business Monitor: SDA 25*, HMSO, London.

of goods and services different to those of their large-store competitors, complement the larger outlets in the retail system. However, to survive, such businesses need to be efficiently managed and to have a clear appreciation of their position in the marketplace, and in particular of the changing needs of their customers.

While the retail systems of many developed, western economies provide evidence to support the theory of retail polarisation, all too frequently, especially in Britain, the small businesses themselves appear to lack the efficiency, expertise and flexibility necessary to ensure their survival and profitability. Characteristically, the retail owner-manager has received no formal training in retailing and left school at or before the age of sixteen. While formal education has been found not to be an important factor in determining business success, previous business experience is significant but research suggests that only about one-third of all prospective entrants have any prior knowledge of the trade.

However, most commentators would agree that there is no one cause of the demise of the independent trader and Dawson (1983) has identified nine reasons for decline, namely:

1. Broad economic and social change (inflation, recession, buying behaviour).
2. Competition from multiples and co-operatives.
3. Increased operating costs (rates, electricity, etc.).
4. Lack of capital for investment.
5. Availability of supplies of goods (price, quantity, delivery, etc.).
6. Urban renewal.
7. Age of entrepreneur (man approaching retirement).
8. Poor locations.
9. Inflexible management attitudes.

Doubtless this list is not exhaustive and there are a wide range of pressures which impinge upon the small business and affect its viability. However, within this context, there are numerous examples of small enterprises which are winning the battle of survival and profitability. One such example is the Spar Foodliner of Treherbert in the Rhondda Valley, South Wales.

Spar Foodliner, Treherbert

In September 1992, the Spar Foodliner at Treherbert won the Independent Grocer of the Year Award. Later in the year, in October, it was runner up in the Best Independent Retailer Award, organised by Booker plc. What makes this such a successful business?

The people

Started in 1972 as a family business, this 2,200 sq. ft (202.4 m^2) store is run by 36-year-old Michael Pritchard. In 1975, at the age of 18, Michael spent a year in West Germany with Spar Hamburg studying business and learning German. From 1976 to 1978 he undertook a two-year course in Supermarket Operations at the College of the Distributive Trades, London, from where he obtained a Diploma in Supermarket Retailing, a Certificate in Meat Pricing and the Royal Society Diploma of Hygiene. Subsequently, between 1978 and 1980, he studied for an HND in Business Studies (specialising in Distribution) before joining the family business. In 1983 he took over full management control. Despite having a young family, Michael is a member of the Spar Guild Committee and attends all Spar Overseas Conventions, area and national meetings.

The store is manned by four full-time and 23 part-time staff. There are three store supervisors (two for evening shifts) and three departmental heads (with responsibility for provisions, frozen foods, and fruit and vegetables). Eighty per cent of the staff have been with the business for more than ten years and 16 of them have passed the basic Food Hygiene examination.

The business

Already a successful, well-established enterprise in 1983, Michael has steered the business through recession and an increasingly competitive environment to its present pre-eminent position as one of Britain's most successful small, independent retail grocery businesses. Currently, the business has an annual turnover of approximately £1.5 million and turnover growth is presently about 1.5 percentage points above the level of inflation. Over the five-year period 1987–1992, trade increased by in excess of 62 per cent with gross profitability rising by 2.3 per cent to 21.3 per cent. The business is open 92 hours per week, from 8 a.m. to 10 p.m. Monday to Saturday and 10 a.m. to 6 p.m. on Sundays. Two-thirds of the weekly turnover comes from normal daytime trading.

There are three checkouts each equipped with Omron Scanning tills and all 20 till departments are used to monitor sales, profitability and stock levels on the 2,450 lines currently stocked. Stocktaking is undertaken quarterly, with stock levels equivalent to approximately 1.75 weekly sales. The store is supplied by the Spar wholesaler, Capper & Co. Ltd, of Talbot Green. In addition to its range of grocery and convenience items, the store carries fresh and frozen foods and operates an off-licence. Both branded goods and Spar own-label goods are stocked. 'While we are convenience orientated,' says Michael, 'we still believe in a strong grocery base. Convenience lines make the greatest cash profit but it is the customer we have to satisfy.'

The store is monitored by a 16-camera closed-circuit television system and shrinkage levels are in the order of 0.85 per cent of retail sales. A Woodley electronics 32-point computerised refrigeration temperature recording system has been installed to ensure compliance with new hygiene regulations and all refrigeration units are equipped with blinds and sava-watt controls. Since 1972, the store has undergone five major refits.

An integral element of the store monitoring procedures is the business plan with its monthly cashflow forecasts. Actual monthly income and expenditure figures are recorded against the forecasts to monitor the progress of the business. Any significant deviations are noted and, when necessary, immediate remedial action is taken.

The market

As indicated above, the store is located in Treherbert at the northern end of the Rhondda Valley in South Wales. Typically, the population of the region is contracting (by 5.2 per cent over the period 1981–1991) and somewhere in the order of 21 per cent of the population are at or above retirement age. Unemployment in the area is around 13.5 per cent, with employment concentrated in mining, the distributive trades, other services, transport and communication and metal goods. Home ownership levels are higher than the national average, at 78 per cent, but car ownership is below average with some 45 per cent of households without a car and only 12.7 per cent with two or more.

Competition in the immediate locality takes the form of five independent grocery outlets, numerous greengrocery businesses, general stores and off-licences, with a 7,000 sq. ft (644 m²) Gateway supermarket one mile down the valley at Treorchy and a 5,000 sq. ft (460 m²) Kwik Save discount store at Toneyrefail, seven miles away. The former is being converted to the Solo discount convenience concept.

Apart from national Spar advertising, the store prints and distributes 6,000 leaflets monthly, incorporating redemption coupons. By monitoring the redemption rate, Michael is able to assess the impact of the advertisement. However, he believes that local promotional activity is the most cost-effective means of increasing sales and encouraging customer loyalty. Accordingly, the store closely involves itself in the activities of the local community and Pritchard's charity events have become well known.

The future

Having successfully developed the business over the past ten years, in what has been a difficult and turbulent trading environment, Michael is concerned to ensure its continued success. He is aware that competition is intensifying. A new 8,000 sq. ft (736 m²) Kwik Save discount store is being built in Tonypandy, four miles away, and planning permission has been granted for another Kwik Save store at Treorchy. More importantly, perhaps, he realises that the world is entering an era of rapid change where change does not mean 'more of the same but better' (Handy, 1990, 5), but rather uncertainty. He is aware, also, that if the business is to succeed, not only will it have to respond to change but it will have to initiate it. Accordingly, Michael had developed, already, a series of plans for the business.

Assessment

Clearly the business is highly successful. As a recent external assessor observed, 'the store represents all that is best in independent retailing. The store performs an indispensable service to the local community. The staff are well trained and enthusiastic. Shopping at the Pritchard's store, in short, is a pleasurable experience.'

This is a view shared, it would seem, by the store's customers. As one customer from Pontypridd put it:

> I am writing because I have to thank you for the care and service you and your staff give the local community. My father is a seventy-eight-year-old pensioner who is able to do his own shopping due to the care and attention he receives from your staff. He says he is treated with respect not like a dithery old man. I have heard a lot about your shop from my father and as I am not local decided to go on a visit with him. I was amazed at the range of products on display but even more amazed to see one of the assistants walking around the store doing the shopping of a man in an electric car which was duly parked inside the store. I really thought the days of individual help were over. However, the store may be old-fashioned in its caring attitude but certainly not old-fashioned in any other way, with its bar codes, air conditioning and easy access for the disabled. Congratulations. I think you have the balance just right and thank you.

Problem

The problems facing Michael when he took over the business in 1983, and those facing him currently, are typical of those most small retail businesses experience, both in Britain and overseas. Why do you believe the Spar Foodliner at Treherbert has been successful?

When he took over the business, Michael had to decide on an appropriate strategy. What strategies were available to him and which would you have advised him to follow? What actions would be necessary to effect the implementation of his strategy?

In order to ensure the continued success of the business, Michael will need to have plans for the future, as he recognises. What suggestions would you make to Michael about how he can maintain and improve the performance of the business?

References and further reading

Brown, S. (1987), 'An integrated approach to retail change: the multi-polarisation model', *The Services Industries Journal*, 7 (2), 153–164.

Davies, G. J. and J. M. Brooks (1989), *Positioning Strategy in Retailing*, Paul Chapman Publishing, London.

Davies, G. and K. Harris (1990), *Small Business: The Independent Retailer*, MacMillan, Basingstoke.

Dawson, J. A. (1983), 'Independent retailing in Britain: dinosaur or chameleon?', *Retail and Distribution Management*, 11 (3), 29–32.

Handy, C. (1990), *The Age of Unreason*, Arrow Books, London.

Kirby, D. A. (1986), 'The small retailer', in Curran, J., J. Stanworth and D. Watkins (eds), *The Survival of the Small Firm: Employment, Growth, Technology and Politics*, Gower, Aldershot, 162–179.

Knee, D. and D. Walters (1985), *Strategy in Retailing: Theory and Application*, Philip Allan, Oxford.

The Co-operative difference
Asset or handicap?

Stuart Eliot
Manchester School of Management

Context

For the purpose of this case we intend to focus on developments in the UK, for the roots of the international Co-operative Movement lie in Rochdale, England. It was there, in 1844, that 28 working men (mostly poor people) decided that the best way of protecting consumers against the unfair trading practices of the time would be to open a shop which was actually owned by its customers. The men, who became known as the Rochdale Pioneers, collected a sum of £28 by weekly subscriptions and used it to open a shop in Toad Lane. At first the shop opened only on one or two evenings a week, but trade developed quickly and before long Rochdale became the model for the formation of many other societies.

What makes the Co-op different?

The essential feature Co-operative societies have in common is that they all operate according to the so-called Rochdale Principles, developed from the original working practices and rules of the Rochdale Pioneers. Of course, it is recognised that principles based on nineteenth-century conditions may require modification to take account of changes in social, economic and political environments. Accordingly, two reviews have so far been undertaken by the International Co-operative Alliance, one in the 1930s and one in the 1960s; with a further review currently underway and due for completion in 1995. However, the author expects that the spirit of the principles will remain close to the wording agreed in the 1960s.

The key principles may be summarised as follows:

1. *Voluntary and open membership* – anyone can join regardless of race, religion or political affiliation.
2. *Democratic control* – the ultimate control of societies lies with the members. They have the power to elect or appoint people to manage their societies, and all members have equal voting rights – *one member, one vote.*

3. *Share capital should only receive a strictly limited rate of interest.*
4. *Surplus* (profits) *should be distributed to members in proportion to their purchases from their society,* the share of profits being referred to as the members' dividend.

These principles represent the fundamental difference between Co-ops and other types of retailer and have been adopted throughout the world by the members of the International Co-operative Alliance; indeed, they are a prerequisite for membership of that body.

The UK Co-operative Movement

The Co-op's share of the grocery trade is similar in the UK to France and Germany, but low compared to the shares achieved in Austria, Sweden, Switzerland and Norway (see Table 2.1). Even so the UK Co-operative sector still achieves turnover figures that put it among the largest retailers in the country (see Table 2.2).

In line with co-operative principles, the ultimate control of the UK Movement rests in the hands of its eight million consumer members, although in practice effective control is exercised by the boards and chief executives of the various societies.

The largest societies are Co-operative Retail Services (CRS) and the Co-operative Wholesale Society (CWS) (see Table 2.3). CRS has always been a retailer, building up its business by accepting the transfers of societies which were struggling and unable to survive independently. In contrast, the CWS was originally set up as a wholesaler to serve the interests of the retail societies. However, it now has extensive retail interests of its own with sales of £1.4 billion, in addition to which it has substantial manufacturing facilities and owns some well-known subsidiaries including the Co-operative Bank.

Table 2.1 Co-operatives' shares of European grocery markets, 1985 (%)

Country	%
West Germany	9
France	8
United Kingdom	8
Belgium	1
Netherlands	1
Austria	21
Switzerland	40
Sweden	28
Norway	24
Spain	3
Italy	5

Source: Euromonitor (1988), 9.

Table 2.2 Results of large UK retailers for year ending 1992 (£m)

	Turnover	Trading profit	Dividend	Retentions	Capital expenditure
Sainsbury	9,202	668	154	269	766
Tesco	7,596	503	122	264	852
Marks & Spencer	5,706[1]	680	195	171	305
Argyll	5,039	331	108	154	442
Asda	4,904	180	47	−475	238
Boots	3,656[1]	403	126	106	173
Kingfisher	3,389[1]	232	63	77	82
J. Lewis	2,280	100	30	35	108
Kwik Save	1,910	99	23	45	105
Storehouse	1,180[1]	10	21	−14	47
Co-operatives	7,089	176	40	36	221

Note: [1] after VAT.

In total, the UK Co-operative Movement comprised 68 separate retail societies at the end of 1991. However, it is important to note that the Movement is not a well-integrated organisation run along the lines of a Tesco or Sainsbury. Rather, it is a collection of independent and completely autonomous businesses. One consequence of this is that co-operatives use a wide variety of trade names – for example, some superstores are called 'Shopping Giant' while others are called 'Leo's'.

Taken together, retail societies have a combined turnover of more than £7 billion. The bulk of the sales are in the relatively slow-growing food market (see Table 2.4), but the Movement also has extensive interests in trades as diverse as funerals and doorstep milk delivery.

These sales are channelled through some 2,600 outlets – a much smaller

Table 2.3 Societies grouped according to 1991 turnover

Turnover category	Number of societies	Turnover (£m.)	% of total turnover	Turnover per society
CRS	1	1,507	21.3	1,507
CWS	1	1,420	20.0	1,420
Over £100m	15	3,171	44.7	211
£50m–£100m	8	532	7.5	67
£20m–£50m	9	336	4.7	37
£2m–£20m	16	109	1.5	7
less than £2m	18	14	0.2	1
	68	7,089	100.0	111

Source: derived from Co-operative Union (1992).

number than twenty years ago when the Co-op had no less than 7,000 shops. One reason for this reduction is that, like many other retailers, the Movement has been endeavouring to replace its smaller units with larger, more efficient superstores. So far it has managed to open nearly 100 of these stores and is one of the largest superstore retailers in the UK.

Nevertheless, the Movement still has a much higher proportion of small shops than its competitors. Nearly 90 per cent of its shops have a sales area of less than 10,000 sq. ft, whereas the average Sainsbury store has an area of 23,000 sq. ft.

In accordance with Co-operative principles, any profits made in a society's shops are shared with that society's members. Traditionally, customer members received a cash dividend every half-year, but in the 1960s many societies found the system too costly and time consuming and moved over to a system of dividend stamps. Nowadays the distribution of profits can take a variety of forms, including stamps, discount vouchers and traditional dividends, although surveys show that dividends still account for the largest share of these so-called members' benefits.

Table 2.4 Co-op turnover, 1991 (%)

Market sector	%
Food	70.1
(of which grocery)	(37.6)
Textiles and fashions	2.6
Menswear	0.7
Footwear	0.9
Furnishing	8.3
Pharmacy	2.2
Funerals	2.1
Motors/Petrol	7.2
Travel	5.2
Other	0.6
Total	100.0

Source: derived from Co-operative Union (1992), 5.

Problems

The heyday of UK Co-ops was in the 1950s when they accounted for 12 per cent of all retail sales and over 20 per cent of grocery sales, the latter being more than all the multiples put together. But problems began to appear with the abolition of resale price maintenance in the late 1950s and early 1960s. This led to the onset of price competition and reduced profit margins, and the Co-op found that many of its smaller shops could not compete.

Matters were made worse by the fact that the finances of many societies were insufficient to fund extensive shop development programmes. To some extent this was due to the fact that (unlike companies quoted on the Stock Exchange which can make use of rights issues) Co-ops had to rely on finance available from loans, members' savings and profit retentions.

The result was that the Co-op found it difficult to shed its outdated image and its performance began to deteriorate rapidly. This is amply illustrated in Table 2.5, which shows that real (inflation adjusted) turnover fell from £976 million in 1957 to £856 million in 1966, since when it has fallen still further to £633 million in 1991. In total this represents a real sales decrease of 35 per cent over a period when consumer spending volumes rose significantly and would have ensured a substantial real sales increase for a more efficient retailer.

Table 2.5 Trends

	Number of societies	Members (millions)	Current prices (£m.)			1957 prices (£m.)	
			Turnover	Profits	Dividend, etc.	Turnover	Profits
1957	936	12.3	976	62	51	976	62
1962	801	13.1	1,054	61	45	935	54
1966	680	13.1	1,108	52	37	856	40
1971	303	11.3	1,195	38	28	704	22
1976	237	10.7	2,413	65	34	722	19
1981	187	9.5	4,039	0	27	643	0
1982	145	9.1	4,158	−6	23	610	−1
1983	129	8.7	4,300	10	20	603	1
1984	112	8.5	4,460	20	18	596	3
1985	103	8.2	4,768	33	17	601	4
1986	100	8.3	4,989	62	18	608	8
1987	91	8.3	5,284	82	19	618	10
1988	85	8.2	5,697	96	20	635	11
1989	81	8.2	6,249	107	26	646	11
1990	77	8.2	6,713	128	26	635	12
1991	68	8.2	7,089	130	28	633	12

Source: Co-operative Union (1992 and earlier editions).

Attempts to solve problems

To begin with, it is important to realise that the difficulties faced by the Co-op have more to do with a failure to take speedy or appropriate action than with some inability to generate possible solutions. Woodcock (1986), for example, has referred to 'the Co-op's penchant for spawning dramatic or grandiose plans to spearhead the future . . . but which invariably seem to vanish into oblivion after years of fruitless talk'.

Typical of this is that, as long ago as the 1950s, the Co-op sought the advice of an Independent Commission (Gaitskell, 1958) on ways of arresting its decline. The Commission argued that one of the key problems needing attention was the fragmented structure of the Movement. Having lots of independent societies inevitably caused problems: costs were higher than in fully integrated organisations of a similar size; many societies were too small to employ the highly skilled people needed in an increasingly competitive environment; and there was insufficient co-operation in vital areas such as marketing.

Therefore the Commission recommended 'amalgamation between societies on a large and rapid scale'. Similar exhortations were also made in two regional plans issued by the Co-operative Union (the Movement's 'parliament') in the 1960s and 1970s (Bamfield 1978a, 1978b).

However, the Commission's recommendations had 'little effect on the speed or scope of amalgamations, most of which came about through the force of economic circumstances and not through any foresight or deliberate planning' (Co-operative Union, 1968). Therefore the Movement's market share continued to decline. As Figure 2.1 shows, the decline in market share was particularly

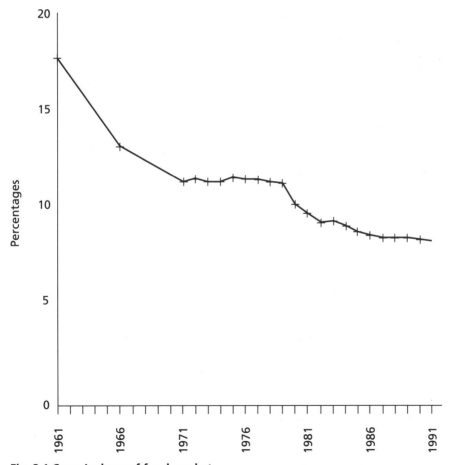

Fig. 2.1 Co-op's share of food market
Source: Co-operative Union (1992 and earlier editions)

rapid in the 1960s, goading the Movement into taking some painful measures. Large numbers of small, uneconomic shops were closed in an attempt to cut costs and many societies were forced by events to transfer their assets to stronger societies.

At the same time, during the late 1960s and early 1970s, some far-reaching initiatives were taken by the Co-operative Wholesale Society:

- A standard 'Co-op' logo and house colour were adopted in an attempt to create a national identity. Previously Co-op marketing had tended to emphasise each society's distinctiveness.
- Under the banner of 'Operation Facelift', societies were helped to refurbish some 5,000 shops, making full use of the new logo, etc.
- Large sums of money were spent on national advertising. Slogans such as the 'Caring, Sharing Co-op' were used in an attempt to convey to shoppers the essential differences between the Co-op and other retailers.

The measures were remarkably successful for a time and succeeded in halting the decline in the market share. But in 1978 Tesco started a price war. The Co-op again found itself unable to compete effectively given its fragmented structure and high proportion of small shops, and its market share resumed its downward trend.

The early 1980s saw the Co-op hitting an all-time low. It went into an overall loss for the first time in its history (see Table 2.5), with the Co-operative Union literature acknowledging that the Movement 'faced a decline that threatened its existence as a nationally recognisable trading entity' (Jaspan, 1991).

Against that background there was yet another restructuring proposal, this time for a merger between the CWS and CRS. Such a union would have made a lot of sense, especially from a retailing standpoint, as the new grouping would have had one-third of the Movement's retail sales and very significant buying power. But, as an old Co-op joke would put it, 'there wasn't much co-operation and even less movement' and the merger talks collapsed in 1986. At the time 'there was a strongly held view among many of the societies that own the CWS that a full merger would not necessarily be in their interests. They feared that the requirements of a retailing organisation with (1986) sales of £1.4 billion would become paramount and that the different needs of different societies would become lost or ignored. Another factor was the belief that the democratic nature of the Co-op and the interests and influence of individual members would be pushed even further into the background' (Woodcock, 1986).

The failure of the merger talks will be seen by some as yet another indication of the Movement's inability to implement difficult measures. Nevertheless, there is a feeling within the Co-op that the struggle to recover from the early 1980s experience has left the Movement in a better state to cope with the demands of the 1990s. The number of societies has continued to fall, even if most of the mergers were forced rather than planned; the falling market share of the early 1980s shows signs of being halted (see Figure 2.1); and profitability has held up in the face of recession.

References and further reading

Bamfield, J. A. N. (1978a), 'The revival of the Co-ops', *Retail and Distribution Management*, **6**(2), 18–23.

Bamfield, J. A. N. (1978b), 'What future for the Co-op?', *Retail and Distribution Management*, **6**(3), 14–18.

Co-operative Union (1968), *Regional Plan for Co-operative Societies*, Co-operative Union, Manchester.

Co-operative Union (1992), *Co-operative Statistics*, Co-operative Union, Manchester.

Euromonitor (1988), *Co-operative Retailing in the UK, 1980–1990*, Euromonitor, London.

Gaitskell, H. T. N. (1958), *Co-operative Independent Commission Report*, Co-operative Union, Manchester.

Jaspan, N. (1991), 'Can honesty pay?', *Northwest Business Insider*, August, 4–8.

Woodcock, C. (1986), 'The limits of co-operation at the Co-op', *The Guardian*, 13 February, 23.

Is there a market for teleshopping?

The home network experience

Jonathan Reynolds
Templeton College, Oxford

Context

The notion that teleshopping might eventually offer a viable alternative channel of distribution for goods and services has been in practitioners' minds for many years. The idea of buying groceries, booking theatre or rail tickets and checking the weather forecast as simply and straightforwardly as turning on the television, has also figured in popular predictions among consumers as to the way in which a 'home of the future' might operate. Many academic commentators have been quite emphatic on the subject: 'We see as a virtual certainty that the era of widespread telecommunications shopping is approaching' (Rosenberg and Hirschman, 1980).

Advances in technology in the mid-1980s were also pointing to the potential for interactive services based either on the fledgling UK cable TV operators, or using an interactive form of teletext called videotex, which was already being developed in the form of BT's Prestel service. In France, the heavily subsidised Minitel initiative developed under the auspices of France Telecom, which used the videotex option, was beginning to attract considerable international publicity.

It was the apparent inevitability of these technological trends which led Alan Coombes to found the Home Network in 1986. Coombes, whose electronic engineering business had already experienced considerable success, was an enthusiast for the 'home of the future'. His own 'smart house' benefited from fully automated energy control and security systems and had featured in the national press. His own inventiveness, combined with an astute knowledge of when to sell on the rights of an invention, had amassed him considerable personal wealth during the early 1980s. In working on security systems, Coombes had stumbled across an ingenious way of making conventional co-axial cabling support two-way communications involving video. This case deals with the way in which Coombes sought to develop and market this approach to teleshopping.

Because of the high cost of fibre-optic cabling, the early UK cable TV franchises had made almost exclusive use of simple copper cabling. Although an inexpensive solution at the time, the use of such cabling with existing transmission equipment effectively prevented the provision of value added services (such as two-way video or data transmission). Three years of intensive technical effort with considerable venture capital support, on the strength of Coombes's previous engineering track record, had resulted in what Coombes regarded as an extremely saleable product – the Network Presentation Process (NPP).

The system

NPP was not based on personal computers, but used conventional technology to provide the impression of a fully interactive cable television service. Full colour, still-frame video images could be called up by customers on their TV screen by using the telephone as the 'return route'.

To shop, customers would tune to the Home Network channel on their cable television service and dial an 0898 number. By holding a touch tone pad against the handset and tapping three-digit codes, they could 'touch' their way to the desired retailer or service provider screen on their TV. Short audio soundtracks could accompany each screen. A 'shopping basket' could be built up by browsing and choosing items from a range of retailers or service providers. Regular orders could be stored within the system. At the end of the 'shopping trip', customers could pay using credit cards or by debiting their own Home Network account. Orders would be delivered direct to the customer's home within 48 hours.

Behind the scenes would lie an impressive amount of technology, developed by Coombes's company (see Figure 3.1). With the Home Network channel selected and the telephone connected to the 0898 number, the management computer at HN head office would link an audio-visual display device at the cable head-end to the picture storage unit sitting on the cable line nearest the customer's home. The picture and related sound generated by the customer's 'touch-tone' request would be routed to the picture storage unit and subsequently forwarded to the customer's television set. The impression would be of an automatic updating of pages, without noticeable delay. Home Network would act as the host for a range of service providers and would take a commission based on sales.

NPP did have its technical limitations. Band width capacity on conventional cable networks meant that each picture storage unit could serve fifteen cabled households – but only one of these households at a time could access the service. However, Coombes's operations research people had shown that this ratio was statistically acceptable given the likely incidence of usage during the day.

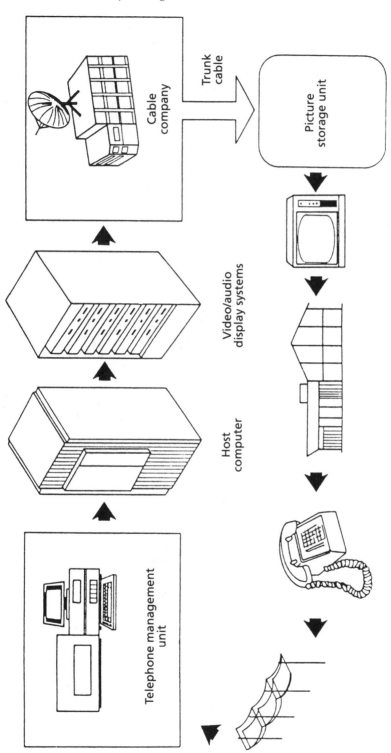

Fig. 3.1 Home Network: Network Presentation Process (NPP)

Starting up

It proved surprisingly easy to obtain the start-up finance for the operation. Financial institutions were eager to lend to a company with such an impressive track record in technical innovation. While some analysts voiced concern over the company's lack of marketing expertise in such a new area, the generally liberal investment climate of the mid-1980s prevailed, encouraged by Coombes's persuasive style. Moreover Coombes had put a significant proportion of his own personal wealth behind the initiative.

But starting up in this kind of market was very different from the others in which Coombes had experience. He needed the support of retailers and service providers to ensure the success of his system – but most importantly, he needed a likely cable franchise area in which to trial the system.

Black Country Cable (BCC) provided that opportunity. In the middle of cabling 250,000 homes in the West Midlands, BCC (majority owned by Baytel, the San Francisco-based regional Bell telephone company) were looking for ways to add value to their service and to improve its penetration of households passed. Coombes lunched with chief executive Michael Pullen in early 1987 and persuaded him to see the prototype system in action. Pullen was impressed by the system's instantaneous response and the picture quality generated. Much of his experience of teleshopping had been of the poor quality 'mosaic-style' videotex, initially championed by Prestel in the UK. A product 'drawn' with crude pixels was hardly an illustrative, let alone tempting, offer to a prospective purchaser. Consequently, a high-quality video image, albeit a still rather than moving one, represented a real step forward as far as he was concerned. He agreed to a trial of 500 units, and a joint venture whereby BCC marketing and engineering personnel would collaborate with Coombes's small engineering team in planning and implementing the development.

Much of Coombes's case to both the cable company and to prospective retailers was based upon the market research he had already commissioned. The research focused on changing consumer attitudes to shopping and technology and on the likely levels of take-up for various kinds of products and services. 'The biggest change', he suggested to one retailer, 'is that consumers have become more convenience oriented. Many households, particularly those on two incomes and with children, have big constraints on their time and are looking for ways to use their limited time more effectively.' He detected considerable enthusiasm for 'armchair shopping' in principle (see Table 3.1) for all kinds of services and among a wide range of socioeconomic groups (see Table 3.2). The only groups seemingly less keen on the service described were of older consumers.

He was particularly taken by the statistics beginning to come out of France, where France Telecom were subsidising the distribution of some one million Minitel videotex terminals a year to French households (see Table 3.3). 'If only 10% of consumers buy their clothes through teleshopping, that means a market worth £2bn a year!' Further, Coombes argued that his NPP system made use of conventional technology in the home. The high degree of penetration of colour

Table 3.1 Attitudes towards teleshopping

'For which of the following would you be willing to shop from home?'

	Positive response (%)
Groceries	75
DIY and household goods	60
Basic clothing	40
Fashion clothing	15
Rail tickets	60
Theatre tickets	75
Banking	80
None of these	20

Table 3.2 Attitudes towards Home Network (based on verbal description)

Respondent	Very interested in using (%)	Quite interested in using (%)	Not very interested in using (%)
Total	23	41	35
Men	22	48	29
Women	24	35	41
A, B, C1	22	40	38
C2, D, E	24	45	31
16–24	30	48	22
25–34	28	40	32
35–54	20	37	43
+55	10	15	75

Source: Base of 1,200 adults in London and the south-east

TV together with the telephone (see Table 3.4) compared to that for, say, the home computer, would provide an instant market for the service.

Bringing retailers on board proved to be difficult, however. Most enthusiastic were the existing mail order companies, now busy renaming themselves 'home shopping companies' in an attempt to reposition their operations upmarket. Such businesses were also used to operating directly with the home and had computer systems which could handle non-store-based ordering and fulfilment. Because Home Network would rely upon retailers or third-party suppliers to distribute the goods, this was a particularly attractive feature and Coombes was quick to sign them up to the system.

Most problematic were food retailers. Consumer research had shown that respondents saw grocery retailing as one of the most attractive of the services

Table 3.3 Use of Minitel 'supers à domicile' (electronic supermarkets)

Frequency	%
Every week	20
Once a month	18
Rarely	37
Not since the first time	25

Table 3.4 Penetration of selected domestic electronics, UK, 1989

Item	Households (%)
Telephone	84
Colour TV	90
2+ TV sets	35
Teletext	19
Video recorder	42
Home computer	28

Source: Home Office

which might be offered. Many consumers detested the conventional grocery shopping trip. It was important to get a food retailer on board. However, many of the largest UK food retailers refused even to meet Coombes. One marketing director sent a curt letter commenting that 'we do not see teleshopping for food as being a viable option for our business until well into the next century. We have better things to do with our time and resources at present.' While others were willing to meet, they either thought that the scale of operation proposed by Coombes was too small, or wanted it located adjacent to their spare warehousing capacity, and in any case were certainly not willing to pay HN commission on sales. In the end, HN signed up an independent operation based in the West Midlands, Dudley Grocery Services, which was looking for a way of competing with the major operators and was willing to offer 1,200 lines.

On the non-food side, there were mixed results. No clothing retailer would agree to discuss the matter further once they had heard the idea. 'Who is going to want to buy clothes straight off the screen, without trying them on?' was the usual response, despite patient attempts by HN to conjure up comparisons with mail order or TV fashion shows. Record and book retailers were more interested, but Coombes felt that book retailing was not appropriate for the 'image' of the service. A local department store company signed up for the trial, as did a national record retailer, which saw the trial as an opportunity to generate local publicity.

He was more fortunate in obtaining agreements with service providers. A

Table 3.5 Home Network trial service providers, 1988

Operator	Sector
British Rail	railway timetables
Croissants	delicatessen
Dudley Grocery Services	grocery goods
Dewers	department store
The Flower Garden	flowers and gifts
Roundabout Records	records, tapes, CDs
Stevensons	mail order catalogue
United Home Shopping	mail order catalogue
Tickettout	ticket agency
West Midlands Transport	transportation services

ticket agency, Tickettout, and the local bus company were amongst the first to sign an agreement. Tickettout, which also operated over the phone and via Prestel in addition to its outlets in ten city centres, saw it as an opportunity to develop one further means of reaching potential customers. In all, some ten service providers were recruited (see Table 3.5).

One further difficulty which affected the recruitment of all retail and service providers was the requirement for them to prepare material for the video stills that formed the heart of the service. Many companies simply did not have the design or mastering capability in-house and Coombes did not have the

---

Welcome to Home Network

'Shopping at the speed of light'

You now have an exciting new way to shop at your favourite stores from the comfort of your own armchair! Imagine how convenient shopping would be if all your favourite stores were no further than your television set! Until now, such an idea would have taxed even the most vivid imagination. But today it is reality: Home Network.

You can browse or buy whenever you like – 24 hours a day – with complete control over the stores, the products and the order in which you see them!

'I suppose there are lots of things people do in bed', laughs busy sales executive Teresa Murray, *'but when I get home late and tired, I know that I can fall into bed, turn to Home Network, phone the service, choose the groceries I need and get them delivered straight to the front door.'*

To begin shopping, call Home Network now on 0800–735422, or speak to your local cable company.

Fig. 3.2 Sample copy for Home Network brochure

capacity to handle the production needs of all ten organisations. A number of third-party agencies were used to put stills together, which meant that there was no co-ordination of style and little consistency in either approach or quality. On the non-food side, only a small selection of merchandise was trialled.

The use of BCC's marketing and engineering personnel proved invaluable. The service was marketed by being included in the standard pack on the cable service that was being sent to all households in the area which the system would pass. Figure 3.2 shows a typical insert. Prospective customers for the service could fill in the appropriate section of the subscription form to receive the service. There was no charge for subscribing, with subscribers only having to pay when using the service, via the 0898 number. Unfortunately, at the time the material was printed, many of the discussions with service providers were still underway and so it was not possible to incorporate their names in the brochure. The copy was necessarily generalised, therefore.

The early experience

The service was launched in spring of 1988, alongside the introduction of the second phase of BCC's programming. Take-up, in terms of completing the form, was encouraging. Indeed, HN was unable to meet the level of initial demand to sign up to the service. Only 500 picture storage units were available, and these had to be attached to the cable line adjacent to a subscriber's residence. Although the system had a theoretical capacity of 500 × 15 users (7,500), there were never fifteen subscribers living adjacent to a unit, which had been installed on a first-come, first-served basis. Consequently, while all 500 units were installed, only 2,000 subscribers were actually accepted onto the system.

Nevertheless, initial usage was encouraging. Dudley Grocery Services in particular found itself besieged with orders in the first few weeks, passed to it from HN's computer system. Operating out of a small warehouse in Smethwick, with a fleet of three vans, DGS found itself hard pressed to meet the 48-hour deadline for deliveries. Orders were not provided by HN's system in a logical picking sequence and DGS's sales assistants spent much time chasing around the aisles of the warehouse. Moreover the orders were relatively small – an average basket size of £7.50, compared with a supermarket average of £35. Subscribers were obviously trying out the service before committing themselves to it. An immediate consequence of this was that DGS found its vans with large numbers of small orders to deliver to a wide range of households – and generally late.

DGS were not alone in this difficulty. For the non-food retailers other than mail order, delivery schedules were unrealistic. Many (particularly Dewers) were more used to 3–6 week delivery schedules and found it difficult to impress upon delivery staff the importance of prompt delivery. After all, this was the only contact the company's staff would have with the customer. A good impression was important.

Early on, the quality and range of merchandise also became an issue. Customers were quick to complain that they had access to only a limited range of goods in both Dewers and from Roundabout Records, based upon their usual trips to those stores. The quality of the video stills was also a problem – particularly for DGS, which had little experience in this area. Furthermore, the quality of goods delivered from DGS, it was claimed, rarely matched the quality seen on the video still. Sometimes prices changed (particularly for fresh produce) after the order had been placed. Consumers were often less tolerant, Alan Coombes felt, of a little-known retail operator than they would have been of a blue chip retailer like Sainsbury or Marks & Spencer. He rapidly got tired of taking champagne and flowers round to disgruntled customers. Poor quality goods also raised the question of returns, which put further pressure on already stretched van crews.

Only the mail order company was happy – in the sense that they had an additional outlet for their products and the opportunity to test out a new technology. Their catalogue production divisions had the expertise to put together video stills of excellent quality and it was often by Stephensons' pictures that consumers judged the remainder of the service.

Company failure

Nine months into the trial, Coombes decided to de-list DGS. It was, he felt, dragging the whole operation down. In any case, following the spate of early orders, DGS's share of the business seemed to have gone into a rapid decline, largely, he was sure, because of the quality issues being brought to his attention. An in any case he had a further offer to make to BCC. In dealing with channel operators, Black Country Cable was simply acting as a conduit for programming. No action other than negotiation over rates and the simple interface issue involved in establishing a transponder link with the relevant satellite was needed. When it came to Home Network, BCC had to be much more involved with technical innovation than it felt was comfortable. A disproportionate amount of BCC's engineers' time was being spent calibrating or re-calibrating picture storage units on behalf of Home Network. Although an 0898 number existed for customer complaints to HN, many calls came to BCC instead.

Consequently, having taken a few of the calls himself, Michael Pullen was less than pleased to have a visit from Alan Coombes seeking additional support from BCC's engineers to re-calibrate the picture storage units. There had been complaints that one subscriber's neighbour had been 'spying' on her purchases by tuning into the HN service. Coombes also wanted help in providing funding for a roll out of the units to achieve what he called a 'critical mass in the market place'. He was convinced that the distribution problems were simply a matter of the low density of subscribers to the service. Pullen was not feeling co-operative. Home Network was bringing in more complaints than the rest of the programming put together. He refused Coombes's offer.

In June 1989, just over 14 months after the launch of the trial service, Home Network went into receivership. Home Network's final press release stated that the company had been unable to find sources of further investment in the operation to finance system development. It criticised the lack of co-operation from cable companies in hosting the system and berated what Coombes termed 'backward-looking retailers' for their unwillingness to get involved with the 'technology of the future'.

Glossary of terms

Home shopping A term now in broad use to cover non-store retailing of all kinds: whether this be by telephone, post or using new communications technology. Many companies formerly known as 'mail order' organisations now refer to themselves as 'home shopping' companies.

Minitel Videotex terminal supplied by France Telecom to French households and businesses seeking to access the Teletel service network.

Prestel BT's public videotex service.

Prodigy A partnership of IBM and Sears Roebuck offering an 'interactive personal service' based upon videotex software running on a personal computer.

Teleshopping The direct marketing of products or services to the home, using new communications technology.

Teletext One-way broadcast of text and mosaic graphics from central computers to a standard domestic TV screen or monitor.

Videodisc Technology allowing the storage and retrieval of significant amounts of high-quality still or simulated moving images, which can be video-standard or computer-generated.

Videotex Two-way transmission of text and mosaic graphics from computer to computer. Can take place over voice or data telephone networks, or via broad band cable.

References and further reading

McKay, J. and K. Fletcher (1988), 'Consumers' attitudes towards teleshopping', *Quarterly Review of Marketing*, spring, 1–7.

Mintel (1992), 'Home Shopping', *Retail Intelligence.*

Reynolds, J. (1990), 'Is there a market for teleshopping?', *Irish Marketing Review*, **5**(2), 39–51.

Rosenberg, L. J. and E. Hirshman (1980), 'Retailing without stores', *Harvard Business Review*, July–Aug., 103–112.

Timmermans, H., A. Boyers and M. Gunsing (1991), 'The potential adoption of teleshopping technology: a decompositional choice experiment', *International Review of Retail Distribution and Consumer Research*, **1**(4), 549–567.

Westlake, T. (1990), 'Electronic home shopping: where does it begin?', *International Journal of Retail & Distribution Management*, **18**(2), 26–32.

Re-inventing the retailing wheel

A postmodern morality tale

Stephen Brown and Barry Quinn
University of Ulster

'I think this is going to be the start of a beautiful friendship,' said Simon Barnes to himself as he finished reading the chapter, closed the book with a triumphant, if unnecessary, flourish and sank back, smiling, into his chair. All being well, the worst period of his professional life, the *annus horribilis* of 1992, the absolute nightmare that had been the last year or so, looked as if it might – just might – be coming to an end. And not before time.

It had all been going so well: his management consultancy firm had more business than it could cope with; he was a much sought after speaker on the conference and 'rubber chicken' circuit; his words of wisdom were regularly solicited by TV companies, radio stations, the financial press, the trade press (where he 'wrote' a ghosted weekly column) and the news media generally; he had the ear of the managing directors of some of the biggest firms in the sector, which was one of the most important sectors of the economy. He was the Tom Peters, the Ted Levitt, the Sir John Harvey-Jones, the undisputed heavyweight guru of the GB grocery business.

Simon, in short, had it all, though he deserved his success (if he said so himself). He had read the market, taken a risk, backed his judgement, exploited the opportunity and reaped the rewards that were his due. And then it all went disastrously wrong, completely, irrevocable and cataclysmicly wrong. 'Still, all's well that ends well,' he reminded himself, 'touch wood'.

He glanced at his watch. Seven p.m. Just time for a celebratory drink before the long drive home. 'Not that there's much to celebrate with,' he muttered, scanning the all-but empty shelves of the office drinks cabinet, 'or been much to celebrate about recently,' he added ruefully. Simon selected, opened and poured, in one practised motion, a bottle of Brains best bitter, low alcohol of course. It reminded him of his carefree days as a business studies undergraduate in his home town of Cardiff and that never-to-be-forgotten occasion when Prince Philip visited the college, made a speech and uttered those immortal words, 'what this country needs is more brains'. Of course, had Simon had less Brains, or more brains, he might have got a first class degree, but he did well enough to get on to the MBA programme at Strathclyde, where his interest in retailing took root, germinated and eventually burst into flower.

Everyone, needless to say, was interested in retailing then. It was 1985 and giants roamed the earth, well, Great Britain at least. Derek Hunt, George Davies, Sophie Mirman, Gerald Ratner, Terence Conran, Ralph Halpern, Anita Roddick and many more bestrode the British retailing scene. Hardly a week went by without some monster takeover bid, innovative retailing concept, buccaneering international foray or designer-led relaunch. The media revelled in retailing, consumers revelled in retailing, retailers revelled in retailing and even the universities revelled in retailing, albeit reluctantly. Retailing was where it was at and it was where Simon was going to be.

After graduating, he was taken on by the Institute of Grocery Distribution, which led to spells at Coopers and Lybrand and Management Horizons, where he specialised in the food and grocery business. Granted, grocery wasn't as 'sexy' as most other retail sectors, but it too had seen some remarkable changes since the 1970s (see Exhibit 4.1). The number of outlets had fallen dramatically, although, thanks to the growth of the grocery superstore, this was offset somewhat by an increase in the average size of those that remained. The multiples had expanded apace, either through acquisition or organic growth, at the expense of independents, the co-operative societies and, increasingly, smaller regional chains. Information technology had revolutionised distribution, stockholding, merchandising and operations; while the success of own-label products had undermined the hegemony of manufacturer's brands and, hence, producers' traditional dominance of the channels of grocery distribution. Profit margins increased inexorably, generous dividends were disbursed and, apart from the occasional scare over incipient superstore saturation or ill-advised international ventures, the 'big five' of Sainsbury, Tesco, Argyll, Asda and Gateway emerged as the darlings of the City and shareholders alike. It was no idle late 1980s boast that Britain possessed the best and most competitive grocery business in the world.

'Those were the days,' Simon thought, as he sipped his drink, 'days of wine bars and bonuses.'

□ □ □

Simon quickly washed his glass and went through his daily departure routine: briefcase packed, tomorrow's diary checked (no appointments, as usual these days), lights off, alarm on, ignition key inserted. Perhaps it was the Brains, perhaps it was his innate Welsh melancholia, but as he swung out of the office car park and settled down for the tedious journey home, he mentally rewound and replayed, yet again, his 'tape' of memories of the last few roller-coaster years.

It was in late 1988 that he realised he had to make the break and branch out on his own. Although happy enough in his well-paid, seemingly secure and, courtesy of two richly deserved promotions (if he said so himself), reasonably elevated position in Management Horizons, Simon had long harboured an ambition to be a management guru. He wanted to be sought after, wined and dined, expensively acquired and genuflected to by retailers in Britain, Europe and beyond. This secret desire was sparked some years previously at a Tom Peters 'excellence' seminar when some rough and ready mental arithmetic revealed the staggering sum that the great man was picking up for the day's work, not to mention his consultancy fees, book royalties and heaven only knows what else. 'I'll have some of that,' Simon thought, 'I'm going to have some of that.'

Simon smiled as he recalled, not for the first time, the lengths he went to in order to develop his (latent) gurubility. The elocution lessons that removed the final traces of Cardiff's Tiger Bay, the media relations course, the dress-for-success programme, the self-improvement manuals, the inter-personal skills training and, not least, the collection of key volumes by management thinkers, which he deconstructed with gusto. Moss Kanter had her dancing giants, Handy had his shamrock organisation, Porter had his value chain and 'diamond' of national advantages. There were dolphin strategies, Taoist doctrines, magnet principles, warfare analogies, and more matrices than you could shake a stick at. The secret of their success, Simon concluded, was some sort of concept, some sort of gimmick, some sort of metaphor that challenged the conventional wisdom, appealed to managers through its apparent relevance, applicability and implications of eternal truth, and, most importantly perhaps, provided ample scope for further exploitation through books, magazines, personal appearances and so on.

Sitting in the IGD (Institute of Grocery Distribution) library one day, gathering material for an overdue report on Carrefour, he came across an article on the so-called wheel of retailing theory (see Figure 4.1). He read the first couple of paragraphs and gave up in despair. 'Why can't bloody academics write in a simple fashion?', he muttered to himself, 'how on earth do they expect managers to read this gobbledegook?' But, as he sat at his desk later that evening, working on the impending Carrefour presentation, Simon found that the wheel theory just wouldn't go away. This notion that new forms of retailing commence with a cut-price orientation, progressively trade up and thus create an opportunity for a new generation of price cutters, kept going round and round in his head. He couldn't get to sleep because of it. And then it struck him like a thunderbolt; the wheel concept can be applied to the grocery industry in Great Britain. Yes, it can. It can!

Think about it. The 1970s was the 'pile it high, sell it cheap' era of price competition, what with Tesco's Operation Checkout, Sainsbury's 'Discount' campaigns and the rapid spread of companies with rock-bottom pricing policies – Asda, Kwik Save, Shoppers Paradise, Victor Value, Lo-Cost and many, many more. The 1980s, by contrast, were characterised by the deliberate avoidance of price competition and all-round trading up. Tesco traded up, Asda traded up, Argyll traded up (through the acquisition of Safeway), Sainsbury continued to trade up, Isosceles and the Co-ops traded up, after a fashion, and, as the

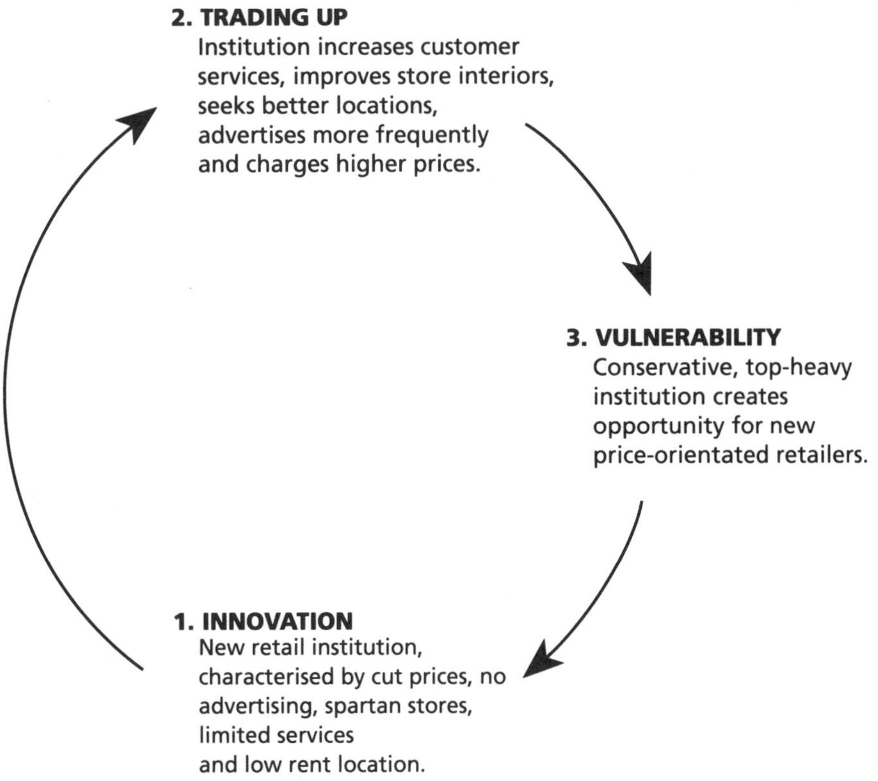

2. TRADING UP
Institution increases customer
services, improves store interiors,
seeks better locations,
advertises more frequently
and charges higher prices.

3. VULNERABILITY
Conservative, top-heavy
institution creates
opportunity for new
price-orientated retailers.

1. INNOVATION
New retail institution,
characterised by cut prices, no
advertising, spartan stores,
limited services
and low rent location.

'the wheel of retailing . . . contends that retail institutions commence as cut-price, low-cost, narrow margin operations which subsequently "trade up". Improvements in display, more prestigious premises, increased advertising and the provision of credit, delivery and many other customer services all serve to drive up expenses, margins and prices. Eventually they mature as high-cost, conservative and "top-heavy" institutions with a sales policy based on quality goods and services rather than price appeal. This, in turn, opens the way for the next low-cost innovator; and so the wheel revolves.'

Fig. 4.1 The wheel of retailing
Source: Brown (1988)

dropping of 'Discount' from its trading name clearly testified, even Kwik Save moved up market. The quasi-industrial outhouses that were 1970s grocery stores, with their inaccessible locations, congested car parks, unattractive interiors, narrow aisles, harsh lighting, cut cases, damaged goods, insufficient checkouts, temperamental trollies, cash only policies and no-frills service, are long, long gone. They have been replaced by accessible, attractive, architecturally distinctive superstores with ample car parking, public transport provision, on-site service stations, extended opening hours, wide aisles, subtle lighting, ergonomic trolleys, broad ranges of temptingly displayed, value added, own brand goods, not to mention the in-store bakeries, florists, pharmacies, delicatessens, cheese counters, fish counters, sandwich counters, wine cellars, bottle banks, salad bars, pizza bars, coffee bars, heel bars, organic vegetables, exotic fruits, local specialities, restaurants, lavatories, mother and baby rooms, customer service desks, healthy eating advice, food preparation guidance, party planning services, cash points, chequeing facilities, credit card payments, funds transfer capability, speedy checkouts, itemised receipts, bag packing, home delivery, charitable donations, Air Miles promotions, high quality advertising (see Exhibit 4.2) . . . . The list is endless. Where will it all end?

Simon Barnes knew exactly where it would end – in a bitterly fought price war as the wheel theory suggested. The wheel was perfect for his purposes. It was a simple metaphor that retailing executives could quickly grasp and relate to. It complemented the industry's mind set (how often had he heard retailers say 'this business goes in cycles' or 'there's nothing new in retailing'). It made clear predictions, had operational implications and ran counter to the prevailing conventional wisdom, which held that the 1990s would be the decade of customer care. Fair enough, the wheel wasn't his idea, it wasn't a new concept, but most management gurus exploit old ideas anyhow. They simply scrape away the academic barnacles, give the thing a polish and start counting their royalties. Retailers couldn't care less where the concept comes from or who thought of it, they only care about its implications. And the implications of the wheel are cataclysmic for GB grocery retailing. One person's disaster, however, is another person's opportunity. The wheel was going to be his passport to serious money. He was going to be rich and famous, famously rich.

'What a night that was,' Simon mused as he turned off the motorway and into the service station, 'didn't get a wink of sleep and the Carrefour presentation next day was a complete disaster.'

□   □   □

Buoyed up by the caffeine, Simon set off on the last leg of his journey home and relived that glorious day in September 1989. They say that timing is everything in retailing and life, and so it proved. Perhaps it was growing concern over the incipient economic downturn; perhaps it was the prospect of invasion by continental discount grocers, like Aldi and Netto; perhaps it was a reaction against the ubiquitous commentators' refrain of 'service orientation', 'total quality' and 'customer care'; perhaps it was events in eastern Europe and the widespread feelings of uncertainty and flux that accompanied the dramatic collapse of communism and the old world order; perhaps it was the intellectual climate of the times, what with Fukuyama's prediction of the 'end of history' and Kennedy's much debated prognostications on the rise and fall of great powers; perhaps it was the simple fact that Monday is traditionally a slow news day, especially at the dog-end of the silly season. But, irrespective of the circumstances, Simon Barnes' retailing 'wheel' and apocalyptic prediction of a grocery price war caused a sensation at the annual *Financial Times* retailing conference. It was picked up by the media and projected as one of the main stories of the day. His carefully honed communication skills were on display on every television news bulletin, his exquisite standard English resonated across every radio wavelength and his artfully retouched publicity photograph materialised on many of the following day's front pages. Acres of newsprint and hours of air time were devoted to his predictions and, despite the protestations of several company chairmen, food share prices tumbled in a frenzy of selling. The FT index dropped 45 points. His star was in the ascendant. Gurudom had arrived.

The next two years were a blur, a delicious, golden blur. His position was resigned, despite an attractive offer to stay, a consultancy practice set up, lectures given, television programmes made, videos produced and CBT training packages developed. Articles and reports outlining his vision and applying it to everything – industry sectors, individual companies, elements of the retailing mix, western civilisation, etc. – were penned by the dozen. He was in demand as a consultant, speaker and media pundit. Hagiographic profiles were produced by the quality press, financial press and trade press; government ministers considered him the first port of call on retailing matters; he was approached by continental European retailers keen to exploit GB grocery opportunities; and, to cap it all, he was brought in to advise on the strategies of troubled giants Asda and Gateway, where his very presence was sufficient to appease increasingly anxious investors. Most importantly, however, he was proved right. As the 1990s unfolded, hardly a month went by without some additional evidence of consumers' increasing price consciousness or retailers' adoption of a cut-price orientation, all of which presaged his predicted pitched battle on grocery prices (see Exhibit 4.3).

Everything was going swimmingly, apart, of course, for the stream of abusive letters from an irate Irish academic accusing him of misinterpreting the wheel theory. Idiot! It was then that he received an invitation to appear on a live, pre-Christmas television debate with the captains of the grocery retailing industry. His PA, worrier that she was, advised against it as she had once seen Lord Sainsbury confront Michael Porter on a television discussion programme. But Simon knew better. Did he not possess consummate communication skills? Is he not telegenic? Was he not the foremost management thinker of his generation? Had he not bearded Derek Hunt, at the time of the Asda–MFI demerger, with the remark, 'does this mean that the legs of Asda chickens will no longer fall off?' What could the chief executives of Tesco, Sainsbury and Argyll possibly do to him?

Nothing, except an answer to the simple inquiry, 'Mr Barnes, you have been predicting a price war for two years now and it has not materialised. Why's that?' Flustered by the directness of the question, Simon tried to dismiss it with an amusing allusion to collusion and, having done so, felt the weight of 150 plus years of grocery retailing experience bear down inexorably upon him. 'Flop sweat' they call it in television. 'Dying' they call it in the theatre. 'Gob-smacked' they call it everywhere else. The press, however, called it something else again – 'Store Chiefs Slash Prices Pundit', 'Barnes' Bubble Bursts', 'Retailing Big-wheel Punctured', 'Simple Simon Spiked by Piemen' and on and on and on. He groaned aloud at the memory, almost swerved off the road and, having regained control, thought of his further humiliation the following day, when his conference speech was interrupted by a deflated bicycle tyre that some joker had rolled down the aisle. When it collapsed in front of the podium, the whole place erupted. His debasement was complete.

In the aftermath of the television debacle, and its embarrassing rerun on the various TV 'reviews of the year', Simon discovered that his meteoric career had well and truly crashed to earth. Clients cancelled contracts, his newspaper column was discontinued, government ministers failed to return his calls, speaking engagements dwindled to zero, honorary degrees failed to material-ise and the publishers rejected his book-length treatment of the wheel theory (the referees didn't like it, apparently). It was of little comfort to him that GB grocery retailers' emphasis on price continued unabated. The Queen, he concluded, had it right when she described 1992 as an *annus horribilis*.

□   □   □

Simon switched off the engine and stared vacantly at his garage doors. The last twelve hellish months scrolled before his eyes. The empty appointments book; the mounting mortgage arrears; his wife giving birth to twins; the long days spent in the British Library looking for a concept to revive his career; the lonely nights spent in his study when he should have been shouldering his parental burden. Ironically, it was while reading the letters page of *The Sunday Times*, one of the newspapers which had revelled in his dramatic fall from grace, that he found the way forward. It appeared just after the Sainsbury price offensive of January 1993, when the company slashed – by up to 50 per cent – the prices of some 500 items, only to have their endeavours dismissed by the media as a sham, a publicity stunt, a phoney price war (see Figure 4.2). Even now, Simon could see the letter in front of him, every word was burnt into his memory . . .

> Dear Sir,
>
> Over the past few weeks, *The Sunday Times* has devoted many column inches to the so-called price war between Sainsbury, Tesco, Asda and other grocery retailers. It seems to me, however, that your coverage is placed in the wrong section of the newspaper. Just as Jean Baudrillard declared that the Gulf War would not take place, was not taking place and did not take place, so too we appear to be witnessing a pseudo price war, a simulated price war, a food price war that is not taking place. In short, a *postmodern* price war! In future, therefore, you should confine your coverage to section seven, The Culture, and the reporting should be undertaken by that postmodernist par excellence, Gilbert Adair.
>
> Yours sincerely
>
> Samuel Beckett
> Co. Londonderry.

Postmodern, postmodernism, postmodernist . . . . what on earth is that? A quick trip to the library revealed that, in today's postmodern world, style apparently takes precedence over substance, image over reality, surface to depth, chaos to order, locality to universality, past to future and consumption to production

Fig. 4.2 Sainsbury's postmodern price war of 1993
Source: *The Sunday Times,* 3 January 1993

(see Exhibit 4.4). Postmodernism is manifest in art (Christo, Fischl), architecture (Pompidou Centre, Clore Gallery), literature (Umberto Eco, Paul Auster), cinema (*Blade Runner, Body Heat),* music (rap, Bjorn Again), television (*Miami Vice, Twin Peaks),* advertising (Levis, Guinness), new products ('Death' brand cigarettes, 'Jolt' cola), shopping centres (West Edmonton Mall, South Street Seaport), leisure facilities ('theme' parks, pubs, restaurants, museums, airlines, etc.) and, why not, come to think of it, grocery price wars. Postmodernism is characterised by pastiche, parody, ambiguity, inauthenticity, irony, ephemerality, subversion, scepticism and self-referentiality. It says that everything you know is wrong, that there are no rules only choices and that the only generalisation is that there are no generalisations. Postmodernism, Simon concluded, was vague, trendy, ubiquitous and open to all manner of interpretations. In short, postmodernism had potential!

☐   ☐   ☐

'Hello dear. How was your day? Any luck?'
'Yes dearest, yes indeed. I think I've managed to re-invent the wheel.'

Case study questions

1. *Was the irate Irishman right, did Simon Barnes misinterpret the wheel of retailing theory?*

2. *Is the wheel of retailing the 'right' theory to apply to recent changes in the British grocery industry, and if not, why not?*

3. *Why has the predicted price war not materialised?*

4. *Will postmodernism provide the 'beautiful friendship' that Simon Barnes is looking for?*

Exhibit 4.1 Structural change in British grocery retailing 1981–91

	1981	1983	1985	1987	1989	1991
Number of grocery outlets (000s)	61.6	52.2	48.5	47.3	46.3	41.1
Market share of multiples (%)	59.2	66.7	70.2	72.9	74.0	76.0
Average pre-tax profit margins (top 5 multiples)	2.6	3.2	4.0	5.3	6.0	6.0
Number of Co-operative societies	187	129	103	91	81	68
Number of grocery superstores (cumulative)	315	372	432	500	644	798
Average sales area of multiple stores (sq. ft)	7,543	8,684	10,180	11,172	12,017	12,948
Own label share of packaged groceries (%)	23.3	26.2	28.0	29.1	29.4	31.6
Number of scanning stores	6	39	249	473	972	2,303
Press and television advertising (£ million)	51.0	67.2	64.2	62.9	71.5	98.4

Sources: IGD (1986, 1992); Nielsen (1989, 1991); Institute for Retail Studies (1992)

Exhibit 4.2 Major multiple retailers: financial performance and customer service provision 1991

	Sainsbury[1]	Tesco	Argyll[2]	Asda	Gateway[3]	Kwik-Save
Turnover (£ million)	7,813.3	6,346.3	4,496.1	4,468.1	3,118.7	1,785.0
Pre-tax profit (£ million)	518.2	436.2	290.8	172.8	3.6	102.0
Pre-tax profit margin (%)	6.6	6.9	6.5	3.9	n/a	5.7
Market share (%)	12.4	12.0	9.0	8.4	5.5	2.9
Number of stores	308	384	823	204	682	703
In-store bakery	222	197	297	172	113	0
Fresh fish counter	89	133	0	91	67	0
Delicatessen	224	288	481	192	592	0
Pizza bar	26	0	117	169	2	0
Restaurant/ Coffee shop	74	103	30	123	16	0
Pharmacy	29	22	50	37	6	0
Creche	1	0	0	27	2	0
Petrol station	76	129	18	87	11	0
Recycling points	236	180	138	132	190	0

Sources: IGD (1992); Mintel (1992)

Notes:

[1] Includes Savacentre　[2] Includes Presto　[3] Includes Somerfield

Exhibit 4.3 Cut-price chronicles, 1991–93

FEBRUARY '91
* Widespread predictions that discount stores are due to make inroads into British grocery retailing, after the opening in 1990 of first Aldi and Netto stores.

MARCH '91
* Aldi's allegations of unfair trading practices are rejected by the Office of Fair Trading.

APRIL '91
* Commentators in the grocery trade warn that the British food retailing industry is moving into its most confrontational stage for a decade. The anticipated growth in the grocery market and the likely improvement in trading margins will be insufficient to sustain the expansion of the leading supermarket chains. Attempts to gain market share from other food retailers are likely to trigger defensive action. Consumers' sensitivity to price is heightening.

▶

MAY '91
- CRS (Co-operative Retail Services) reveals that it intends to expand its Pioneer discount superstore concept. The initial target is 12 Pioneer stores within one year to 18 months.

JULY '91
- Aldi complain again to the Director General of Fair Trading about alleged price fixing by GB food manufacturers.

- Gateway converts its 40,000 sq. ft store in Bulwell near Nottingham into a discounter, Food Giant, offering a full range of 11,000 lines.

AUGUST '91
- Tesco's earlier than usual price cut campaign, on 500 own label lines, leads to fears of a price war. Grocery share prices fall and a *Daily Telegraph* headline reads, "Tesco starts supermarket price war".

- Sainsbury respond to Tesco's "Why Pay More" promotion and furore over price war with statement, "there is a price war but the point is there is always a price war . . . food retailing is a highly competitive business."

- Talk of a price war dismissed by industry and the City. However, Asda fuels speculation by following Tesco with price reductions on 60 lines.

- Kwik Save growth continues as the company buys 18 stores in the north of England. Significant change in range and pricing expected along with more aggressive prices.

- Findings from a *Sunday Times* survey suggest that British shoppers are paying up to twice as much for basic goods as consumers in other western countries, though claims dismissed by Sainsbury.

- As a result of claims of high price setting by GB food retailers, an investigation by a House of Commons Select Committee is mooted, as is the possibility of a referral to the Monopolies and Mergers Commission.

- CRS announces that it is seeking to extend its Pioneer range of discount outlets, following the success of the first four stores. A number of other co-operative societies reveal plans for discount operations.

OCTOBER '91
- Tesco introduce a "value range" of 69 secondary brands on a trial basis in selected outlets near discounter stores.

- Wm. Low announce a price freeze on all lines except fresh meat, produce and cigarettes.

- Rumours are rife that Lidl, the 800 unit German discounter, is intending to set up in Britain, with the Midlands as its base.

- Asda plans to convert up to 80 of its 204 stores into a new discount operation designed to hit back at increasing competition from continental retailers and other price-cutters in its core markets, the north and the Midlands.

NOVEMBER '91
- United Norwest Co-operatives is to open a chain of 11 Discount Giant cut-price food stores.

- US warehouse club, Costco, is reputed to be targeting London, Birmingham and Manchester for its first moves into GB.

- A third major Co-op moves into discounting, though, unlike its forerunners, Central Midlands uses only part of each store to carry a range of heavily discounted goods.

- Asda announces a price freeze in the run up to Christmas.

▶

- Kwik Save launches its most aggressive campaign ever by advertising direct price comparisons in national newspapers for the first time. Adverts compare prices with the major superstore groups, not other discounters.

- Budgens launches itself into the discount sector with a new 2000-line store format.

DECEMBER '91
- Gateway and Aldi team up to operate three joint stores in the north east of England.

JANUARY '92
- Sainsbury introduces price promotion for one month, with deeper than usual cuts. Rival supermarkets dismiss price war hysteria in the media.

- Safeway launch "more value" promotion, with 500 lines on offer each week.

- Asda announce a repositioning with increased emphasis on price.

- A Verdict research report indicates that grocery shoppers have become more price conscious over the past 5 years.

FEBRUARY '92
- Discounter Shoprite continues its expansion programme in Scotland after a slow start hampered by planning and acquisition problems.

- United Norwest to open its second Discount Giant store, a 22,000 sq. ft outlet.

- CRS launches a major price initiative in its 18 Leo's superstores nationwide, guaranteeing the lowest price on a total shopping basket of around 20 basic items.

- Costio, the US warehouse club, announces plans to expand into the British market.

MARCH '92
- Londis urges its independent retailers to counter-attack supermarkets by taking advantage of a multi-pronged promotional campaign.

- Helmut Nanz, of Nanz Group, predicts that price will become the dominant factor in GB grocery retailing over the next ten years.

- Aldi and Netto announce plans to relocate into larger depots so as to further their ambitions of opening 200 or more stores apiece.

- Argyll's Lo-Cost launches a new generation of larger, purpose-built discount stores.

MAY '92
- Asda shifts its emphasis towards brands as part of its major overhaul of trading strategy. Stores will address "basic food needs and the return to price competitiveness will be sharpened even more."

- Lidl & Schwarz abandon plans to enter the GB market.

- More than 200 Gateway stores considered unsuitable for conversion to Somerfield fresh food stores or Food Giant discounters are to be converted into two other fascias – Solo, a limited range discounter, and David Greig, a high street supermarket.

JUNE '92
- North Eastern Co-operative expands its Discount Superstore format to fight off the influx of other discounters into the area.

- Asda opens an experimental discount store, Dales, marking the chain's first move back to the price platform upon which it used to trade successfully until the mid-1980s.

- Isosceles looks to extend its broad assortment Food Giant chain from 15 to 38 stores.

- French hypermarket operator, Carrefour, acknowledges that it is weighing up its own discounting opportunities in Britain.

▶

JULY '92

- Star Discount, the 18 store Humberside-based chain, confirms that it is planning to launch a US-style warehouse club.

- Argyll is placing greater emphasis on its Lo-Cost discount format.

AUGUST '92

- The Giant Food Trading Co. opens in a converted Grandways store.

- Central Midlands Co-op launches another pilot concept, First Discount.

- Marks & Spencer breaks with tradition by embarking on an all-out autumn price offensive. The chain promises to freeze or cut prices on the vast majority of products in all 300 of its stores.

SEPTEMBER '92

- Aldi is negotiating to take up to 70 stores from a major GB retailer.

- Aldi and Netto slash prices after meeting head-to-head on two sites.

- Ed Stores of Paris, part of Carrefour, launches Ertico to look at discounting opportunities in Britain.

OCTOBER '92

- Costcutter to launch a new "price-conscious" imagery in a dozen experimental stores across the country.

- CRS's next Pioneer outlet will open in Dorset.

- Tesco experiments with a regional pricing structure in the West Midlands.

DECEMBER '92

- Archie Norman, Asda's chief executive, states that grocery retailers have underestimated consumers' increasing price consciousness – large scale discounting is here to stay.

- Sainsbury announce price cuts of up to 50% on a selected range of 750 products. Share prices fall with price war fears.

- Carrefour's discounting debut in GB is delayed until 1993.

JANUARY '93

- Tesco and Safeway respond to Sainsbury's price cuts with reductions on 1000 items.

- Sainsbury price cuts dismissed as a "meaningless publicity stunt" by the *Sunday Times* and "a con" by *The Sun*. Competitors, food industry commentators and marketing authorities are also highly critical of Sainsbury's price "hype". MPs renew call for government investigation into supermarket prices.

Sources: Various trade publications

Exhibit 4.4 What is postmodernism? Some definitions

THE GOOD

"something that seems to entail buildings which have been constructed of Lego from designs commissioned by the Mayor of Toytown, and novels about novelists experiencing difficulty writing novels".

Source: Watkins (1991)

THE BAD

"postmodern thinking involves rethinking – finding the places of difference within texts and institutions, examining the inscriptions of indecidability, noting the dispersal of signification, identity and centred unity across a plurivalent texture of epistemological and metaphysical knowledge production".

Source: Silverman (1990)

THE UGLY

"postmodernism is not a gesture of the cut, a permanent refusal, nor (most of all) a division of existence into polarised opposites. The postmodern scene begins and ends with transgression as the 'lightning flash' which illuminates the sky for an instant only to reveal the immensity of the darkness within: absence as the disappearing sign of the limitlessness of the void within and without: Nietzsche's 'throw of the dice' across a spider's web of existence".

Source: Kroker and Cook (1986)

References and further reading

Brown, S. (1988), 'The wheel of the wheel of retailing', *International Journal of Retailing*, 3(1), 15–37.

Institute of Grocery Distribution (1986), *Food Retailing Review*, IGD, Watford.

Institute of Grocery Distribution (1992), *Food Industry Statistics Digest*, IGD, Watford.

Institute for Retail Studies (1992), *Distributive Trades Profile 1991: A Statistical Digest*, IRS, University of Stirling.

Kroker, A. and D. Cook (1986), *The Postmodern Scene: Excremental Culture and Hyperaesthetics*, New World Perspectives, Montreal.

Mintel (1992), *Grocery Retailing*, Mintel, London.

Nielsen Marketing Research (1989), *The Retail Pocket Book*, NTC Publications, Henley-on-Thames.

Nielsen Marketing Research (1991), *The Retail Pocket Book*, NTC Publications, Henley-on-Thames.

Silverman, H. J. (1990), *Postmodernism – Philosophy and the Arts*, Routledge, London.

Watkins, A. (1991), 'Mr Heseltine may get his secret wish', *The Observer*, 20 October, 21.

Part Two

FORMULATION OF RETAIL STRATEGY

The strategic importance of an appropriate retail image is at the core of 'Repositioning MFI' by Gary Davies. Like MFI, most retailers have faced the challenge of repositioning in response to changes in the marketplace, or the arrival of new forms of competition.

Switzerland provides the setting for Steve Burt's case 'Migros: a socially responsible retailer?'. The case highlights the links between corporate mission/philosophy and retail strategy, and asks whether the approach could work outside of this specific cultural setting.

'Consumerism in the cosmetics and toiletries industry' by Barbara Lewis and Catherine Woodman examines how retail strategies have both accommodated and built upon consumers' concerns for health and the environment. The case also provides the opportunity to evaluate and interpret original market research data.

In 'Brashs: an expanding success', Michael Collins describes one of Australia's most profitable retailers of the last decade. The case illustrates how competitive advantage was gained through the application of strategic marketing and management principles.

Repositioning MFI

Gary Davies
Manchester Business School

Context

In November 1986 the *Investors Chronicle* described MFI as 'the UK's largest furniture retailer', and added 'It dominates the self assembly sector and currently specialises in kitchen and bedroom units. Its goal is to become a complete home furnishing superstore.'

Furniture and furnishings

Expenditure by British families on furniture, floor coverings, soft furnishings and household textiles accounted for only around 3–4 per cent of total household expenditure in the 1980s. This compared with some 28 per cent on food, 22 per cent on housing costs and nearly 10 per cent on clothing and footwear. Expenditure on tobacco was about the same as that on furniture and furnishings; expenditure on alcoholic drink was worth twice as much.

Furniture and furnishings competed for the customer's disposable income together with other domestic durable goods, including televisions, videos, washing machines and so on. Such electrical appliances had been attracting a growing proportion of the family budget, while expenditure on furniture was relatively static.

The furniture market

The furniture market (worth over £3,700m in 1987) could be sub-divided into four roughly equal sectors: bedroom furniture, kitchen furniture, upholstered furniture for the living room, and other lounge and dining room furniture. Of these sectors, kitchen furniture had shown the most growth.

One of the brighter areas of the furniture market was in self-assembly, or KD (knocked down) products, accounting for over a quarter of the market. Most of the KD sales were in bedroom or kitchen products. Their growth in popularity was ascribed to various factors, including lower prices, immediate delivery and an improved perception of the quality of KD furniture. However, KD products did have their drawbacks; upholstered furniture was generally unsuited to the KD concept and KD furniture often lacked in its design. The significant advantage of KD furniture remained its price. The increased manufacturing costs of producing a product that could be assembled by the lay person were more than covered by the fact that the manufacturer did not pay the labour costs of assembly.

In any one year about 50 per cent of households purchased an item of furniture. Specific stages in life prompt an important furniture purchase, such as marriage, moving house, or an increase in the size of the family. The younger groups therefore tend to be most prominent in purchasing new furniture. The elderly and those in the lowest socioeconomic group were half as likely as the 'average' to make any furniture purchase.

British households tended to spend less on furniture than say German or French households and to buy fewer items. Poor design and a failure to promote furniture generally were seen as reasons for the less than buoyant market.

While furniture was rarely seen as a fashion item in the 1980s, fitted bedrooms and replacement kitchens became two exceptions to this general rule. The growth in both sectors benefited the KD market with its inherent cost advantages over ready-built units.

A further price advantage was available to the DIY enthusiast who felt able to install fitted units. Some companies offered an optional fitting service, some included fitting in their price. A minority supplied only ready-assembled units, either made to measure or with separate fascias and worktops, to provide the fitted look.

In the four main furniture sectors KD furniture held varying shares of the market. In kitchen furniture KD accounted for as much as 60 per cent. With respect to bedroom furniture, upholstered products could not generally be sold in self-assembly form; but of the bedroom units, FIRA (The Furniture Industry Research Association) estimated that around 11 per cent were sold for self-assembly by 1982.

Current KD technology meant that all upholstered furniture was difficult to manufacture. However, FIRA estimated in 1983 that sales of KD upholstered furniture could grow to 9 per cent of the market sector by 1986. Finally, in dining and living room furniture, up to 1982 FIRA actually reported a decline in sales of self-assembly wall units even though the total wall unit market was still expanding. In the slightly larger 'occasional' subsector (bookcases, coffee tables), self-assembly had grown to take 50 per cent of sales.

Trends in furniture retailing

Furniture posed a number of problems to the retailer, in that it was expensive, had a relatively low stock turnover and was also bulky to stock. The traditional high street furniture store was particularly affected by these factors, to the point where mixed retailers such as department stores found it difficult to justify giving substantial floor space to furniture. On the other hand, such a fragmented market with few well-known or dominant brands and a wide range of furniture types, implied a need for considerable display space to do justice to the product area. High margins were therefore essential to the retailer, typically double those in mainstream retailing. These high margins also made it tempting to discount, a dangerous strategy unless the retailer could achieve increased sales levels and competition were unwilling to match the lower prices.

The need for large areas of display space coupled with the need to avoid the high overheads of the high street led to a growth in large out-of-town furniture stores. Such operations, with MFI as a prominent exponent, tended to concentrate on KD furniture. Modern DIY (Do it yourself) multiples also saw the synergy between their operations and the DIY element intrinsic to KD furniture and entered the self-assembly kitchen market. While department stores held their share of furniture sales into the 1980s, it was the traditional high street independent who felt the effects of a static market, higher costs and the out-of-town competition.

Manufacturers' brands

There were few prominent manufacturers' brands in furniture by 1986. In some sectors, notably those of fitted bedrooms, kitchens and lounge suites, the market was highly fragmented and typified by small companies who both manufactured and retailed locally.

Table 5.1 attempts to encapsulate this fragmentation by citing the leading manufacturer brand in each major sector in 1983. In all but upholstered furniture the share held by MFI was significant, if not dominant. In upholstered furniture the market share of Queensway, the main out-of-town retail furniture arm of the Harris Group, was important. Therefore, due to the fragmentation of manufacturing, the furniture and furnishings market was best analysed by concentrating on retailers rather than on the manufacturers they purchased from.

Further evidence to substantiate this line of reasoning is provided by statistics on advertising expenditure. Such was the imbalance between the advertising activity of retailers and manufacturers, that in 1985 expenditure by the three leading retailers exceeded the total for all furniture manufacturers.

Company history of MFI

MFI traced its origins to two entrepreneurs who dealt in army surplus sales after the 1939–45 war. Soon the company came to specialise in furniture, largely through mail order. Business boomed in the late 1960s and the company went public in 1971, by which time it also had a number of small high street sites mainly in secondary locations. In the mid-1970s the oil crisis and the advent of VAT conspired to depress the furniture market, particularly the mail order sector from which MFI derived over 80 per cent of its business and nearly all its profits. Attempts to rejuvenate the business by offering free approval and 28 days free credit backfired and bad debts mounted. Damage to furniture reached unacceptably high levels as the company's transport operators did away with the van boys who had helped drivers load and off-load merchandise. In 1974 the mail order business went bankrupt, leaving some 20 or so stores surviving hand to mouth – the embryo of a company that was to grow

Table 5.1 Brand and retailer market shares, 1983

Sector	Leading manufacturer and (brand names)	Estimated share	Estimated MFI share
Non-upholstered bedroom furniture	Stag	8	–
Self-assembly bedroom furniture	Schreiber	6–8	50
Upholstered bedroom furniture	Silentnight	30	–
Self-assembly kitchen units	Schreiber	6–8	25
All kitchen furniture	Moben/Dilusso (formerly Kitchen Queen)	6	16
Upholstered furniture	Christie Tyler (Cambria-Model, Braemore, Action Furniture, Outline, Contour, Colonial, Pendle and own label)	20	2
Dining/living room	Stag	6	5
All domestic furniture	Various	–	11

Sources: FIRA, Mintel, MFI, author's estimates

twentyfold in ten years and revolutionise furniture retailing on its way.

The one important asset remaining from their mail order days was the KD concept. However, three further principles were also established which became the cornerstones of the business. MFI was one of the first retailers to move out of town, not to the retail parks of the 1980s, but first to industrial units where planning permission was feasible. Out-of-town sites were considered necessary because of the scale of the operations envisaged and the need for car parking space. Car parks were essential if the company was to deliver on its next principle, that of offering a takeaway service. MFI turned its back on the traditional method of furniture retailing, with limited display and waiting lists for products selected mainly from catalogues. Instead every item on offer was to be displayed and most, if not all, were stocked on site to be taken away on purchase. The final principle was to advertise strongly, majoring on a price-led appeal to attract customers to the out-of-town stores.

The formula worked, enabling the company to recoup its opening costs generally within some six months of launching a new store. The 1970s saw a rapid growth in store numbers and the gradual replacement of smaller units, so that the large stores opening in 1986 increased the average store size to over 40,000 sq. ft. Early stores, which were converted warehouses and even cinemas, were relocated to purpose-built units.

In 1980 MFI purchased the Status Discount organisation, one of its leading competitors. But more significantly, Status was also the only other UK outlet for the Hygena brand of KD kitchen and bedroom fitted furniture.

In April 1985 MFI was the junior partner in Britain's biggest ever retail merger with ASDA, at the time the country's third largest food retailer. The ASDA Group included Allied Carpets, which with 74 stores was following the parent company in developing out-of-town sites. The synergy between the two retail operations seemed limited to an out-of-town orientation and the potential for MFI to benefit from Allied's carpet expertise. Carpets had been a minor product area for MFI, which had previously franchised some of the space in their stores to competitors, Harris, for carpet retailing. However, it seemed that the motives behind the merger were more subtle, with both parties seeing the move as a defence against a hostile takeover in an era of acquisition in the retail sector.

MFI were one of the first retailers to adopt electronic point of sale (EPOS) but the more obvious application of computer technology from a customer's perspective was the sales support system. Once a customer had decided to purchase one or more products, the customer or a salesperson completed a selection slip, the information required being the unique selection number of each item, the quantity required and the unit price. The salesperson then entered this data via one of two or three terminals on the shop floor to check the availability of each item in the adjoining warehouse. If all the items were in stock the customer paid the total bill and proceeded with the sales docket to the warehouse, where they would wait for the goods to be picked from the warehouse racks.

Any out-of-stock items could be placed on order and a daily printout gave availability of all the company's line items. The computer system provided reorder levels for replenishing stock directly from a manufacturer (in the case of some carpet and kitchen and bedroom lines) or, more usually, from the company's large centralised warehousing outside Northampton.

Distribution

MFI's huge National Distribution Centre occupied a 42-acre site and a one million sq. ft capacity warehouse.

The company owned and operated its own fleet of 40 ft vehicles, each painted white with the slogan 'MFI won't be beaten' in red on the sides. Deliveries at least twice a week to each of the 135 stores stretching from the south of England to Scotland were standard. Hygena products were delivered to stores separately; whereas carpets, of which most stores carried very limited stocks, were generally delivered to stores either from Northampton or directly from the manufacturer. For items out of stock which were not given a specific reorder time, the customer would be quoted 28 days for delivery, but in practice, the store expected to better this more often than not.

MFI did not undertake deliveries to customers' premises until 1987. Instead, customers were expected to use their own transport (roof racks could be purchased from the store), or they could hire a small MFI delivery van.

With KD furniture, spare parts could be a prominent issue. In a few instances the incorrect number of screws, clips, hinges, and so on, would have been packed with the product. More often, customers would lose or damage one. Company policy was to offer spares free of charge against proof of purchase of the original product. Damaged goods, unless clearly caused through the actions of the customer, were also replaced without charge. By 1987 the company could claim substantial improvement in both product quality and in the elimination of packing problems (failure to provide the right parts for each product).

Advertising and promotion

MFI's advertising expenditure rate was high for a retail organisation (see Table 5.2). Typically the company purchased some 12 pages of newspaper advertising each week in publications such as the *Mail, Mirror, Star, Sun, Express* and *Today*, supporting this with forays into television advertising. Adverts majored on price by announcing sales and special offers. Special loss leader lines were to attract customers to the stores. A money-back guarantee offered the customer a full refund and the purchase item free if the item could be found cheaper elsewhere within 28 days. Price reductions featured in advertisements were often spectacular; a video cabinet reduced from £96.99 to £39.99; a barstool from £44.99 to £14.99; a storage divan from £59.99 to £29.99.

In MFI, sales price reductions were sometimes offered against notional prices for a fully assembled unit. In-store promotion repeated the same price messages contained in the national advertising, with banners promoting sales prices. Various sales occupied most of the trading year.

In-store tapes played over the public address system were used to put across a softer message, often extolling the quality of the merchandise and not just its price. The development of an image element in the company's promotion could also be detected in a series of full colour advertisements, mainly in women's magazines and Sunday supplements, featuring the Hygena product range. Although the advertisements often featured price, they contained a stronger emphasis on design than the company believed was compatible with their black and white advertising in daily newspapers. The MFI name was less prominent in their colour advertisements, which were being used primarily to remind the reader where the Hygena range could be purchased.

MFI had a reputation for being sales orientated. Sales personnel were given a smart uniform, and were paid commission: top sales people could earn substantial salaries, quadrupling their basic wages. Promotion prospects in a growing company also provided an additional incentive. However, sales people were trained not to be at all oppressive in their personal selling; customers were given time to walk around the store and often had to ask for assistance.

Table 5.2 MFI advertising expenditure (£m.)

1985	1984	1983	1982	1981	1980	1979
18.7	16.4	12.9	10.0	9.6	6.7	4.7

Advertising as a percentage of sales revenue 1985						
Habitat	MFI	Queensway	Times	Maples Waring Gillow	Wades
0.6	5.3	4.1	3.8	2.3	1.2

Sources: MEAL, Verdict

MFI's price-led promotion, media selection and concentration on the lower price end of the market implied a downmarket clientele, but MFI had a broad appeal across all strata of society. In fact, their customers represented all socioeconomic groups roughly in proportion to national norms, except that the lowest, group E, was underrepresented and group C2 (skilled manual workers) was slightly overrepresented. However, the appeal to various groups did seem to vary by product area, with the higher groups buying more of the fitted bedroom and kitchen units.

Merchandise policy

MFI were dominant in the KD sector of furniture, a market which had tripled in size from 1980 to 1985 to represent 23 per cent of all furniture sales. The Hygena brand, exclusive to MFI in Britain, held around 25 per cent market share in self-assembly kitchens. MFI's total market share (fitted and self-assembly kitchens) was around 16 per cent. Kitchen units and appliances (the latter also branded under Hygena) represented around 40 per cent of MFI's sales. Bedroom furniture represented some 30 per cent of turnover, and dining and living room furniture less than 20 per cent. Sales of upholstered furniture, generally unsuited to the KD approach, were limited, although an expanded range was introduced in 1986.

Sales of carpets had increased since the ASDA merger, the company had also moved into soft furnishings and lighting in a few of its stores with encouraging results. Of all merchandise, 85 per cent was British made, with much of the remainder being imported from Eastern Europe where the unit costs of producing the more basic items were extremely low.

With British suppliers, MFI emphasised the value of working with, rather than just purchasing from, their manufacturers. This, the company claimed, allowed the manufacturer to concentrate on their area of expertise and MFI to do the same. Malcolm Healy, chairman of Hygena, was quoted in 1984 as saying: 'Our friends at MFI know what the market wants and we know the best way to make it.' New technology helped Hygena to produce formed edging and a carved appearance on their products, features normally associated with more expensive, hand-finished lines. But while quality had improved, real prices had tumbled. Noel Lister, chief executive of MFI, cited two examples:

'Take a standard sink base unit. That was about £30 in 1976. Today it's retailing at £24.95, which, allowing for inflation, is really about a third of the original price' and 'A double wardrobe in 1978 was around £66. Now a similar sized unit of better quality costs £49.99.'

In stores, bedroom and kitchen furniture was displayed in room settings around the sides of the display area. The centre floor contained the lounge and dining room furniture, as well as the carpets and soft furnishings if stocked. Each item had a product name: the Erica desk; Bianca wall units; the Victory mattress, the Albany range of tables, wall units and upholstered chairs. Each was separately price ticketed with the tickets containing the basic product data and item number needed for the computerised sales support system. Merchandise displays were defined centrally, different sizes of store carried different sizes of product range but all stores carried the same core lines.

Quality control was a key issue in selling KD furniture and MFI were conscious of the need to improve their market image for product quality and customer care. Heavy emphasis was thus placed on staff training and the Quality Control department in Northampton had been expanded substantially in 1984.

Competition

As mentioned previously, the furniture and furnishings market did not contain many prominent manufacturers' brands, few of which held wide distribution or market shares. Many lines were exclusive to a retailer, Hygena and MFI being the most prominent example.

In terms of total numbers of shops, the high street stores predominated. However, the high street sector's 95 per cent or so of store numbers translated into only 80 per cent of floor space and still less in terms of market share.

If furniture and carpets were taken as one market, MFI and Harris Queensway vied for market leadership, being the only companies to hold more than a 5 per cent share. Harris Queensway, through a number of separately named outlets (of which Queensway, the out-of-town chain, was the largest), was stronger in carpets. Queensway itself majored more in lounge and dining room furniture but had recently introduced a number of Symphony kitchen concessions into some of its 100 or so stores. Queensway represented a substantial proportion of the Harris Group turnover and represented the most obvious challenge to MFI.

Times Furnishing was a subsidiary of Great Universal Stores, one of Europe's largest retailing groups. A recent merger with GUS's other furniture interest, Cavendish Woodhouse, had given the group third place in the furniture and furnishings market under the Times name. They could be regarded as the most prominent of the high street specialists with over 300 stores. In 1987 Times was purchased by the Harris Group. Also important in the high street were Wades (once part of the ASDA group) which had undergone a rationalisation since a management buyout in 1985, and Maples Waring & Gillow. Each had under 100 stores apiece. Both companies had been experiencing low profits and commentators pointed to them as examples of the structural difficulties of being a furniture retailer in the modern high street. In 1987 Wades was acquired by Waring & Gillow. Many of the latter's stores were extensively refurbished under the Gillow name.

A smaller, but more prominent, furniture retailer was Habitat, the original retail outlet for Sir Terence Conran, widely regarded for his innovation in store and product design. A series of takeovers and mergers found Habitat a part of the Storehouse Group in 1986, together with Mothercare and British Home Stores (BhS) (children's wear and variety chain retailers respectively).

Furniture and floorcovering represented less than half Habitat's turnover and its market share was less than a fifth of MFI's, but still, Habitat was an interesting case. Its rapid growth, very high sales per square foot and high customer flow rates in 55 stores effectively highlighted the potential for more targeted, design-led furniture retailing. To extend their promotion of what had become termed the Habitat 'lifestyle' approach, Habitat were rumoured to be considering a major move to out-of-town shops (most of their sites were secondary high street locations) and to be opening concessions in BhS stores.

More intense speculation surrounded the planned arrival of Swedish based IKEA, the world's largest furniture retailer, into Britain. The company's product range was seen as similar to that of Habitat, but was some three times as large. The typical store had an out-of-town location of over 150,000 sq. ft, enormous by British standards. The company specialised in KD furniture with a similar takeaway format to that of MFI. By 1987 one store, in Warrington, Cheshire, was under construction, another was planned for Brent Cross outside London and IKEA was also looking (albeit with some difficulty) to establish other sites in the south of England.

By 1985 IKEA was a $1 billion company. Founded by Ingvar Kamprad in Sweden in 1949, it was now trading from 71 stores in 18 countries. The catchment area for each store was large. For example, when the first American outlet opened in Philadelphia it attracted customers from as far away as New York. All stores had restaurants and supervised playrooms for children.

A substantial marketing tool was their catalogue, available at the entrance and sometimes distributed within the catchment area. The retailer aimed to have the lowest prices for the products it sold, but at the same time saw itself as a fashion retailer. One manager was quoted as saying 'Coming from IKEA is like a party' and according to the magazine *International Management*, 'Its simple designs, colour and fabric-coordinated home accessories were an instant hit with the young, upwardly mobile market segment, known as the "jean academics"'. They labelled the company as 'trendy'.

Products all bore a quality assurance label and some could be seen on test in each store. The company had a distinctive culture, frugal but egalitarian. Titles were frowned upon. Its Swedish origins were emphasised in the blue and yellow store paintwork and poster advertisements, matching the colours of the Swedish flag. Price was an important theme in much of IKEA's advertising but design and innovation were also strongly emphasised.

Meanwhile, Britain's biggest retail chain, Marks & Spencer, had also begun to test the market for furniture, offering a delivery service on upholstered furniture and a wide range of KD products to take away. Marks & Spencer had experimented with a number of new product areas, but they had found it difficult to match their returns from clothing and food. However, opening stores out of town, where operating costs were lower, was seen as one way to sell products such as furniture profitably. Finally, fashion retailers Next had also entered the market for furniture and fabrics.

What next?

In terms of profitability, measured by profit and sales per square foot and per employee, MFI was performing well, but there did not seem to be the potential for further spectacular rates of growth. By 1987, MFI management considered that there were some four years of potential growth left for the company in its mainstream activities in Britain.

Penetration into the higher socioeconomic groups with the present trading format seemed one line of approach. The company's market research had indicated that while the majority of the population liked the MFI offering, a minority were not attracted – even though they could be in the market for the products MFI had on sale. The newer, larger stores with their wider range of merchandise and lower emphasis on the more utilitarian product lines con-trasted somewhat with the company's mainstream advertising. Moreover it was possible that changes in the law governing what constituted a 'sale' could affect the legality of this advertising.

The 1986 ASDA–MFI Group Annual Report contained a separate statement from MFI's managing director, John O'Connell, stating the intention to be-come a 'complete home furnishing superstore'. Experimental layouts and decors had been introduced into two stores with promising results, which would be used in new stores. One-third of stores in 1985/86 had been refurbished, extended during the previous year, or were brand new. A similar rate of development was planned for 1986/87.

Image mapping

In 1988 a study was made of the furniture market in the north-west of England where IKEA had opened their first store. The research method involved identifying a large number of words or phrases (concepts) that shoppers used when considering furniture. This was done by conducting a number of group discussions. A list of concepts was then screened to identify which concepts appealed to everyone, which appealed to some furniture shoppers and which appealed to no one.

The first group contained the eleven concepts listed in Table 5.3 and were taken to describe the 'ideal' furniture store – what everyone agreed a furniture

Table 5.3 Concepts describing the ideal furniture retailer

- Value for money
- Quality product
- Quality service
- Easy assembly (of knocked-down furniture)
- Stock availability
- Durability of goods
- Product design
- Car-parking facilities
- Product knowledge
- Delivery service
- Life-style compatibility

Table 5.4 Segmenting concepts

• Practicality of goods	• Replacement parts availability
• Staff availability	• Comfort of goods
• Offers discounts	• Good display
• Sale of accessories	• Late-night shopping
• Good store atmosphere	• Aftersales service
• Accessibility of store	• Immediate collection
• Attentiveness of staff	• Range co-ordination

store *should* be about. The second group contained a longer list of concepts, each of which appealed strongly to some shoppers, but not to all (Table 5.4). For example, not everyone wanted discounts or immediate collection but, as some did, such concepts could be usefully used to segment the furniture market.

The final stage of the research involved interviewing a quota sample of furniture shoppers to find which retailers they saw as similar, which as different and (using the segmenting concepts) why. The market map produced from the computer analysis of the results is shown in Figure 5.1.

The 'ideal' furniture retailer can be taken to subsume all the concepts in Table 5.3. The segmenting concepts in Table 5.4 are included in Figure 5.1 as vectors. For example, because ELS and MFI were associated with offering discounts, that vector is close to them. House of Fraser outlets were associated with giving aftersales service, Marks & Spencer with attentive staff, Habitat and Next with range co-ordination and accessories, IKEA with the same and with practical goods. IKEA was also associated with immediate collection and late-night shopping, attributes it shared with MFI.

Figure 5.1 indicated that the market was divided into a number of segments. Queensway, ELS and MFI formed one segment distinguished by the discounts

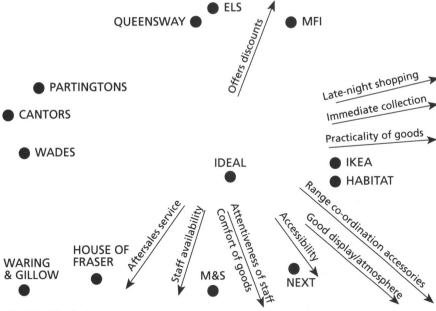

Fig. 5.1 Market map

offered and little else. ELS and Queensway did, however, concentrate on soft furnishings, while MFI were stronger in fitted kitchens and bedroom furniture. IKEA, Habitat, Next and, to some extent, Marks & Spencer, represented a group where co-ordination, display and atmosphere were important. Marks & Spencer, House of Fraser and Waring & Gillow had staff attentiveness and aftersales service in common. A final group, largely middle market retailers trading in the high street, were not closely associated with any concepts; they seemed to have no clear image. IKEA and Habitat were seen as having a similar image. Both were relatively close to the average view of what the ideal furniture retailer should be.

Issues for MFI

Strategically, MFI's position in the furniture market was dominated by its reputation for discounting. Its retail format was similar to that of IKEA, with an emphasis on immediate availability, although MFI's product mix was far more focused on fitted kitchen and bedroom furniture. IKEA were known to be keen to develop more stores, each equivalent in size to four or more MFIs. The new store outside Warrington appeared to be highly attractive to shoppers, a perception confirmed by the positioning study. So what should MFI's response be, both nationally and locally? What should they do about their national image and to their Warrington store, located near the town centre, not on a particularly good site and in need of refurbishment?

The company also had other concerns. The merger with ASDA had not been a success. In November 1987 ASDA sold 75 per cent of MFI to a management buyout. MFI simultaneously purchased Hygena, leaving the new company with substantial debt.

MFI's response

MFI decided to reposition its business. Within its stores it adopted IKEA's approach of presenting all furniture in room settings rather than by product type, as it had been doing. In 1988 the company purchased the manufacturing business Schreiber and moved to a greater reliance upon branding. MFI used the Shreiber brand name for higher price point kitchen and bedroom furniture and the Hygena name for slightly lower price, but similar, goods. By 1990 a comprehensive range of rigid (factory-assembled) kitchen ranges were available under the Schreiber name, with the Hygena product being self-assembly. Other 'brand' names, such as Greaves & Thomas and Ashton Dean, were introduced for upholstery, textiles and co-ordinated textile products. Low price point products were grouped together in a self-selection area under the Pronto name.

Television advertising was used to present a softer image for MFI. One series of advertisements particularly encouraged lapsed or non-customers to 'Take a look at us now'. Within the stores, specialist kitchen salespeople were employed. A fitting service was also launched.

Chairman Derek Hunt explained the move at a conference in 1989:

> We bought Schreiber to open the door on a whole new range of customers. Not just the younger C1 C2 Hygena shoppers, but the older A B C1 Schreiber groups as well. The Schreiber brand is specifically targeted at people who want style and quality from their furniture.

Five factors had influenced the company's thinking: greater consumer affluence, people becoming more houseproud, and with heightened aspirations, greater demand for choice, and an ageing population.

By 1991 one trade source estimated that the Schreiber brand accounted for 27 per cent of MFI's sales. Small wonder that kitchen and bedroom furniture were also estimated to account for over 70 per cent of all sales.

The marketplace for furniture had grown steadily in the 1980s, but by the end of the decade a number of prominent names were floundering, notably market leaders Lowndes Queensway, which collapsed in August 1990. MFI itself recorded losses for 1990 and 1991, but with turnover still growing, it was successfully refloated in 1992. Habitat was suffering from substantial losses in its British operation and closed a third of its sales area. IKEA were said to have overtaken Habitat in sales volume and in 1992 the business was purchased by IKEA. But was MFI's situation a result of the wider problems of the furniture market or had its repositioning produced the wrong result?

References and further reading

Aaker, D. A. (1982), 'Positioning your product', *Business Horizons*, 25, May/June, 56.

Buzzell, R. D. and B. T. Gale (1987), *The PIMS Principles*, The Free Press, New York, 124.

Davies, G. J. and J. M. Brooks (1989), *Positioning Strategy in Retailing*, Paul Chapman, London.

Davies, G. (1992), 'Positioning, image and the marketing of multiple retailers', *International Review of Retail Distribution and Consumer Research*, **2**(1), 13.

Ries, A. and J. Trout (1986), *Positioning: The Battle for Your Mind*, 2nd edn, McGraw Hill, New York.

Migros
A socially responsible retailer?

Steve Burt
University of Stirling

Context

For most people outside Switzerland the name Migros will mean little. Yet to the Swiss themselves, and indeed most visitors to the country, the name is very familiar. Like Marks & Spencer in the UK, Migros has become a national institution dominating Swiss retailing and many other aspects of Swiss life. In 1992, the group achieved a total turnover of over SFr 15 billion and a retail turnover of SFr 12 billion. This represented 15 per cent of all retail sales, and no less than 23 per cent of food sales in the country (see Table 6.1). Such a level of market dominance would attract the attention of the public authorities in many countries, yet the philosophy and behaviour of Migros has so far negated the need for any intervention.

The company origins

The Migros story starts in 1925 when Gottlieb Duttweiler returned to his native Switzerland following a less than successful period as a Brazilian coffee

Table 6.1 Migros - performance indicators

	1981	1984	1986	1988	1990	1992
Total turnover (SFr m.)	8,906.4	10,109.7	10,923.6	11,882.0	13,682.8	15,124.9
Retail turnover (SFr m.)	7,605.5	8,655.7	9,403.4	10,181.0	11,460.0	12,468.3
Market share (%)						
Retail sales	n.a.	15.0	15.0	15.3	16.0	15.6
Food sales	n.a.	21.9	21.4	21.5	22.2	23.4
Non-food sales	n.a.	8.3	8.7	9.2	9.7	8.9
Post tax profit (SFr m.)	111.9	154.0	210.4	183.0	256.7	214.4
Social levy (SFr m.)	66.9	74.5	83.4	84.0	98.4	106.5
Membership (millions households)	1.15	1.20	1.39	1.50	1.52	1.54

Source: Annual Reports

planter. His career in retailing began when he saw a market opportunity in undercutting the high prices charged for basic foodstuffs by Zurich retailers. Migros, a name derived from 'demi-gross' (half wholesale), was born in rather unconventional fashion via five lorries selling six basic grocery products – sugar, coffee, pasta, rice, coconut-oil and soap – at heavily discounted prices said to be at least 25 per cent below those of established traders. The phenomenal success of the 'shops-on-wheels' venture encouraged him to open the first Migros store the following year.

The extent of Duttweiler's popularity with his customers was equally matched by the resentment from his competitors. They tried to drive Migros out of the market, through physically intimidating the driver-salesmen and by enlisting the support of suppliers and local authorities. A frequently re-counted illustration of these early problems is that of Migros's entry into Berne, when opponents in the town persuaded the local authorities to ban his lorries for obstructing traffic. When Duttweiler refused to accept the ban he was fined, to which he responded by asking local housewives who disagreed with the fine to contribute 10 centimes towards payment. Needless to say, the response was overwhelming and the local authorities backed down.

Duttweiler similarly refused to bow to more significant attempts to force him out of the market. When the large established manufacturers and importers, encouraged by other retailers, refused to supply Migros, Duttweiler bought his own manufacturing capacity and switched to smaller manufacturing companies. In 1933, by which time Migros had grown to around 100 stores, the food manufacturing industry and the retail and wholesale lobbies succeeded in promoting a legislative bill, the Branch Store Prohibition Act, to prevent Migros opening more stores and thus maintaining the status quo. Duttweiler's response to this provocation was twofold: he formed a political party, the Independent Alliance, and diversified into other lines of business not directly affected by the Act.

The scope of business activities

The Branch Store Prohibition Act was eventually repealed in 1945, and Migros grew rapidly in the post-war period. As Table 6.2 shows, Migros's retail activities are still firmly based in food retailing, with over 500 stores (classified by size from the largest 'MMM' markets to the smallest 'S' stores) accounting for 87 per cent of sales. In memory of the company's origins and founding principles the group still retains 88 mobile shops serving over 1,400 mainly rural communities without Migros stores, even though they contribute less than 1 per cent of sales. Migros also wholesales its food products to other retailers and supplies the Giro group of affiliated retailers. Other retail activities which have grown over time include a restaurant subsidiary of over 200 outlets, most located within the larger stores, and around 40 non-food speciality stores (DIY, home appliance and garden centres).

Migros has long been a market leader in product development and informa-

Table 6.2 Migros – store network

Number of stores	1981	1984	1986	1988	1990	1992
Food stores:	466	470	479	494	504	514
MMM markets	26	31	34	35	35	37
MM markets	162	164	165	169	176	181
M stores	150	161	169	182	192	205
S stores	128	114	111	108	101	91
Mobile shops	111	107	107	101	91	88
Restaurants/snacks	175	n.a.	187	190	196	202
Non-food speciality stores	40	35	32	33	36	38
Petrol stations	30	25	24	24	24	n.a.
Giro affiliates	17	n.a.	n.a.	58	56	n.a.

Sales by store type (%)	1981	1984	1986	1988	1990	1992
Food stores:						
MMM markets	19.4	21.5	23.4	23.7	23.5	23.7
MM markets	47.2	46.4	45.2	44.5	44.5	43.7
M stores	16.2	16.1	15.7	15.8	16.3	16.5
S stores	5.8	5.2	4.8	4.4	3.8	3.4
Mobile shops	1.8	1.5	1.3	1.2	1.0	0.8
Restaurants/snacks	4.0	4.2	4.3	4.6	4.7	4.9
Non-food speciality stores			2.7	3.2	3.4	3.7
Petrol stations/ auto centres	5.7	5.1	1.6	1.4	1.4	1.5
Direct/ wholesale deliveries			0.5	0.5	0.6	0.4
Giro store deliveries[1]			0.5	0.6	0.6	1.0
Leisure time	–	–	0.1	0.1	0.1	0.1

Note: [1] Retailers carrying Migros products

Source: Migros Annual Reports and Migros Public Affairs Department

tion provision, priding itself on the high quality and low prices of its retail brand range. The company developed retail brands relatively early in its history when it was forced to seek out alternative manufacturers and suppliers to the established brand manufacturers. The Migros range is supplemented by exclusive contracts for the Swiss market with a number of international brands, such as Del Monte and Pepsi, where possible. Information on products and activities is disseminated through a weekly magazine, translated into each of the three languages spoken in Switzerland, and with a combined print run of 1.45 million copies.

A standard range of compulsory basic lines is carried in all stores no matter what the size, to which the regional co-operatives and store managers can add products to extend ranges. Despite the range of shop size and locations within the organisation a standard pricing policy is applied, so that Migros products cost the same in the mobile stores as they do in the largest 'MMM' superstores. The basic product range, however, excludes certain products: on establishing the company Duttweiler refused to sell tobacco or alcohol products because of their effect on health, a policy still applied today.

The moves toward vertical and horizontal diversification stimulated by the attempts to block Migros's early expansion have also continued apace. Migros now controls twelve manufacturing companies accounting for around 30 per cent of all goods sold, including meat processing, bakery products, pasta, chocolate, milk products, canned goods, drinks and cosmetics; it also has a number of transportation and shipping companies. Horizontal diversification, which began in 1935 with the formation of Hotelplan to provide cheap holidays, was aimed generally at non-competitive sectors of the economy or where particular consumer issues existed, and was at its most vigorous before Duttweiler's death in 1962. In 1951 Klein Taxis was formed, as Duttweiler believed taxi fares were artificially high; in 1954 Migros diversified into petrol with Migrol; and into book retailing with Ex-Libris in 1955. The financial service sector followed with the formation of the Migros Bank in 1957 and Secura (insurance) in 1959. All these subsidiary retailing and service activities are retained today.

The organisation

In 1941, Duttweiler and his wife, Adele, surprised many by turning Migros into a co-operative – although cynics suggest that preferential tax rates may have been a motive. Certificates with a nominal value of SFr 30 were distributed to 100,000 registered customers and an organisational structure consisting of a central body and eight regional co-operatives was formed. In 1992, over 1.5 million households (75 per cent of the total in Switzerland) are members of the 'Migros Community' and ultimately have control of the company via the annual membership ballot. It is common for around 25 per cent of members to vote in the annual ballot, depending on the issues involved.

The organisational structure of Migros today consists of two elements: twelve regional co-operative societies and a central body 'The Federation of Migros Co-operatives' (see Figure 6.1). The Federation of Migros Co-operatives (FMC) manages the manufacturing activities and national retailing interests such as the non-food chains, while the regional societies manage the food retail operations in their respective areas. In terms of size the Zurich region is the largest with 16.5 per cent of sales, followed by St Gall (11.6 per cent) and Berne (11.6 per cent). The smallest regions in terms of sales are Valais (3.3 per cent) and Ticino (3.7 per cent).

As with all co-operatives, membership democracy underpins the constituent elements of the organisational structure. The three main management committees of the Federation of Migros Co-operatives are derived from these twelve regional co-operative societies. The Assembly of Delegates is seen as the Migros parliament and has 113 members, largely derived by election from

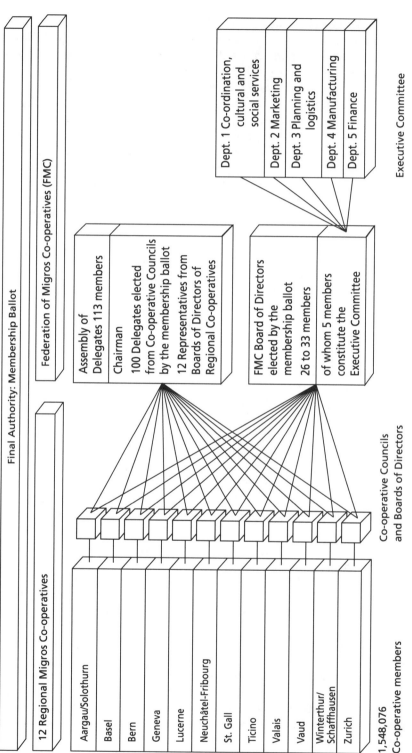

Fig. 6.1 Migros – organisational structure
Source: Migros Annual Report, 1992

the regional societies plus a nominated representative from each society. The Board of Directors, from which in turn the five-member Executive Committee is drawn, is similarly derived from the regional societies. Each of the five members of the Executive Committee oversees one of the five Management Divisions which manage the day-to-day activities and strategy of the Federation of Migros Co-operatives.

Migros and market dominance

From the performance data provided in Table 6.1 and discussed briefly in the introduction, Migros is clearly a powerful agent in Swiss retailing and in the economy as a whole. The annual report for 1991 shows that Migros purchased 26 per cent of Swiss agricultural output. Given that the group does not sell alcohol or tobacco (usually important customer traffic generators for food retailers) the market share figures are even more impressive. Market dominance of this kind would in most countries raise questions concerning the use and possible abuse of market position.

In 1979, a group of co-operative members expressed concern that Migros was becoming too large and too dominant within the economy, arguing that more local autonomy was required within the organisation to counter this problem. This rebellion amongst sections of the membership, known as the Migros-Frühling (Migros-Spring), aimed to take advantage of the democratic structure of the group to obtain representation in the Assembly of Delegates and press their case. Although they were unable to obtain any representation on the various management bodies, the level of support which Migros-Frühling achieved and the issues they raised appear to have influenced various strategic initiatives and activities in the 1980s.

Investment and expansion in new stores, particularly the largest 'MMM' superstores, has slowed since the early 1980s. This may simply be a reflection of market saturation and the lack of expansion opportunities, but it should be noted that membership ballots voted to restrict the growth in investment to 2 per cent per year in 1980 and rejected a motion to allow overseas expansion in 1981. More significant, perhaps, was a study undertaken on supplier dependency, published in the Social Report of 1980 (see Table 6.3). Suppliers for whom Migros accounted for over 30 per cent of their output were deemed to have a 'heavy dependence' on the co-operative. Indeed, the average sales to Migros for this category of supplier was found to be 60 per cent of their output. In Migros's view such heavy dependence meant 'a degree of over reliance for the consequences of which Migros would not wish to be responsible', and announced that in the long term they would seek to limit purchases to 30 per cent of any supplier's output. Not surprisingly this voluntary restriction alarmed many suppliers, especially as Migros had a tendency to ask for exclusive rights to supply within Switzerland.

The Migros attitude to the distribution of profit has also seen commentators referring to the company as 'eccentric'. The 1987/88 fall in post-tax profit was

Table 6.3 Migros supplier survey, 1980

Size of supplier company	Percentage of total	Percentage of suppliers having		
		Marginal dependence (<10%)	Moderate dependence (11–29%)	Heavy dependence (30%+)
Fewer than 50 employees	31.5	10.9	23.8	58.5
50 to 499 employees	64.4	81.8	73.6	39.6
500 or more employees	4.1	7.3	2.6	1.9
Total	100.0	100.0	100.0	100.0

Source: Migros Social Report, 1980

dismissed as a problem by the management, as they argued that previous profit levels 'were almost too good for a co-operative'. The most unconventional aspect of the company, with respect to its financial performance, is, however, the existence of the social levy. Again instigated by Gottlieb Duttweiler, this requires Migros to donate 0.5 per cent of the retail co-operatives sales and 1 per cent of wholesale (FMC) sales to the social levy. This levy is then distributed between a range of educational foundations, cultural activities and social projects. Examples of these schemes are foundations such as the Gottlieb Duttweiler Institute, the Green Meadow Parks (of which there are now three in Switzerland) and the Eurocentres (international language schools). Cultural activities that receive funding cover a wide range of cultural and fine art events including 'Clubhouse' concerts and 'Club Schools' for adult education; while social programmes include activities for pensioners, holidays for the handicapped, sponsorship and grants for young people, and selective aid programmes for AIDS, drug rehabilitation and famine relief, and so forth. In 1989 the membership ballot voted for a further SFr 1 million, in addition to the annual social levy, to be donated to selective aid projects for the next four years. Participation rates in these various activities and schemes are high, providing Migros with a role and exposure in the community which few conventional retailers can match.

The future

Undoubtedly Migros is a remarkable company in many ways. Its approach to business and attitude towards the community are firmly rooted in the ideals of its founder Gottlieb Duttweiler. Some recent commentaries have, however, suggested that the co-operative may now be at a crossroads as the influence of the founder fades. Although Gottlieb Duttweiler has been dead for 30 years, his wife only passed away in 1990 at the age of 98. This severed the final link with the founding family (as the Duttweilers were childless) and most of the current management team have no direct experience of Duttweiler himself.

Whether a change in approach will occur is open to debate. The regional cooperative societies near the border have recently acquired sites for store development in France and Germany and a number of self-help programmes have been organised with retailers in the former eastern bloc and Soviet Union. In 1992, two joint ventures were formed with Konsum in Austria, which will give Migros an interest in almost 200 Austrian supermarkets. Although only small steps, these moves do contrast with the 1981 membership rejection of international expansion. Similarly, Migros acquired the two Carrefour hypermarkets in Switzerland in May 1991 and have given over some of the floorspace in the converted stores to Pick Pay. The significance of this move is that Pick Pay retails a range of branded foods which includes alcohol and tobacco. Thus, while not retailing these products themselves, they may now be found under the same roof as the traditional Migros offer. These events have been seen by some as cracks in the original Migros philosophy and approach to retailing.

Whatever the long-term future for Migros, the company appears to be so firmly engrained in Swiss society that the opening sentence of Bryan Smith's 1982 article is likely to be applicable for many more years: 'Switzerland might aptly be described as the land of "M" standing for money, mountains and Migros.' Few retailers have achieved such institutional status within their market.

References and further reading

The Economist (1983), 'The mighty Migros', 26 March 1983, 78–9.

The Economist (1992), 'Strength through eccentricity', 12 December 1992, 93–4.

Elvin, R. (1986), 'Migros: the multiple that wheeled its way to Europe's summit', *The Grocer*, 12 July 1986, 44–6.

The Grocer (1987), 'Was this multiple abusing its power?', 10 January 1987.

Häsler, A. A. (1985), *'L'Aventure Migros'*, Fédération des Co-opératives Migros, Zurich.

Marguerite, C. (1992), 'Migros: cap sur l'international', *Libre Service Actualités*, 1294, 5 mars 1992, 34–5.

Rigoureau, A. (1990), 'Gros: des Suisses au-dessus de tout soupçon', *Libre Service Actualités*, 1202, 22 mars 1990, 42–8.

Smith, B. (1982), 'Migros: Switzerland's retailing giant', *Retail & Distribution Management*, 5, December 1982, 8–17.

Migros Annual Reports and Social Reports.

Consumerism in the cosmetics and toiletries industry

Barbara Lewis and Catherine Woodman
Manchester School of Management

Context

This is case is focused on the UK cosmetics and toiletries industry, which comprises a wide spectrum of personal care products including household toiletries, cosmetics and fragrances. A number of developments which affect the growth of the industry are highlighted, in particular environmental and green trends. Data is then presented from a survey of customers of a retail toiletries company and a number of questions posed relating to recent trends and consumer concerns and actions.

The cosmetics and toiletries industry

Growth in the cosmetics and toiletries industry has been stimulated by developments in the environment and society, which may be summarised under a number of headings.

Demographic and social trends

- *Improved housing conditions and living standards,* leading to higher standards of personal care and hygiene.
- *The importance of personal appearance and grooming.*
- *Demographic trends.* There is an increasing number of young consumers and an increasing proportion of older customers. Also, an increasing number of working women, who are more aware of cosmetic and skin care products and who have money to spend on them.
- *The emergence of the 'new man',* and men taking a greater interest in personal hygiene and appearance and grooming, and being more receptive to new products and sales approaches.
- *Increased interest in healthy living.* There are changes in consumer awareness, knowledge and attitudes with respect to health (diet and exercise), alternative medicines, natural products and the environment.

Marketing developments

The cosmetics and toiletries industry has traditionally marketed its products using the image of glamour and sophistication, conveyed to the consumer through both advertising and product packaging. Recent marketing developments, however, relate to:

- *Product innovations* (e.g. skin care, sun care, anti-allergy products.)
- *Retailer own brands* (e.g. Boots, Marks & Spencer, Body Shop).

Environmental/Consumer concerns

In recent years there has been a dramatic increase in public awareness of environmental issues and this has had an important influence on the cosmetics and toiletries industry in relation to:

- *Product ingredients.* Natural ingredients were used in skin care and hair care preparations long before the cosmetics industry existed and there is now an increasing demand for a return to natural ingredients.
- *Product testing.* Consumers increasingly want cosmetics and toiletries that have not been tested on animals and may be prepared to pay a premium for these. Pressure group activity (e.g. the British Union for Abolition of Vivisection) has led to a more sensitive approach by manufacturers and retailers.
- *Packaging.* Consumers are concerned, for example, about materials, waste, and damage to the ozone layer.

As a consequence of these concerns, some companies do consider the environment and animal rights in addition to profitability. They do not necessarily promote idealised notions of beauty or claim that products will perform cosmetic miracles. Some *do* strike fair deals with suppliers, conserve resources and reduce waste, save customers money, and promote environmental, community and charitable causes.

The Natural Cosmetics and Toiletries Company

Natural Cosmetics and Toiletries supports and promotes a number of environmental and social causes as follows:

- None of its ingredients or products are tested on animals.
- It uses only natural ingredients.
- All its raw materials are micro-biologically tested.
- The formulations are tested on humans for safety, irritation and allergies.
- They lobby for recognition of proven alternatives to animal testing.

In addition, they are at the forefront of a number of consumer/green issues ranging from Greenpeace, Friends of the Earth, Amnesty International,

Shelter, Stop the Burning, and Refill-Re-use-and-Recycle. Further, they use the minimum of packaging, use plastic instead of glass, recycle containers and use recycled paper.

Through all of these activities they create a store/company image that people associate with the corporate name. Such an image usually influences consumers' perceptions of products in the shops, and to some extent consumers choose stores and buy products to re-enforce a self-concept. This may well be to symbolise an *ideal* self (how one would like to be) rather than a *real* self.

Natural Cosmetics and Toiletries was interested in knowing the extent to which its consumers demonstrated *concern* and *action* with respect to the company ideals and philosophy. A structured survey questionnaire (see Exhibit 7.1 below) was designed to assess:

- Aspects of buyer behaviour (e.g. frequency of visits, reasons for purchase, use of competitors).
- Activities which customers took part in that contribute to a 'green' life-style.
- Customers' values regarding environmental issues.

Findings from 178 respondents are presented in the following tables.

Case study questions

1. *Evaluate recent demographic and social trends and their impact on the cosmetics and toiletries industry.*

2. *What are the important consumer 'green' issues in the industry? How are they addressed by consumers, organisations and pressure groups?*

3. *Interpret the results from the survey of Natural Cosmetics and Toiletries customers.*

4. *Outline any inconsistencies in the survey data and suggest possible explanations for them.*

Exhibit 7.1 Natural Cosmetics and Toiletries – Customer Survey[1]

Questions about the purchase you have just made

1. What have you just purchased? (open-ended)

Creams/lotions	27.0	Bath/shower	16.9
Shampoos/conditioners	23.0	Colourings	15.2
Perfume/oils	21.9	Facial products	14.6

2. Number of items bought (open-ended)

1 – 48.3	3 – 17.4	5 – 3.9
2 – 24.7	4 – 5.1	6 – 0.6

3. Total price paid for these goods

Less than £2	18.5
£2 – £5	42.7
£5.01 – £10	30.9
More than £10	7.9

4. Did you purchase these goods?

for yourself	67.7
on behalf of someone	4.5
for a present	19.3
combination of above	8.5

Questions about your visits to Natural Cosmetics and Toiletries

5. How often approximately do you visit Natural Cosmetics & Toiletries?

once a week	7.9
once every 2–3 weeks	41.8
once every 1–3 months	44.0
once every 6 months	5.1
once a year or less	1.1

6. Do you usually buy something?

every visit	46.4
most visits	36.7
some visits	14.1
occasionally	2.8

7. How long have you been a customer of Natural Cosmetics & Toiletries?

less than a year	9.1
1 – 5 years	75.0
6 – 10 years	15.3
more than 10 years	0.6

[1]All response figures are given as a percentage of total responses.

8. Why do you buy goods from Natural Cosmetics & Toiletries? (open-ended)

Not tested on animals	53.9
Quality/performance of alternatives	37.1
Price/value for money	33.7
Range/originality	24.2
Ethics/environment	23.0
Natural ingredients	21.9
Good for skin type	19.1
Design/novelty	15.7
Good for presents	14.6
Recycled/simple packing	12.9
Nice smells	12.4
Helpful staff	10.1
Shop environment	8.4
Refilling facility	7.3
Information	5.1
Non-animal ingredients	5.1
Testers/many sizes	5.1
Supports Third World trade/human rights	3.4

9. Do you use the Refill Service?   Yes – 32.0

10. Have you ever taken back containers to be recycled?   Yes – 24.7

11. Do you buy toiletries from other shops or organisations?   Yes – 93.2

12. Which shops or organisations do you also buy toiletries from? (open-ended)

Boots the Chemist	69.7
Superdrug	30.9
Supermarkets	20.8
Marks & Spencer	14.6
Other (department stores, mail order, health food shops, chemists)	23.6

13. For what reasons do you buy toiletries from these sources in preference to Natural Cosmetics & Toiletries? (open-ended)

Convenience, save time shopping	53.9
Price, special offers, discounts	34.8
Brands/products available	28.7
Performance and quality of alternatives	21.3
Range/choice	10.1

▶

Questions about your home life

14. Do you recycle any of the following on a regular basis at home?

Newspapers	52.8
Glass	38.2
Plastics	12.9
Aluminium cans	29.2
Clothing	32.0
None	29.2

15. Are you a member of any of the following organisations and/or receive information from them?

World Wide Fund for Nature	12.4
British Union for the Abolition of Vivisection	8.4
Greenpeace	9.0
Friends of the Earth	6.2
National Trust	6.2
Lynx	5.1
None	69.1

Have you ever?

16. Made any home improvements to save energy   Yes – 60.2

17. Purchased particular goods for environmental reasons   Yes – 86.0

18. Converted your car to run on unleaded petrol   Yes – 44.9

19. Used public transport or cycled INSTEAD of a car
    for environmental reasons?   Yes – 29.3

20. Bought 'Ecover' or another 'environmentally friendly'
    washing powder   Yes – 43.0

▶

21. Have you done any of the following in the past 12 months?

	None	1–5 times	6–10 times	More than 10 times
Been for a walk in the country	9.6	44.4	16.9	29.2
Been involved in any conservation work	88.8	9.6	1.1	0.6
Bought goods from an environmental organisation	42.7	43.3	8.4	5.6
Discussed environmental issues with friends or family	16.3	43.3	17.4	23.0
Bought goods that support Third World trade	46.6	39.9	5.6	7.9
Written to your MP about an issue concerning the environment, animal testing or the Third World	90.4	8.4	0.6	0.6

▶

22. Please indicate your agreement with the following statements

	Agree completely	Agree somewhat	Agree a little	Disagree a little	Disagree somewhat	Disagree completely
I look for value for money rather than anything else when purchasing goods	9.7	27.5	31.4	14.8	8.5	8.0
I am willing to spend more on products that have 'not been tested on animals'	45.4	24.3	18.2	3.7	5.3	3.2
I would not buy goods from shops whose business ethics I disagreed with	53.2	16.0	14.7	5.2	4.0	6.8
I like toiletries to look expensive	6.8	10.8	18.7	9.7	13.0	40.9
I like to buy recycled toilet paper	34.7	19.9	17.1	11.3	4.6	12.5
The actions of individuals do not make any difference to protecting the world	6.3	2.8	5.2	11.9	15.9	58.0
I am satisfied with present labelling on 'green' products	13.0	18.2	21.0	14.8	19.3	13.7
I cannot be bothered to recycle things	3.4	7.9	14.1	20.3	17.5	36.7
The Government is not doing enough to pass legislation that will protect the environment	50.0	20.4	10.8	8.0	8.5	2.2
Manufacturers should be held responsible for the effect their products have on the environment	62.1	20.3	9.7	0.6	2.8	4.5
I always buy the same toiletry brands	22.0	22.7	14.1	14.1	11.3	10.8
There should be more recycling facilities	72.3	15.8	8.5	1.1	–	2.2
I like to buy products with a certain 'image'	6.3	13.7	21.0	11.9	12.5	34.7
I would not return empty bottles or containers to shops, even if there was the opportunity	2.8	1.1	9.1	11.9	14.1	61.1
I like to keep up with fashion	15.6	31.0	26.4	5.2	8.6	13.2
How much I like a product is more important than the price	40.8	30.1	14.2	9.7	4.6	0.6
I only buy toiletries that have 'not been tested on animals'	38.4	22.6	14.7	12.5	5.6	6.2
I would never buy recycled writing paper	1.1	2.8	3.9	7.9	9.7	74.6
Buying goods that support Third World trade does not make much difference to individuals there	6.7	6.3	16.5	13.0	18.2	39.2
I would be happy to have no excess packaging on toiletries	74.6	12.5	5.6	2.8	1.1	3.4

Brashs
An expanding success

Michael Collins
Australian Centre for Retail Studies, Monash University

Context

Brashs has been one of Australia's fastest growing and most profitable retailers of the last decade. It was ranked 222 in Australian Business's Top 500 list for 1990. Its sales had reached $429,750,000 with pre-tax profits of $15 million. The company had stores in every state. Not only was it the dominant specialty chain for consumer electronics, recorded music and musical instruments, but it had also entered book retailing by taking over several large book retailers and expanded into New Zealand.

From the beginning (1862–1957)

Its extraordinary success has been no accident. It has been the result of far-sighted leadership, disciplined management, and outstanding retail practice. That leadership began with Marcus Brash, who founded the company in 1862 to import and sell pianos and reed organs. Trading commenced in 1880 at 108 Elizabeth Street, Melbourne, which remains the company's flagship store. Over the following twenty-five years, Brashs built up a strong reputation for quality pianos. It flourished in an era when home entertainment among the middle and upper classes was an important social activity. Melbourne itself was the manufacturing and financial centre of Australia, particularly after the First World War.

During this period and up to 1955, the City held a dominant share of Melbourne metropolitan retail sales. Although there were a number of strong inner suburban shopping concentrations, such as Prahran, Moonee Ponds and Camberwell, most people went to the City to shop for anything other than immediate household needs. Brashs was well placed to take advantage of this City trade, although it had plenty of competition.

However, from the beginning, the company sought opportunities to develop the business to gain a competitive edge. It widened its original range from musical instruments to gramophones and records early in the century. In 1927 it took the important pioneering step of opening the first radio department in order to exploit the 'wireless boom'. The department ranked amongst the best in Australia and became the forerunner of the company's consumer electronic division. This in turn led to the further extension of the product range in the 1930s, to include radiograms, record players and music. In the same period Brashs also set up a recording studio in its Elizabeth Street store and began producing its own aluminium discs.

After the Second World War, the Company picked up franchises for imported goods. It recognised the great opportunity in white goods and gained a Kelvinator agency as only one of three retailers to sell their much sought after brand (the others being Myer and A. H. Gibson, later Vealls). Thus Brashs took full advantage of the rapidly growing demand for refrigerators. Myer was the dominant retailer but Brashs won a substantial segment of the market by offering trade-ins on ice-chests and even radios. Demand was so great that customers had to put down deposits and wait months before delivery. Brashs won a reputation as the store to go to through surprising its customers by getting them their refrigerators earlier than the original promised delivery dates. Brashs sold 1,000 refrigerators a year from their 5th floor! White goods became 75 per cent of the business as Brashs expanded the range to cover washing machines and small appliances.

The older 'brown goods' or radio department was transformed in 1956 when the Olympic Games came to Melbourne, and with it, the introduction of black and white television. Australia's wealth led to rapid penetration of television into virtually every household and Brashs took full advantage of this opportunity.

The company also diversified into furniture as it owned another building. However, this was soon discontinued and the building sold off to provide cash to buy out the well-known Frankston radio and TV retailer, Harold Peakes. This first move into the suburbs was made to take advantage of the emerging TV boom and marked the beginning of Brashs as a specialty chain.

The making of a chain (1958–1978)

The post-war population explosion, high immigration numbers and a level of affluence such that car ownership became commonplace, led to the shopping centre revolution which changed the face of retailing in Australia. In Melbourne, Myer established the first regional shopping centre at Chadstone in 1960, followed by Northland, Southland and Eastland. Brashs was among the first specialty retailers to lease shops in these centres.

To expand sales and exploit the accelerating market for consumer electrical goods, Brashs had also to address its credit problem. Up to this period the company had carried its own hire purchase but this had created a massive contingent liability. To overcome this, it was floated to become a public company in 1958 and part of the new funds were used to establish Music

Acceptance as the company's finance company.

It then took the highly significant strategic decision to drop white goods. Brashs had always based their business on service; this meant not only in-store personal service but also providing installation and aftersales service, which involved heavy investment. Brashs had initially built its white goods business on Kelvinator but when Kelvinator decided to expand their distribution to other retailers, Brashs changed to Frigidaire. However, by the mid-1960s, manufacturers had begun doing their own servicing by setting up installation divisions. Furthermore as supply now began overtaking demand, discounters emerged in the marketplace, so Brashs could no longer maintain margins. Indeed Brashs was even seen to be 'ripping off' the consumer with their higher prices, which was clearly an untenable position. They decided therefore to take white goods out of all their stores, except the Southland store to which they transferred all their stock. To Brashs' surprise, sales in their other stores held up despite now only offering brown goods. This experience proved to management the value and opportunity of being a real *specialist* store. It was a lesson Brashs has never forgotten.

The discounters also competed with Brashs in brown goods and this led to the adoption of another important strategy: the development of exclusive brands and products to get away from direct price competition. Brashs established a wholesale arm to selectively distribute these exclusive lines in sufficient volumes to do justice to their retail agencies. The products covered all the merchandise sections of the business. Joint ventures were formed with the principal overseas suppliers, including Norlin Music (Lowrey Organs), Teac (audio) and Roland (electronics). Brashs also had its own exclusive brand, Silver, in audio products. These strategies became critical following the 1974 Trade Practices legislation which removed manufacturer control over prices, thereby accelerating discount retailing and the introduction of discount department stores.

To expand its business further, in 1964 Brashs took the significant step of acquiring Suttons and in 1969, Kilners, two prominent music businesses with long traditions. Suttons had been confined to pianos until 1952 when it introduced musical instrument departments in order to position itself as a music store. It had three stores in Victoria and three in New South Wales, but had encountered financial difficulties. The purchase not only added new stores but also expanded Brashs' range to include a music division. This was enhanced by the acquisition of Allans in 1976 – a music publishing house with stores in Victoria, South Australia and Tasmania. Allans, established in 1850, was Australia's oldest and most prestigious music firm. By acquiring it, Brashs took its first step towards a national presence.

Sales of its core consumer products rose strongly over this formative period which had begun with the introduction of black and white TV in 1956 and ended with the introduction of colour TV in 1975, marking the start of a new era in home entertainment. Sales were also achieved by the steady increase in store numbers. As more shopping centres opened, Brashs became a sought-after tenant which gave it an important negotiating advantage. By 1978, the company had stores across Melbourne, in Victorian country centres and its Allans stores interstate. It had thus become a substantial and financially strong Victorian music, TV and hi-fi chain, able to offer suppliers not only large volume orders but also immediate settlement. This gave the company a significant competitive advantage over independent electrical retailers.

During this period Brashs had also ventured into wholesaling. This was a defensive move to get exclusivity over selected brands and hold on to its agencies. However, wholesaling required holding higher stocks, carrying debtors and different selling and management skills to retailing. After sustaining substantial losses, in 1977 it decided to close this division down and put the total focus back on retailing. Nevertheless it had played an important strategic role. As Geoff Brash pointed out:

> the Wholesale Division gave us an opportunity to provide exclusive brands in all product areas of our business. It gave us as a retailer a wholesale antenna and as a wholesaler we had a retail antenna; it made us unique in the marketplace.
>
> From the wholesale business we developed joint ventures which were very successful indeed. We came apart because of the temptation of colour television in 1975 and allowed the Wholesale Division to over expand and eventually endanger the business. We made a quick decision to close it.

A decade to dominance (1979–1989)

After 15 years of steady growth, in 1978 the company's pre-tax profit was halved from the previous year's peak. For the first time Brashs found itself in a difficult position and had to review its whole operation. It realised that its past growth and financial success had been largely due to the strong growth in consumer demand and the company's extensive opening of new stores to exploit that demand.

The immediate problem was to recover sales and improve profitability. To do this, it embarked on an aggressive promotional campaign and severe cost-cutting programmes. Unprofitable assets were sold off and tighter budgetary controls introduced.

Mr Peter Bennell in a speech to the AIM National Convention in 1986 described the next step. He pointed out that:

> As a result (of these initial actions), earnings and return on investment rose; however, they were still not satisfactory and the moves were obviously shoring up exercises. To achieve better returns, the company had to reassess its whole operation by undertaking a detailed strategic analysis of its business, establish new objectives, develop a strategic plan and then detailed operational plans. Our immediate task at Brashs was to define objectives, group- and then division-wise. These were quantified to achieve the desired return on investment – that is, on shareholders funds, net profit, growth, sales and market share growth.
>
> If necessary, these objectives would be modified after the analysis of our industry outlook and our competitive position was completed: in fact they were.
>
> Having defined our objectives, our next task was then to determine our growth

strategy. This was achieved by defining the driving force or common thread which our company possessed and which would indicate the direction in which the company could move. The common thread was identified by examining our product market scope using the traditional areas of growth which were available. These were: increased market penetration, opening of new markets, widening the product range and acquisition or diversification. We also needed to examine the competitive advantages which the Group enjoyed.

Firstly, we commenced by undertaking a general audit of our business. This involved a detailed study of our markets, our potential customers and our competitors plus a detailed analysis of our own strengths and weaknesses. It also involved a major review of our organisation and our staff. Our line managers were very much involved in this strengths and weaknesses review.

Every aspect of the company was therefore placed under the microscope. In-depth research was undertaken to determine consumers' purchasing habits and preferences. The critical issue was to identify how Brashs could develop a competitive edge, since essentially it was selling the same products and brands as its competitors. This analysis enabled it to define five components, which Peter Bennell described as:

Firstly, visual merchandising by making our stores more appealing, attractive and exciting to customers.

Offering the customer the largest range of products in our specialty areas. This led to the creation of our superstores.

More dominant promotions: that is, more frequent, larger, more aggressive promotional price-type advertising. Our research showed that we were perceived to be expensive: we were not in fact, but were seen to be and we had to change that perception. We, in fact, renamed our consumer electronics stores Brashs Discounts.

The buying/merchandising department had to be more effective; that is, buy on more beneficial terms with the right advertising back up and provide the right stock.

Better information systems to measure the *hero* products that will give better returns.

However it was also recognised that people were critical to the successful implementation of strategies, particularly those in the stores. To quote Peter Bennell again:

We saw the calibre of our sales staff as the most important factor in differentiating us from our competitors and providing a major competitive advantage: this is, in the selection, training, motivation and rewarding of our sales staff within our Group. The Store Manager – who spends a good deal of his time selling – and our sales staff are absolutely critical to our success.

We therefore had to acquaint our staff right down to the salespeople with what our future objectives were, as well as our plans to achieve these objectives in general and then, in detailed terms, set out our detailed operational plans for division and store and individual targets. Staff were briefed on where we were at that time, where we could go, how we could go. They knew what was expected of them and were given their detailed operational programmes.

Senior and middle managers were given detailed assessment of our business and alternatives at a weekend in the country.

We also introduced a new sales training course with a great deal of emphasis on the technical skills of floor selling, product knowledge particularly product benefits and how to sell them. This involved extensive role playing. We changed our remuneration package to reward entirely on gross profit results for sales staff and net profit for store managers; thus setting apart the capable from the mediocre. We also introduced recognition and achievement awards with financial incentives. We make a great effort to recognise our top achievers with award presentations and publicity in our in-house magazine. To provide greater staff involvement a staff share scheme introduced several years earlier was extended. This was available to all staff who had been with the company for three years or more.

This recognition of the importance of investing in people later led to the development of the company's own one-year Diploma in Management Skills involving field projects, classroom training and assessment.

The company has also had a deep commitment to ethics and sought a carefully crafted balance between aggressive selling and dedication to customer service. This is the essence of the company's culture. Geoffrey Brash wrote: 'above all, I know my Father, who in his sixty years in the business, believed passionately about integrity, high standards of service and sharing benefits with staff. It was he who introduced employee shares long before my time. I really believe that the sound foundation of the business comes from this culture.' In 1984 Brashs stated that its operating philosophy was based on 3Ps: People, Product and Promotion. Promotion, particularly advertising, played a vital role in Brashs becoming a household name in the 1980s.

Market research had shown that Brashs was regarded as too expensive and hence its near disastrous loss of sales and market share. Its advertising agency persuaded the company to use TV, which no other major retailer had previously used. Geoff Brash approached suppliers to help subsidise the campaign in which Mike Springfield III from the original cast of 'Hair!' was the presenter. He had to promise it would increase sales by 25 per cent in three months. As Mr Brash said:

That was a gamble. Our business actually increased by over 50 per cent so we were able to continue the programme with backing support from suppliers. Our business boomed. The change of image was dramatically successful. We then engaged Sammy Davis Jnr., who would not promote a product but promoted the concept of Brashs. At the end of the Sammy Davis Jnr. advertisement we would put a slide on TV advertising the product. The programme was a flop and we changed agencies. The new agency discovered that the advertisement was so entertaining that nobody saw the product! When the product slide was inserted in the middle of the advertisement the business recovered immediately.

Nevertheless, despite the lessons inherent in this story, the campaign slogan 'Right On, Mr B' had created a very high awareness level of Brashs. The company then embarked on a programme of aggressive pricing using catalogues, promotions and specials. By the end of the decade Brashs was the third largest spender on advertising.

With the company now leaner and meaner, more professional in its planning and control, and with a strong external image, Brashs' growth and profitability were restored. It was now able to channel and focus its resources towards the long-term objective of achieving national dominance in the home entertainment business.

Brashs started out on the major geographical expansion strategy beyond Victoria by acquiring R. H. Elvy in 1980. Elvy's was a long-established retailer of organs and pianos in New South Wales, where it had a store in Sydney and one in Parramatta. In 1981 Brashs acquired a well-known store in Brisbane, B. B. Whitehouse & Co., which it expanded in 1985 to include musical instruments and a print music department.

The company also started opening record stores interstate and acquired Edels in 1984, a 22-outlet record store chain in New South Wales. This made Brashs Australia's leading retailer of pre-recorded music with 61 stores across Victoria, NSW, SA and Tasmania. In 1986 Brashs opened the largest music and record store in Australia with its Pitt Street store in Sydney.

The company continued to acquire other music businesses, particularly in new geographical markets as well as opening new stores to expand its market base. In 1987 it bought out Geoffrey Buttons and Commodore TV consumer electronics stores in Sydney suburbs and opened its first superstores in South Australia. In 1988 Brashs purchased Palings music stores in Sydney and Brisbane and Douglas Hi-Fi in Victoria. In 1989 it acquired Douglas Hi-Fi in Western Australia, Dandy Sound in Victoria and Miranda Hi-Fi in Sydney.

Perhaps the most significant strategic decision in this decade was to develop, broaden and deepen its range of consumer electronics (audio/video) products by launching its superstore concept. The first of these 10,000 sq. ft stores was opened in Blackburn, Victoria in 1982. Its success was immediate and led to similar stores being opened in Adelaide and Sydney as well as Melbourne. Apart from their strong merchandise impact, these free-standing 'highway' stores presented a discount price image to combat such discount chains as Billy Guyatt and Norman Ross.

This strategy was in response to the extraordinary growth of demand in consumer electronic products due to 'their cost efficiency as well as their utility' as noted in the 1984 Annual Report. This report noted that VCR units had grown from 50,000 to 700,000 units per year in just four years, to achieve 40 per cent household penetration, the highest in the world. Brashs introduced microwaves into its range in 1983 as these were also produced by a number of their consumer electronics suppliers. It also took advantage of the growth in pre-recorded music and in blank tapes which had risen from one to nine million over this four-year period.

By 1986 Brashs had deliberately realigned its business to concentrate on the more profitable product categories and to shift its emphasis to consumer electronics products where it was clearly seen as being at 'the forefront of these waves of change'. These now included the introduction of camcorders, compact disc players, fax machines, and cellular phones as well as larger screen stereo colour TVs. The technological revolution also changed the market for instruments with the introduction of electronic organs and other products, which also boosted Brashs' music division.

The 1988 Annual Report traced this technological revolution from the invention of the vacuum tube to the silicon chip and integrated circuit. It predicted that 'today our history is becoming part of the fabric of Australian daily life and as the home becomes the focal point of a family's activities a greater proportion of discretionary income will flow into consumer electronics.' Brashs had always been quick to recognise the potential of new products. The company estimated that 40 per cent of its consumer electronics products were not in existence just five years ago.

Brashs' primary aim had been to offer the consumer as wide a range as possible in both products and price. This has been largely possible through its cultivation of strong partnership relations with key suppliers. Although it reduced its shareholding in its major joint venture in 1983, special relationships with Teac, Norlin and Roland in particular contributed significantly to Brashs' success, and in turn to the progress of these key suppliers.

At the same time the company has sought to give value. It has been able to offer lower prices through importing and working with suppliers to offer promotional products. 'Our philosophy is to give more value for money than anybody else and more quality in terms of products, service, and after sales attention' (1988 Annual Report).

During this period, Brashs' store network had been rationalised into three major categories. At the top were the superstores discussed earlier. The second category were the combined stores of 3–4,000 sq. ft, typically located in regional shopping malls which carried both consumer electronics and records. The third group were record only stores of 1,000 sq. ft which were mainly in shopping malls. This had been necessary because there were many stores trying to sell records, hi-fi and TV products out of very limited space, creating overcrowding and uninviting ranges.

Over the years but behind the scenes, Brashs had also been investing in information technology (IT). From its earliest days as a chain it recognised the importance of setting up not only financial, but also sales and stock control systems, which have all grown in sophistication. Apart from enabling management to keep a tight rein on expenditure, IT has helped the company to decentralise its management and give greater responsibility to those at the operating end of the business.

The company has also sought to be a responsible corporate citizen. One of its chief initiatives was to establish The Brash Foundation in 1986 to contribute to the development of music in Australia, including The Sound House to help music making.

Presentation of stores has been an important element of Brashs' strategy. The company has aimed at giving an 'immediate overwhelming impression' of product availability, range and price. This, together with the third element of ambience, not only make the stores inviting and exciting but also create the strong identification of Brashs as a 'destination' store. Brashs has continually invested in upgrading and refurbishing its stores to ensure they always have a fresh, exciting and modern appearance. Stores that do not perform are closed as soon as leases permit. Careful attention is paid to layout, product adjacencies and merchandising to guide customers through the store and simplify the customer purchase decision.

By the end of the decade Brashs had established itself as the nation's dominant retailer in home entertainment. The keys to that success have been described and are apparent in this story. They were summed up by the chairman, Geoffrey Brash, at an International Roundtable in 1984 as:

- Concentrate on strengths and markets which we can dominate.
- Recruit and develop people of quality and dedication.
- Improve the quality of relations with staff, suppliers, customers and shareholders.
- Develop and use information systems.
- Develop leadership qualities in executives.
- Be innovative and continue to take risks.

The extent of the success is illustrated in Tables 8.1, 8.2, 8.3 and 8.4.

Thus the 1989 Annual Report was able to reflect that 'structured dynamic growth was the hallmark of The Brashs Group in the 1980s'. It had taken a significant lead in the Home Entertainment Revolution, but could its growth be sustained?

Table 8.1 Brashs' market share: 1989

Item	Market ($m.)	Brashs ($m.)	Percentage of business	Percentage share
Consumer electronics	1,650.0	198.2	58.8	12.0
Pre-recorded music, videos, etc.	855.0	101.4	30.1	11.9
Musical products and print music	300.0	37.5	11.1	12.5
Total	2,850.0	337.1	100.0	12.0

Table 8.2 Brashs' consumer electronics estimated market share, 1989 (units)

Item	TV	VCR	Camcorders	Microwaves	CD players
Victoria	23.0	27.0	32.0	6.0	38.0
National	10.0	14.0	17.0	3.0	20.0

Table 8.3 Brashs' store outlets, January 1990

Number of stores by division		Number of stores by state	
Records	83	New South Wales (with ACT)	36
Consumer electronics	43	Victoria	48
Superstores	23	Queensland	13
Musical products	13	Western Australia	8
Print music	7	Tasmania	4
		Northern Territory	6
Total	169		115

Table 8.4 Brashs' sales, profit and financial ratios, 1979–1989

	1979	1989	Percentage change
Sales ($200)	40,017	340,329	+750.5
Profit before tax ($m.)	2,386	12,387	+419.2
Return on equity (%)	14.4	17.4	
Earnings per share (cents)		38.8	
Asset/sales (%)		26.5	
Debt/equity (%)		27.3	
Store (number)	33	115	

Diversification for the 1990s

Throughout the last decade, the company had focused its business on consumer electronics and recorded music to establish its reputation as a 'first choice' store for these products. Although its range included the anomaly of microwave ovens, its business was clearly based on home entertainment.

Nevertheless the company's strategic analysis and environmental scanning had picked up the emerging trend towards home entertainment in a wider context. There were strong indications that the 1990s would see people returning more to the home as a focus of activity, encouraged by a return to more conservative, family-orientated values and by a growing concern about personal security. Furthermore, technological advances in communication and computers were likely to lead to more activities being conducted from the home, including work, shopping and entertainment.

It was therefore logical for Brashs to broaden its scope or mission beyond consumer electronics and music products to develop the business for the new decade. Such broadening was crucial to long-term growth due to the relatively small size of the Australian domestic market and the increasing problem of 'cannibalisation' of sales as outlets proliferated into every area of Australia.

The company identified that the most closely allied business in home entertainment with similar retail practices was books, particularly as these were now becoming available in recorded media. Therefore, in 1989 Brashs diversified into book retailing by acquiring one of Australia's best-known book chains, Angus & Robertson, with its fifty-two company owned outlets and fifty-three franchised stores. This was soon followed by Bookworld, a chain of thirty stores owned by the British Paul Hamlyn Group, making Brashs Australia's largest bookseller. The company's press release of 6 June 1990 stated:

> The Directors believe that book retailing represents an appropriate extension of Brashs' core activities, in particular Angus & Robertson. At this stage of development, it provides scope for Brashs to expand one of Australia's best-known and respected book retailing chains.
>
> Angus & Robertson stores have offered customers a wide range of products at competitive prices since 1886. More recently, the Group has opened eight stores trading under the 'Colourcode Book Discount' banner to compete in the discount price market. Sales have grown steadily over the past five years.
>
> Angus & Robertson's operations are similar to Brashs' recorded music division, with both businesses operating in high traffic locations and balancing stock ranges between the current best sellers and back catalogues.

Clearly the company was now poised for a new and exciting period of growth.

At the same time, the company had also recognised the opportunity to go off-shore. In 1990 it acquired from Thorn-EMI the record retailing operation of HMV in New Zealand. The stores were changed to Brashs and remerchandised accordingly to mirror the Australian chain. Synergies included management expertise and experience, together with a closely linked supplier base.

It was considered that despite deteriorating economic conditions, the company was now well poised for the new era. Its confidence was reflected in Brashs' 1989 Annual Report, which stated that its corporate objectives were as follows:

- To achieve sales of $1 billion in the 1994–5 fiscal year.
- To earn a satisfactory return in excess of 25 per cent, after tax, on shareholders' funds.
- To be the leading specialty retailer in home entertainment and home communications in Australia.
- To value equally our employees, customers, suppliers and shareholders.
- To contribute to the community.
- To attract, reward and retain the best possible people and to provide challenging and satisfying work opportunities in a stimulating and friendly environment.
- To strive for excellence in all we do.

Will Brashs achieve these objectives? What challenges does it face? What further initiatives will it have to take? What lessons can be applied from its past development? Which strategic concepts can you identify that Brashs consciously applied in order to achieve its current position?

Exhibit 8.1 gives a synopsis of Brashs' financial performance from 1979 to 1990.

Exhibit 8.1 Brashs' financial performance ($000) 1979–1990

	1990	1989	1988	1987	1986	1985	1984	1983	1982	1981	1980	1979
Sales	429,750	340,329	263,442	180,553	162,667	147,725	128,003	102,792	78,290	65,678	49,829	40,017
Profit before interest and tax	15,019	12,387	10,533	8,807	8,664	7,251	5,740	5,151	4,425	3,764	3,272	2,386
Net profit after tax	9,247	7,632	5,901	4,358	4,613	3,905	3,092	2,752	2,389	2,032	1,761	1,728
Interest paid	2,661	1,086	970	965	832	779	576	560				
Total assets	141,584	96,128	70,776	60,600	52,476	48,327	41,417	34,149				
Inventory	80,815	51,888	40,640	31,419	26,494	25,008	22,628	17,387				
Shareholders funds	61,482	43,838	29,439	28,137	28,137	24,708	20,484	18,662	17,174	15,912	13,191	12,023
Earnings per share (cents)	42.5	38.8	32.9	25.0	26.8	22.8	18.0	16.0				
Selling area (sq. metres)	51,468	43,044	33,444	23,059			19,414					

Source: Annual Reports for financial years ending 31 July

Part Three

MANAGEMENT OF STRATEGIC CHANGE

A case of dynamic growth and development is provided by 'Argyll Group plc', by Colin Clarke-Hill and Terry Robinson. They present alternative directions for growth, including choices between building or buying brands, and strategies for entering mainland Europe.

Acquisition strategy and the subsequent problems of integrating very different organisational cultures are the focus of Gerry Johnson's 'Harpers' takeover of Coopers'. The case emphasises the links between organisational culture and strategy, developing the concept of a culture web.

The problems of managing an international grouping of partly autonomous retailers are illustrated by Lluís Martínez-Ribes in 'Intersport Spain'. The case invites a strategic audit of the group's strengths, weaknesses, opportunities and threats within the Spanish market.

Problems are also the focus in 'Ratners: a successful retail strategy derailed?', written by Chris Carr and Neil Botten. The case demonstrates the need for sound financial analysis to help avoid some of the potential pitfalls of an ambitious acquisitions strategy.

Argyll Group plc

Colin Clarke-Hill and Terry Robinson
University of Huddersfield

Context

The decade of the 1980s saw many significant changes in the UK economy. Many companies, in every sector of the economy and particularly in retailing, rose from obscurity to gain national or international prominence. Among them was the Argyll Group. Since 1978, Argyll, through a series of astute acquisitions, had become the third largest food retailer in the UK by 1992, with sales of over £5 bn and a market capitalisation (December 1992) of £4.45 bn. By 1992, Argyll Group operated throughout the UK from 819 stores that had a combined sales area of 8.44 million square feet. In addition to supermarkets, Argyll also had interests in the cash and carry and specialist frozen food distribution sectors. In the fourteen years since 1978, Argyll's pre-tax profit had risen from zero to £365 m.

Growth and development of the company

The origins of Argyll can be traced back to the early 1970s when a management team, comprising James Gulliver, Alistair Grant and David Webster became responsible for the development of Oriel Foods which was acquired by the RCA Corporation in 1974. Following three years of success, they left Oriel/RCA to lay the foundations of the current Argyll company. These foundations were laid on a pattern of acquiring underperforming companies and rebuilding their businesses. The Argyll team's first move into the food industry came in April 1978 when they took control of Morgan Edwards, a loss-making listed grocery distributor based in Shrewsbury. Many of Morgan Edwards' underperforming Supavalu stores were closed, Edwards' discounting policy was reversed and controls on costs and margins were tightened. Much of the restructuring and debt reduction of the Morgan Edwards business was funded by the sale of their non-retail businesses, while at the same time a compatible business (Paddys, based in the north Midlands) was acquired to give the embryonic retail group some economies of scale.

Early in 1979, another heavily geared and loss-making company, also quoted on the Stock Exchange, came under the team's management control, namely Louis C. Edwards & Sons (Manchester), a meat-processing and wholesaling company with retail butchers shops. A strategy similar to that followed at Morgan Edwards was observed; the loss-making processing and wholesaling operations were disposed of or closed and margins in the butchers shops rebuilt. In the same year two successful biscuit manufacturers, Yorkshire Biscuits and Furniss & Co., were acquired for £3 million.

In 1980, Louis Edwards acquired two freezer chains: Cordon Bleu, with 46 outlets in the north-west Midlands and Dalgety Frozen Foods with its 33 freezer centres in the south-east. It was at this point the Argyll Group itself was formed with the merger of Louis Edwards and Morgan Edwards.

Further acquisitions came in the early 1980s with Freezer Fare and Bonimart, both of which were integrated with Cordon Bleu to create a chain of more than 130 freezer centres. Some short time later, its biscuit interests were enlarged through the acquisition of Paterson's Scottish Shortbread, subsequently integrated with Yorkshire Biscuits and Furniss.

A key development in the expansion of Argyll came in February 1981 with the purchase of Oriel Foods from the RCA Corporation. A number of similarities existed in the way in which Oriel Foods had developed and that of Argyll itself; culturally and structurally the two businesses were compatible. The purchase of Oriel for £19.5 million represented 80 per cent of Argyll's then stock market valuation. The Oriel acquisition contributed £4.5 million in profits and £22.1 million in net tangible assets. More significantly perhaps, Argyll inherited a strong senior management team, many of whom were former colleagues. Oriel's retail and wholesale operations – Lo-Cost discount stores, Mojo cash and carry and Snowking frozen foods – fitted neatly into Argyll's portfolio. The acquisition provided Argyll with scope for rationalising its overheads, integrating distribution and increasing its purchasing power.

The Lo-Cost brand strengthened Argyll's presence in the discount sector, complementing its Supavalu stores. Argyll merged these two brands under the Lo-Cost fascia, an exercise that was to be repeated five years later with the merger of Safeway and Presto.

The Oriel acquisition also brought into Argyll food manufacturing capacity in the shape of edible oil processing, and tea and coffee businesses. Although these interests did not fit in with its existing operations, Argyll was able to manage this diversity efficiently.

Argyll's strategic aim at this time was to create a substantial retailing and wholesale distribution business. The internal development of the existing businesses, while satisfactory, did not facilitate Argyll's effective competition with the industry leaders at the time. In 1981 Argyll's total sales were £102 million. In September 1981 the company took a 20 per cent stake in Linfood Holdings, a wholesale, retail and cash and carry group, now known as Gateway, with sales of £1 billion. In October of that year Argyll launched its first contested takeover valuing Linfood at £91 million against its own stock market value of £46 million. Argyll's stake in Linfood rose to 30 per cent and this was followed a month later by a referral to the Monopolies and Mergers Commission. Argyll was unwilling to finance the cost of its shareholding in Linfood while the investigation continued and subsequently withdrew its bid. In January 1982 Argyll purchased 67 Pricerite stores for a consideration of £3 million.

In the spring of 1982, Cavenham Foods put its Allied Suppliers business up for sale. Allied Suppliers was one of the UK's largest grocery retailers trading under such brands as Galbraith and Templeton in Scotland, as well as Presto and Lipton in England. Its portfolio consisted of 923 stores with sales of £847 million and a market share of 4.6 per cent, with its regional strength in Scotland and north-east England. Argyll and Cavenham agreed terms in May 1982, valuing Allied Suppliers at £101 million. Argyll funded the deal by issuing 95 million shares, which raised £81 million, with the balance being paid in cash. After this acquisition Argyll's gearing reached 100 per cent. The Allied purchase gave Argyll the critical mass to compete effectively in the UK food retailing industry. However, a number of strategic problems still remained to be solved (details of which are documented in the strategy section below). A further acquisition was made in 1984 when Argyll took over the Hintons supermarket group for £27.5 million.

A parallel development at Argyll was the creation of an alcoholic beverages distribution business involving the distillation and distribution of scotch whisky and rum, as well as the wholesaling and retailing of wines and spirits in the UK. A strategic acquisition in the US was also completed with the £24.6 million purchase of Barton Brands of Chicago, a manufacturer of bourbon, gin and rum, and a distributor of imported beers, wines and spirits.

In 1987, Argyll disposed of its drinks businesses and food manufacturing interests to concentrate on grocery retailing. In the same year, Argyll purchased Safeway Stores, a subsidiary of a US company of the same name, for £651 m. Safeway had a strong brand name in the UK and was renowned for its innovation and the quality of its retailing operations. It had a UK market share of 3.4 per cent with sales in 1986 in excess of £1 billion and pre-tax profits of £43.8 million. Safeway traded from 133 stores with an aggregate selling area of 2 million sq. ft. Its geographical coverage was as follows:

    86 stores in London and the south;
    25 stores in the Midlands and the north;
    22 stores in Scotland;

and the modern company was thus created.

At the beginning of the 1990s Argyll, along with Ahold of the Netherlands and Casino of France, formed the European Retail Alliance (ERA) in order to co-operate in areas such as marketing, distribution, production and information technology. This alliance involved a £35 million investment in cross-shareholding among the three groups. In addition to the ERA, a buying

Table 9.1 Argyll Group plc – 5-year summary financial history, 1988–92

Profit & Loss Account	1992 £m	1991 £m	1990 £m	1989 £m	1988 £m
Net sales	4,729.2	4,496.1	3,920.0	3,500.9	3,236.3
Operating profit	331.0	285.3	224.6	187.8	161.9
Net interest received	33.5	5.5	19.0	20.7	13.7
Profit before taxation	364.5	290.8	243.6	208.5	175.6
Exceptional item	–	–	(16.1)	(29.8)	(43.5)
Profit before taxation	364.5	290.8	227.5	178.7	132.1
Taxation	(102.1)	(81.4)	(68.3)	(53.6)	(54.9)
Profit after taxation	262.4	209.4	159.2	125.1	77.2
Extraordinary item	78.3	–	4.1	–	22.4
Profit for the financial year	340.7	209.4	163.3	125.1	99.6

Balance Sheet	1992 £m	1991 £m	1990 £m	1989 £m	1988 £m
Fixed assets	1,751.7	1,389.7	1,117.8	818.2	597.6
Net current liabilities	(132.4)	(356.7)	(314.0)	(186.4)	(61.8)
Total assets less current liabilities	1,619.3	1,033.0	803.8	631.8	535.8
Creditors (due after one year)	157.6	207.4	114.3	109.9	90.9
Deferred taxation	15.4	10.2	6.4	5.8	4.5
Total shareholders' funds	1,446.3	815.4	683.1	516.1	440.4
Total capital employed	1,619.3	1,033.0	803.8	631.8	535.8
Net cash/(borrowings)	199.2	(165.7)	(11.3)	59.8	130.4

	1992 pence	1991 pence	1990 pence	1989 pence	1988 pence
Earnings per share:					
before exceptional item	24.2	21.6	18.0	15.7	12.8
after exceptional item	24.2	21.6	16.8	13.5	8.9
Dividend per share:					
net	9.75	8.49	7.07	6.05	5.17
gross	13.0	11.32	9.44	8.07	6.96
Net tangible assets per share	129.9	83.8	70.5	55.1	47.7
Share price range:[1]					
high	432.0	315.0	250.8	251.8	209.8
low	273.0	234.9	193.2	159.1	154.2

Source: Company Accounts

Note: [1] Share prices are as at 31 Dec. taken from the Extel Card for Argyll plc, except for 1992 where price was taken as at 31 Dec. from the F.T. listings.

organisation based in Switzerland entitled Associated Marketing Services (AMS) was created involving the three ERA members and nine other European food retailing companies.

Table 9.1 gives a five-year summary of Argyll's financial history, and further data for the last three years is given in Exhibit 9.1 at pp. 102–3.

Strategy and style

By 1992, of the original three founding members of Argyll, only Grant (now Sir Alistair Grant) and David Webster remained. James Gulliver, Argyll's first chairman, left in 1986 after losing a bitterly contested takeover for Distillers plc. It was Gulliver's vision and entrepreneurial skill which had created the Argyll Group. When he left, Grant, his natural successor, assumed control of Argyll. It was Grant's strategy that steered Argyll deeper into food retailing, masterminding the takeover of Safeway and dismantling Gulliver's ventures into international drinks and food manufacturing.

The grocery retailing industry in the UK was dominated by the large multiples, with J. Sainsbury, Tesco and Argyll the top three players. 'The pecking order,' said Grant, 'was not written in stone. Back in 1979 Asda was the most profitable retailer followed by Tesco and then Sainsbury.' By 1992 that position was reversed and Argyll had emerged as a major player. (Exhibit 9.2 shows the key financial ratios of these three retailers, along with the ratios for the food retailing industry as a whole.) Grant said that he took no pleasure in seeing rivals lose money and strongly refuted the idea that running supermarkets was like 'owning a toll bridge where you cannot possibly fail'. Argyll's success, he contended, was 'not simply achieved by financial sleight of hand. Since we bought Allied Suppliers in 1982, we have overtaken Waitrose, Kwik Save, Gateway, Morrison and Asda. What is more we have raised the net assets of the business from £117m to £1.5 bn.' Grant likens Argyll to a 'horse that wins hurdle races. The acquisitions are the hurdles, but you actually win the race by the speed you gallop between the hurdles.' Argyll started 1993 five percentage points behind Sainsbury and Tesco, but Grant believed that Argyll was capable of narrowing the gap.

It was Grant's view that Argyll had at least a decade of growth ahead of it in its supermarket business. 'What warms our hearts, is that Safeway stores still only cover forty per cent of the population compared with sixty per cent for Sainsbury.' This growth was likely to be concentrated in the south-east of England where Safeway was relatively weak, but paradoxically, where it was most profitable. Grant's strategy was to intensify the battle with Sainsbury on Sainsbury's home territory. Over the next three years to 1995/96, in many south-east towns where only two superstores compete for the consumers' grocery shopping basket, Argyll intended to add a third – Safeway.

The corporate strategy and the retailing strategy at Argyll are inextricably linked. Since the takeover of Safeway, it was always the objective of the company to create a distinct Safeway culture that differentiated it from its

Table 9.2 Sales turnover and operating profit by class of business 1989–92

	1992	1991	1990	1989
Sales turnover				
Safeway (£m.)	3,905.0	3,496.6	2,805.8	2,071.0
Other food activities (£m.)	1,134.3	1,260.9	1,337.5	1,625.4
Total (inc. VAT) (£m.)	5,039.3	4,757.5	4,143.3	3,696.4
Operating profit				
Safeway (£m.)	275.3	222.5	158.8	105.6
Margin (ex. VAT) (%)	7.5	6.7	6.0	5.4
Other food activities (£m.)	51.9	59.0	61.7	79.9
Margin (ex. VAT) (%)	4.9	5.0	4.9	5.2
Property and other income (£m.)	3.8	3.8	4.1	2.3
Total for the year (£m.)	331.0	285.3	224.6	187.8

Note: Other food activities includes stores other than Safeway as well as food retailing and the group's wholesale activities.

rivals. Argyll's strategy had always been based around a central 'recipe of success'. Acquisitions allowed the firm to grow quickly to achieve critical mass and to obtain a good geographic spread of stores; strong management to attend to margin improvement and operating efficiency; the creation of an infrastructure that allowed the management to attend to the cost base; and marketing to facilitate brand growth in the three retail market areas Argyll traded in. The Safeway strategy was central to Argyll's success. Table 9.2 shows the breakdown of sales turnover and operating profit by class of business for the period 1989–1992.

The Safeway business

The acquisition of Safeway brought Argyll into the premier league of UK food retailing. The Group had acquired an excellent brand, an innovative management team and an excellent portfolio of stores. Argyll's primary objective was to place its Presto brand into the new stores group it now controlled and expand Safeway's selling area from 2 million sq.ft to 6 million sq.ft. This would be achieved primarily by converting 100 of Presto's largest stores into Safeway and by adding capacity by building new stores.

The acquisition now meant that Argyll had three sets of everything. Rationalisation was uppermost in the minds of Argyll's senior managers. Safeway and Presto's distribution systems were merged and Safeway practices were introduced into Presto's store operations. In 1987, a typical Safeway store's sales per square foot were 55 per cent higher than a typical Presto unit and its operating profitability some 76 per cent greater. This was largely explained by the different sales mix at Safeway, concentrated as it was on fresh produce.

Other areas of commonality were also addressed, namely, marketing and central administration. Argyll saw the relationship as an interlocking cycle

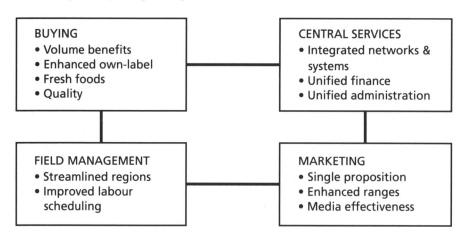

Fig. 9.1 Operational benefits

involving four key components – buying, central services, marketing and field management (see Figure 9.1).

Argyll increasingly built its corporate and retailing strategy around its newly acquired Safeway brand. By 1992, 85 per cent of Argyll's profits came from the Safeway business. The larger Presto stores were progressively refurbished and converted to become Safeway units, and along with new store openings, the average sales area for a Safeway store rose to 20,000 sq.ft. The Presto brand was scaled down in terms of store size, operating medium-sized outlets of around 5,000 sq.ft. The discount shops, Lo-Cost, were in the small category of about 3,000 sq.ft. The store profile meant that the Safeway marque competed directly with Sainsbury, Tesco and Asda, whereas the Lo-Cost brand competed with Kwik Save, whose shopping basket profile was very similar. Argyll was one of the few food retailers in the UK to operate a dual branding strategy. The Co-op, Gateway and recently Asda (with the Dales brand) are all now attempting such a dual branding strategy.

Linking the Safeway and Presto operations permitted Argyll the economies of scale and scope it needed to be an efficient national operator. It allowed Argyll's other store chain, Lo-Cost, to operate separately as it was more geographically focused in the north of England and in Scotland. The store conversion and infrastructure programme cost the Group some £1 billion. By 1991, the conversion programme had run its course. Further growth in stores now had to be via new openings.

Argyll had thus operated concurrent strategies of store conversion, new openings and store closures. Much of the finance for this programme came from cashflow and borrowings. In 1991, the Group raised £386m. net of costs in a 1 for 6 rights issue. This new capital was to be used to fund the next phase in the company's development plan, which envisaged some 20 new store openings a year. The cost of each new store amounted to around £1.5m. for the site and about £10m. for construction. Each new store took on average 55 weeks

Table 9.3 Safeway store development, 1987–1991

	1987	1988	1989	1990	1991
Sales area (000 sq. ft)	2,006	2,873	4,265	5,436	6,001
net increase (%)	3.1	43.2	48.5	27.5	10.6
New stores opened	2	21	19	23	18
Average size (000 sq. ft)	29	23	29	30	28
Presto transfers and conversions	–	22	51	34	9
Average size (000 sq. ft)	–	18	18	17	18
Size analysis					
over 20,000 sq.ft	27	49	82	110	130
10–20,000 sq.ft	75	94	124	146	152
under 20,000 sq.ft	31	33	34	35	28
Number of stores	133	176	240	291	310
Average size of all stores (000 sq.ft)	15	16	18	19	19

Note: By 1992 the planned conversion of Presto stores to Safeway stores was completed and Argyll plc added a further 17 new Safeway stores to their portfolio, increasing the sales area by a further 642,000 sq. ft. The Group planned a further 25 new Safeway store openings in 1993.

Source: Company Reports

to complete. All the large retailing groups have ambitious store opening programmes.

Table 9.3 depicts the scale of the Safeway store development programme since the acquisition was made and the Presto conversion programme completed.

The Argyll retailing strategy of creating a Safeway culture to differentiate it from its rivals involved an apparent 'value-added' approach. The approach consisted of added service provisions in-store, a strong own-label presence and quality fresh produce displayed in an attractive manner. This included bakeries, post offices, dry-cleaning services, cafés and, in some stores, crêches. In keeping with its rivals, Argyll's new sites had retail petrol for its customers. Safeway's other distinguishing feature was its close links with its customers through the customers' panel. Safeway operated between 15,000 to 20,000 lines and serviced around 6 million customers per week. By March 1992 the following specialist departments were evident in the Safeway stores: delicatessens 317; bakeries 275; petrol stations 31; pharmacies 53; coffee shops 49; post offices 10; and dry cleaners 10.

Meanwhile, the international alliance Argyll formed with partners Ahold and Casino had begun to reap some early benefits. Fifty Casino own-label recipes were transferred to the Safeway brand in the UK. Buying economies from the AMS grouping were also expected to filter through in the near future as the Alliance strategy matured.

In keeping with the overall strategy of the Group, Argyll had invested heavily in scanning technology, becoming the first national player to achieve

Table 9.4 Stores profile for the Argyll Group, 1988–1982

	1992	1991	1990	1989	1988
Safeway					
Number of stores	322	310	291	240	176
Sales area (000 sq.ft)	6,424	6,011	5,436	4,265	2,873
Average size (sq.ft)	20,000	19,400	18,680	17,771	16,324
Presto					
Number of stores	212	215	227	270	488
Sales area (000 sq.ft)	1,132	1,157	1,356	2,041	3,520
Average size (sq.ft)	5,300	5,400	5,970	7,560	7,213
Lo-Cost					
Number of stores	285	298	320	353	288
Sales area (000 sq.ft)	888	913	935	1,003	801
Average size (sq.ft)	3,100	3,100	2,921	2,841	2,780
Total					
Number of stores	819	823	838	863	952
Sales area (000 sq.ft)	8,444	8,081	7,727	7,309	7,194

100 per cent scanned sales. This would effectively allow further savings to be made in logistics and distribution systems. A new enlarged division was created in 1992 to apply the advantages of scanned data more strategically and to help further enhance the quality of service to Safeway customers in the area of fresh produce. Improved stockholding from scanned data had improved inventory control.

Other food activities

The bulk of the Group's sales and profits came from the Safeway business. This did not mean that Argyll had neglected the Presto and the Lo-Cost operations. The sections of the business not involved in Safeway included Snowking, Mojo cash and carry, and a small retail liquor and wholesale drinks business. In 1991, Argyll divested itself of the drinks businesses and finally severed the link with the strategy of former chairman, James Gulliver.

The conversion of Presto stores had depressed sales turnover in this part of the Group. No new store openings were planned under the Presto fascia and only two new shops were commissioned under the Lo-Cost marque in 1990/91. However, the Group planned to change this strategy in 1993/94 and strengthen its position in both the mid-sized and discount sections of the retail market; thus five new Presto stores and ten new Lo-Cost stores were to be built in 1993. Further store openings were also likely as the discount brand was strengthened to meet challenges from Kwik Save, Asda's Dales brand and the new continental entrants into the UK grocery market, namely, Aldi and Netto. Table 9.4 shows the stores profile of the Argyll Group.

The retail grocery industry market

Introduction

To fully grasp the issues and the dynamics of the UK retail grocery market it is necessary to focus on the supplier side (the food industry), as well as the retailers.

By the early 1990s the food industry had undergone a number of important structural changes at the domestic as well as the European level. The industry, through merger and acquisition activity, had sharply increased in concentration and with this, the smaller, under-resourced competitors had become increasingly vulnerable due to the rising costs of branding.

At the European level, the industry also witnessed a sharp increase in merger and acquisition activity, as well as the formation of cross-border marketing and distribution agreements and attempts by the large groups to create pan-European brands. The European food groups were increasingly challenged by their large US counterparts, which saw the growth potential in Europe as an opportunity for pursuing their own global development. This opportunity was in part due to the opening up of eastern European markets.

Structural change on the retail side was no less significant. At the domestic level, the UK saw a polarisation of the retail environment, increasing retailer concentration intensified their power over suppliers, increasing sophistication in interactions with suppliers, and the creation of very efficient distribution and logistical systems, making UK retailers among the most profitable retailers in Europe. At the European level, cross-border expansion and the formation of pan-European retailing alliances were among the most significant structural changes.

The UK grocery market

The UK retail grocery sector in 1978 had some 71,000 retail outlets spread between the multiples, the co-operatives and the independents. By 1990, this total figure had fallen to 42,446. Market share by value for the multiples rose from 52 per cent to 75 per cent during that period, with corresponding falls for the co-operative and independent sectors. This gain in market share was primarily at the expense of the small shopkeeper. While the number of store units had fallen during the period, the average size of trading unit had risen, so that by 1990, the UK grocery market had an aggregate of 58.4 million sq.ft of sales space. This represented about 5,838 sq.ft per 1000 of the population. In 1978, average operating margins were around 1.8 per cent, with Tesco as the market leader. Asda was the most profitable retailer in the sector with pre-tax margins of 4.9 per cent. By 1992, the positions had changed markedly, Sainsbury having become the market leader in terms of both market share and profitability.

The 1980s was a decade of mergers and acquisitions that saw the development of the 'super group'; Kingfisher, Dixons, Burton, Tesco, Sainsbury, Argyll and Marks & Spencer, to name but a few, were all mergers and acquisitions players, either in the domestic market or in the cross-border sector. The significant point behind the 1980s was that the leading food retailers had moved away from being merchants to become fully responsible for product development, supply chain management, and distribution. Their enhanced margins reflected this increased role, which they relished. Previously, food retailers were subsidiaries of companies that operated in the food business, now the main grocery retailers were fully focused food retailers.

The multiples saw their market share grow to such an extent that by 1990, 7,200 of the largest stores were responsible for nearly 85 per cent of total sales in a market valued at £40bn. In keeping with this concentration of retailer power, town-centre landscapes changed. The large multiples sited their large new superstores in new edge-of-town sites or in suburban centres, each new store being in excess of 25,000 sq.ft, with parking for several hundred cars and facilities such as petrol for motorists. The grocery retailers had branched out into petrol retailing, challenging the established players like Shell and Esso.

Table 9.5 gives the market share positions of the main players in the UK grocery market for the years 1987–1991.

Table 9.5 UK grocery market share, 1987–1991 (%)

	1987 %	1988 %	1989 %	1990 %	1991 %
J Sainsbury	13.9	14.3	14.5	16.0	16.7
Tesco	13.5	14.3	14.9	15.3	16.2
Safeway	9.9	10.9	11.0	11.0	11.3
Asda	7.6	7.8	7.9	10.5	10.5
Gateway	11.5	11.8	11.2	8.0	7.3
Kwik Save	3.0	3.0	3.5	3.9	4.4
Waitrose	2.7	2.6	2.6	2.5	2.5
Morrison	1.6	1.7	1.9	2.2	2.3
Iceland	0.5	0.6	1.8	1.9	1.9
Other multiples	7.7	5.2	5.0	1.0	3.2
Co-operatives	12.1	11.7	11.3	11.0	10.7
Independents	14.6	11.4	14.0	13.7	13.0

Sources: Verdict, IGD Research Services

Trends and other issues

The UK recession of the early 1990s was acute, and had seriously affected a number of industrial sectors. Poor retail sales, low consumer confidence and high real interest rates had their effects on the retail sector. The food sector was one of the few areas of the economy largely unaffected by the recession, but some analysts expressed concern about the sector's continued growth, although most agreed that it had at least ten further years of growth and expansion. However, if the economy continued in its depressed state into 1993 and beyond, the sector was likely to be affected by the recession and tougher market conditions.

Financial results by the top groups in this sector had shown little increase in volume on a like-for-like basis. Sales volume rises had been generated from new store openings and from geographic expansion. This trend was likely to continue for the foreseeable future, as all the main players had ambitious new store opening programmes. J. Sainsbury, for instance, had earmarked £800m. a year for new stores.

However, new stores, larger stores and more stores all contributed to increasing benefits of scale, which, together with changing sales mixes towards higher margin fresh produce, ready-prepared dishes and other services, enabled store groups to maintain their margins. Absolute scale economies would be likely to plateau as stores reached optimum size and advantages from infrastructure and information technology investment peaked.

While low consumer confidence and the continuing poor performance of the economy brought their own problems to the food retailers, other more pressing issues continued to dominate the sector. These were the arrival of the continental discount groups Aldi and Netto in the UK and the small-scale emergence of the warehouse idea from the US. The warehouse idea was the ultimate 'pile it high and sell it cheap' concept. Other competitive threats from the continent of Europe, in the form of the French groups Leclerc and Continent and the German group Tengelmann, were not to be dismissed. A likely entry strategy into the UK market by a large European player would be through the acquisition of one of the weaker UK groups. Likely candidates were the troubled Gateway group and possibly Asda. Both firms have struggled in the recession due to high debt gearing and poor sales performances.

The high UK grocery margins proved attractive to powerful European groups accustomed to relatively low margins. European food retailers believed that their UK rivals were less competitive and that the UK was a 'soft' market. As Peter Martin of the Belgian group Delhaize put it: 'We would like to be as profitable as Sainsbury, but unlike British stores we have to operate in a highly competitive market. We have more competition in Belgium, both from other supermarkets and independent shops. The result is a tradition of low prices.' Sergio Dias, a Carrefour executive, agreed with this statement: 'There is more emphasis on convenience stores in the UK, while in France we have many more hypermarkets which deliberately pursue a low margin policy.'

A number of factors could be said to contribute to higher margins in the UK than elsewhere in Europe. Distribution and logistical systems, widespread use of scan data, complex supplier relationships, own-brand development, and the demise of the independent, all being significant contributory factors. Many mainland European groups are still family owned and are not listed companies, and thus enjoy less market pressure on them than their UK rivals. A further reason could be that while UK customers want value for money, they are less price driven than their European cousins. UK store groups have responded to this customer characteristic by developing the appropriate strategy.

The competitive battleground had been enlarged, as grocery retailers attempted to increase their service package and to draw in more customers. By 1997, it has been estimated that UK grocery retailers would command around 20 per cent of the retail petrol market. Supermarket petrol retailing offered the customer petrol from a basic filling station at prices of 10–15 pence a gallon cheaper than existing branded petrol stations. In 1992, Tesco operated 151 petrol stations with plans to build a further 20, Safeway operated 37 stations, with plans for 20 or so new sites, and J. Sainsbury had 100 petrol stations in service with plans for a further 100 units. Market leaders Esso and Shell are potentially threatened.

Retailer alliances

The continued long-term organic growth in national markets was believed to be limited, growth via the merger and acquisition route was also seen as being restricted due to competition regulation at both the domestic and the EC level. This meant that grocery retailers have turned to alliances and formed international buying groups as an alternative growth strategy. These alliances operated on a voluntary basis, some of which involve cross-shareholding. Their objective was to allow for operational, buying and marketing synergies to accrue to member firms. Table 9.6 shows the extent of such alliances, excluding the European Retail Alliance, which is shown separately.

The European Retail Alliance

Argyll, Casino and Ahold were the founding members of the European Retail Alliance (ERA), which they set up at the end of 1989. This alliance, while being voluntary, included an element of cross-shareholding between each of the members. The ERA was linked to another operational organisation, Associated Marketing Services (AMS), which in turn had a further nine affiliated retail members. Table 9.7 shows the membership and its geographic coverage.

The eleven AMS members collectively controlled 13,439 retail outlets, which were visited by 50 million customers each week, thus servicing more than 130 million consumers in total. They had an estimated combined purchasing power of about 11 per cent of the European food market.

Table 9.6 Major pan-European buying groups

Buying group	Location	Members	Purchasing power in Europe (est $USbn.)
Intercoop	Denmark	Coop(I), Coop(CH) CWS(UK), EKA(SF) FDB(DK), FNCC(F) KF(S), Konsum(A) NKL(NI), SOK(SF)	51.8
Deuro-Buying	Switzerland	Asda(UK), Carrefour(F) Makro(NI), Metro(D)	39.6
CEM (Coopération Européenne de Marketing)	Belgium	Conad(I), Crai(I) Edeka(D), UDA(E) Booker(UK)[3]	34.3
Difra	France	Ariaud(F), Casino(F) Catteau(F), Co-op Normandie-Picardie(F) Delhaize(B), Montlaur(F) Rallye(F), SCA Monoprix(F) Zanin(I)	22.6
Eurogroup	Germany[1]	GIB(B), HOKI(Dk), Rewe(D) Vendex (NI)	23.7
Intergroup Trading	Netherlands	Despar(I), Spar(A), Spar(B) Spar(D), Spar(E), Spar(UK) Spar(NI)	20.7[2]
EMD (European Marketing Distribution)	Switzerland	Selex(I), Markant(NI) Markant(D), Selex(E) Sodadip(F), Uniarme(P) ZEV(A)	15% of European food market

Notes: [1] Two additional purchasing offices in Italy and Spain. [2] Specialises in purchase of fresh fruit and vegetables; worldwide figure. [3] Joined January 1992.
Source: Euromonitor (1991), Burt (1991)

The relationship between the individual retailer and the AMS was managed by a designated senior executive in each company. These co-ordinators met formally on a four-week routine cycle, or more frequently if necessary. In addition to the activities of the co-ordinators, relationships existed at the product buyer level among the retailers in order to pool experience and to discuss matters relating to supplier selection, promotions, quality specifications, physical distribution, new product launches and the development of fighting brands. The AMS identified a number of areas of mutual benefit to member firms and their suppliers. The possible areas of opportunity AMS identified were as follows:

Table 9.7 Membership of the Associated Marketing Services Group

Group member	Country of domicile	Number of stores
Ahold	Netherlands	945
Allkauf	Germany	235
Argyll	UK	853
Casino	France	3,223
Dansk Supermarked[1]	Denmark	250
Hagen Gruppen	Norway	264
ICA	Sweden	3,100
Kesko	Finland	3,445
Mercadonna	Spain	125
Migros	Switzerland	541
Rinacente	Italy	696
Superquinn	Republic of Ireland	12

Note: [1]Dansk Supermarked left the AMS in 1992.
Source: AMS (1991)

- Development of existing business.
- Co-ordination of supplies.
- Co-ordination of promotional support.
- Introduction and market testing of new products.
- Standardisation of product and packaging.
- Introduction of suppliers to new markets.
- Co-ordination of distribution.
- Development of merchandising and promotional presentation materials.
- Co-ordination of own brand development.
- Material sourcing for own brand suppliers.
- Assistance in production and distribution.
- Operation of stockholding.
- Management of temporary supply shortages.
- A forum for retailer/supplier issues.

The AMS itself worked through marketing co-ordinators assigned by participating companies to work on behalf of the alliance on a full-time basis. These co-ordinators in turn had direct access to the marketing and buying executives of the member firms and worked closely both with and through them.

Trends in tastes, life-styles and choices for the European consumer appeared to be converging and own brand retailers wished to reflect this trend in much the same way as the branded producer. A number of illustrations of this are evident from recent AMS successes. In October 1991 the AMS announced the launch of a pan-European kitchen towel through all AMS stores, with the exception of Migros. This low-priced towel provided product information in the languages of the AMS members on its wrapping. Ten million packs were produced in the first year of supply. In conjunction with a French manufacturer the AMS also launched a baby's disposal nappy under a unified brand name throughout its stores. The manufacturer put in dedicated production capacity for the production of this product. Other areas of co-operation would be developed in future: orange juice, light bulbs, dry cells and food brand and recipe exchanges were all planned. An executive at the AMS summed up this development as follows: 'For a long time, manufacturers we spoke to said it was impossible to create a common product for Europe. Now we have demonstrated what top brand suppliers were not able to do.'

The driving forces for such buying alliances were that they spread the risk of development, accelerated learning and could potentially overcome very real mobility barriers. As one executive from the AMS put it: 'The purpose of the company (AMS) is to work with manufacturers and suppliers of branded, non-branded and own label goods and services to identify opportunities to improve the efficiency of the supply chain, to reduce the cost of goods and services and to share in the benefits from this co-operation.'

Endpiece

Towards the end of 1992 the Argyll Group acquired nine stores in northern England from the Jackson Grandway Group, converting one into a Safeway store and the other eight into the Presto format.

On December 18 1992, Tesco announced the acquisition of a controlling interest in the French grocery retailer Catteau for a consideration of FFr 1.47 bn. Catteau controlled 90 stores in northern France and is a member of the buying alliance Difra. This was Tesco's first foreign acquisition, but could this move into Europe be the beginning of a trend for the big UK food retailers? How will the other two majors respond?

Towards the end of 1992, J. Sainsbury announced that it was to launch an aggressive package of price cuts early in the new year (1993). The announcement raised fears that a damaging price war could follow.

Exhibit 9.1 Argyll Group plc – financial data for 1990–1992 (£m.)

(a) Profit and Loss Accounts 1990–1992 (year ended 31 March)

	1992	1991	1990
Sales turnover	5,039.3	4,757.5	4,143.3
Value added tax	(310.1)	(261.4)	(223.3)
Turnover ex. value added tax	4,729.2	4,496.1	3,920.0
Cost of sales	(3,662.8)	(3,551.6)	(3,121.0)
Gross profit	1,066.4	944.5	799.0
Net operating expenses	(735.4)	(659.2)	(574.4)
Operating profit	331.0	285.0	224.6
Investment income	2.5	2.6	–
Net interest receivable	31.0	2.9	19.0
Profit on ordinary activities before taxation and exceptional item	364.5	290.8	243.6
Exceptional item	–	–	(16.1)
Profit on ordinary activities before taxation	364.5	290.8	227.5
Taxation	(102.1)	(81.4)	(68.3)
Profit before extraordinary item	262.4	209.4	159.2
Extraordinary item	78.3[1]	–	4.1
Profit for the financial year	340.7	209.4	163.3
Dividends	(108.3)	(82.5)	(68.6)
Retained profit for the year	232.4	126.9	94.7
Retained profit, beginning of year	404.7	277.8	183.1
Retained profit, end of year	637.1	404.7	277.8

Note:[1] Extraordinary item comprises £100m. received by the company from Guinness plc in settlement of a claim resulting from the failure of the company's bid for the Distillers Company plc in April 1986, net of £1.9m. in costs and £19.8m. in taxation.

(b) Balance sheets 1990–92 (year ended 31 March)

	1992	1991	1990
Fixed assets			
Tangible fixed assets	1,684.3	1,324.7	1,047.9
Investments	67.4	65.0	69.9
Total fixed assets	1,751.7	1,389.7	1,117.8
Current assets			
Stocks	262.9	308.2	283.1
Debtors	150.4	117.6	90.8
Investments and deposits	516.5	122.0	} 229.9
Cash at bank and in hand	78.0	92.0	
Total current assets	1,077.8	639.8	603.8

Exhibit 9.1 (continued)

Current liabilities			
(due within one year)			
Bank overdrafts	(63.8)	(73.5)	(59.4)
Loans	(173.9)	(98.8)	(67.5)
Other creditors	(902.5)	(824.2)	(790.9)
Net current assets/(liabilities)	(132.4)	(356.7)	(314.0)
Total assets less current liabilities	1,619.3	1,033.0	803.8
Creditors (due after one year)			
Loans	(157.6)	(207.4)	(114.3)
Deferred taxation	(15.1)	(10.2)	(6.4)
Net worth	1,446.3	815.4	683.1
Capital and reserves			
Called-up share capital	278.3	237.3	236.3
Share premium account	530.9	173.4	168.8
Profit and loss account	637.1	404.7	277.8
Total shareholders' funds	1,446.3	815.4	683.1

Exhibit 9.2 Key ratios – Argyll, the industry and key competitors

(a) Argyll Group

No.	Description	2/4/88	1/4/89	31/3/90	30/3/91	28/3/92
701	Return on s'holders equity (%)	23.49	24.37	23.61	25.56	17.96
707	Return on capital employed (%)	29.63	24.49	25.78	25.89	20.63
713	Operating profit margin (%)	4.43	4.48	5.24	6.27	6.91
716	Pre-tax profit margin (%)	4.85	5.11	5.80	6.47	7.62
717	Net profit margin (%)	3.15	3.32	3.77	4.30	5.17
725	Stock ratio (days)	27.68	27.45	26.36	25.02	20.29
727	Debtors ratio (days)	4.83	5.62	6.97	7.78	9.51
729	Creditors ratio (days)	55.38	61.21	61.98	58.11	57.66
741	Working capital ratio	0.88	0.75	0.64	0.62	0.86
762	Sales per employee (£)	54,379	55,225	60,625	68,021	72,083
763	Operating profit per employee (£)	2,408	2,474	3,175	4,268	4,982
764	Capital employed per employee (£)	9,170	11,857	14,160	17,955	27,945
792	Cash earnings per share	14.97	17.34	21.19	26.34	30.24

▶

Exhibit 9.2 (continued)

(b) Food retailing – UK

No.	Description	10/6/87	24/6/88	7/7/89	7/7/90	11/7/91
701	Return on s'holders equity (%)	19.60	18.13	19.72	18.56	17.42
707	Return on capital employed (%)	23.26	21.46	21.27	20.46	19.76
713	Operating profit margin (%)	4.76	4.85	5.39	5.62	5.92
716	Pre-tax profit margin (%)	5.04	5.27	5.62	5.55	5.62
717	Net profit margin (%)	3.30	3.46	3.74	3.63	3.74
725	Stock ratio (days)	24.94	22.07	22.41	22.55	21.67
727	Debtors ratio (days)	6.73	7.82	8.78	8.76	8.94
729	Creditors ratio (days)	48.84	44.45	48.37	50.34	48.57
741	Working capital ratio	0.70	0.83	0.67	0.60	0.66
762	Sales per employee (£)	59,632	66,210	65,054	69,658	74,747
763	Operating profit per employee (£)	2,841	3,209	3,509	3,913	4,421
764	Capital employed per employee (£)	13,903	17,533	19,288	22,108	25,243

(c) J. Sainsbury

No.	Description	19/3/88	18/3/89	17/3/90	16/3/91	14/3/92
701	Return on s'holders equity (%)	18.71	19.82	20.48	20.81	16.42
707	Return on capital employed (%)	22.28	20.46	21.90	22.90	21.43
713	Operating profit margin (%)	5.67	6.12	6.30	6.92	7.11
716	Pre-tax profit margin (%)	5.85	5.95	6.05	6.47	7.26
717	Net profit margin (%)	3.96	4.01	4.04	4.38	4.98
725	Stock ratio (days)	18.25	18.45	16.24	16.85	15.20
727	Debtors ratio (days)	2.42	6.28	5.00	5.43	3.39
729	Creditors ratio (days)	45.72	46.90	44.78	45.20	42.73
741	Working capital ratio	0.37	0.36	0.42	0.41	0.55
762	Sales per employee (£)	58,004	64,101	69,303	71,690	77,099
763	Operating profit per employee (£)	3,290	3,921	4,369	4,964	5,482
764	Capital employed per employee (£)	17,628	22,488	23,567	24,861	30,454
792	Cash earnings per share	17.02	20.12	25.33	30.64	30.96

▶

Exhibit 9.2 (continued)

(d) Tesco

No.	Description	27/2/88	25/2/89	24/2/90	23/2/91	29/2/92
701	Return on s'holders equity (%)	16.65	17.03	17.40	13.04	15.45
707	Return on capital employed (%)	19.54	21.80	22.34	17.42	19.05
713	Operating profit margin (%)	4.95	5.57	5.86	6.27	6.76
716	Pre-tax profit margin (%)	5.44	5.62	6.05	6.57	7.68
717	Net profit margin (%)	3.53	3.72	3.93	4.27	5.14
725	Stock ratio (days)	15.86	14.87	14.38	13.31	11.40
727	Debtors ratio (days)	3.52	2.12	1.43	1.53	1.89
729	Creditors ratio (days)	37.37	43.03	45.18	44.16	45.36
741	Working capital ratio	0.50	0.48	0.34	0.68	0.60
762	Sales per employee (£)	57,802	62,356	64,908	72,371	81,548
763	Operating profit per employee (£)	2,858	3,475	3,807	4,539	5,509
764	Capital employed per employee (£)	17,220	18,430	20,064	30,794	36,349
792	Cash earnings per share	14.26	15.94	19.45	24.47	26.53

Source: Datastream, Output from *Program 190*, reproduced with permission

References and further reading

The Argyll Story (1991), Argyll plc.

Burt (1991), 'Trends in the internationalisation of grocery retailing: the European experience', *International Review of Retail, Distribution and Consumer Research*, **1**(4), 487–515.

Euromonitor (1991), *Europe's Major Retailers 1991*, Euromonitor, London.

Harpers' takeover of Coopers[1]

Gerry Johnson
Cranfield School of Management

Context

By the early 1990s the once buoyant fashion retail market in the UK was suffering heavily from recession, with companies declaring dramatically reduced profits, laying off staff and closing shops. In this troubled market Harpers remained relatively successful. Moreover it saw the opportunity to build its business through acquisition as competitors' profits and share prices dipped dramatically. In 1990 they launched a bid for Coopers.

Harpers

Harpers was a successful retailer of mens and womens fashion wear. It had two chains of stores. The first, Harpers itself, had 500 high street shops and catered for the middle-class fashion-conscious male. The second, 'Bazaar', consisted of 200 high street shops and focused on the middle-class fashion-conscious woman. The stores had a reputation for being 'ahead of their time', setting the pace in fashion for their target markets, reading the market well and running an efficient retail operation. For many years they had headed the profit league in their sector. Prior to 1990 the strategy had been to develop market share by internal development, through opening new branches, branch refurbishment and careful market positioning. However, in the view of Tom Sutton, the chief executive: 'the time had come when we had to find a new market: we could not simply grow within the markets in which we operated.'

Coopers

Coopers was a long-established chain of menswear shops. The 500 shops concentrated mainly on downmarket casual clothes for men, sold through retail premises which, although fairly small, were well positioned in high

---

[1] This case is intended as the basis for class discussion rather than to illustrate either effective or ineffective handling of an administrative situation. The two company names used are pseudonyms but the material is based on the author's knowledge of actual retail business. © Gerry Johnson, 1993.

streets and shopping malls. The company had a long history of steady profit growth and a reputation for concentrating on the market it knew well. While suffering in the recession of the early 1980s, Coopers seemed to have come through it. Indeed, it had done rather better than some of its more adventurous competitors in the late 1980s: but by 1990 profits had taken a dip and the company looked vulnerable.

The bid

Tom Sutton's view was that Coopers was a natural acquisition, offering substantial benefits and considerable synergy:

> Coopers' traditional market has shown itself, in the long run, to be much less vulnerable to the ups and downs of the market than most clothing chains. It is not high fashion, but then a large percentage of the population aren't either. It is a well run, efficient operation which seems to know how to provide for the needs of its market. Its sites are good and often complementary to our own. Some of them could be used for either Coopers or Harpers shops so there is a potential transferability of assets there anyway. The management know their business: there is a good deal of expertise there. Provided we ensure that we maintain the name and image of Coopers in the market place, I believe that the coming together of the two operations can only benefit both.

In 1990 Harpers launched a bid for Coopers. This was done on the back of a careful market study of Coopers' operation and market sector. It showed that their customers were loyal and that the dip in profits was, in the main, a simple function of the recession. A careful study was done of the finances of Coopers, which showed a healthy position and a potential release of funds from freehold assets. The view was also that the senior executives in Coopers would not put up a hard fight in the acquisition: and that many of the shareholders would welcome it.

Integrating the acquisition

Bill Masters, the marketing director of Harpers, and a close friend of Tom Sutton, was rather more wary of the acquisition than Tom. He accepted the market logic, and like Tom believed that Harpers had to move into a new market sector. However, he knew that the problem with acquisitions was often the integration of the two companies. He was also concerned that the culture at Harpers was unique: 'Indeed it is one of our reasons for success,' he believed.

Bill had been a member of a workshop for senior executives at Harpers, at which he and his colleagues had explored the important links between organisational strategy and culture (see Exhibit 10.1 below) and had carried out a cultural audit by drawing up a culture web (see Exhibit 10.2).

This confirmed his views that the company was seen by its own managers as a confident and often arrogant leader in its sector; with a dominant, respected, though sometimes feared, centralised and personalised leadership from Tom and Bill; an informal style of organisation, yet one which achieved tight control; and a set of routines that kept them close to the market, and expected devoted, hard-working managers who 'do it the Harpers way'. 'It is a sort of benign dictatorship in many ways. A lot of informality; a lot of hard work; but don't rub Tom up the wrong way,' as one manager put it.

This was reflected in the way strategies were developed. Managers saw strategies developing through an essentially visionary process – a process which began with Tom and Bill, but was generally owned throughout the business. The planning function acted as a counter-balance to this, focusing as it did on understanding the market in fine detail. There was however 'a way of doing things around here' which had a powerful influence on the development of the firm. The pressures from the environment were not seen to be oppressive: 'We keep on top of the market here: that's why we have our market research and planning experts.'

Bill persuaded Tom that a similar sort of study should be done in Coopers as soon as possible after the takeover. Two workshops were organised at Coopers after the acquisition: one for the board and one for ten senior executives. The purpose of the workshops was to debate the future strategy of the company and the way the integration of the two companies should be planned. As part of the workshop culture webs were drawn up for Coopers (see Exhibit 10.3 below) and the managers discussed how strategies had developed in their organisation. The executives saw strategies coming about through a process of adaptive change: 'We try things out: some work and we develop them, some don't and we drop them: but we don't take risks.' This occurred within a long established culture and a set of routines revolving around the merchandising and buying functions: 'Buying is our strength in this firm; we do it well and we have a great deal of expertise in it: we know how to buy for our market.' All this took place within a structure that was essentially hierarchical, with the three functions of retail operations, merchandising and finance being represented by powerful leaders; leaders often seen battling it out between themselves. The environment in which they operated was seen to be a dominant influence on strategy. As one manager put it: 'Our market sector has served us well: but we are heavily dependent on it and when they suffer, as they are now, then we suffer: it's cause and effect.'

The culture web reflected much of this. Loyalty to the firm was assumed and the dominance of the merchandising operation seen as central. As one manager stated: 'Traditionally we have been at risk of placing too much emphasis on buying. Some managers here think that if you get the merchandise right you could sell it out of fish barrels.' There was also the assumption that in difficult times the market will always respond to price; indeed Coopers was known for the number of sales it ran during such periods. Hence in times of trouble 'get the wagons in a circle and put up the posters'. All of this took place within an organisation that was undeniably political, with the three functions frequently at loggerheads and problems often resolved through a 'mafia' of long-service managers. The cost control in the organisation was tight and traditional, reliant on a reporting system built up over the years and managers concentrating on up-to-the-minute performance figures: 'We even ring in for sales figures on Saturday night – not that there is anything that we can do about it on Sunday.' Many of the symbols and stories associated with the organisation were rooted in history, particularly to do with the founders of the business, heroic 'wheeler-dealer' buyers and more recently a 'villainous ex-chief executive' who was blamed for many of the current problems. But there were two things in particular that worried Bill: one was the heavily hierarchical nature of the organisation, even down to quite senior managers calling the chief executive 'sir', and the second was managers' attitudes towards customers – they even referred to their merchandise as 'yobbos' uniforms'.

Tom and Bill both attended the debriefing of the two workshops. As Tom's chauffeur drove them back afterwards, Tom turned to Bill and said 'I think this might be more tricky than we thought'.

Exhibit 10.1 Organisational strategy and culture

It is not possible to cover all the work which Bill did on his workshop here. However, below are extracts from notes he received at the workshop explaining some of the links between organisational strategy and culture. They also introduce the notion of the culture web.

Managers have a set of core beliefs and assumptions which are specific and relevant to the organisation in which they work and which are learned over time. While individual managers may hold quite varying sets of beliefs about many different aspects of their organisational world, there is likely to exist, at some level, a core set of beliefs and assumptions held relatively commonly by the managers. This has been called 'ideational culture', or a paradigm. This paradigm is essentially cultural in nature in so far as it is the 'deeper level of basic assumptions and beliefs that are shared by members of an organisation that operate unconsciously and define in a basic "taken for granted" fashion an organisation's view of itself and its environment'. It is likely to evolve over time, might embrace assumptions about the nature of the organisational environment, the managerial style in the organisation, the nature of its leaders, and the operational routines seen as important to ensure the success of the organisation.

It is this paradigm which, in many organisations, creates a relatively homogeneous approach to the interpretation of the complexity that the organisation faces. The various and often confusing signals that the organisation faces are made sense of, and are filtered, in terms of this paradigm. Moreover since the paradigm evolves over time and is reinforced through the history and perhaps the success of the organisation, it also provides a repertoire of tried and tested responses to signals experienced by managers. It is, at one and the same time, a device for interpretation and a formula for action. At its most beneficial, it encapsulates the unique or special competences and skills of that organisation and, therefore, the bases by which the firm might expect to achieve real competitive advantage. However, it can also lead to significant strategic problems.

The strategies that managers advocate and those that emerge are typically configured within the bounds of this paradigm. Changes going on within or without the organisation may affect the organisation's performance; however, even if managers, as individuals, perceive such changes they may not necessarily acknowledge them as impinging on the strategy or performance of their organisation.

The likelihood of the paradigm dominating the development of strategy and causing resistance to significant change becomes clearer when the wider cultural context in which it is embedded is considered. The taken-for-granted assumptions and beliefs, which are the paradigm, are likely to be hedged about and protected by a web of cultural artefacts. The *routine* ways that individuals, departments or functions in the organisation behave towards each other, customers, suppliers and so on; the *rituals* of organisational life that provide a programme for the way members respond to given situations and prescribe 'the way we do things around here'. the more formalised *control systems* and rewards which delineate the important areas of activity

▶

Exhibit 10.1 (continued)

focus. The *stories* told which embed the present in organisational history; the type of language and expressions commonly used and the organisational *symbols* such as logos, offices, cars and titles which become a short-hand representation of the nature of the organisation. Moreover it is likely that the most *power* in the organisation is associated with the key constructs of the paradigm. It would, therefore, be a mistake to conceive of the paradigm as merely a set of beliefs removed from organisational action. It lies within a cultural web which bonds it to the action of organisational life. It is, therefore, continually, if gradually, evolving.

Exhibit 10.2 Harpers' culture web

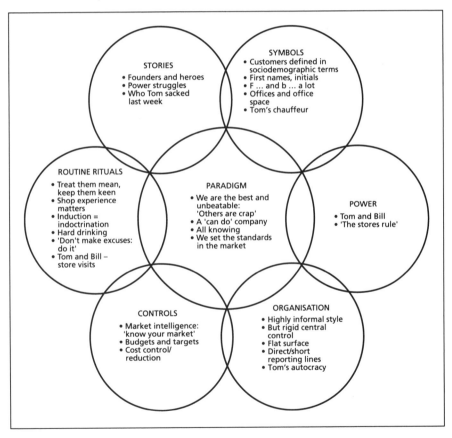

Exhibit 10.3 Coopers' culture web

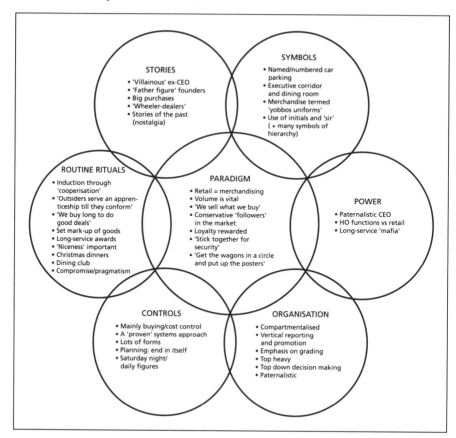

STORIES
- 'Villainous' ex-CEO
- 'Father figure' founders
- Big purchases
- 'Wheeler-dealers'
- Stories of the past (nostalgia)

SYMBOLS
- Named/numbered car parking
- Executive corridor and dining room
- Merchandise termed 'yobbos uniforms'
- Use of initials and 'sir' (+ many symbols of hierarchy)

ROUTINE RITUALS
- Induction through 'cooperisation'
- 'Outsiders serve an apprenticeship till they conform'
- 'We buy long to do good deals'
- Set mark-up of goods
- Long-service awards
- 'Niceness' important
- Christmas dinners
- Dining club
- Compromise/pragmatism

PARADIGM
- Retail = merchandising
- Volume is vital
- 'We sell what we buy'
- Conservative 'followers' in the market
- Loyalty rewarded
- 'Stick together for security'
- 'Get the wagons in a circle and put up the posters'

POWER
- Paternalistic CEO
- HO functions vs retail
- Long-service 'mafia'

CONTROLS
- Mainly buying/cost control
- A 'proven' systems approach
- Lots of forms
- Planning: end in itself
- Saturday night/ daily figures

ORGANISATION
- Compartmentalised
- Vertical reporting and promotion
- Emphasis on grading
- Top heavy
- Top down decision making
- Paternalistic

Intersport Spain

The management of strategic change in groups of retailers¹

Lluís Martínez-Ribes
ESADE, Barcelona

Context

Everyone present in the conference room of the Gran Hotel Canarias in Santa Cruz de Tenerife on the morning of Thursday, 11 May, 1989 applauded when Jurg Stucki, Intersport International Corporation's chief executive officer (CEO), rose and walked towards the speakers' rostrum. There had been much rumour concerning the subject of his speech. Everyone was convinced that he would address a number of issues of vital importance to the future of Intersport Spain. They were on the verge of learning Intersport's plans for the future.

> I would like to start by reminding you of the meaning of 'global marketing' in an international context, because it is precisely here that Intersport will have to make a concerted effort in the next few years. A product – and don't forget that shops are products too – must be able to satisfy similar market segments with similar needs even in different countries. We are going to spend a lot of time talking about the 'Intersport Shop Formula' for the 1990s while we're here on this wonderful island, and there is one thing I want to make absolutely clear: the first thing we have to do is define our general strategy. After that, we can decide on a communications strategy, but it will have to be consistent with our general plans. The Shop Formula is an important part of our strategy, but it is not the only part. We're a group and we have to act like one.

While listening to the CEO, Miquel Verdaguer, Managing Director of Intersport Spain, began thinking. Although Intersport operated in 16 countries, its general development strategy for Spain was not clear. It was becoming increasingly obvious that such a strategy was necessary, but it was also evident that many points

---

1 Case written by Rafael Peces and Gloria Gratacós, under the direction of Prof. Lluís Martínez-Ribes. This case is intended to serve as a basis for discussion and is not an example of good or bad management of a particular situation.

had to be clarified before one could be developed. Nevertheless, it looked as though the time had come to decide on a strategy.

One alternative would be to keep going as before: the member retailers would continue to have virtually free hands and headquarters would act basically as a purchasing centre, albeit one that provided a number of complementary services. Another option would be for the organisation to practically turn into a franchise system. Should that happen, headquarters would take on a more important role in terms of decision making and the member retailers would go along with these decisions. In other words the company would become what in retailing jargon is known as 'more vertical'. Midway between these two extreme alternatives were a series of other possibilities which Miquel Verdaguer similarly pondered.

It seemed obvious to Verdaguer that simply defining a strategic option for the future would not be enough in itself. Success would also depend upon how the strategy was implemented, what steps it would involve, which measures would be given priority and what resources would be allocated.

Verdaguer turned to Arseni Sallent, the Chairman of the board of Intersport Spain, who was sitting next to him, and murmured, 'This is just the beginning. We need to get a broad picture of the future, look at the figures and then make our move. It won't be long before we'll have to stop acting like ostriches.' Arseni Sallent nodded and continued listening to the speaker.

What is Intersport?

Intersport Spain is a retailers' co-operative, which currently has 82 members with a total of 127 shops throughout the country. Founded in May 1970, it had the stated object of 'centralising purchases of sporting goods in order to resell them to member owners of retail sporting goods stores'. By 1981 Intersport had survived a management crisis by rethinking its general aims and bringing in a new management team. At that time there were 37 members and headquarters' sales amounted to 150 million pesetas (1981), but by 1988 this had risen to some 1,426 million pesetas (see Exhibits 11.1 and 11.2 below).

The highest level of management is the Executive Council, which retailers elect at their general meeting of members. The CEO is appointed by the Executive Council and given broad powers. The following departments answer to the CEO:

- Administration and finance (this includes personnel management and taxation).
- Operations management (purchasing, inventories, imports, promotions).
- External relations (relations with partners and prospective partners, advertising, etc.).
- Communications (catalogue and shop design).
- Warehousing and logistics.

In Intersport Spain there are also members' committees, which advise on purchasing and advertising policies.

Headquarters currently employ 27 people, some of whom are permanent employees, others temporary. The working atmosphere is good and absentee-ism low. The human resources policy is based on team work, delegating responsibility and promoting from within the company.

Intersport Spain in turn belongs to an international association of co-operatives, Intersport International Corporation (IIC), which has its headquar-ters in Switzerland. IIC was officially founded in September 1968, but the French, Swiss and German organisations had begun working closely together as far back as the early 1960s. Up until now, all the national organisations have been self-sufficient; however, since IIC owns the Intersport® brand it can revoke the licence of any national organisation whose performance is not up to standard.

In 1986 the Intersport Group's retail sales amounted to over 4.5 billion Swiss francs. Over 3,500 sporting goods stores throughout the world belonged to the Intersport Group.

The Intersport philosophy

Manufacturer relations

It is commonly said that 'Manufacturers of name brands are the most impor-tant members of Intersport.' Name brands are the basis of the Intersport product range. Consumers feel that Intersport stores are particularly good because they largely stock items produced by leading manufacturers such as Atomic, Adidas, Salomon, Head, Karhu-Titan, Puma, Fila, Nike, Fischer, Donnay, Rossignol, and so on.

What does Intersport offer manufacturers?

- *Continuity and stability.* Intersport aims to establish long-term relation-ships based on mutual trust. Company policy is one of loyalty to its suppliers.
- *Quantity and quality in orders.* Intersport orders considerable quantities which account for 6 per cent of the Spanish sporting goods market. More-over these quantities are concentrated in a few orders placed during the season or in advance, which enables suppliers to plan their production better.
- *Centralised payments.* Intersport has never failed to pay any of its suppliers.
- *Lower costs and higher sales.* Selling to individual retailers is costly and time-consuming. Intersport purchasing centres permit manufacturers to reach a large number of retailers through a single transaction.
- *Savings on distribution costs.* All the national headquarters have their own central warehouses.
- *Sales promotion.* Intersport advertising directly promotes sales of manu-facturers' articles in Intersport outlets.
- *Joint advertising.* An effective marketing programme gives manufacturers

of name-brand articles numerous chances to benefit from joint advertising with Intersport.

- *Market information.* The Intersport Group regularly reviews sales trends. What are customers currently buying most? What will they want in the near future? Intersport furnishes manufacturers with valuable market information.
- *Close relations.* Intersport wants solid, lasting relationships with leading manufacturers, offering them a great deal of security and the chance to make long-range production plans.

Member relations

Owners of shops are hardly likely to be experts in such varied fields as data processing, accounting, purchasing, inventory management, advertising, and so on. They need to be able to delegate many of these responsibilities to a central office. The sporting goods market is extremely complex. It is difficult to acquire a thorough knowledge of any aspect of this market and at the same time shape a vision of the sporting goods industry as a whole. Sporting goods retailers who do not belong to any organised group have a hard time fighting competition of all kinds and have little chance of success or even survival. The Intersport system is based on co-operation, offering retailers the strength of a big business without forcing them to sacrifice the advantages of their independence.

The company's golden rule is that Intersport retailers are responsible for running their own businesses because no one else could do as good a job. However, national headquarters and the international organisation take charge of those operations which can be carried out more efficiently and economically as co-ordinated actions. In line with this basic principle the retailers' job is clearly distinguished from that of headquarters.

As the group's parent company, IIC is permanently in touch with the national Intersport organisations, supporting and co-ordinating their activities. IIC is mainly in charge of the following functions:

- designing and developing broad policy lines;
- designing shared strategies;
- managing purchases of sporting goods and sportswear throughout the world;
- occasionally financing international purchases;
- marketing/advertising; and
- market research.

The Spanish head office offers member retailers a range of services, chief among which are the following:

- It builds up an effective product range based on members' orders (quarterly conventions).

- Intersport has a nose for new developments and trends in the sporting goods world and reports them to its members.
- It provides members with the latest in new products.
- It centralises purchasing.
- It can negotiate the best prices and terms.
- It has a central stock from which member retailers can be supplied (Stockinter).
- It designs co-ordinated marketing actions (catalogues, point-of-sale displays).
- It does special advertising for international sports events.
- It studies and analyses the market.
- Intersport centralises payments, keeping down administrative costs.
- Members receive advice on legal ordinances, tax law, labour legislation and business law.
- It studies the feasibility of setting up Intersport outlets in particular areas.
- Members are given advice on how best to display their products and decorate their shops and on what products to stock.
- Intersport trains its employees and members.
- It promotes exchange of information.
- An Intersport point-of-sale computer program is available to all members.
- The next step will be to provide on-line connections with the head office.
- Intersport exhibits at major trade fairs.

As you can see, many of these services involve purchasing, which is one of the main concerns of any sporting goods store. Purchasing is therefore given highest priority by the various national headquarters and the international organisation. Bulk purchasing keeps Intersport retailers competitive. When 16 countries band together to purchase in bulk, lower prices and a considerable number of other advantages are guaranteed.

Nowadays sporting goods and sportswear are manufactured all over the world. The only way really to get to know this extremely complex market is by keeping in constant touch with the latest developments. The 16 international Intersport organisations keep the purchasing team permanently abreast of the latest trends, enabling them to respond quickly to any changes in consumer behaviour.

Intersport retailers in Spain purchase between 1,200,000 and 42,000,000 pesetas worth of goods from national headquarters annually. Purchases average about 8 million pesetas per retailer each year, with about a quarter of members spending between 10 and 20 million pesetas. Only three retailers spend more than 20 million pesetas in a given year.

Miquel Verdaguer frequently tells his management team that it is no longer enough just to make joint purchases. 'You also have to sell jointly. Together we have strong purchasing power. We have to work together to make our selling power equally strong and turn our shops into efficient sales machines.'

IIC and the national headquarters design their advertising campaigns in close collaboration with Intersport retailers. Advertising increases the impact of the national marketing strategies. The Intersport group invests more than 120 million Swiss francs per year (about 9 billion pesetas) in advertising.

Because end customers need professional advice on sports products, the Intersport Group has an extensive training program for all its members and employees.

The marketing mix

Intersport's marketing philosophy reflects the characteristics of the Intersport group.

1. As IIC's Chief Executive Officer likes to say, one of Intersport's strongest points is its product range; the idea that 'Intersport has the best selection of attractive brands' is in itself an extremely persuasive proposition. The Intersport product range includes Intersport's own brands as well as name brands. However, as Miquel Verdaguer points out, although the Intersport brand was originally used for all sorts of products, this policy was eventually changed. In order to avoid flooding the market with Intersport products, the company opted to create different brands for different product groups. Intersport brands are currently sold under the following names : Tecno-Pro (racquets and ski equipment), Rombo (running shoes and balls), Cis and Etirel (sportswear), McKinley (camping and mountaineering equipment) and Trex (underwater sports). These brands aim to fill the market niche for average quality, reasonably priced items, all carefully selected with an eye to market needs. Headquarters can provide member retailers with a stock of Intersport-owned brands and popular name brands (via its centralised Stockinter warehouse) large enough to last 2–3 months. Of the retailers' stock, 32 per cent consists of items distributed directly by Intersport headquarters, while approximately 20 per cent is supplied directly by the manufacturers on special terms for Intersport retailers. The remaining 48 per cent of the stock is not channelled through headquarters. Although it does recommend some of the products, headquarters does not as yet earn anything on them.

2. Intersport's policy is to offer medium- to high-priced goods, but with an extremely competitive price/quality ratio; Intersport shops are no more expensive than their competitors. The company applies an active pricing policy with a number of special offers on particularly attractive products.

3. Because Intersport aims to offer both a wide range of products and good service, the company has definite standards for selecting member retailers and places a great deal of emphasis on training.

4. Speaking at the international Intersport convention in Tenerife the CEO emphasised the importance of developing a corporate image for all member retailers. Shop decor and merchandising details are important in creating a

pleasant, carefree atmosphere where sports goods can be bought and sold. With this in mind, a study is being made to determine the shop design able to strike the best balance between corporate strategy and corporate image. This design will include recommendations on how the shop should be laid out and the merchandise displayed.

5   Advertising is one of the most important ways to shape and communicate a corporate image. Intersport advertises mostly at sports events and through its catalogues. Produced by the head office, the catalogues are sold to member retailers at a reasonable price for circulating amongst current and/or prospective customers. Suppliers help finance the catalogues by paying approximately 500,000 pesetas for each page featuring their products. The head office also supplies member retailers with a series of advertisements suitable for publication in magazines and newspapers. Costs of publication are paid by the individual retailers.

Industry trends

When analysing future trends in the sporting goods industry, it is commonly assumed that Spain will follow the French retailing model.

France

Half of all sports goods sold in France are sold in specialised sports shops, while the other half are sold by large outlets (superstores), clothing shops and mail order companies. Specialised shops may be Intersport retailers, franchisees, independents or branches of major companies.

The driving force in retailing sports goods is the need to have enough purchasing power to be able to negotiate the best terms with suppliers. Intersport Spain's managing director likes to say that: 'Intersport's strongest point is that it's an international organisation and as such is able to search for the best, most reasonably priced manufacturers and keep abreast of the latest trends in order to respond quickly to consumer needs.'

The leading distributors of sporting goods in France are Intersport, Decathlon and Go Sport (see Exhibit 11.3 below). Intersport is the largest in terms of sales and number of retailers. Although Go Sport has only been operating since 1983 it has registered considerable growth and has a 4 per cent share of the French market. Intersport's share of the market is 7 per cent, while Decathlon registers 5 per cent. Both Decathlon and Go Sport are multiple retailers, although they differ in the way they evolved. Decathlon expanded through internal growth while Go Sport grew by methodically acquiring its competitors.

Independent retailers account for 54 per cent of the retail outlets in France but only 25 per cent of total sales. Industry experts predict that two-thirds of these independent retailers will go out of business in the next two years.

Spain

In Spain, a considerable percentage of sports goods are sold through department stores. El Corte Inglés alone accounts for 8.5 per cent of the total market.

There are four purchasing groups in Spain in addition to Intersport. They are Detall Sport, Prestige Golden Team, Syncro Sport Group and Sports Deval. Moreover some corporate chains exist (that is, Copy Sport and Go Sport). All the purchasing groups share the following characteristics: members have exclusive rights within their particular territories (and can veto the membership of any nearby shop), and must meet certain requirements in terms of annual gross sales averages and years of experience in the sporting goods business.

Detall Sport

Detall Sport was founded over ten years ago. As of September 1989, it has 28 member retailers, and a market share of approximately 1.75 per cent. One of the members of Detall Sport's Executive Committee explains that: 'Our philosophy is based on saving time and money for retailers by getting them to join together in a purchasing group.'

Associated with the French group, Techniciens Sport (with headquarters in Grenoble and more than 350 member retailers in a number of different countries), Detall Sport is nevertheless a completely independent organisation. It operates through purchasing conventions and two yearly catalogues, although more services may be added in the future. Share capital amounts to 9,800,000 pesetas and it is a non-profit organisation. At the moment it does not have an independent headquarters, although this seems likely to change in the near future.

Detall Sport buys name brands but gives no special preference to any particular manufacturer and can therefore channel consumers towards the supplier of its choice. Its prices are slightly lower than those of Intersport. Advertising consists primarily of a catalogue aimed at end purchasers.

Prestige Golden Team

Recently founded, Prestige Golden Team has 35 member retailers as of September 1989 and 54 outlets.

Prestige Golden Team offers only two general ranges, one each for the summer and winter. However, to counteract the 'staleness' resulting from so few stock changes, they stimulate their 'mid-season' turnover with regular special offers. Type of products available are as follows:

- Own brands supplied by Golden Team Internacional.
- Exclusive models of international brands.
- Other models produced by national and international manufacturers selected by the group.

Member retailers have the following characteristics:

- Good financial condition.
- A minimum of two years in existence.
- Gross sales of over 50 million pesetas per year.
- Proven professional skill.
- Individual PGT retailers have exclusive territorial rights, being able to veto the entry of other PGT retailers into their area.

The managers of all these purchasing groups agree that it is important to belong to a group in order to gain a stronger negotiating position with suppliers. Furthermore because the industry is excessively fragmented, the survival of independent retailers will become increasingly difficult once the Single European Market takes effect in 1993. Spanish retailers frequently talk about the possibility of foreign companies like Decathlon eventually moving in to the Spanish market.

The Go Sport chain, a branch of an international company, did not get off to a very successful start in Spain, but has recently opened an outlet occupying more than 1,000 square metres in the Madrid-2 shopping mall, popularly known as La Vaguada.

Exhibits 11.4 and 11.5 give data on the expansion and penetration of Intersport in the Spanish market.

The Intersport project comes of age

The issues which are certain to influence future trends in this industry were thoroughly examined at the international meeting of Intersport in May 1989. Among them were the focus on quality, market segmentation, increasing concern with health and fitness, and information.

However, the crux of the meeting was when Jurg Stucki acknowledged that 'there is no such thing as a single Intersport corporate identity or image at either national or international levels', and he emphasised the need to establish one in order to take advantage of the group's strength and make the most of its communications strategy. Experiences in other countries have shown that a strong corporate identity makes for more effective communications, which in turn lead to a greater share of the market. This need is perceived differently on international and national levels. Although agreement was unanimous at the Tenerife meeting, it was also very clear that Intersport would develop differently in different countries. As an example, a number of Intersport franchise outlets in Austria are 100 per cent supplied by their headquarters, which also monitors their sales on a daily basis.

The Spanish management team agree unanimously that a common image is an essential part of corporate strategy and a key to success, but are simultaneously aware that it may differ from the Intersport image in other countries because the Spanish organisation is a co-operative association. The more business-minded member retailers understand the need for a corporate image to distinguish them from their competitors, while the more conservative-minded members are less willing to sacrifice their individual identities to the Intersport brand. A number of well-known retailers have opted to stress their Intersport membership more than their individual identities, which certainly has not hampered their success.

Requisites for becoming an Intersport retailer

Intersport retailers must be Intersporty in outlook and behaviour, willing to participate in professional education programmes, technically knowledgeable and enthusiastic about sports and the Intersport brands. As Intersport aims to be a solid, serious-minded group the ideal members are therefore well-respected professional retailers who are either the leaders, or potential leaders, in their particular territories. They must be of proven solvency, run a suitable shop in a territory where there is no other Intersport retailer and be willing to integrate in the Intersport Group.

Retailers should have annual gross sales totalling at least 60 million pesetas and should be experienced in the field of sporting goods. The typical Intersport member retailer (see Exhibit 11.6 below) has a minimum of 200 square metres of shop space, earns a 4–5 per cent profit on sales and registers returns on investment which are twice his/her return on equity. All member retailers must invest one million pesetas in Intersport shares, make a non-refundable donation of 150,000 pesetas and pay monthly dues of 20,000 pesetas.

There is one important difference between Intersport Spain and the Intersport organisations in other countries. In France, the head office gets 60 per cent of its financing through membership dues and 40 per cent through the margin earned on products sold to its members; while in Spain, membership dues account for only 10 per cent of financing with the margin on products accounting for the other 90 per cent. Of the membership fees, 70 per cent are allocated to advertising. Members are increasingly demanding new and better services from the head office.

The governing bodies of Intersport have little power over member retailers. A sense of conviction and good personal contacts govern the relations between headquarters and the member retailers. Supplies of merchandise are only cut off when a member retailer is officially declared insolvent.

Exhibit 11.1 P & L Account (pesetas)

	1987			1988		
	Movement	%	Totals	Movement	%	Totals
Stockinter sales	93,861,071	10.80	10,136,340	135,233,268	12.30	16,650,437
Import sales	514,716,064	18.36	94,511,790	540,106,180	19.10	103,161,619
Centralised payments	139,100,107			243,175,936		
Rebates	471,314,000	2.51	11,832,044	507,978,880	2.50	12,699,472
Dues			13,671,529			17,544,662
	1,281,991,202	Income:	130,151,703	1,426,494,264	Income:	150,056,130
Services supplied						1,031,500
						151,087,630
Annual expenses and depreciation			98,368,795			122,548,787
Operating profit			31,782,908			28,538,843
Financial costs			15,950,852			20,221,686
			15,832,056			8,317,157
Assorted adjustments			699,134			1,816,303
Earnings before taxes (EBT)			15,132,922			10,133,460

Exhibit 11.2 Balance Sheet (pesetas)

Assets	31/12/87	31/12/88	Liabilities	31/12/87	31/12/88
Fixed assets			*Shareholders' equity*		
Buildings and			Capitalised profits		1,836,280
equipment	18,721,197	118,130,138[1]	Share capital	65,350,000	70,000,000
Patents and brands	500,000	500,000	Legal reserve	–	2,482,530
Guarantees	895,000	915,000	Year's profits	15,132,922	10,133,460
Shares IIC	4,991,000	5,270,000			
				80,482,922	84,452,270
	25,107,197	124,815,138	*Provisions*		
Inventories			Reserve for		
Stock on hand	74,018,333	102,006,290	exchange rate		
			differences	–	3,011,500
	74,018,333	102,006,290	*Long-term liabilities*		
Receivables			Loans from		
Customers–			partners	38,094,535	33,050,498
members	140,347,929	59,193,695	Debentures to		
Exchange bills			members	–	29,686,338
receivable	14,177,695	36,694,432	Warehouse		
Misc. debtors	9,511,138	9,200,613	mortgage	–	48,000,000
Unpaid calls on					
share capital	21,537,046	3,325,000		38,094,535	110,736,836
Doubtful debtors	3,095,886	4,053,780	*Short-term liabilities*		
			Suppliers	94,896,785	3,463,276
	188,669,694	112,467,520	Import loans	53,979,974	106,833,755
Cash and banks			Exchange		
Cash and banks	29,864,954	33,703,496	bills payable	2,742,874	2,669,229
			Misc. creditors	31,219,270	66,205,973
	29,864,954	33,703,496	Taxes & welfare		
Suspense accounts			payable	10,895,433	4,417,967
Prepayments		4,970,440			
Contingency fund		2,044,468		193,734,336	183,590,200
Import expenses to be attributed		9,187,696	*Suspense accounts*		
			Deferred		
		16,202,604	payments	5,348,385	7,404,242
				5,348,385	7,404,242
Totals	317,660,178	389,195,048		317,660,178	389,195,048

Note: [1] A new headquarters building with a warehouse and offices was inaugurated.

Exhibit 11.3 Sporting goods groups in France

Company	Systems	Number of outlets	Sales (FFr m.) (real or estimated)
Adidas Style	Franchise	10	20
Athlete's foot	Corporate branch	21	69
Athlete's foot	Franchise	26	50
Cabanon	Co-operative	130	350
Chausport	Corporate branch	6	?
Chausport	Franchise	12	17
Comprasport	Co-operative	125	250
Courir	Corporate branch	18	66
Decathlon	Corporate branch	58	1,300
Disport	Corporate branch	11	140
Go Sport	Corporate branch	45	1,000
Intersport	Co-operative	520	1,710
KWay	Franchise	11	20
Lacoste	Franchise	24	40
Leclerc Sport	Franchise	4	35
Matos	Franchise	16	25
Mi Temps	Corporate branch	35	180
Mistral Shop	Franchise	10	20
Pro Shop	Co-operative	30	25
Quai 34	Franchise	34	68
S Sport	Co-operative	39	250
Shineige	Co-operative	250	390
Spao	Corporate branch	17	125
Sport 2000	Co-operative	500	950
Sport Chalet	Corporate branch	2	?
Sports Contact	Co-operative	30	30
Start Sport	Co-operative	13	20
TDS	Co-operative	450	900
Trigano	Corporate branch	129	?
Vieux Campeur	Independent	12	180
Vitasport	Corporate branch	6	27
Weider	Franchise	20	40

Exhibit 11.4 Intersport Spain expansion

Predicted growth in the Spanish market (in million pesetas)

1987		72,000	2,000 ptas. per capita
1988	10%	79,200	–
1989	12%	88,704	–
1990	11%	98,461	–
1991	10%	108,307	–
1992	9%	118,055	–
1993	9%	128,680	3,575 ptas. per capita

Intersport Spain Group

	Sales (Retail price)	Market share (%)
1987	4,085	6
1988	4,752	6
1989	5,677	6
1990	6,695	7
1991	7,798	7
1992	8,972	8
1993	10,294	8

Intersport Spain headquarters

	Estimated total sales to members	Members loyalty to headquarters (%)	Headquarters gross sales	Growth over previous year (%)
1987	2,269	26.0	600	
1988	2,670	28.0	725	21.0
1989	3,153	29.0	915	26.0
1990	3,719	30.0	1,115	21.0
1991	4,332	30.0	1,299	16.0
1992	4,984	30.0	1,495	15.0
1993	5,718	30.0	1,715	14.0

Exhibit 11.5 List of Intersport shops in Spain, winter 1989

City	Shop(s)
ALBACETE	Deportes Reyse / Camping y Deportes Albacete
ALGORTA	Deportes Gaztañaga
ALMERIA	Deportes Flipper
AYAMONTE	Pulido Sport
BADALONA	Sports Maresma
BAQUEIRA BERET	Esports Monitor
BARACALDO	Bide Onera
BARBERA DEL VALLES	Intersport Baricentro
BARCELONA	Sports Esplai / Match / La Tenda (3) / Esports Fenix / Esports Teens (3) / Esports Spot / Esports Edelweiss / Sports Canavese / Ski Center Intersport
BEASAIN	Urrutia Kirolak
BENICASIM	Deportes Castello
BENIDORM	Deportes Beni-Algar / Deportes El Rincon / Sports Experts
BERGA	Sol i Neu
BERMEO	Kirol-Etxea
BILBAO	Guisasola Sport (2)
BURGOS	Alex Sport
BURRIANA	Deportes Helios
CANDANCHU	Roldan Sport
CASTELLON	Deportes Castello
CERDANYOLA	Esports Cistue
CORDOBA	Deportivo Hnos. Ponce (3)
LA CORUÑA	Deportes Gudi (3)
DENIA	Les Tendes Reig / Deportes Reig / Playsport Reig
EIBAR	Ascasibar Deportes
ELCHE	Armeria y Deportes Andrés / Deportes Unisport
ELDA	Armeria y Deportes Torres (2)
ESPLUGUES DE LL.	Esports Spot
FIGUERES	Sports Prada
FORMIGAL	Sport Masonet Ski (2)
GANDIA	Sport Richard
GAVA	Esports Quince
GIRONA	Esports Ferrer
GRANADA	Moto-Deporte
GRANOLLERS	Auto-Moto Sastre
L'HOSPITALET DE LL.	Tot-Esport (2)
HUELVA	Deportes Hobby
HUESCA	Deportes Jorri
IGUALADA	Drac-Esport
IRUN	Deportes Gonzalez
JACA	Piedrafita Sports
LEJONA	Deportes Gaztañaga
LEON	Deportes Conty (2)
LOGROÑO	Deportes Helio
LORCA	Deportes Zurano
LUGO	Miguel Sport / Deportes Bourio / Bourio Caravanas-Jardineria / Intersport Miguel
LLEIDA	La Tenda
LLORET DE MAR	Sports Marques
MADRID	Pilos Sport / La Tienda
MANRESA	La Tenda
MATARO	La Tenda
MIRANDA DE EBRO	Sport 82
MONDRAGON	Loramendi Kirolak
MONZON	Deportes Monzón
MURCIA	Deportes internacional (2)
OLOT	Sportman Balcells
ONTENIENTE	Armeria y Deportes Rull
ORENSE	Bousso Sport
OVIEDO	Deportes Tuñon
PALAFRUGELL	Sports 17
PALMA DE MALLORCA	Intersport
PAMPLONA	Deportes Irabia (3)
PANTICOSA	Sport 2
EL PRAT DE LLOBREGAT	Unisport
REUS	Esports Sentis (2)
RUBI	Esports Edelweiss
SABADELL	Esports Alpins
SAN ISIDRO	Deportes Conty
SAN SEBASTIAN	Casa Alzugaray
SAN BOI DE LLOBREGAT	Esports Quinze
SANTA C. GRAMANET	Sports Masip

Exhibit 11.5 (Continued)

SAN CUGAT DEL VALLES	Esports Set	TERRASSA	Esports Alpins
		TORRENTE	Deportes Herca
SAN FELIU DE LLOBREGAT	Running Sports	VALENCIA	Deportes Ferando
		VALL D'UXO	Deportes Castello
SAN JOAN DESPI	Running Sports	VALLADOLID	Sport 2,000
SANTIAGO DE COMPOSTELA	Deportes Piteira	VIC	Sports Everest
		VILADECANS	Esports Quinze
SEVILLA	Deportes "Z" Zulategui	VILANOVA I LA GELTRU	Olaria Esports
TARRAGONA	Deportes Mestres L'Esport	YECLA	Deportes Cumbre (2)
		ZARAGOZA	Intersport-
TARREGA	Sports Club		Miraflores

Exhibit 11.6 How to do better business: responses to member survey

Intersport began surveying its member retailers about one year ago. Their responses are now available. Members have been classified in 3 categories, according to the gross sales declared in 1987:

Group A – more than 75 million pesetas per year.
Group B – 36–75 million pesetas per year.
Group C – 35 million pesetas per year or less.

(a) Floor space (shop average)

	Group A	Group B	Group C	Average
1. Floor space dedicated to selling	185 sq. m	214 sq. m	103 sq. m	173 sq. m
2. Floor space dedicated to warehousing	167 sq. m	101 sq. m	69 sq. m	105 sq. m

(b) Sales data (pesetas)

	Group A	Group B	Group C	Average
Ratio advertising costs/sales (%)	1.59	1.96	2.80	2.30
Sales per employee	10,190,000	8,650,000	7,760,000	8,550,000
Sales per salesperson	13,060,000	11,330,000	9,040,000	10,720,000
Sales per square metre (total floor space)	199,000	132,000	124,000	140,000
Sales per square metre (selling space)	313,000	218,000	245,000	243,000

Ratners
A successful retail strategy derailed?

Chris Carr
Manchester Business School

and

Neil Botten
University of Westminster

Context

On the night of 25 November 1992, Gerald Ratner resigned as chief executive of the Ratners Group due to the 'continued negative press' he had attracted in the wake of a remark made in April 1991 at the Institute of Directors' conference. Shareholders had seen their shares decline from just over 400p in 1987 to 18p.

Mr Ratner was quoted (*Independent*, 26/11/92) as saying: 'I am obviously saddened to be leaving a business of which I am so proud. However, the continuing negative press I have attracted leads me to believe that this is in the interests of the group and the people working in it.' James McAdam, chairman, added: 'It's his decision. It's sad for everybody. It's the end of an era. He's been in the group for 26 years and built it up from small beginnings.' A compensation payment of £375,000 was made 'in recognition of the particular circumstances that have led him to resign'.

Since April 1984 when he became full managing director, Gerald Ratner had transformed a modest jewellery chain into Britain's leading player, with a major position even in the US. At the same time, his entrepreneurship and marketing flair had revolutionised high street jewellery retailing. Although Gerald Ratner's successor was now established, the loss of such a personality, just as the crucial Christmas selling season was beginning, must have left the group in some consternation.

Mr McAdam faced difficult strategic questions. What exactly had gone wrong in the company, previously proclaimed one of the winners of the 1980s? How was such a marketing-orientated company to face up to tough financial decisions in virtually a turnaround situation, without destroying those critical strengths which had led to earlier success?

The company's earlier background

Founded by Gerald's father, Leslie Ratner, on his son's birthday 43 years earlier, the company had operated as a traditional retail jeweller in a conservative, highly fragmented, dull and backward industry. Gerald Ratner entered the family business at the age of 16 as a salesman, but for many years made little impact. He was restless and lacked patience with the conservative nature of the industry. One of his main interests at the time was to play poker with his close friends Michael Green and Charles Saatchi. Occasionally a brilliant player, he often lost heavily when his openness allowed his opponents to read him like a book. Nevertheless, he became joint managing director in 1982, working alongside his father. The combination was not successful; there were many rows, particularly when he felt his views were not given due attention. In its financial year to April 1983, Ratners made a loss of £350,000.

They were not alone, however. During 1982 the whole of the jewellery trade suffered poor results. Ernest Jones, for example, announced halved profits on nominal sales growth of only 4 per cent and rationalisation steps aimed at improving efficiency. Caution spread through the industry, with other companies such as Zales also de-stocking. Most shares reached 'new lows' – James Walker 43p and Ratners 39p.

Poor performances were blamed on reduced consumer demand as a result of recession, higher VAT, and the severe weather conditions during the previous Christmas buying period. Gold prices (shown in Table 12.1) were at a high, meaning that stock bought at previously low prices had to be replaced at higher cash cost. Manufacturers (including Ratners' own manufacturing operation) were hit by lower orders from retailers. Its problems were exacerbated by a fundamental shift in retail order patterns, resulting in more rush orders in late December. Jewellers dealing with the Christmas rush were becoming more conscious of the need for fast turnover of stocks, which were paid for in advance.

Despite such changes, industry observers such as David Cassidy (*Retail Jeweller*, 1 July 1982) were optimistic that with better conditions on the way the traditional approach to jewellery retailing was still the answer to all these problems:

> You in the jewellery trade, as customer surveys indicate, are in a very, very happy position. Price is not high in the purchaser's decision. You have the opportunity to observe the change in lifestyles and to build an environment and an attractiveness which will ensure your profitable survival. But I believe you have a bigger opportunity, you are predominantly independent. You are small, and in retailing small is beautiful ...you can motivate staff in ways that we (British Homes Stores) would find impossible. If you lose out to the major chains who can only offer a price advantage you will only have yourselves to blame, and I do not believe you will.

Not everyone agreed, however. A report in *The Daily Telegraph* in September 1982 described the jewellery industry as: 'lacklustre and jaded after 2 years of recession and is bracing itself for another round of company closures and

Table 12.1 Average annual gold price, 1980–1990 ($/ounce)

1980	1981	1982	1983	1984	1985	1986	1987	1988	1989	1990
615	460	376	424	361	317	368	447	437	382	384

Source: World Gold Council.

redundancies as the luxury trade continues its down hill slide'. John Smith of the British Jewellers Association argued that many firms were only surviving by virtue of the courtesy of their bankers and another flat Christmas would force them under (*Retail Jeweller*, 9 September 1982). The root of the trouble was that recession had opened the way to the department stores and mail order catalogues, which offered mass produced, imported, gold and silver items. This had greatly reduced the perceived value of the craftsman-made products of the old school. A report by Mintel viewed such developments more optimistically, pointing to the expansion of the overall market as companies such as Argos attracted new types of customers; but, like ICC, Mintel saw little scope for organic growth in the independent sector.

Mintel expected greater polarisation, with some outlets specialising in luxury items. Multiples needed greater visual identity. Although the retail jewellers presented a smart and sparkling face to the world, consumers found difficulty in distinguishing the branches of one multiple from another. Arthur Conley's managing director, for example, achieved higher margins by shifting upmarket: changing its name (to Walker and Hall), its store appearance, and improving its product range and quality (*Retail Jeweller*, 15 July 1992): 'many people agreed jewellers had been their own worst enemy for the last year or two because of their suicidal decision to bring in lower prices'. Some jewellers emphasised the increasing importance of a store's appearance: 'a jeweller's store should be a luxurious place'. A modern refit of an Ipswich store was claimed to have brought about a 40 per cent increase in turnover within two years. A good window display was cheaper than advertising and could be more effective.

ICC argued the industry was ripe for modernisation. Consumer spending would be boosted by new marketing methods, as had occurred in other retail sectors. Better credit facilities, heavier promotion and advertising and re-newed emphasis on shop displays would all be adopted by the more tradi-tional multiples in an attempt to combat the new entrants. One such new entrant was a new division of Johnson Matthey, a direct response sales operation named Rembrandt, selling entirely other manufacturers' products and making more liberal use of credit facilities.

John Bischoff, chief executive of the Company of Master Jewellers, likewise argued (*Retail Jeweller*, 4 November 1982) that jewellers would have to be 'prepared to accept change, to reduce their product ranges and to take a look at alternative products if they are to increase the traffic flow through their shops and keep their businesses alive in the '80s'. There were too many retailers on the high street: independents were subsidising the multiples who were able to buy more competitively. Discounting operations were on the increase and catalogue showrooms – such as Argos – had a broad range of products which cut across the traditional jeweller's range of products. Prospective customers were able to carry the attractively laid out catalogues around with them to make price comparisons. For them, the traditional store's front door was still a barrier.

Ratners' pre-tax profits improved in the company's financial year to April 1984 to just over £1 million, representing a return on capital of 7.1 per cent as sales recovered 7.2 per cent to £2.76m. In the same month, Gerald Ratner ousted his father in a boardroom coup and became sole managing director.

Starting with only 130 jewellery branches, he created one of the world's top jewellery retailing chains and was to transform a fragmented and confused industry in the process. For a time most people in the industry remained oblivious, distracted by the creation of the industry's exciting new giant, H. Samuels, which had just bought James Walker to take them to nearly 400 outlets.

Gerald Ratner's early retail formula

Within a week of taking charge, so the story goes, Gerald Ratner quizzed managers as to which competitors were doing well. Told of a shop in Newcastle taking £1m a month which had Geordies queuing half-way to Sunderland, he jumped on a train to discover its secret and was instantly converted to a formula which was to become his hallmark. In fact, any such store was more likely to have been part of a small chain in the south-east created by Terry Jordan, Gerald Ratner's chief buyer back in 1976 when he had charge of Ratners' manufacturing arm, Jedales. Jordan believed that 'the jewellery industry divides up into small segments and you should stick to one of them' (*Management Today*, April 1987). Convinced that a retailer should not manufacture and practising what he preached, Jordan left to sell bought-in, low-priced jewellery in his own shops – very basic affairs with all the stock displayed in the windows. The success of the formula (by 1984 there were 26 shops) made an indelible impact on Ratner.

Gerald Ratner acquired Terry's in December that year, on the basis that Jordan 'would give Ratners any knowledge of experience that would be of benefit to them . . . Terry Jordan was very good, and I wanted him back.' Jordan spent 18 months training Ratners' buyers and merchandisers – 'I went through everything, showing them the best lines, good suppliers, got the windows straight and so on.' To secure better discounts, the group used central purchasing and increased the number of suppliers from 5 to around 50, with an emphasis on merchandise that would turn over rapidly. Jordan joined the board, staying with the company until his retirement in January 1990. For his part, Gerald Ratner 'got rid of the peripheral rubbish, like the six stores in Holland, the spectacle shops', while also making the decision to axe Jedales.

Ratner wanted to transform what he felt to be an intimidating public image: 'Jewellery used to be an occasion, a once-in-a-lifetime investment.' Jewellers' product orientation was reinforced by the training of the traditional, poorly paid jeweller who emerged more skilled in repairs and valuations than in selling. The image, of engagement rings bought from sombrely dressed assistants, who whispered the price lest other customers might hear, had to be changed. Traditionally, mark-ups were around 100 per cent and prices rose by 10 – 15 per cent per annum regardless of the retail price index. However, for younger people whose spending power was increasing, jewellery as an investment was 'no better than a fur coat'. A reduced gold content, keen pricing and greater fashion appeal were needed to open up the market.

Using the Terry's chain initially to pilot these ideas, Ratners began to offer jewellery cheaply, with no frills but nevertheless inviting outlets where the customer would feel comfortable. Key buyers were changed and many younger managers, in their thirties, were brought in. Gerald Ratner substantially increased financial incentives, supporting these with an extremely hands-on style of management.

The high value of the real jewellery stock carried prevented stores from being converted to self-selection as had occurred in other retail trades. Therefore, the window back remained an integral part of any promotional display. This lead to the deep 'tunnel' entrance to the shop doorway, providing more display space and browsing space in the event of bad weather. This did not, however, provide any means of distinguishing one retailer from another. Branding was virtually impossible with the large number of manufacturers and the high advertising spend necessary to establish a brand. Ratners solved this problem, together with the repositioning downmarket, by giving the appearance of a permanent sale. Shop fronts were covered, all year round, with posters promoting particular products on the basis of their price, money back guarantees, price matching and credit. Store design was taken to a fine art, but Gerald Ratner viewed this as more than just a matter of image (*Independent*, 29 November 1992): 'Price is crucial. Image isn't. You can't sell a new logo or colour scheme.' A new store design would be mocked-up in the basement of one of the company's warehouses, approved, photographed and passed to each store manager for implementation.

Imports of fine jewellery had started and were increasingly exploited to keep costs and prices down. The 'flash for cash' image was born, encouraging impulse purchasing at the lower end of the range. To reduce working capital associated with seasonality, logistics were refined ever further. Stocks at the stores were kept to a minimum with frequent replenishment from the warehouse where stock levels had been increased. By 1986, electronic point of sale systems were installed and the stores were being restocked twice a week rather than the previous fortnightly cycle.

Later this low cost, highly flexible system enabled them to target a new but growing market segment, where the product could be promoted as an everyday, disposable, fashion accessory.

Such an approach was to be honed through the 1980s, but by 1986 Gerald Ratner had already successfully consolidated his expanded business base and had turned in performances which could not fail to impress the City. Exhibit

12.1 on pp. 143–7 provides for an analysis of the company's financial perform-ance over the full period of the case, including credit ratings of more relevance later. Exhibits 12.2 and 12.3, on pp. 148–51, show trends in its share price as compared with the *Financial Times* all-shares index and four other companies, and trends in its price earnings ratio.

Market developments in the 1980s

A critical evaluation of Ratners' strategy throughout the 1980s requires some appreciation of the market context.

First, Gerald Ratner had set the company unambiguously on a path aimed at industry leadership, but much of the industry continued to remain frag-mented, as shown in Table 12.2. Ratners' activities concentrated initially on 'real' rather than 'costume' or fashion jewellery. 'Real' jewellery is made from solid, or latterly hollow, but not plated gold, silver or platinum. The pieces may or may not be set with precious or semi-precious stones. As well as real jewellery, most independent outlets will carry giftware, silverware, watches and clocks.

'Fashion' or 'costume' jewellery consists of all other jewellery whatever made from, normally including gilt and gold plated items. Sales of costume jewellery, although initially unimportant, increased steadily over the decade as shown in Table 12.3. This was mainly due to the trend towards coordinated clothes and accessories moving down the age profile, which was itself chang-ing (see Table 12.4). The lower price, initially, of the costume jewellery helped the positioning of the sector. The dress taste of people such as the Princess of Wales and Joan Collins brought about an additional upmarket fashion jewel-lery sector, where by 1988 prices upwards of £300 were not uncommon. The fashion jewellery sector attracted department stores and fashion stores such as Next, Miss Selfridge and Top Shop, together with specialist accessory shops such as Salisburys, Butler & Wilson, Tonq and Ciro. There are more branding opportunities in this sector than in real jewellery but it is still relatively insignificant.

Table 12.2 Jewellery outlets, 1980–1988

	1980	1982	1984	1986	1988(est.)
Number of businesses	4,830	5,157	4,596	5,133	5,100
Number of outlets	7,746	7,804	7,215	8,096	8,100
Total employees (000s)	41	37	34	38	–

Source: Mintel.

Table 12.3 Retail sales of jewellery by type at current prices (£m.)

	Real	Diamond	Fashion
1983	898	216	143
1984	972	287	174
1985	1,054	313	200
1986	1,108	346	226
1987	1,172	398	258
1988	1,322	494	288
1989	1,495	560	325
1990(est.)	1,568	555	340

Sources: Business Monitor, Diamond Promotion Service, Mintel.

Table 12.4 Female demographic structure of population (000s)

Age	1980	1985	1990
0–5	1,657	1,760	1,887
5–14	4,099	3,543	3,434
15–24	4,344	4,547	4,143
25–34	3,967	3,900	4,362
35–44	3,311	3,770	3,937
45–54	3,177	3,180	3,246
55–64	3,244	3,223	2,985
65+	5,120	5,191	5,383

Source: Mintel.

Ratners made increasing use of jewellery manufactured overseas, exploiting the trend towards imports particularly in the 9-carat real jewellery sector (see Tables 12.5, 12.6 and 12.7). As the group grew it could negotiate good conditions, not only with some 2,000 UK manufacturers, but with tens of thousands of manufacturers around the world. Prior to the 1987 crash, the group was buying and selling 250,000 carats of diamonds a year and 27 tonnes of 9-carat gold. The volume of business attracted new styles of performance from manufacturers, hollow gold jewellery was first offered by Ratner. Design innovation was vital for the group selling 'disposable' jewellery. When Princess Diana became engaged to Prince Charles, the design of the ring was copied and delivered to the stores in just four days. A day later 10,000 had been sold at £28.50. The original was valued at £30,000. Prices of most items were held year on year and in some cases fell, as increased efficiency allowed reduced margins to be taken. By April 1990 Victor Ratner, deputy managing director, was able to claim that: 'a particular bracelet sold for £38.95 at Christmas 1988 was sold at £29.95 the following Christmas with only a slight loss of weight, and would be cheaper again at Christmas 1990' (*Financial Times*, 24 April 1990). By then jewellery had become the third most popular gift item, having overtaken books and records.

Table 12.5 Number of items hallmarked and percentage imported

	Hallmarked (m.)			Imports (%)		
	Gold	Silver	Platinum	Gold	Silver	Platinum
1983	14.61			26.3		
1985	17.03	3.25	0.008	29.8	14.7	0.0
1987	18.00	3.54	0.006	30.2	13.6	4.9
1989	23.95	3.82	0.008	35.9	16.9	4.1
1991	19.09	3.27	0.007	39.5	19.2	2.9

Source: British Hallmarking Council.

Table 12.6 Hallmarking of gold items and percentage imported by carat (kg)

	22car.	%	18car.	%	14car.	%	9car.	%
1985	4,702	17.0	2,353	24.1	164	31.1	41,556	39.4
1987	4,226	23.6	2,831	27.7	120	59.0	50,136	38.9
1989	6,967	32.9	4,470	28.7	211	52.1	76,698	45.2
1991	8,113	40.3	3,869	28.2	226	63.7	66,315	48.1

Source: British Hallmarking Council.

Table 12.7 Volume of gold items by carat (%)

	22car.	18car.	14car.	9car.	Total
1985	9.6	4.8	0.3	85.3	100.0
1987	7.4	4.9	0.2	87.5	100.0
1989	7.9	5.1	0.2	86.8	100.0
1991	10.3	4.9	0.3	84.5	100.0

Note: The data misleads as regards the overall dominance of the sector by 9car. standard items. In reality the percentage taken by 9car. will be as much as 20 per cent higher. The Council do not hallmark items of less than one gram in weight, which accounted for much of the hollow jewellery in circulation in the later years of this table. There is a higher incidence of imports in the 14car. sector since this is the main European standard.

Table 12.8 Average monthly percentage of annual sales, 1986–90

Jan	Feb	Mar	Apr	May	Jun	Jly	Aug	Sep	Oct	Nov	Dec
6.3	6.1	6.4	6.1	6.3	7.2	7.6	7.6	7.7	7.4	9.3	22.0

Source: Business Monitor.

A final feature of the market, which also has some effect on the timing of acquisitions, is its seasonality (shown in Table 12.8). Given that costs accumulate relatively evenly through the year, often 90 per cent or even more of profits arise in the last two calendar months. Jewellery companies making acquisitions later in the year may thus have the opportunity to take into their accounts the higher proportion of profit earned in the later part of the calendar year.

Ratners' acquisition-based rapid growth strategy

On the 13 January 1986, having established a sound base, Ratners family announced in the *Financial Times* its intention to become Britain's biggest jewellery chain, with plans to add 40 new shops to the existing 173 then trading. Funding for the expansion was to come from the 1 for 4 rights issue at 112p.

In the event most of this expansion was through acquisition. In May 1986 Gerald Ratner paid £4.3 million to take a 27.7 per cent stake in H. Samuel. He had bought the shares from the owning family members who had been disappointed by recent trading results. The majority of the shares were held by chairman Anthony Edgar who controlled 38 per cent together with his mother's 5 per cent. By the end of the month Edgar had agreed terms at £149 million. Edgar initially became chairman of the combined group, but in August accepted a £585,000 golden handshake, leaving Gerald Ratner as both chairman and chief executive.

The financing costs of the acquisition were reduced by sale and lease back of H. Samuel's freehold shops releasing £27m, half in that financial year and half in the next. Goodwill provisions result in net asset additions to Ratners' consolidated balance sheets being less than the consideration paid: full details for all Ratners' major acquisitions are therefore included in Exhibit 12.4 below. In interpreting accounts it should also be appreciated that, set against the increased profit that may arise immediately on acquisitions, there are likely to be increased interest and dividend outlays, particularly in subsequent years arising from considerations paid. These figures are grouped together in Exhibit 12.5.

The H. Samuel operation continued to trade under its own name but the merchandising and marketing programme, so successful at Ratners, was now applied to the acquired stores. By January 1987, turnover was reported as having increased 40 per cent at H. Samuel and 50 per cent in the Ratner outlets. Gerald Ratner described the deal as the 'steal of the century . . . When we took it over it was making profits of around £10 a square foot compared to Ratners' £80. Now it is making £32 and we've plans to raise it up to £100 with new ranges' (*Marketing*, 19 March 1987).

There was now clear segmentation of the market. While the group had previously concentrated on the lower end of the market with Terry's and Ratners, Watches of Switzerland was aimed upmarket and specialised in watch brands such as Rolex, Patek Phillipe and Audemars Piaget. The middle market was catered for by H. Samuel and its subsidiary James Walker. This pattern of segmentation was to continue into the 1990s and, with the exception of Terry's, the same names would be carried on (see Table 12.9), with clearly priced segments.

By May 1987, Ratners had made a bid for Combined English Stores, a large group comprising Zales, J. Weir and Collingwood jewellers which amounted to some 360 outlets. It also had other retail interests, notably Salisbury, the fashion accessory chain. Although the CES board gave an irrevocable recom-

Table 12.9 Average transaction values at Ratners Group outlets

Trading name	1990
Watches of Switzerland	950
Zales/Ernest Jones	50
H. Samuel	25
Ratners	18
Salisbury	7

Source: Ratner Group.

mendation to the Ratners offer, a higher bid by George Davis of Next was successful. There was no counter-offer, as an increased offer would have caused problems with EPS dilution. There was also some concern that the acquisition of the full group might lead to an OFT referral to the MMC as suggested by the Goldsmith Group of Jewellers, owned by Oriflame (*Financial Times*, 2 May 1987).

Another rights issue, this time on a 3 for 10 basis, announced at the end of May, provided funding for the acquisition of Ernest Jones, with 61 locations trading in prime sites. This chain was already well established in the middle to upper end of the market, the only segment not covered at that time by the Ratners Group. In addition, it operated in shopping precincts where Ratners were underrepresented. Again the separate trading identity was to be maintained, but the Ratners merchandising and logistics skills would be applied to the group. All Ernest Jones stores had recently gone through a refurbishment programme. In July it was announced that the bid would not be referred to the MMC.

The *Financial Times* (4 July 1987) suggested that this would probably be the company's last major acquisition in the UK, and went on to announce that the company had agreed terms for the acquisition of the Sterling group in the US. Sterling, the fourth largest jewellery group in the US, operated in a market sector with which Gerald Ratner was very familiar. He was reported as saying that the US market was ripe for 'a shakeout and consolidation'. The $20bn per annum retail market was highly fragmented, in the hands of the independents and small chains, and very similar to the market in the UK. Additionally, the market had enjoyed a 7.9 per cent compound annual growth rate over the previous five years. Sterling had 117 stores, operated in 15 states and operated under a number of store names. Despite the market trend of the time which was poor, the rights issue was 91.7 per cent taken up.

The following month Ratners acquired Westall, a specialist US jeweller with 71 outlets. The acquisition offered operational synergies as both Sterling and Westall catered for the same market segments but in adjoining geographical areas. By November, Ratners was the second largest jeweller worldwide with 930 outlets, of which 213 were in the US.

Ratners continued to make progress, transferring its merchandising techniques to Samuels. By early 1988, profits per square foot had increased from £32 to £62 at Samuels, while Ratners had risen to £92. The market share for the group was now 19 per cent compared to 2.5 per cent when Gerald had become chairman. Logistics were improved throughout the group and incentives were extended to all staff. Bonuses and merit awards based on performance were paid every eight weeks to top branches and managers now spent more time selling than administering. Within the Ratners and Terry's branches the average age of the staff was low, which helped both to keep staff costs down and promote a fashionable image. The size of the group was such that they were now able to offer for £94.50 a diamond ring which other multiples would have to sell for £200.

The further acquisition of Ostermans took the group to 310 outlets in the US, while the target of 1,000 stores in the UK came closer with the acquisition of Stephens Jewellery (13 shops in the south-east). The loss-making chain was acquired for a nominal cash sum and brought the number of outlets to 830.

In the Ratners outlets the preference for sales volume rather than margins continued. Sale and lease-back kept gearing in the UK low and the US sale of consumer credit balance would bring in $75 million.

The frustrated acquisition of Combined English Stores was reversed in October 1988 when the troubled Next group under George Davis sold Zales (130 stores), Salisburys (235 stores) and the 73 stores trading as Collingwood or J. Weir. It had been agreed that if the bid was referred, then only the purchase of Salisburys would proceed. Ratners paid £150.8 million for the stores and raised its third rights issue in 18 months, this time on a 1 for 4 basis. There were concerns in the City (*Financial Times*, 12 October 1988) that Ratners had bitten off more than it could chew and that the dilution would cause the same problems as those from which George Davis was suffering.

The acquisition of Salisburys marked a new direction for Ratners. Salisburys was an accessories retailer; its only connection with the main group was its sale of costume jewellery. The company had always maintained that the sale of costume jewellery and real jewellery would not mix. However, now there was a blurring between the low end of the real market and the costume jewellery market. There was certainly a price overlap; the cheapest gold earrings in Ratners branches were just 99p – 'cheaper than a prawn sandwich', as Gerald Ratner used to joke (*Retail & Distribution Management*, May/June 1989).

1988 proved to be a good year in terms of results. Turnover was up by approximately 76 per cent and nearly 20 times the 1983 total. Profits were up more than 60 per cent and were more than 40 times the 1985 total. Of this the UK was responsible for 57 per cent and 59 per cent respectively. On a like-for-like basis, H. Samuels had achieved 32 per cent growth in sales and the rest of the chains 20 per cent, with the exception of Terry's which had only managed 6 per cent. Zales and Salisburys had only been in the fold for 10 weeks but in that time had contributed £5 million to profits, emphasising the importance of the last quarter. Ratners had been unable to 'de-seasonalise' the sales to any great extent and was quoted later (*The Sunday Telegraph*, 29 November 1992) as saying: 'Christmas Eve is the time I know my fate. I am afraid I drive everyone mad.' Ratners traditionally made 80 per cent of its profit in the last five weeks before Christmas, and 10 per cent on Christmas Eve. The year's results could be forecast fairly accurately on Christmas morning.

The group had now reached its peak in terms of the number of UK stores (see Table 12.10) and a rationalisation process began.

Table 12.10 Number of outlets as at 1 January

	1985	1986	1987	1988	1989	1990	1991
H. Samuels			333	364	411	419	437
Ratners		143	199	220	238	248	
Terry's			70	80	89		
Ernest Jones[1]				59	59	195	200
Zales[1]					170		
Watches of Switzerland		19	20	21	23	24	
Salisburys					234	219	220
Other						56	
Total UK	153	170	565	730[2]	1,230[2]	1,150	1,180[2]
Total US				212	317	471	1,000[2]
Total	153	170	565	9,42[2]	1,547[2]	1,621	2,180[2]

Notes: [1] Zales and Ernest Jones trade as a single operation, and outlets are being consolidated under the Ernest Jones name. [2] These numbers are approximate.

Terry's was to disappear as a brand name; its relatively poor performance compared to Ratners meant that half of the outlets would be merged with other parts of the group and the balance sold off. The Zales and Ernest Jones operations were effectively combined and had the same product range, a particularly prominent feature of which would be diamond rings. The balance of the product mix in Salisburys was to be shifted towards costume jewellery and away from some of the other products which the group carried. All of the recent acquisitions were being fitted into the EPOS systems operated by the company to bring the operational efficiency up to the level achieved by H. Samuels and Ratners.

Ratners had stated targets of a 50 per cent market share of the UK market in the next few years and 10 per cent of the US market in five years. This did not seem too improbable based on their market performance (see Table 12.11). The buoyant market of 1989 was benefiting from the increased affluence of the population and had been growing at 20 per cent per annum.

In contrast with some of the more recent retailing set-backs such as Next, Dixons, Storehouse, Laura Ashley and Harris Queensway, Ratners enjoyed some notable advantages: it was not in a small segment of a fickle market; its supply lines were short and well managed; it was not a manufacturer; EPOS gave it flexibility; and there were no serious competitors.

October 1989 brought the announcement of further expansion in the US.

Table 12.11 Market share of retail jewellery market by retailer (£m.)

	1988	1989	1990
Independent specialists	610	615	622
Ratners	466	649	750
Other multiple specialists	238	245	234
Catalogue showrooms	173	189	192
Mail order	178	180	174
Department stores	201	205	212
Other	294	307	306
Total	2,160	2,390	2,490

Note: All figures include sales of watches, clocks, silverware and gifts.
Source: Mintel.

The 87-branch Weisfields operation had been purchased for $55 million, bringing the local total of stores to 450. The acquisition increased the geographical spread of the group by taking it into 50 shopping malls where it had not previously been represented down the West coast. The target of 1,500 stores in the US was mentioned. An attempt to frustrate the deal by Kays, the main competitor in the US, came to nothing but forced the price up to $57.50 per share.

In the run-up to Christmas 1989 Ratners decided to quadruple the advertising spend for the group to £6 million, much of which was to be directed through television. Traditionally TV had not played a substantial part in advertising, the press having previously taken around 90 per cent of annual expenditure. Never significant advertisers before this, the group had always concentrated on point-of-sale promotion, discounting and catalogues. Vouchers offering £50 off with every £150 spent were available during 1989 and 1990. Catalogues were available on stands outside branches and were increasingly distributed free with women's magazines. Subsequently in May 1990 it was announced that new catalogues would be produced on a fortnightly basis throughout the spring and summer in an attempt to maintain volume. In 1990, ten million catalogues were issued in the run-up to Christmas, a figure which increased to an estimated 17 million in 1991.

Despite encouraging results in early 1990, the *Financial Times* (24 March 1990) argued for a change of strategy when the finance director Andrew Coppell, a mergers and acquisitions specialist, was replaced by Gary O'Brien, a retail specialist. In July, however, the group pressed on by acquiring Kays, the 500-store chain in the US, making the company the second biggest jeweller in the US. Zales, the market leader, had 1,700 stores, whereas Ratners would have 900. The geographical fit of the new acquisition was seen as logistically sound, but some analysts were less than happy about the financial sense of the deal. Kays had been loss making and rumoured to be heading for a Chapter 11 filing (*Financial Times*, 3 July 1990). In the event there were difficulties convincing bond holders in Kays of the suitability of the deal and completion was not finally announced until the end of October.

Despite further efficiency improvements, Ratners' 1991 profits shrunk for the first time in nearly ten years, creating an atmosphere of gloom. While speaking at an Institute of Directors' meeting in April 1991 Gerald Ratner repeated a throwaway line he had used before, referring to some of the cheaper products that he sold as crap. On a day when there was little other news of any consequence, this became a front page headline for the tabloids, which were to hound him thereafter.

In January 1992, James McAdam became executive chairman, working alongside Gerald Ratner who continued as managing director in charge of day-to-day operations. A strategic review was instigated, aided by outside consultants. A cost-cutting and rationalisation programme was embarked upon as the company started to pursue margins as well as sales. In the meantime, however, Kays in the US was proving indigestible and the worrying cost increase seen in the previous year's second half had carried forward into the new year. In the year to February 1992, Ratners declared a loss of £123 million. Its share price continued plummeting throughout the year to a low point of 10p. A first-half loss was recorded. In the rationalisation, 1,000 jobs were to go and some of the guarantees and credit terms would be trimmed. In June, Watches of Switzerland, representing sales of £22 million, was sold off to Asprey for around £23 million.

By the end of 1992, the share price improved a little, as new support was gained from financial institutions. US operations began moving into profit and UK operations, though still loss-making, began to show signs of stabilising. Nevertheless, as James McAdam took over full control on 25 November, few could doubt the need for a new strategy and for a new style of management. An acclaimed success story in the 1980s, how could the company be put back on track?

Exhibit 12.1 Ratners' consolidated accounts and ratio analysis, 1983–1992 (£000s)

(a) Profit and Loss Account

	1/2/92	2/2/91	3/2/90	28/1/89	31/1/88	31/1/87	6/4/86	6/4/85	6/4/84	6/4/83
Number of weeks	52	52	53	52	52	43	52	52	52	52
Turnover	1,128,634	1,113,922	898,102	635,160	360,205	158,178	44,840	32,312	27,612	25,942
Pre-tax profits	–122,328	112,057	121,488	86,010	52,742	22,674	4,284	2,139	1,067	–350
Interest paid	40,609	30,200	30,447	16,502	7,282	4,154	551	290	267	204
Non-trading income	13,835	8,002	9,185	5,306	1,912	338	10	29	0	0
Operating profit	–95,554	134,255	142,750	97,206	58,112	26,490	4,825	2,400	1,334	–146
Depreciation	39,319	28,932	23,060	16,536	8,871	3,899	1,361	1,171	1,117	1,082
Trading profit	–56,235	163,187	165,810	113,742	66,983	30,389	6,186	3,571	2,451	936
Employees remuneration	210,119	188,722	148,181	96,206	58,402	25,036	7,990	6,342	5,299	4,739
Number of employees (actual)	20,352	19,405	16,903	14,838	9,478	3,643	1,286	1,058	861	835
Value-added	176,997	372,668	330,290	220,530	131,809	58,178	15,054	10,610	8,332	6,196

Source: ICC data taken from Lotus One Source UK Private + Database.

Exhibit 12.1 (continued)

(b) Balance Sheet

	1/2/92	2/2/91	3/2/90	28/1/89	31/1/88	31/1/87	6/4/86	6/4/85	6/4/84	6/4/83
Number of weeks	52	52	53	52	52	43	52	52	52	52
Fixed assets	235,887	262,226	209,642	195,033	144,015	95,840	6,658	5,185	4,949	5,119
Intangible assets	0	0	0	0	0	0	0	0	0	0
Stocks	425,725	443,476	374,388	251,920	174,464	78,209	17,748	15,413	13,639	12,517
Debtors	56,134	74,006	38,165	19,362	26,727	2,971	130	227	87	49
Other current assets	310,079	276,111	149,562	74,284	33,634	19,628	2,004	1,463	985	889
Total current assets	791,938	793,593	562,115	345,566	234,825	100,808	19,882	17,103	14,711	13,455
Total assets	1,058,553	1,073,986	777,248	545,407	380,895	198,876	26,935	23,055	20,520	18,574
Creditors	91,890	92,236	76,899	62,698	38,208	20,841	3,892	3,835	1,306	1,671
Short-term loans	476,114	48,805	49,748	81,168	58,968	47,442	3,192	1,726	2,210	904
Other current liabilities	155,521	209,963	165,040	124,856	58,522	21,671	3,500	2,499	1,905	2,219
Total current liabilities	723,525	351,004	291,687	268,722	155,689	89,954	10,584	8,060	5,421	4,794
Net assets	335,028	722,982	485,561	276,685	225,197	108,922	16,351	14,995	15,099	13,780
Shareholders' funds	302,553	397,648	297,900	184,635	163,508	95,813	14,178	12,526	13,296	13,142
Long-term loans	5,878	321,829	165,115	70,241	48,708	1,273	1,050	1,150	470	476
Other long-term liabilities	26,597	3,505	22,546	21,809	12,981	11,836	1,123	1,319	1,333	162
Capital employed	335,028	722,982	485,561	276,685	225,197	108,922	16,351	14,995	15,099	13,780

Exhibit 12.1 (continued)

(c) Consolidated sources and applications of funds

	2/2/91	3/2/90	28/1/89	31/1/88	31/1/87	6/4/86	6/4/85	6/4/84	6/4/83
Number of weeks	52	53	52	52	43	52	52	52	52
Source of funds									
Profit on ordinary activities before tax	112.06	121.49	86.01	52.74	22.67	4.28	2.14	1.07	(0.35)
Extraordinary items pre-tax	(10.10)	(0.70)	–	(2.45)	(0.89)	(0.40)	(0.01)	0.29	0.11
Adjustments for items not involving the use of funds									
Depreciation	29.23	23.06	16.54	8.87	3.90	1.36	1.17	1.12	1.08
Other	0.31	0.18	–	–	–	–	(0.02)		
Funds from operations – total	131.50	144.03	102.55	59.17	25.69	5.41	3.28	2.51	0.90
Funds from other services									
Net book value of tangible assets	18.88	33.64	10.21	12.83	30.16	0.16	0.59	0.13	0.21
Share issues	237.08	123.67	142.17	210.69	114.71	–	1.50	–	–
Loans/increases in creditors over 1 year	2.75	2.54	24.61	49.84	–	–	1.25	–	–
Other	16.42	27.43	42.31	0.65	–	–	–	–	–
Total sources	406.63	331.31	321.85	333.18	170.56	5.57	6.62	2.64	1.11

Exhibit 12.1 (continued)
(c) continued

	2/2/91	3/2/90	28/1/89	31/1/88	31/1/87	6/4/86	6/4/85	6/4/84	6/4/83
Number of weeks	52	53	52	52	43	52	52	52	52
Application of funds									
Purchase of fixed assets	71.98	63.28	52.14	49.52	10.75	3.11	1.02	1.08	0.99
Acquisitions	116.24	52.50	177.12	181.71	144.62	0.02	4.37	–	–
Tax paid	19.58	15.31	10.86	5.11	2.38	0.77	0.17	0.31	0.45
Dividend paid	35.25	26.56	10.56	6.60	2.55	0.81	0.68	0.68	0.68
Repayment of loans	1.98	2.83	1.12	0.51	0.10	0.10	–	0.08	0.07
Redemption of pref' shares	–	25.00	–	–	–	–	–	–	–
Other applications	24.00	22.10	8.91	–	–	–	–	–	–
Increase in working capital	137.62	123.71	61.14	89.73	10.16	0.76	0.38	0.49	1.08

Source: Company Accounts.

Exhibit 12.1 (continued)

(d) Key ratios and credit rating

	1/2/92	2/2/91	3/2/90	28/1/89	31/1/88	31/1/87	6/4/86	6/4/85	6/4/84	6/4/83
Number of weeks	52	52	53	52	52	43	52	52	52	52
Profitability ratios										
Pre-tax profit margins (%)	−10.8	10.1	13.5	13.5	14.6	14.3	9.6	6.6	3.9	−1.4
Return on capital (%)	−36.5	15.5	24.6	31.1	23.4	25.2	26.2	14.3	7.1	−2.5
Return on total assets (%)	−11.6	10.4	15.3	15.8	13.9	13.8	15.9	9.3	5.2	−1.9
Return on shareholder funds (%)	−40.4	28.2	40.0	46.6	32.3	28.6	30.2	17.1	8.0	−2.7
Earnings/share (p)	−50.4	23.6	29.2	25.6	20.4	14.2	8.1	3.9	3.1	1.4
Credit ratios										
Working capital/turnover (%)	6.1	39.7	30.7	12.1	22.0	5.7	20.7	28.0	33.6	33.4
Liquidity	1.1	2.3	1.9	1.3	1.5	1.1	1.9	2.1	2.7	2.8
Quick ratio	0.5	1.0	0.6	0.4	0.4	0.3	0.2	0.2	0.2	0.2
Total debt/net worth (%)	159.3	93.2	72.1	82.0	65.9	50.8	29.9	23.0	20.2	10.5
ICC credit score (100 is best possible; below 20 is critical)	21	65	61	43	63	53	60	60	56	

Source: ICC data taken from Lotus One Source UK Private + Database.

Exhibit 12.2 Ratners' trends in share price

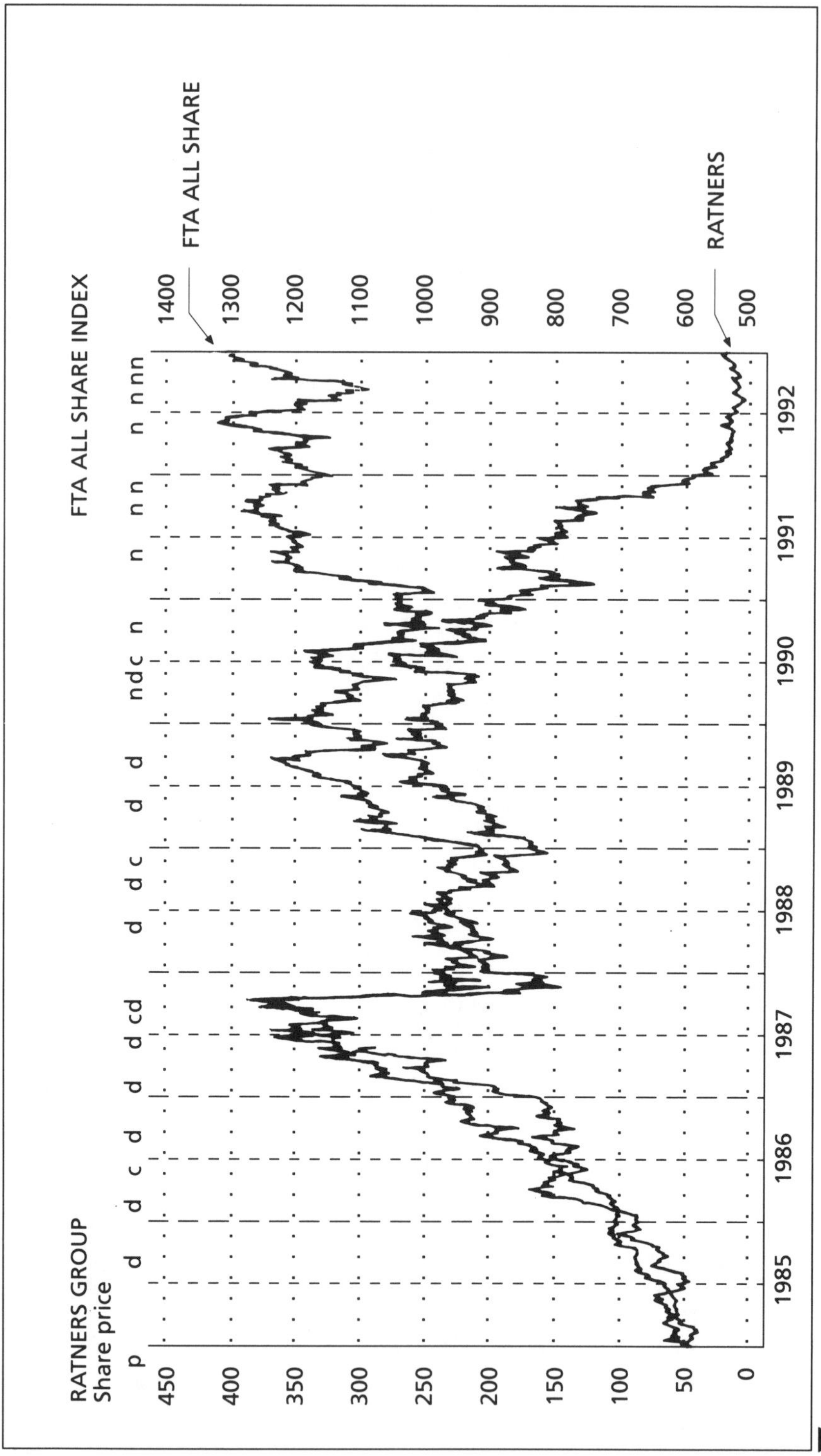

RATNERS GROUP
Share price

FTA ALL SHARE INDEX

FTA ALL SHARE

RATNERS

Exhibit 12.2 (continued)

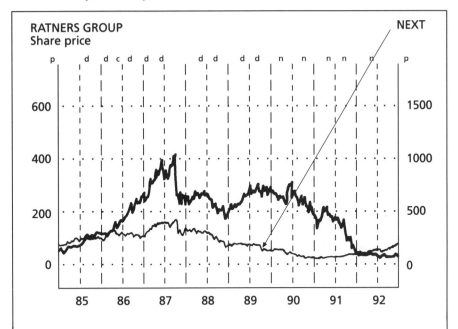

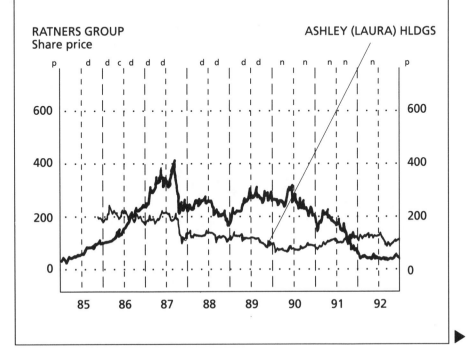

Exhibit 12.2 (continued)

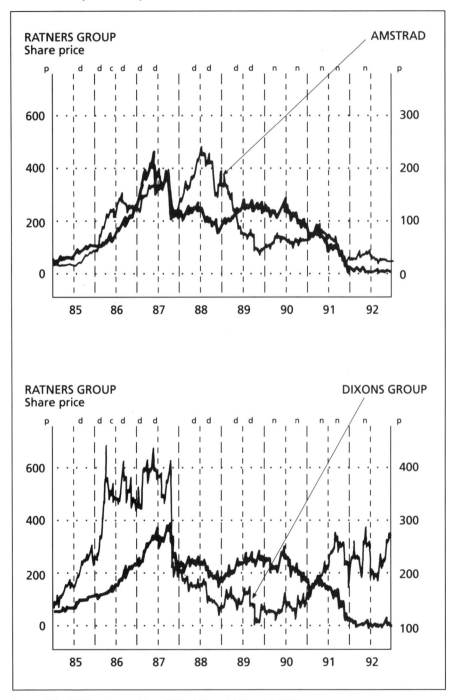

Source: MicroEXTEL price graphics – ©EXTEL Financial (071 251 3333).

Exhibit 12.3 Ratners' price earnings ratios, 1983–1992

Year	1st Qtr	2nd Qtr	3rd Qtr	4th Qtr
1983	31.2	n.a.	n.a.	n.a.
1984	n.a.	52.4	49.1	26.6
1985	32.7	50.4	57.0	29.7
1986	35.7	30.9	40.1	27.7
1987	34.5	52.4	17.6	17.7
1988	10.9	11.3	11.7	8.5
1989	7.7	9.4	9.4	9.0
1990	8.9	8.1	9.0	6.4
1991	5.5	5.5	5.9	11.7
1992	2.7	1.5	1.1	n.a.

Note: Highest value 57.0 on 1.7.85; lowest value 1.1 on 1.7.92.
Source: Datastream.

Exhibit 12.4 Ratners' acquisitions and goodwill write-offs

Accounts year	Acquisition	Total spent on acq.s in a/c year	Goodwill write-off	Net assets added to Balance Sheet
		£m.	£m.	£m.
1985	Terry's	4.36	2.81	1.55
1986	–			
1987	Samuels	138.96	38.65	100.31
1988	Ernest Jones Sterling Westall	181.65	160.00	21.65
1989	Osterman's Time (Jersey) Salisburys Zales	177.12	170.56	4.56
1990	Weisfields Ringmakers & Allen	39.80	32.00	7.80
1991	Kays	110.17	165.92	(55.75)
1992	–			

Source: Company Accounts.

Exhibit 12.5 Ratners' interest and dividend payments

Accounts year	Interest paid	All dividends	Interest + dividends	Profit attributable to shareholders
	£m.	£m.	£m.	£m.
1992	40.61	22.70	63.61	(125.95)
1991	30.20	44.41	74.61	68.92
1990	30.48	28.61	59.09	79.06
1989	16.50	18.82	35.32	54.19
1988	7.28	9.92	17.20	29.12
1987	4.15	4.59	8.74	13.61
1986	0.55	1.05	1.60	2.67
1985	0.29	0.76	1.05	1.32
1984	0.27	0.68	0.95	0.95
1983	0.20	0.68	0.88	(0.33)

Source: Company Accounts.

Part Four

INTERNATIONALISATION OF RETAILING

In 'Carrefour: internationalising innovation', Steve Burt illustrates how this company has 'exported' a major concept, the hypermarket, and also 'imported' a number of innovatory concepts. The case also provides a vehicle for discussing the choice of markets for internationalisation.

'Toys 'R' Us' by Andre Tordjman depicts the growth and process of internationalisation of this 'category killer' retailer. The case invites analysis of differences in the demand, supply and competitive characteristics of the various toy markets in Europe and the US.

In presenting 'Sainsbury's move into New England', Nicholas Alexander portrays the role of internationalisation within the overall development strategy of Sainsburys. The case focuses upon the choice of the US, rather than EC markets, and the use of the acquisition mode of entry.

In contrast, 'Littlewoods in St Petersburg' depicts the first steps by this British retailer into the huge but difficult Russian retail market. Nigel Holden describes the background to the development, the partnerships involved and the particular management challenges of operating within a newly marketised economy.

Carrefour
Internationalising innovation

Steve Burt
University of Stirling

Context

It is often said that retailing is a rapidly changing sector of the economy, and that managing such change is central to success. The advent of the Single European Market in 1993 coincided with the 30th anniversary of the opening of the first hypermarket in France and the effective birth of a retail format which is now a common feature of retailing in most of western Europe. The hypermarket concept – commonly defined as an outlet retailing both food and non-food products from a sales area of at least 2,500m² supported by extensive car parking – was inspired by the views of Bernard Trujillo at the Club MMM seminars in Dayton Ohio in the 1950s. Marcel Fournier and Louis Defforey, who had formed Carrefour four years earlier, attended these seminars and put Trujillo's ideas into practice at Sainte-Geneviève-des-Bois outside Paris. This innovative retail concept was an instant success, achieving sales of FFr 40 million in the first year of operation. Largely on the basis of this retail formula, Carrefour has grown into one of the largest grocery retailers in Europe, with sales exceeding FFr 117 billion in 1992 (see Table 13.1).

The basic strategy of Carrefour, which has remained largely unaltered over the past three decades, was summed up in the 1984 annual report:

Carrefour, a Single Objective:

Offer quality products and services to consumers at lowest prices, and the convenience of choice in large well-stocked, well-managed stores.

Three concepts serve this objective:

- *Discounting*. Carrefour leader in the 1984 and 1985 *Que Choisir* (consumer magazine) ratings in France. Leader in Brazil in the 'Sunab' (official body concerned with retailing) 1984 rating.

- *Multispecialisation*. In every product line, Carrefour is a specialist; butcher shop, bakery, delicatessen, fishmonger . . .

- *Giving people responsibility*. The store is the level at which decisions are made.

Table 13.1 The Carrefour Group: financial highlights (FFr m.)

	1975	1980	1985	1986	1987	1988	1989	1990	1991	1992
Sales (ex. VAT)	7,639	20,405	42,832	49,240	53,445	61,565	70,140	75,848	100,377	117,139
Profit	131	342	520	675	761	911	1,181	1,352	1,207	1,335
Net assets	562	1,535	3,590	4,376	5,407	6,762	7,765	8,654	10,379	12,615
Total assets	2,622	6,947	15,661	18,622	20,690	24,620	28,007	30,947	48,924	52,076
Borrowings	523	710	1,792	1,613	1,543	1,386	1,918	2,455	9,294	8,701

Source: Annual Reports, various years.

This basic approach has been followed in both France and the international markets which the company has entered. The hypermarket as a retail concept has changed little over the past thirty years. The addition and development of specialist product ranges has occurred within a trading format still fundamentally based on low prices. Similarly a central tenet of the Carrefour operating philosophy throughout its history has been the emphasis placed on decentralised management. Broadly speaking, each hypermarket operates as a profit centre with the store manager responsible for performance. The group has often been referred to as a 'confederation' of individual stores operating within certain common denominators, allowing the group to benefit from 'the delegation of responsibility and federation of effort'.

Expansion in the domestic market: the hypermarket at home

In the 1960s and 1970s the French market was strongly regionalised, with few retailers operating store networks beyond their 'home' regions. Carrefour saw the potential to develop a more national network on the basis of the innovative hypermarket concept. Most of the store expansion in the late 1960s and early 1970s occurred via franchising the Carrefour name and trading concept in the north and north-east with Promodès and Cora, together with the formation of joint venture companies (such as Sogara, Soracma, GSD and Sograma) with a range of regional operators based in the south and west of France. Of the 43 stores trading as Carrefour in 1973 only 18 were company owned.

For large store retailers, 1973 was an important year in France. The politically strong small shopkeeper organisations had lobbied the government against large store developments since the late 1960s, and with elections impending the government conceded with the enactment of the Loi Royer. As Marcel Fournier commented in the press at the time: 'one says that it will act to regulate an economic and social problem. I rather have the impression that one wishes to regulate an electoral problem.' This legislation strengthened the position of the urban commercial planning commissions established in 1969 to determine planning permission for retail developments. Effectively applications for stores of over 1,500m² (1,000m² in communities of under 40,000 people) and extensions of over 200m² to existing stores were to be brought before the commissions, which were dominated by small business representatives. Although an appeal to the Minister of Commerce was allowed the legislation significantly raised the costs of development through delays in planning applications, application and appeal costs and the effective creation of a market for authorised sites. Most of the leading hypermarket operators argued that they were treated less fairly by the planning commissions than smaller organisations.

Although hypermarket openings in France have continued, the strategy of Carrefour appears to have changed in the post-Royer period. In 1974 and 1975, Promodès and Cora – now also operating under their own tradenames – gave up the Carrefour franchise. A process of absorbing some of the smaller joint venture operations also began, and in 1984 a 19 per cent stake was taken in Comptoirs Modernes, a regional grocery retailer which was also involved in one of the larger joint venture operations. The slow organic growth in store numbers was supplemented when possible by other activities. The collapse of the French consumer co-operative movement in the mid-1980s saw the surviving societies either affiliate or sell their stores to the leading hypermarket operators. Consequently, in August 1985 Carrefour formed a joint venture, Carcoop, with the Union Coopérative des Supermarchés (four hypermarkets) and Coopérative du Nord (three hypermarkets). Carrefour took over the operational management of these stores, which adopted the Carrefour tradename a year later.

Throughout this period the buying and selling of individual hypermarkets was a common feature of the French market. But this pattern was altered quite dramatically by events towards the end of the 1980s, when a wave of takeovers and mergers amongst the major operators began. Prior to 1991 Carrefour's acquisition activity in the hypermarket sector had been restricted to individual stores; but then in March, Carrefour paid FFr 1.05 billion for the bankrupt Montlaur company with its eleven hypermarkets and three supermarkets in the south-west. The acquisition involved an undertaking to keep all eleven stores and staff for four years, although it has subsequently been announced that seven of the stores will be sold. The drama continued in June of the same year when Jacques Abihssira, the owner of three hypermarkets, left the Leclerc organisation and formed a 70 : 30 per cent venture with Carrefour. In that same month, Carrefour also acquired the troubled Euromarché Group for FFr 5.22 billion.

In terms of scale, this acquisition is the most significant seen in French grocery retailing. The Euromarché Group, with a turnover of FFr 34.6 billion, consisted of 76 hypermarkets (54 of which were company owned, accounting for 360,000m^2 of floorspace and sales of FFr 25.6 billion), 47 Bricorama DIY stores (30 company owned) and 57 Eris cafeterias/restaurants (43 company owned). Although smaller in size on average than the existing Carrefour hypermarkets, the Euromarché stores represented an almost perfect geographical fit in terms of location. In a single stroke the Euromarché-owned stores increased the number of Carrefour hypermarkets in France by 68 per cent and hypermarket floorspace by 52 per cent.

The steady growth in store numbers in France throughout the past three decades placed little strain on the decentralised management approach followed by Carrefour. However, it may require some adjustment following the dramatic change in the scale of the operation post-1991. The late 1980s had already seen some operational changes, with pooled purchasing in some regions and logistical changes involving regional delivery and distribution of fresh foods. The growing role of the regions was further emphasised following the Euromarché acquisition, with the restructuring of Carrefour France into three main regions: West, East and North, each composed of six sub-regions with an extra 'region' comprising the smaller Euromarché stores.

Table 13.2 Carrefour: international activity indicators, 1983–1992

	1983	1984	1985	1986	1987	1988	1989	1990	1991	1992
Sales ex. VAT (FFr m.)										
France[1]	26,984	31,262	35,255	40,310	43,922	44,708	48,217	52,215	69,811	81,063
Spain	3,409	4,312	4,959	5,995	7,646	10,090	12,680	15,740	19,643	22,494
Brazil	2,002	3,226	3,564	4,501	4,392	5,503	7,998	6,699	8,612	7,869
Argentina	209	506	391	666	543	941	826	626	1,200	2,503
Profit/loss (FFr m.)										
France[1]	270	326	439	512	522	739	836	959	211	341
Spain	59	135	128	198	267	302	377	464	581	704
Brazil	88	97	83	152	128	185	267	151	296	279
Argentina	5	(15)	14	6	15	7	32	6	24	79
Hypermarket numbers[2]										
France	56	57	64	69	70	71	72	74	133	118
Spain	18	18	20	21	24	25	26	29	34	40
Brazil	9	9	10	12	15	17	19	22	24	28
Argentina	1	2	2	3	3	3	4	4	4	6
Sales area (000m²)										
France	503	512	555	594	622	628	637	697	Not available	Not available
Spain	150	142	156	162	190	204	215	250		
Brazil	89	89	96	118	145	162	179	208		
Argentina	12	18	18	25	25	25	33	35		

Notes: [1] 1988–1992 – Carrefour France sales and profit figures calculated on different basis from previous years.

[2] In 1992 a number of former Euromarché hypermarkets were sold.

Source: Annual Reports, various years.

And abroad: international expansion

Internationalisation of the hypermarket concept has been a clear element of the Carrefour strategy (see Table 13.2). In January 1991, prior to the Montlaur and Euromarché acquisitions, the group controlled 55 hypermarkets outside France, compared to 74 within the native market. This move overseas started early. Only six years after the first hypermarket opened in France, the group ventured into Belgium in a joint venture with Delhaize le Lion; Switzerland in a similar arrangement with Mercure; and the UK via a minority shareholding in Hypermarket Holdings, with Wheatsheaf Distribution (ultimately part of the Dee Corporation). The network spread further afield in the 1970s with joint venture operations in Italy (1972), Spain (1973), Brazil (1974), Austria (1976) and Germany (1977). Attempts to find a suitable partner in the US were also rumoured to have failed in the 1973/74 period.

Following this strategy of market spreading, the group rationalised its overseas operations to focus on a limited number of markets. A number of joint ventures have been discontinued. The 50 per cent share in Distrimas in Belgium (three stores) was sold to Delhaize le Lion in 1978, followed by the 20 per cent stake in Interkaufpark (one German store) in 1979. The single Austrian store operated by Verbrauchermarkt was sold in 1980, and Wheatsheaf acquired the 10 per cent stake held in the British operation (six stores) in 1983. Attempts to build up the Italian subsidiary were made by merging its single store with the three owned by Standa in a joint venture, Euromercato, but divestment soon followed in 1984. Finally and most recently, the stake held in the oldest surviving international venture, Hypermarchés de Participations, operating two stores in Switzerland, was sold to Migros in 1991.

In contrast, heavy investment continued in three markets, Spain, Brazil and Argentina, and in the late 1980s, two new markets, the US and Taiwan, saw investment. The Spanish subsidiary, Pryca, represents the largest and most successful of Carrefour's overseas investments. A continued commitment to this market saw the formation of a second Spanish joint venture, Promotora de Hipermercados, with Simago in 1975 and the acquisition of Euromarché's 44 per cent stake in Iberica de Hipermercados when Euromarché abandoned the Spanish market in 1978.

Stores continued to be opened via a number of separate operating subsidiaries, but since the mid-1980s, a policy of organistional consolidation ensued. In 1986 Carrefour raised its share in the largest company, Promotora de Hipermercados (now renamed Pryca), which in turn operated a number of other subsidiaries, to 70 per cent and in July 1990 the group merged all the various Spanish subsidiaries into Centros Commerciales Pryca. Carrefour retains a 77 per cent stake in this venture, with the remaining 33 per cent held by March, the large Spanish financial group. All Spanish stores now trade as Pryca ('Precio Calidad' – Price and Quality), with a heavy emphasis on low prices. The operation is organised on a regional basis to accommodate both regional variations in taste and the regional nature of the planning system. Despite its relative youth, Pryca is the largest food retailer in Spain.

In Latin America, investment has continued despite the difficulties of operating in markets experiencing hyperinflation. In Brazil, annual inflation rates soared to levels of above 200 per cent in the mid-1980s and 1700 per cent in 1989, while in Argentina a figure of 5000 per cent is recorded in the annual report for 1989, and 800 per cent in 1990. Such figures have rendered a marketing strategy based on low prices almost impossible to promote, as prices are virtually obsolete from the moment they are set! In both countries, economic difficulties have focused Carrefour's efforts on the need for a dialogue and partnership with suppliers to maintain stocks. Notwithstanding these problems, investment has continued. The hypermarket has been an innovation in these markets, reinforced by the development of focused shopping centres to support the stores. Growth in store networks has been largely self-financed, although in Argentina in early 1988 the subsidiary did increase its capital via a share issue in which Perez Companc, a large Argentinian company, acquired a 20 per cent stake.

Although for the most part investment has been focused on these three markets, in the late 1980s two further markets were entered with varying degrees of initial success. In 1986 and 1987 sites were acquired in the US, as a number of French hypermarket operators began to test the American market. The first Carrefour store opened in February 1988 in Philadelphia, but struggled to meet expectations. In response, the food range was widened and a shopping mall added to the store. Although performance improved, a number of commentators felt, and still feel, that the hypermarket concept is not suited to the American market. Different problems befell Carrefour's second site in Long Island, being re-zoned as a residential area in 1988, two years after purchase. This made it virtually impossible to open the store and the asset price of the site was devalued by 75 per cent. It came as no surprise when it was announced, in early 1993, that the American operation was to be discontinued.

Much more successful in the short term has been the entry into Taiwan, a market of 20 million people with 10 million located in four principal cities. In August 1987 a 60 : 40 joint venture with President Enterprise Corporation called Presicarre was established and the first store was opened in December 1989 in Kaohiung. By 1993 five stores were trading successfully, although certain adaptations have been made including maintaining an 'outdoor market' look for the fresh produce range. Although car parking facilities are smaller than normal, averaging 200 spaces, this has not been a problem as many consumers shop by motorcycle. Future plans for the Asian region include a move into Malaysia.

Investment in innovation

The hypermarket concept itself was an innovative form of retailing when it was launched on the French market in 1963 and Carrefour has been keen to stress its capacity to be innovative in the grocery market in general. Three aspects of strategy development reflect this theme over the past three decades: the introduction of retailer brands; the launching of financial service activities; and investment in innovative retail concepts.

Carrefour has been a prime mover in the introduction and evolution of retailer brands in the French grocery market. 1976 saw the launch of a range of 50 'generic' products under the 'produits libres' banner. By the end of the first year this range accounted for 4 per cent of sales and 40 per cent in their respective product categories. As other competitors followed suit, Denis Defforey was proud to claim: 'It is always good to be imitated, because when one of your competitors imitates you, he does not innovate.'

This initiative was followed in 1982 by the launch of an own-brand clothing and textile range under the 'Tex' name. In 1985 a true retail brand under the 'Carrefour' name was launched to provide a high-quality retail brand and replace the generic range – a strategy familiar in British retailing – and by 1990 this range had grown to 3,000 lines.

This experience in retail branding has similarly been transferred overseas. In Spain a 'Pryca' brand of 123 lines advertised as 'the best quality at the best price' was launched in May 1985, followed by a clothing own-brand range ('First Line') in October 1988. In Brazil the strategy began with the 'Bonjour' own-brand range of linen in May 1987, with the 'Extra Plus' casual clothing range appearing a year later. The grocery market was approached via an 82-line generic range in August 1988, and a 39-line 'Carrefour' brand six months later. In the highly price conscious and more volatile Argentinian market a low price own-brand range was launched as late as 1990.

A second innovative thrust to the Carrefour strategy has been the development and integration of a range of financial services for customers. In 1981 an in-store credit card, the 'Carte Pass', was introduced in a six-store pilot. The acceptance of the card has seen the number in circulation rise steadily from 200,000 in 1985 to 440,000 in 1987 and around 700,000 in 1990. The financial services subsidiary S2P was strengthened in 1985 by its conversion into a 60 : 40 per cent joint venture with Cetelim, a leading French credit/financial services company. As a result the range of services has been extended over the years to include personal loans, ATM withdrawal facilities and personal savings plans. Again, the transfer of this experience to other markets followed with the launch of a 'Pryca' card in ten stores in May 1989 and the formation of a Spanish financial subsidiary the following year, plus the piloting of a 'Carrefour' card in Brazil during 1990.

Neither have Carrefour been slow to take an interest in other potentially innovative forms of retailing as they have appeared on the market. Early indications of this strategy were provided in the late 1970s by investments taken in Castorama and Erteco. In 1977 Carrefour acquired a 47 per cent stake in Castorama, the pioneer of large out-of-town DIY outlets. Similarities in operating methods and synergy from developing Carrefour and Castorama stores on adjacent sites both motivated this action. The relationship between the two companies has not, however, always been smooth. The founding Dubois family retained firm control over management, although tensions appeared to ease in 1988 when Carrefour exchanged their stake in Castorama with the family for a 32.2 per cent share in Castorama-Dubois, the ultimate holding company. In 1992 the Bricorama DIY stores acquired in the Euromarché acquisition were sold on to Castorama, strengthening its position as the leader in the French DIY market.

Similarly, in 1978, Erteco, a new company trading from small limited-line discount stores, attracted Carrefour's attention. A 45 per cent stake was acquired and the chain expanded from 18 stores in 1979 to 75 stores in 1982. Financial performance lagged behind the physical expansion of the store network, but Carrefour confirmed their belief in the concept by assuming management of the operation in 1983 and buying out the other shareholders. In subsequent years investment in the original 'Ed' trading format continued with the introduction of 'Ed' retail brands, frozen products and the segmentation of this discount end of the market into three formats: 'Ed – l'Epicier' (limited-line discount stores), 'Ed – le Maraîcher' (fruit and vegetables) and 'Europa Discount' (larger suburban discount supermarkets). These formats now extend to over 350 units with sales of FFr 4 billion in 1992 and have provided the basis to respond to the recent arrival of Aldi on the French scene. The Erteco concept was itself transferred to Spain as 'AD' (Attorro Diario) in 1987 and expanded to a chain of 37 stores, before being sold to Dia (the Spanish limited-line discount store chain of Promodès) in 1991.

Such investment in innovative concepts has not been restricted to the French market. Carrefour has also been willing to look overseas for innovative forms of retailing which may ultimately reach the European market. Two companies in the US caught the eye of Carrefour management in the early stages of their development. In December 1984 Carrefour Netherlands, an investment subsidiary, acquired $30 million worth of shares and convertible bonds in Costco, which gave Carrefour an 18 per cent stake in 1985. Costco at this time had 21 wholesale club stores. By 1993 Costco operated 89 stores, and was strongly rumoured to be considering entry into the European market via the UK. A planning application for a store in Manchester was made to the relevant authorities early in 1993. Carrefour's commitment to this company was reinforced by a take-up of share options in December 1989 to maintain a 20 per cent stake. More recently, Carrefour acquired 18 per cent in Office Depot, a rapidly expanding retailer of office equipment through large stores. Both of these activities may be seen as long-term investments in innovative retail forms which may hold potential for transfer into the European market.

Other examples exist of diversification activity in Europe, with Carrefour willing to take minority stakes in a number of primarily large store retailers. An attempt to enter the restaurant/cafeteria market by forming a wholly owned subsidiary Brapa in 1980 was abandoned in 1985, and other early attempts at diversification with minority shareholdings in Meijac (freezer centres) and Disport (sports goods) were sold in 1982. In the late 1980s a new spree of minority investments occurred. In December 1987 a 25 per cent share in Reno France, a subsidiary of the German large store discount shoe retailer Reno, was acquired, but this was sold in December 1990. In the same year a 45 per cent stake was acquired in But, a furniture and household appliance chain and buying group. This stake has since been diluted to 31 per cent. In 1989, 45 per cent was acquired in Média Concorde, a vehicle for Kaufhof and Metro to enter the French electrical goods market; and 27.5 per cent was taken in Carpetland, an established carpet retailer operating in France, Belgium and the Netherlands. The returns from these investments have been variable, but they do illustrate the willingness of the Carrefour Group to look for opportunities beyond its core hypermarket activity.

Carrefour – at the crossroads?

Like many French retailers the founding families have retained an important role in managing the company, yet over the past decade, an outsider, Michel Bon, became closely associated with Carrefour and its strategy. Since 1984, he has occupied the post of either deputy or chief executive officer and in 1990, with all the family members having reached the retirement age of 65, Michel Bon became the chairman of the Group, the first non-family member to hold this post. It therefore came as some surprise when his 'departure' was announced in dramatic circumstances in September 1992. The digestion of Euromarché and to a lesser extent Montlaur had taken longer than expected, with the Group's 1992 interim results showing turnover up 37 per cent, but profits down 53 per cent. To many commentators, Bon had been made a scapegoat for a strategy that required more time to deliver return on the investment.

Bon has been replaced by Daniel Bernard, an executive from outside the company, and the supervisory role of the board of directors has been strengthened by the formal construction of a supervisory board (to represent shareholders, mainly the Fournier and Defforey families) and an executive committee. To ameliorate the short-term balance sheet problems, it has been announced that the Group was to sell non-essential investments, such as Castorama and possibly But. Bricorama and Eris, acquired as part of Euromarché, have already been sold. For a company with a history of showing patience and taking a long-term view of investments, this response has been uncharacteristic.

References and further reading

Burt, S. L. (1984), 'Hypermarkets in France – has the Loi Royer had any effect?', *Retail and Distribution Management*, Jan–Feb, 16–19.

Burt, S. L. (1986), 'The Carrefour Group – the first 25 years', *International Journal of Retailing*, **1**(3), 54–78.

Burt, S. L. (1991), 'Trends in the internationalisation of grocery retailing: the European experience', *International Review of Retail Distribution and Consumer Research*, **1**(4), 489–515.

Salmon, W. J. and A. Tordjman (1989), 'The internationalisation of retailing', *International Journal of Retailing*, **4**(2), 3–16.

Tordjman, A. (1988), 'The French hypermarket: could it be developed in the United States?', *Retail and Distribution Management*, **16**(6), 8–12.

Toussaint, J. C. (1984), *'La politique générale de l'entreprise – un cas concret: Carrefour'*, Chotard et Associés Editeurs, Paris.

Treadgold, A. (1988), 'Retailing without frontiers', *Retail and Distribution Management*, **16**(6), 8–12.

Treadgold, A. (1990), 'The developing internationalisation of retailing', *International Journal of Retail and Distribution Management*, **18**(2), 4–11.

Toys 'R' Us[1]

Andre Tordjman
Groupe HEC School of Management

Context

> Six years ago in Great Britain when our only office was the table in my dining room, everybody said to me that the introduction of Toys 'R' Us would never work and that I should go back to my old job.
>
> Articles were written in most newspapers concluding unanimously that this 'American' formula would never catch on on the other side of the Atlantic. We are now present in France, Germany and Great Britain and we intend to increase our presence in the coming years in terms of the number of stores, as well as the number of countries.
>
> (David Rurka, president of Toys 'R' Us Europe)

Set up in 1948 by Charles P. Lazarus, Toys 'R' Us had become the first toy retailer in the US. In 1990 it controlled almost a quarter of this $17.7 billion market. But with expansion prospects in the US constrained by the predominant market share already occupied, the internationalisation of the company had become its principal means of growth. Thus an international division had been created in 1983, with the objective of introducing stores in other countries of the world. After the US, Europe was the world's second largest market. Its 61 million children therefore represented a priority target for the American company.

In order to repeat their American success in Europe, Toys 'R' Us settled on the objective of controlling 20 per cent of the $12 billion market (see Table 14.1). However, while the Single European Act intends to transform it into a global market, the diversity in national situations between EC countries will ensure that differences remain, not least in terms of retailing. These differences could raise particular difficulties for the Toys 'R' Us company in terms of its establishment policies.

Faced with a diversified European market, albeit one in the process of being homogenised, what are the market entry conditions faced by Toys 'R' Us? What could be the best strategy to put into action? What are the chances of success for the leading American toy retailer?

---

[1] This case was written in collaboration with Julien Levy, candidate for the doctoral programme at Groupe HEC.

Table 14.1 Toy sales in the world ($ billion)

	1986	1987	1988	1989	1990	1990 (% of total)
North America[1]	13.71	14.35	16.35	17.67	18.45	48.8
Europe	9.68	10.14	10.74	11.35	11.92	31.6
Far East	5.81	6.11	6.46	7.12	7.41	19.6
Total	29.20	30.60	33.50	36.10	37.80	100.0

Note: [1]Includes Canada and Mexico which account in 1990 for $1.03 bn and $0.22 bn respectively.
Source: Bernstein Research.

Toys 'R' Us in the US

Expansion of Toys 'R' Us

The history of Toys 'R' Us began in 1948, when Charles P. Lazarus opened a children's furniture store in his father's bicycle repair shop in Washington, DC. Four years later, in 1952, he added toys to the goods already sold and called it the 'Baby Furniture and Toy Supermarket'.

At this time, Lazarus was still searching for the 'right formula': he was trying to define a new concept of toy and game distribution on the US market. The concept took shape in 1958 with the opening of a 2500 sq.m. supermarket selling everything for children under the sign of Toys 'R' Us. The store had a very wide-ranging stock, with the prices fixed at 20–50 per cent below those asked by conventional toy stores. The idea was to offer customers a large selection of toys, games, furniture and children's clothes, at low prices during the whole year, in a single store.

By 1966, Toys 'R' Us had four stores in Washington, DC, realising an annual turnover of $12 million. It was at that point that Lazarus decided to sell the chain to Interstate Stores, in order to increase the financial capacity of the company. He continued, however, to manage and develop the company in order to reach 47 stores in 1973 with a turnover of $130 million. Interstate fell bankrupt in 1974. In 1978, after rather a long phase of reorganisation, a new company emerged under the direction of Lazarus. The chain owned 72 stores in 1978 and since 1979, around 30 stores have opened each year. At the end of 1990, the chain had 451 stores open in the US and 88 abroad. It controlled 164 clothes stores under the name Kids 'R' Us. The turnover of the company, for the 1990 accounting period, totalled $5.5 billion, of which $4.15 billion was for the domestic Toys 'R' Us division, $577 million for the Kids 'R' Us division and $773 million for its international operations. The operating profit in 1990 was $585 million, of which 81 per cent was for the toy division. Table 14.2 summarises the growth between 1986 and 1990.

Table 14.2 Toys 'R' Us total sales and operating profit (1986–1990)

	1986	1987	1988	1989	1990
Toys 'R' Us					
Domestic					
Number of stores	271	313	358	404	451
Total sales ($m.)	2,191	2,652	3,272	3,785	4,150
Operating profit ($m.)	277	340	409	473	474
Kids 'R' Us					
Number of stores	–	–	112	137	164
Total sales ($m.)	135	257	360	470	577
Operating profit ($m.)	3	3	7	26	34
Toys 'R' Us					
International					
Number of stores	21	34	48	68	88
Total sales ($m.)	101	210	368	534	773
Operating profit ($m.)	4	7	27	47	77
Total sales ($m.)	2,445	3,137	4,000	4,788	5,510
Total operating profit ($m.)	285	352	443	546	585

Source: Bernstein Research.

Competition in the US

Small independent retailers have more or less disappeared in the US, proving unable to compete in terms of selection, price and management efficiency. With regard to specialist chains, Child World and Lionel are the main competitors of Toys 'R' Us in the US. They have opted for the same strategy as Toys 'R' Us, establishing stores near important shopping centres, in separate buildings near motorways. Kay-Bee Toy, which locates its smaller, higher-priced stores actually inside shopping centres, and FAO Schwartz, which puts the accent on the location and sale of top-of-the-range toys, have met with a certain degree of success. Overall, these other specialists held around 11 per cent of the market both in 1985 and in 1990.

Discount stores, which use their toy departments to attract customers and generate sales during the Christmas holiday period, present the greatest form of competition for Toys 'R' Us. With more than 10,000 outlets all over the US, they owned 37 per cent of the toy market in 1990. The main companies are K-mart, Wal-mart, Target Stores, Zayre corporation. Store space devoted by discounters to toys can range from 3000 sq.ft with 3,500 SKUs (stock-keeping units) during the Christmas season, down to 1000 sq.ft with 1,500 SKUs during the remainder of the year. Carrying the most popular items, they use toys as loss leaders to bring people into the store and generate traffic at key times of the year. Their toy departments produce high sales per square foot, but low gross margins and inventory turns. The discount stores provide strong competition and force Toys 'R' Us to be more aggressive on price.

The department stores also tend to use their toy departments as a seasonal attraction. During most of the year they devote little selling space to toys, only expanding the square footage at Christmas time. The conventional department stores face the problem of a high cost structure, making them relatively uncompetitive in terms of toys. As they have to compete on both fronts with discounters and speciality chains, they do not have any competitive advantage to attract customers into buying toys from their stores. As a result, the market share held by department stores in the US has decreased over the last five years, from 15 per cent in 1985 to only 8 per cent in 1990.

Likewise, the share of variety stores fell from 4 to 2 per cent, while that of catalogue showrooms fell from 7 to 4 per cent. In contrast, the market share of Toys 'R' Us in the US grew from 13 to 22 per cent during the same period of time.

Key elements in business strategy

Toys 'R' Us is considered to have a highly disciplined business formula. The Toys 'R' Us concept of toy retailing is a combination of factors which make the company very powerful (see Figure 14.1). These factors include marketing, organisation and efficient management. In terms of marketing, the company has a very good retailing mix of assortment, communication, price, service and location policies. In terms of organisation, elements include management information systems facilitating effective inventory control and a computerised distribution centre which makes purchasing more efficient. Additionally, the company has cultivated managers devoted to the growth of Toys 'R' Us and

Fig. 14.1 The strength of the concept

has motivated associates by providing stock incentives to all employees.

This combination of superspecialist, supermarket and service mentalities can be grouped under the heading 'Don't give the customer any reason to shop some place else'.

Stores

A Toys 'R' Us store is a toy supermarket. As a supermarket, it presents its merchandise as self-service and at low prices. As a specialist, it offers a large choice of products (18,000 SKUs) with all the important brands of the toy sector being sold.

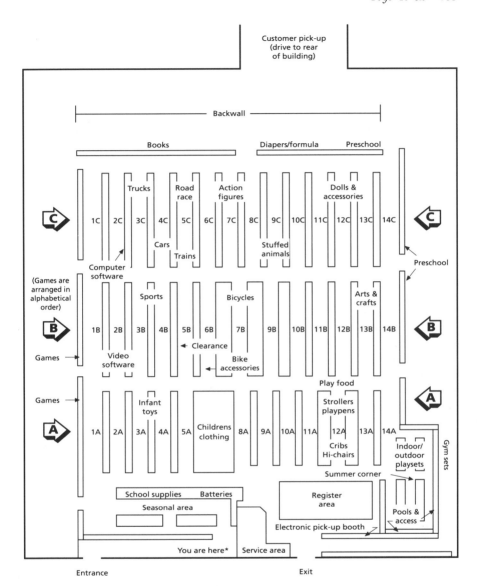

Fig. 14.2 Toys 'R' Us identical store lay-out

Toys 'R' Us has certain characteristics common to all of its stores. A typical Toys 'R' Us is situated near a shopping centre, in its own separate building. The stores have an area of floor and storage space of about 4,500 sq.m., with all stock out on the shelves.

All the stores have an identical lay-out (see Figure 14.2), established by head office, so that customers can find what they want without wasting time or requiring much assistance from employees. Products are categorised according to family and allocated distinct aisles. Signs indicate the categorisation of the aisles and give a code number. At the store entrance a print out is available with an alphabetical list of toys, showing the number of the shelf concerned.

Assortment policy

The stores offer an exhaustive range, covering the child's world from birth onwards. Articles are classed in broad categories: character/collectable toys (action and fantasy figures for both boys and girls), art and craft items, bicycles and other vehicles, construction games, miniature cars and trains, children's furniture, clothes (2–7 years), dolls and soft toys, educational games, electronic games, board games, toy tea sets, nursing items and baby food, pre-school (toys for children aged 0–5 years), party games and snacks, confectionery, sports items, and so on.

Selection remains highly important throughout the whole year, even though certain items are seasonal: notably outdoor games being linked to spring and summer. As Toys 'R' Us carries the largest choice of toys all year long, customers are able to find any product they look for under the one roof.

The presence of in-store stock, displayed on very high shelves, gives the visitor a very real impression of strolling with his trolley between 'walls' of toys. For sizeable articles, the customer takes a ticket which he gives in at the cash desk, before moving on to the collection room to pick up the merchandise. The organisation of shelves encourages impulse buying: confectionery is found either right by the entrance or just before the cash desks. The shelves are always full and the toys listed are rarely out of stock.

Pricing policy

Pricing policies are clear: it is a matter of offering low prices throughout the year on brand-named toys, just as much as on the others. Toys 'R' Us is rightly classed among discounters, but it never offers promotions. The presence of in-store stock, its not particularly extravagant decor, entirely computer-controlled stock, the need for few staff, and the strong buying power of the network, are all elements which allow prices to be kept low.

Toys 'R' Us follows a policy of highly reduced margins on nursing items, particularly nappies. Discounts on these types of article aim to attract the custom of new parents in order to gain their store loyalty and become the supplier of toys for their children at all ages.

Service policy

The service policy of Toys 'R' Us aims for maximum customer satisfaction, 'satisfied, or your money back', while minimising the need for sales help. The customer is provided with a receipt showing which toy was purchased at which cash desk, so that they can obtain a refund months after the sale, even if the product has been used. In the days following Christmas, certain cash tills are reserved specifically for returns.

Organisation

Purchasing, marketing and merchandising are entirely centralised. Sellers and demonstrators are not allowed in stores. The personnel are versatile: working on the cash desks, replenishing stock, reception desk, and so on.

In keeping with its supermarket mentality, Toys 'R' Us was an early user of scanners and point-of-sale information in order to facilitate inventory management. Complementing this, the company built a computerised distribution centre to help speed up its inventory turnover. This system allows automatic stock control by daily deliveries, so that articles are never missing from the shelves.

As a result, to reduce its costs, Toys 'R' Us has successfully established a productivity loop, whereby the lowering of costs has allowed prices to be lowered, resulting in higher productivity, which in turn leads to even lower costs. In comparison with some of its competitors, Toys 'R' Us has sales and a gross margin per square foot twice as high (see Table 14.3).

Relations with suppliers

Lastly, Toys 'R' Us believe strongly in stable relations with the manufacturers and suppliers of toys. For most of these suppliers, Toys 'R' Us is their largest client. Its size allows it to influence the manufacturing process with regard to the design of toys, and to benefit from good purchasing conditions.

For many manufacturers, both large and small, Toys 'R' Us has been a real help in supplying continual work throughout the year, thereby reducing the effects of the seasonal nature of toy sales. The supplies anticipated during the year allow, in the same way, for Toys 'R' Us to obtain supplementary discounts with regard to high season prices. This continual buying gives manufacturers the opportunity to collect information on toy trends during the year and test out new products. Toys 'R' Us thus give manufacturers an indication of the success of new toys and allow more efficient planning of production for the Christmas season.

The sheer weight of the Toys 'R' Us market share allows the company to

Table 14.3 Toys 'R' Us productivity, 1990

	Toys 'R' Us	Child World	Department store	Discount store
Average sales/store ($m.)	9.73	4.66	–	–
Average sales/sq. m. ($)	2,120	1,133	570	2,030
Gross margin/sq. m. ($)	640	320	190	540

Source: Bernstein Research.

negotiate extremely favourable prices and terms of payment. In this way, a whole part of Toys 'R' Us stock is financed by the manufacturers. What is more, Toys 'R' Us specifies in its sales contracts that it will return to the manufacturer those products which are returned by customers. For this reason, the customer policy of 'satisfied or your money back' is largely taken on by the manufacturers themselves.

The international expansion of Toys 'R' Us

To nurture and develop the expansion of the company, the management of Toys 'R' Us decided to introduce the company abroad, in order to become a worldwide retailing chain. The international division was created in 1983.

In 1984, Toys 'R' Us opened four stores in Canada and one in Singapore. In 1985, three new sales outlets were opened in Canada and the introduction of Toys 'R' Us began in Britain with the opening of five stores. The pace has been kept up since then. By the end of 1990, Toys 'R' Us had opened 88 stores abroad. Seven regional subsidiaries have been set up, concerning: Canada, Singapore, Germany, Hong Kong, Taiwan, Great Britain, and France. In 1991, other countries such as Spain and Italy were forecast to open stores.

The contribution of international operations has increased dramatically from 1986 to 1990. Sales have grown sevenfold from $101 million to $773 million, representing 15.6 per cent of total Toys 'R' Us sales in 1990. It is forecast that Toys 'R' Us operations abroad will represent 31.2 per cent of total sales in 1996. In this respect, the European operations, which represented 37 per cent of international sales in 1986 and 63 per cent in 1990, will constitute two-thirds of Toys 'R' Us sales in 1996 (see Table 14.4).

Toys 'R' Us stores opened in Europe correspond (apart from the obvious exceptions caused by planning) to the same standards found in the US: the same store architecture, surface area, arrangement of shelves, tills, gondolas, door locks, plastic bags, and so forth, through to the same machines for counting the tickets coming directly from the American suppliers who work for the company. Store size, location and merchandising, however, sometimes need to be adapted to local legislation and local demand.

Table 14.4 Sales for Toys 'R' Us International (%)

	1986	1990	1996 (estimation)
Canada	63	37	19
Europe	37	63	66
Japan	0	0	12
Other	0	0	3
Total	100	100	100
Total ($m.)	101	773	3,756

Source: Bernstein Research.

For example, entire shelves reserved solely for baseball equipment can definitely not be justified on the French market. These adaptions are nevertheless limited, the international standardisation of products allowing for a very large standardisation of merchandise. Store-planners grouped by country, who plan every centimetre of gondolas, are placed hierarchically under the authority of store-planners grouped in zones, themselves being accountable to store-planners on a world scale.

Each country in which Toys 'R' Us is set up has the aim of opening five stores per year. The opening must take place in September in order to make the most of the return to school and to be ready for the peak season (November–January). The last country in which Toys 'R' Us has opened in the European zone must then sponsor the next country in which it is to be set up, by sending executives and specialists to ease the establishment of the structure and opening of stores.

The director of Toys 'R' Us for each country is generally a local executive with retailing experience. He is aided by an American supervisor, whose role is to ensure that procedures are followed. These procedures, put together in a number of manuals, define all aspects of stores and infrastructure activity and are standardised on a world scale. Each hierarchical level has its corresponding procedures, one of the fundamental roles for executives being to respect these procedures.

Toys 'R' Us in Europe, Japan and Canada

In Europe, seen as a priority objective for the company, Toys 'R' Us has opened 28 stores in Great Britain, 18 in Germany and 10 in France. Openings are planned in Italy, Spain, the Benelux countries, Portugal and Ireland.

Great Britain

The UK, the third largest European market worth 1.45 billion ecus, was the initial point of market entry into Europe in 1985 for Toys 'R' Us. Since then, the development of the company has been very rapid and sales have grown from $19 million in 1985 to $245 million in 1990. With 10.8 million children under 14 years, a high population density, a good transportation system and a similarity in language and culture, the UK was a good country in which to gain experience in Europe. With 28 stores in 1990, Toys 'R' Us controlled 14 per cent of the British toy market and it is forecast that the company will open five stores per year over the next five years.

Germany

Toys 'R' Us was first introduced in Germany in 1986. This country represented a good opportunity for various reasons. Germany has only nine million children under 14 years, but expenditure per child is the highest in Europe (216 ecus). The German market is therefore the second largest in Europe, worth 1.95 billion ecus. Competition is similar to that faced in the past by Toys 'R' Us in the US: two-thirds of toys in Germany are sold by independent retailers and conventional department stores. Finally, during the last five years, Germany has had the highest growth in Europe (+33 per cent from 1984 to 1989 in constant money). With 18 stores realising $160 million in sales in 1990, Toys 'R' Us controlled 6.5 per cent of the German toy market. Its aim is to open 60 stores in reunified Germany.

France

Toys 'R' Us was first introduced in France in 1989. France represents the largest toy market in Europe, in terms of the number of children (11.6 million) as well as in terms of sales (2.3 billion ecus). However, in constant money, the market decreased by 8 per cent from 1984 to 1989. In this very important market, Toys 'R' Us face not only the problem of competition from hypermarkets, but also the difficulty of obtaining good locations due to restrictive legislation (Loi Royer). In December 1990, the sales figure for the 10 stores opened was FFr 374 million ($1 = FFr 5.5), with a loss of FFr 56 million. The cumulated loss in 1989 and 1990 was FFr 105 million. Contrary to the typical American set-up where stores are systematically located close to, but outside, shopping centres, the stores in France are sometimes found actually inside these shopping centres. Almost all stores are near a hypermarket, managers seeing the competition they present as beneficial: in effect, although Toys 'R' Us sells at more expensive prices than hypermarkets, they can serve to attract additional customers to the shopping centres.

Toys 'R' Us in Japan

In late 1989, Toys 'R' Us took the decision to enter into Japan and by 1991 had set up five stores, with a long-term goal of at least 100 Japanese outlets. The company decided upon a joint venture with McDonald's (Japan) to implement this expansion programme. Worth $6 billion, the Japanese toy market offers good opportunities for growth. However, the process for non-Japanese companies to go into business in Japan is complicated, as the opening at national level of large format requires permission from the Federal Government. Obtaining this permit is very time consuming as it also requires the approval of local merchants. In the past, opposition from local merchants has blocked the entry of a large retailer for as long as ten years. After extensive negotiation, Toys 'R' Us finally received approval to open five stores in Japan. However, ultimately it is likely that the company will face further economic and non-economic resistance to its entry.

Toys 'R' Us in Canada

Toys 'R' Us started its international operation with Canada in 1984. The company operated 32 stores in 1990, realising $300 million in sales, representing a 27 per cent market share. The growth of Toys 'R' Us is expected to be five new stores per year, reaching total sales of $700 million in 1996.

The European toy market

During the last three decades, the European toy market has undergone large transformations, most notably in that national industries have gone from small, little-known craft enterprises, to a worldwide domination of multinational manufacturers. This evolution is explained by environmental factors which have contributed to the creation of a large, relatively homogenous market. The principal factors are: the economic growth of western countries; the convergence in both the way of life and the demographic characteristics of households; and the internationalisation of cultures through the media.

Demographic elements

With 61 million children (0–14 years), the European market is the largest in the world, exceeding that of the US (51 million) and Japan (25 million). Five countries make up 80 per cent of this population: France, Great Britain, Italy, Germany, Spain. In all of these countries, some common demographic tendencies are to be noted, in particular a fall in population growth rates, resulting from a fall in the birth rate, accompanied by an ageing of the population. The size of the market in terms of the number of children will fall by nearly 7 per cent in the next ten years, but an increase in expenditure per child should lead to growth of about 3 per cent per year in current ecus.

Market size

On a worldwide scale, the market is stable but some important disparities exist between countries: Germany has experienced an impressive increase, while France and Italy have both undergone a certain fall in the market. The French toy market is the most important in Europe, worth 2.3 million ecus, four times the size of the Spanish market. As Table 14.5 shows, consumption per child varies from modest to high according to the country (220 ecus for Germany, 64 ecus for Spain).

Market divisions

In all the European countries, the following can be noted: a strong increase in educational and board games, revival of interest in traditional games, growing

Table 14.5 The European toy market

Country	Children under 15 years age (millions 1990)	Expenditure per child (ecus 1989)
France	11.6	195
UK	10.8	220
Italy	10.3	170
Germany (West)	9.0	85
Spain	8.7	64

Sources: AJM, Eurostat and ERC.

interest in video games, and a growth in the market for fashion toys. Four principal product categories represent more than 50 per cent of the market: board games, pre-school (games and toys for the under-5s), dolls and character games (action/fantasy figures for both girls and boys consisting of a large number of characters).

Although the same categories of toys are bought in all the European countries, their share in national markets varies considerably. The doll, for example, accounts for 25 per cent of spending on toys in Spain, as opposed to a figure of less than 10 per cent in France. This can be explained culturally by a perpetuation of the traditional role of the woman, more strongly felt in the first country. Likewise, the model railway accounts for 16.4 per cent of expenditure in Germany, compared to 1.4 per cent in Spain, reflecting the importance of adult collectors in the German market.

In all of these countries, toy sales have a highly seasonal nature, associated

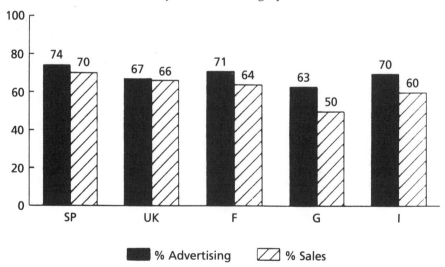

Fig. 14.3 Percentage of advertising and sales concentrated in the last quarter, in the European market

Source: Different national studies.

with the giving of presents at Christmas, Saint Nicholas Day and Epiphany; at least 60 per cent of sales are concentrated in the last two months of the year (see Figure 14.3). This is despite the efforts to reduce seasonality, such as selling educational games, launching new products throughout the year, and promotional and advertising campaigns during the first six months of the year.

Industrial production

Although it has experienced several down turns during the last decade resulting in the closure of many companies, the European toy industry remains significant, if fragmented. European toy production (3.8 billion ecus in 1988) is even larger than production in the US (3.6 billion ecus in 1988) and considerably greater than that of Japan (2.4 billion ecus). The ratio of imports to exports in each country, however, with the exception of Spain, is negative.

A number of toys have strong local connections, and it is here that national manufacturers remain leaders of the market. This is the case for miniature cars, train sets and car sets. For the more universally bought categories of products, such as construction games, pre-school toys or dolls, international manufacturers are assured market domination. According to the country, national manufacturers see themselves as more or less privileged by consumers and retailers alike, and are generally in possession of a greater share of the market in their own country than in the rest of Europe. This is particularly the case in Germany and Great Britain.

One of the principal characteristics of the toy market, however, is the increasing concentration of the industry and the determination of multinational manufacturers to acquire large volumes of sales. These objectives are reached by means of aggressive marketing strategies. The growing fashion toy sector, linked strongly to marketing techniques, such as those of Ninja Turtles and Nintendo, is clearly dominated by multinational companies, generally of American and more recently Japanese origin. The five leading manufacturers hold 40 per cent of the world market (see Table 14.6).

The stabilisation of the market and the disappearance of small manufacturers will lead to head-on competition between multinational toy manufacturers. Consequently, they will have to increase expenditure on technological and commercial research, defend their trade marks and products (involving a vigorous fight against imitations and copies), spread their range of products between classic toys with a long lifespan and fashion toys, and continue the movement towards mergers and the buying up of national and international manufacturers. Above all, they will continue to increase their supply and to move into or become more heavily involved with new types of toys. This will spread the risks between sectors and enable them to fight more successfully against seasonality. It will also create economies of scale relating to administrative costs, research and commercialisation. Furthermore, this policy

Table 14.6 The five main toy multinationals – turnover and market shares ($m.)

	1985 ($m.)	1990 ($m.)	1985–1990 (%)
Nintendo	850	3,256	31
Hasbro[1]	1,477	2,309	9
Mattel	1,051	1,471	7
Lego	683	1,100	10
Fisher-Price	485	569	3
Five largest	4,546	8,704	14
Total market			
Wholesale	16,566	21,715	6
Retail	28,759	37,774	6
Five largest market			
share (%)	27	40	

Note: [1] Includes Tonka.

Source: Corporate reports and Bernstein estimates.

will give those manufacturers producing a large range of goods some power to counter that of the retailers.

European toy retailing

European toy retailing presents a number of similarities:

- Toy sales in department stores are stagnant everywhere.
- Non-specialist discount selling (hyper, super, mail order) is on the increase everywhere.
- The independent specialist either merges to form associations or disappears completely.
- The influence of wholesalers, as a consequence, is falling.
- The emerging forms are the toy supermarket and hyperspecialists.
- Efforts to reduce the seasonal nature of sales, seen as favourable for the specialist seller, have proved to be of little efficacy.

The presence of these similarities has not prevented the existence of particular characteristics specific to individual countries.

While consumers, as with products, show a tendency towards globalisation, toy retailing formats still remain highly national in character. Contrasts in retailing systems remain distinct, and what is more, they are strongly linked to the functioning of the retail system in its entirety. Market shares of retailing formats therefore vary noticeably and the leading format differs from one country to another (see Table 14.7).

Table 14.7 Market share of different types of toy retailing, 1989 (%)

	France	UK	W.Germany	Italy	Spain
Hypers/supers	48	8	21	8	17
Department stores	8	6	23	9	13
Variety stores	4	16	–	–	3
Specialists	17	29	44	50	35
Mail order	3	7	3	–	–
Catalogue showroom	–	19	–	–	–
Others	20	15	6	33	32

Source: Different national studies.

France

The increasingly important role of hypermarkets has affected toy retailing in France. Toy retailers have suffered from this situation and have reacted by forming retail associations, which would appear to be in an even weaker position. The role of wholesalers has declined, retailers increasingly buying direct from manufacturers.

Although the market share of hypermarkets is somewhat stagnant, it is nevertheless this business format that has been best able to respond to the demands of the largest national market in Europe. Hypermarkets are characterised by a large selling space (2500 sq.m. minimum), presenting a large selection of food and non-food items sold at discount prices. In 1991, there existed some 900 hypermarkets in France, realising 26.7 per cent of total food retail sales and 12.2 per cent of total non-food retail sales.

This very important role in toy retailing held by hypermarkets can be explained by their general popularity in France, linked with competitive prices and the support of toy multinationals. The presence of the all-important toy department in hypermarkets is only really effective during the final months of the year.The threat presented by hypermarkets to toy retailers, however, is linked less to what they offer – a greater selection – than to their aggressive pricing policies. Toys are sold at very low prices, with extremely reduced margins, making appealing products for attracting the customer.

During the Christmas period, hypermarkets account for 70 per cent of all toy purchases, compared with 30 per cent during the rest of the year. Hypermarkets, in association with manufacturers, tend to develop their toy departments throughout the year, but this department still only usually constitutes 1–2 per cent of their turnover.

Germany

Specialist retailers – some 5,000 of them – have been able to maintain a very important market share, more than 44 per cent, even though they have had to face up to a reduction in their margins owing to the arrival of discounters.

Many have reacted to the challenge by putting the emphasis on advice, service, in presenting specific products and in training better sales assistants.

Toy retailing is very well organised in Germany: 95 per cent of specialist retailers are members of retailing associations, the most important being Vedes (38 per cent of the market). These associations act as central buying groups for their associate retailers. They have strong links with wholesalers, occupying a strong position with 40 per cent of the market, and have succeeded in both concentrating and strengthening their level of productivity.

When Toys 'R' Us entered the German market, chains of specialist stores rapidly developed toy supermarkets themselves, offering discount prices, with product selections and a range of services particularly adapted to the needs of the German market. Department and variety stores continue to occupy a significant share of the market (23 per cent). Mail order firms, hypermarkets and supermarkets (24 per cent) are in the process of developing their toy departments. Highly specialised retailers are emerging in the particular areas of construction toys, models and train sets.

United Kingdom

Toy retailing in the UK has undergone enormous change in recent years. It has experienced a fall in the number of retail companies with distribution becoming concentrated between the hands of an even smaller number of retailers. The outstanding feature of this market has been a price war which nobody has been able to halt. Many independent retailers have suffered a fall in both their activity level and in their margins.

The retail toy market is dominated by three major companies: Woolworth, Argos and Toys 'R' Us. Argos is a chain of retailers which sell toys through catalogues at discount prices, with showrooms in town centres. Catalogue and showroom retailing is dominated by Argos; its market share has increased from 8 to 12 per cent in the last five years.

Variety stores, a particularly strong business format in the UK, control a 16 per cent and increasing share of the market, notably because of the willingness of Woolworth to put special emphasis on its toy departments. Woolworth, with 800 outlets, has a firmly established reputation and a solid market share which will almost certainly increase with a greater emphasis on its own brand toys and improvements in productivity.

A strong trend towards discount trading puts emphasis on the development of own brands (Woolworth has secured the exclusive rights to the Chad Valley brand), while the highly specialised stores focus on the educational value of the toy in response to the customer's demands (Mothercare which launched 'Toy School' and The Early Learning Centre both specialise in the pre-school market). Multi-specialists, that is to say stores which sell toys and other product lines such as books, records, and so on, are generally losing ground. W. H. Smith, for example, has chosen to concentrate on games, a division in which it still occupies a strong position.

Italy

Toy retailing is highly fragmented, essentially between the hands of vaguely associated independent specialists and a multitude of stores which are not primarily toy specialists, such as pharmacies, stationers, general stores and service stations. This fragmentation of the network (some 60,000 retail outlets) has in the past been particularly favourable for the development of wholesalers and the importance of their role within the market (300 wholesalers dominating 70 per cent of the market).

Independent stores, however, which account for a little over half of toy sales, now appear to be under serious threat with the increasing competition from specialist chains and new entrants such as hypermarkets and Toys 'R' Us. The trend would therefore seem to favour a regrouping of independent stores and a greater degree of specialisation.

With this evolution, the position of wholesalers appears to be equally under threat, since it is linked to that of independent retailers and national manufacturers who are fast losing their share of the market to toy multinationals. The most dynamic have turned to wholesale importing and have become involved in retail distribution.

Large chains have been set up, involving themselves not just in the opening of toy supermarkets but also in production (Linea Gig). Tutto Chicco is a franchise specialising in infant and pre-school toys, which was initiated by the national leader in pre-school toys. Department stores have a 9 per cent and growing share of the market. Hypermarkets, small in number owing to legal restrictions, are becoming more powerful (8 per cent of the market).

Spain

Retailing in Spain is largely dominated by the independents, of which a very large number are non-specialist retailers. Specialist retailers make up the greatest share of the market (more than 35 per cent), making for the most part 50 per cent of sales in November and December and 50 per cent the rest of the year. Many small retailers risk disappearing completely if discounting practices are not regulated. Hence retailers are taking the initiative and attempting to set up retail associations (Gremio Barcelona).

Department stores, however, are in a strong position. Two chains dominate the market: El Corte Ingles and the Galerias Preciados, which together account for 100 outlets. They have realised a figure of 13 per cent in toy sales. Hypermarkets, of which there are 91, have made a spectacular breakthrough in the market in just a few years. Manufacturers have favoured this type of outlet and hypermarkets have developed their own toy departments. They have already claimed 17 per cent of the market.

Spanish retailing is in the middle of a massive transformation, in an underdeveloped market. Toys 'R' Us selected Valencia, Madrid and Barcelona for its first Spanish openings in 1991.

The Single European Act and European diversity

Retailing on a European scale began in the 1970s, with the export of certain successful market formulas. However, in comparison with the exchange of products, this development remains limited. Will it be accelerated by European retailers spurred on by the unified European market? If not, will the Europeanisation of retailing come about thanks to American retailers, motivated by a new market without trade barriers?

American retailers which began the internationalisation of retailing after the war by introducing their own formulas to Europe, met with difficulties in trying to enter certain countries. These difficulties were linked to the cost of property, to highly restrictive legislation with regard to the opening of stores, to local management problems and to the need for capital to finance the national expansion of mother companies. Enterprises like Jewel Company, J. C. Penney, Sears Roebuck, Safeway and Woolworth have either reduced progressively or entirely stopped their investments on the other side of the Atlantic.

With the creation of the large European market, we can only wait to see whether or not American enterprises become interested once again in Europe. Toys 'R' Us is just one of the chains able to modify the European field of competition.

The European market is close to the American market, which did so well for Toys 'R' Us, in terms of size, homogenisation trends and the internationalisation of brands and products. Regulations, however, still differ noticeably from one country to another. Those concerning competition essentially touch entry into the market, the regulation of prices, opening hours and taxation; in some cases they differ noticeably according to the country. The refusal of sale is illegal in certain countries but is authorised in others. In the majority of countries, opening hours are governed by law, but they are unrestricted in Sweden, Belgium and in France for retailers which do not have any salaried employees. Finally, forms of taxation and the application of VAT vary widely.

The Single European Act rightly has the aim of reducing these disparities. It will not be possible to erase them in a single stroke alone. The converging pressure from European consumers and organisations, however, will lead to the eventual passing of more simple legislation, better adapted to the demands of the world market. A reduction in these disparities can therefore be foreseen before too long.

Apart from these statutory disparities which weaken the global character of the European market, some even more important differences must be mentioned, of a historical and cultural nature: there will always be greater differences between Ireland and Greece, for example, than between two states in America. These differences touch upon cultural traditions that influence the structure of the toy market; the proportion of the budget given over to buying toys differs greatly from one country to another.

Moreover the leading forms of toy distribution vary noticeably from one country to another, the consequence being that a retailer wishing to establish itself in Europe must prove its competitive advantage in a heterogenous European market, against the many different successful and unsuccessful competitors.

Toys 'R' Us has opted to enter the European market with its American formula, considering that the concept of the toy supermarket will do well in the different European countries against the different competitors. Even if the concept fundamentally keeps to the same format, some slight adaptations may be necessary. But this belief leaves certain questions to be answered. One must question the pertinence of this choice of penetrating the European market, and on the chances of Toys 'R' Us reaching the share of the market the American enterprise has set its sights upon.

Case study questions

1. *What are the important characteristics in terms of size, evolution, supply or demand of the toy market?*

2. *What were the key stages in the development of Toys 'R' Us in the US? What were the key factors in their success?*

3. *Should Toys 'R' Us internationalise itself in Europe? Which form of internationalisation should it adopt? Within which European markets should Toys 'R' Us develop most actively?*

4. *Toys 'R' Us has demonstrated its capability of penetrating the UK market. The company has experienced quite a high level of success in Germany and it looks as though the opportunities for Spain are also quite good. However, Toys 'R' Us has had some difficulties in growing in France where the competition from hypermarkets is very high. As the French toy market is still the largest in Europe, France may be seen as a priority market. Can Toys 'R' Us compete with the hypermarket in France? What strategy might Toys 'R' Us adopt to combat the challenge of the hypermarket?*

Sainsbury's move into New England

Nicholas Alexander
University of Surrey

Context

It would not be entirely inappropriate to describe J. Sainsbury plc as a family retail business with international interests, rather than as an international retail operation. The articles of association, which limited shareholding to the lineal descendants of the founder, their husbands and wives, disappeared in 1973 when J. Sainsbury became a public company. The company, however, still retains strong links with the founding family who continue to own a significant number of shares.

Unlike some retail operations, within which the initial family links have long been broken by events such as acquisition, merger, or management buy-outs, J. Sainsbury plc retains strong personal links with its past. This nurtures its particular corporate culture. Therefore, the history of the company and the role of the Sainsbury family have an enhanced significance.

Innovation and development

Sainsbury has seen sustained growth throughout its history, from independent grocer, through small and large multiple, to the leading operation among the UK's 'big five' grocery retailers. It was throughout its first hundred years an English grocery retailer. It maintained an orientation toward the food market, which also led to the company's investment in farming, through such as Brecklands Farms, and preparation of the food products, through such as Haverhill Meat Products.

The company has, however, been prepared to innovate and learn through experience and observation. Own brands and store format development are two clear examples of the company's approach to innovation and development.

Own brands

J. Sainsbury has a long history of own-brand development and this is reflected in the high level of own-brand products it maintains today. In its early history, while other grocery retailers became dependent on manufacturer packaged-good brands, Sainsbury, although also passing down that particular road to some degree, retained a retail brand approach outside the provision of fresh food, and thereby may be said to have traded 'own label' groceries from the 1920s (Boswell, 1969).

Among UK grocery retailers today, only Marks & Spencer has a higher percentage of own-brand sales than the J. Sainsbury operation. In 1987, at the time of the Shaw's acquisition, 55 per cent of sales value was accounted for by own brands (IGD, 1989a), compared to the multiple store average of 31 per cent and its competitor Tesco's figure of 34 per cent (IGD, 1989b).

Store format

Sainsbury was also in the forefront of innovation in self-service operations. Alan Sainsbury visited the US in 1949 when he was joint-general manager. During a three week tour to 'New York, Boston, Buffalo, Chicago, Philadelphia', he recognised the potential of self-service retailing and the need to adapt the system within the UK context, appreciating that retailers who ignored the self-service development would be at a competitive disadvantage (Boswell, 1969).

Sainsbury's first self-service store was opened in 1950 in Croydon. Environmental factors, such as rationing, held back the modernisation of retailing in this period, so that by 1954 only four Sainsbury stores operated this format (Boswell, 1969). By 1969 the company was operating 162 service shops out of a total of 244 branches (Sainsbury, 1992). Whether this change was fast enough and whether early self-service stores were keeping pace with the needs of the consumer, is illustrated by the comments of some observers at the time, for whom the Sainsbury shopping experience was characterised by the crush of fellow customers (Winsbury, 1967).

By the late 1960s, however, it was no longer the supermarket that was representative of the spatial and operational changes that were occurring in retailing. The superstore and the hypermarket were the new challenge before grocery operators. Sainsbury has played an important role in the development of the post-supermarket, out-of-town, food operation in the UK, but it has not blindly sought size without benefit.

The size distribution of Sainsbury stores has remained comparatively narrow. By the beginning of 1987, the date of the Shaw's acquisition, 81 per cent of J. Sainsbury stores over 5,000 sq. ft fell below the 25,000 sq. ft point (IGD, 1988). Only 13 per cent of Asda stores fell into this range and 62 per cent of Tesco stores. J. Sainsbury in February 1987 had only five stores of more than 35,000 sq. ft, none of which were more than 40,000 sq. ft. In comparison Tesco had 63 stores of more than 35,000 sq. ft, of which 14 were over 50,000 sq. ft.

Sainsbury has continued to modernise its stores. Of Sainsbury's 263 stores over 5,000 sq. ft in 1987, only 137 were more than ten years old and only 29 were more than 30 years old (IGD, 1988).

At the time of the Shaw's acquisition Sainsbury was still primarily a southern-based operation. The operation was ranked number one in only one region, the south-east, and its market share only took it into the top four ranked grocery operations in four British regions (IGD, 1988). Compared with operations such as Tesco, which had the largest or second largest share of the grocery market in five standard regions, or indeed the Dee Corporation (later Gateway), which had the largest or second largest share of the grocery market in six regions (IGD, 1988), Sainsbury did not have a truly national base and competitive position. Of J. Sainsbury's 283 stores, 171 were in the south-east, with none in the north-east and Scotland (IGD, 1989a).

New objectives

In the late 1970s Sainsbury drafted a new strategic plan (*Financial Times*, 1987). It considered the option of moving away from the core J. Sainsbury supermarket grocery operation. The plan recommended a diversification into DIY, hypermarkets and overseas operations. While use of the Sainsbury name in the overseas market was considered, the idea was finally dropped. Sainsbury was to follow the recommended strategy over the next ten years, leading to the acquisition of the Shaw's supermarket chain in New England.

While Sainsbury's grocery operation has been characterised by organic growth, the company has been prepared, where appropriate, to expand its geographic presence through acquisition. Sainsbury's expansion into the Midlands in the mid-1930s was the result of the acquisition of a chain of shops already operating in the market (Boswell, 1969). In the 1970s and 1980s Sainsbury embarked on an ambitious strategy which would involve the company in joint-venture operations at home and acquisition abroad. In some respects it represented a move away from the cautious organic growth that had characterised the operation in previous periods. However, in other respects the cautious 'learn as you go' approach was still evident in those moves which transformed the company in little more than a decade.

Savacentre

By the late 1970s diversification was already under way with the Savacentre chain, a joint operation with British Home Stores. The first of the combined superstore/variety stores was opened in 1977. Two years after the public flotation of the company in 1973, Sainsbury entered into an agreement with British Home Stores to develop Savacentre, on the basis of a 50 per cent holding. This arrangement lasted until March 1989 when Sainsbury acquired the remaining share of the company.

A month before Sainsbury's acquisition of 100 per cent of Savacentre shares, a seventh store had been added to the chain, bringing the total sales floor space to 543,000 sq. ft. The new store at Merton in Surrey added 107,000 sq. ft (Sainsbury, 1992). The Merton store was the first new Savacentre store since the sixth store was opened in 1985.

Homebase

In 1979 Sainsbury entered the UK DIY market in a joint venture with GIB, a Belgian retail group. Sainsbury held the majority holding in a 75 : 25 per cent split. GIB had experience with DIY retailing, while Sainsbury was able to bring an awareness of the UK market.

In 1982 there were two Homebase stores trading with 90,000 sq. ft of sales area; by 1987 this figure had risen to 32 stores and 1,424,000 sq. ft (Sainsbury, 1992). While it should be borne in mind that around 40 per cent of Homebase sales areas are not under cover, this was an impressive growth record, which made the operation an important player in the DIY market.

Shaw's

In 1983 Sainsbury acquired a 21 per cent stake, for £13m., in Shaw's, a New England supermarket chain. At the time of the purchase Shaw's had only 41 stores and a new store opening programme of one store every 15 months. Geographically the group was limited, trading in the environs of Boston. It was a chain which, as Sainsbury executives agreed at the time, was 'underweight' (*Financial Times*, 1987). While the chain could claim to be the market leader in its limited market area, in New England it had only 7 per cent of the grocery market, behind Purity Supreme with 8 per cent and Hannaford Brothers' Stop 'N' Shop operation, which led the market on 14 per cent.

By early June 1987, when Sainsbury's treasurer, Ewan Davidson, announced the company's acquisition plans for Shaw's, Sainsbury already had a 28.5 per cent holding. Since Sainsbury's first acquisition of shares in 1983, Shaw's had grown to 49 stores and in 1987 had a store development programme of three replacements and three new outlets. Sainsbury was to buy the 20.2 per cent controlling share of the business owned by the Davis family at a share price of $30 ($76.5m.). A tender offer for the remaining shares was made at $30. They were already guaranteed 74 per cent of the shares which would cost $184.4m. to obtain. Control of 100 per cent of the company would cost $261m. which, according to *The Times* (1987), was equivalent to £132m. To meet the initial cost of the purchase Sainsbury placed 20.179 million shares with Warburg Securities, in order to raise $188m.

Press coverage was favourable at the time of the purchase. Sainsbury had clearly flagged their interest in the company and had already had an impact on it. There were, by 1987, two British directors on the board of Shaw's and policy was being influenced. Since Sainsbury's initial investment in the company, eight Super Shaw's stores had been opened, each of over 50,000 sq. ft, above the Shaw's norm of 36,000 sq. ft.

Shaw's was perceived as a suitable vehicle for Sainsbury. Shaw's was focused on quality service and value for money and was not afraid of innovation. In many respects, Shaw's was not a typical US grocery retail operation in that it did not compete primarily on price, although it claimed it could maintain prices 2 per cent beneath the competition because it maintained costs at 4 per cent lower.

Shaw's did not, however, have the return on sales which Sainsbury could boast, 2.85 per cent compared with 6.19 per cent. However, when it was taken into account that Sainsbury owned its properties, in contrast to Shaw's rented outlets, ROCE was 32 per cent in Shaw's and 26 per cent in Sainsbury.

Shaw's, however, was a small regional player, although the US market can not in reality boast truly national operations. Nevertheless, Shaw's at the time of the acquisition was expanding into new markets and specifically had a store planned for Rhode Island. Its regional competitor already had a 1987 opening programme of seven stores in New York State. The New England market was nevertheless an attractive market, with disposable personal income per head of population, at the time of the takeover, 18 per cent above the national average (Bureau of Census, 1990).

International options

Essentially, Sainsbury had two international options in the 1980s; the US, or Europe.

The US market

European retailers have taken a considerable interest in the US grocery market, in terms of both observing innovative techniques and acquiring retail operations. This was particularly the case in the 1970s when Sainsbury made the decision to internationalise its operation.

Given the history of retail innovation in the US operating there offers retailers certain advantages, the opportunity to witness new techniques in operation being significant among them. Sometimes there has also existed, amongst retailers, a belief that the US market has offered greater political and economic stability than European markets. Retail operations have recognised their vulnerability in regulatory environments that do not favour larger businesses. Family businesses in such circumstances will be anxious to build an international portfolio of investments to mitigate such regulatory constraints. To UK retailers the US also offers a common language and, arguably, some similarity of culture. Expansion in North America – both Canada and the US – by British firms such as Marks & Spencer emphasises the attraction of this particular market place.

The EC market

The Single European Market is an important step toward the integration of the EC. While it will not create a single market in terms of consumer life-styles, tastes and preferences, it will remove artificial barriers that have inhibited the free movement of goods around the EC.

In recent decades the EC has seen a period of rapid development, both in terms of new membership and in terms of integration. While there are and will remain certain tensions within the Community, and some member countries will appear more 'European' than others, the Community may be said to have helped move western Europe towards greater political and economic stability, hence providing retail operations with attractive markets in which to operate.

The economic prosperity of the EC market remains uneven, with countries such as Greece and Portugal – when comparisons are made on the basis of GDP, market prices and purchasing power parities – recording levels around half the EC average (Eurostat, 1992). This disparity is even greater when regions are compared. Figures for regions such as Hamburg or the Ile de France look impressive, even when compared to their respective national averages. On the basis of 1988 figures, the south-east of England was the sixth most prosperous region in the EC after Hamburg, the Ile de France, Brussels, Bremen, and Lombardia (Eurostat, 1992).

Nevertheless, if EC integration continues, UK retailers will no longer be able to see the UK as their domestic market but simply as a small part of that potential market. Indeed, given the integration on a European basis of large suppliers to European retailers, UK retailers may be forced to think on the basis of European expansion in order to counter the negotiating muscle of those large suppliers. Aware of this, UK food operators have entered into alliances with other European retailers for purposes such as joint buying and the development of own-brand products.

The EC is home to a number of large food retailers, some of which have diversified into other retail sectors and expanded internationally. Operations such as Tengelmann, with 60 per cent non-domestic turnover, and Carrefour, with 31 per cent, should be compared with Sainsbury's non-domestic turnover of 12 per cent (Lowe, 1992).

Post-Shaw's acquisition

Between 1988 and 1992 Sainsbury added 13 stores to the Shaw's operation bringing the total to 73 (Sainsbury, 1992). From a selling space of 1,592,000 sq. ft the operation had grown to 2,229,000 sq. ft. In the year 1990–1 alone, six stores were remodelled and a further six opened. The six new stores, representing an addition of 207,966 sq. ft of sales area, were in Brockton West, Carver, Hudson, Leominster, and Salem (Massachusetts) and Mill Creek (Maine). A quarter of a million sq. ft distribution centre for perishables also came on line in the 1990–1 development period. This was followed in 1991–2 by three new stores in Beverley, Stoneham (Massachusetts) and Seabrook (New Hampshire), adding a further 86,900 sq. ft, while enlargements were undertaken at three stores. Despite this new store development programme, Shaw's remains an operation based in Massachusetts, Maine, New Hampshire and Rhode Island.

Turnover from the US operation was $1.77 billion in 1991, an increase of 6.5 per cent. In 1992 sales rose to $1.81 billion, an increase of only 2.4 per cent. Operating profit was $55.4m. in 1991 and $37.2m. in 1992 representing a fall of 33 per cent. These are not the kind of growth figures Sainsbury has been used to in the UK. In the US profit figures are built on margins of around 3 per cent, compared with margins of more than 7 per cent in the UK.

Nevertheless, despite the figures coming out of New England, Sainsbury's commitment has remained. In 1990 Shaw's saw over 300 own-label products appear in store, the result of a programme aimed at creating a distinct own-brand identity for Shaw's. Sainsbury's experience with own brands was fully utilised with Sainsbury's personnel involved with the programme. The number of lines grew quickly, more than doubling in eighteen months, and reaching more than 800 lines by early 1992. At the same time an emphasis has also been placed on the development of management teams in the buying function. This development focus on product lines and own brands is particularly appropriate in the New England food market. Retailers such as Big Y Foods, of Massachusetts, and Hannaford Brothers, of Maine, aware of the recession-hit and price-conscious consumer, have placed an emphasis on generics and private labels (Bennett, 1992). The 1980s saw an increasing market acceptance of these products and recognition of their qualities in the New England market.

Sainsbury's systems knowledge has also been used to develop the Shaw's operation. New technology-based distribution and in-store systems have been put in place. In 1992 Shaw's installed a new system to link the operational headquarters in Massachusetts to its distribution centres in Maine and New Hampshire. Among other applications this provides support for the verification of customer payments and reordering (Duffy, 1992). The system will cut by an eighth the time taken to download branch information. However, as David Jenkins, the chairman of Shaw's, has publicly stated, the food industry in the US is lagging behind the rest of the retail sector in the introduction of Electronic Data Interchange (EDI) (Anonymous, 1992). While Shaw's may be able to push ahead with technological innovation, it is still dependent on developments in the US supply chain to achieve the full benefits of some new technology. Fred Hartz, Shaw's vice-president of non-perishables, has similarly made public his views that operational efficiency in the next century will depend on co-operation in the industry. Through the simplification of key processes, he maintains that Shaw's could save $800,000 per annum in administration costs (Weinstein, 1992).

During the period of their involvement with the company, Sainsbury have made a considerable impact on Shaw's. Sainsbury's absorption of Shaw's has even seen the adaptation of a familiar Sainsbury slogan: 'Good Food Costs Less at Shaw's'.

Conclusion

In November 1992 Sainsbury released their half-year sales figures. These interim results (Sainsbury, 1992), the first to be announced by the new chairman David Sainsbury since he replaced Lord Sainsbury, were impressive. The company's operating profits from its UK food stores were 19 per cent higher. In contrast, Homebase with an increase of only 3 per cent and Shaw's with a 17 per cent fall in trading profits, were less impressive. Shaw's turnover was up only 0.3 per cent. The performance of Homebase was blamed on price competition in the DIY sector, while Shaw's results were blamed on recession in the US market.

David Sainsbury assumed his new responsibilities, after 23 years of his cousin's chairmanship of the company, at a time when the company could claim to be in a strong commercial position. This is despite the unfavourable economic climate on both sides of the Atlantic and at a time when the company faced the imminent realities of the Single European Market. His predecessor had taken over when the business was a food operation, firmly set in the English south and Midlands, operating 82 supermarkets and 162 service shops. In 1969 J. Sainsbury sold only a quarter of the lines it sold in 1992, through outlets that were on average little more than 8,000 sq. ft, and enjoyed only a quarter of its current market share (Sainsbury, 1992).

The new chairman took control of a diverse operation which had cautiously, yet profitably, investigated opportunities in other retail markets, that is, non-food at home and food retailing abroad. It had become, in the process, one of the UK's leading retail operations. It was, however, still heavily dependent on its core grocery operation. It had gained international exposure, but compared to the French retailer Carrefour, or the German operation Tengelmann, it was still disproportionately reliant upon its domestic stores.

References and further reading

Anonymous (1992), 'Fallen from leading edge to trailing edge?', *Supermarket Business*, **47**(8), 24–25.

Bennett, S. (1992), 'Massaging the merchandise mix', *Progressive Grocer*, **71**(1), 31–34.

Boswell, J. (1969), *JS 100, The Story of Sainsbury*, J. Sainsbury Ltd.

Bureau of Census (1990), *Statistical Abstract of The United States 1990*, The National Data Book – United States Department of Commerce, Bureau of Census.

Duffy, J. (1992), 'T-1 keeps Shaw's on top of grocery game', *Network World*, **9**(31), 9 & 12.

Eurostat (1992), *Basic Statistics of the European Community*, 29th edn.

Financial Times (1987), 20 June, 8.

IGD (1988), *Store Trends*, Institute of Grocery Distribution, Watford.

IGD (1989), *Key Account Profiles, Sainsbury*, Institute of Grocery Distribution, Watford.

IGD (1989), *Key Account Profiles, Tesco*, Institute of Grocery Distribution, Watford.

Lowe, J. (1992), *European Retail Alliances*, Economist Intelligence Unit, Special Report No. 2207.

Sainsbury (1992), *Annual and Interim Reports*.

The Times (1987), 20 June, 25.

Winsbury, R. (1967), 'The self-service of Sainsbury', *Management Today*, April.

Weinstein, S. (1992), 'Realistic partnering: how to do business better', *Progressive Grocer*, **71** (2), 80–86.

Littlewoods in St Petersburg
A major development in UK–Russian retail co-operation

Nigel Holden
Manchester School of Management

Context

This case study describes how Littlewoods, one of the largest UK retailers, opened two shops (one for hard currency purchases and the other for rouble customers) in Gostinyi Dvor, the leading department store in St Petersburg, Russia's second and most westernised city. The following aspects will be covered: background to the development; locational considerations; staff and management structure; staff recruitment; product policy, sales and buyer behaviour; and the general business climate.

The interest of the Littlewoods development is associated with several factors: its unusual method of entry into a highly uncertain retail environment; its involvement with the local political authorities; its appeal to the rouble as well as hard currency customers; the need to recruit sales staff for unfamiliar activities; the problems with Russian suppliers; the attitudes – and purchasing power – of Russian customers; and the company's role in educating Russian consumers.

Background

On 10 October 1991, Littlewoods opened two shops in St Petersburg in the form of a joint venture with Gostinyi Dvor[1], the city's leading department store, as its principal partner. Operated by Littlewoods Trading, this joint venture is 60 per cent owned by Littlewoods, 30 per cent by Gostinyi Dvor and 10 per cent by Mayak Tailoring Association, a St Petersburg clothing manufacturer.

Littlewoods, whose initial investment is quoted as up to £1m., was at the time of opening these two shops believed to be prepared to 'commit up to £5m.

---

[1] Gostinyi Dvor (literally 'merchant's court') was built between 1761 and 1785, representing a particularly fine example of early classicism architecture (Vityazeva, 1986). It operated originally as an exchange and proffering and selling was banned (Pylyayev, 1889/1990). In 1941 the central portion of Gostinyi Dvor received a direct hit from a German incendiary bomb (Salisbury, 1969). A long overdue restoration is now under way.

over the next few years to establish a chain of stores, first in Leningrad and then throughout the Soviet Union' (*The Sunday Times*, 16 June 1991). Be that as it may, Littlewoods is generally credited with being the first main-stream western retailer to enter the Russian market by way of the store-within-a-store concept (Reuter, 1991). For a firm as traditionally home-bound as Littlewoods, this foray into the Russian market was no opportunistic shot in the dark: it was a calculated decision relating to the planned development of the company as a major international retailer in the twenty-first century.

The entire operation, which took two years to negotiate, is regarded as a pilot operation, but one with clear long-term objectives. Strategically, Littlewoods is applying a 15–20 year time-frame to the initial development stage of the Russian market, while seeking to extend business operations significantly within three to five years from start-up. As we shall see the entire venture has got off to such a good start that within 18 months of start-up Littlewoods has already launched another substantial retailing operation in St Petersburg.

In addition to Gostinyi Dvor, Littlewoods also signed a separate retailing joint venture with the Mayak Tailoring Association of St Petersburg. Under this scheme Mayak is concerned with clothing manufacture for sale within Russia and for export to the UK and western Europe (Littlewoods press release, October 1991). This venture, known as Littlewoods Enterprises, is 70 per cent owned by Littlewoods and 30 per cent by the Russian partner. To Littlewoods the joint ventures represent an opportunity to become a central retailing force in 'by far the most undersupplied market in the world' (*The Daily Telegraph*, 2 October 1991).

The first of the two shops (area: 110 sq. m.) sells, for roubles, men's and women's clothing manufactured to western standards and Littlewoods' design and quality specifications; the other (area: 70 sq. m.) is a hard currency shop selling electrical goods, clothing, beauty products, food, tobacco, beers and wines and spirits (Littlewoods press release, October 1991). Approximately 50 per cent of the hard currency items are imported from the UK – the chain store and the Index catalogue (see below). The remaining 50 per cent come from other suppliers, such as Yardley and Pierre Cardin. After McDonalds, with their celebrated fast-food establishment in Moscow, Littlewoods is the second western retailer to accept roubles in Russian shops (*The Daily Telegraph*, 2 October 1991).

The entire deal was approved earlier in 1991 by the Russian Federation's Ministry of Finance. In the negotiations a key role was played by Mr Anatoly Sobchak, the influential mayor of St Petersburg, who had made a point of visiting Littlewoods head office in Liverpool in April 1991 (*The Daily Telegraph*, 2 October 1991). Desmond Pitcher, Littlewoods' group chief executive, hailed the joint ventures as 'a major development in Anglo-Russian retail co-operation' (*Littlewoods News*, 1991).

Locational considerations

Littlewoods chose St Petersburg rather than Moscow as its first foothold in Russia for three main reasons. First, its proximity to Finland meant that the company could bring in fresh supplies of freshly chilled foods, notably meats, by lorry. Second, Littlewoods preferred to develop its activities in Russia's most westernised city even though there are far fewer resident foreign business people than in Moscow. Third, its location places it in the midst of a once fashionable area of the city that is undergoing a major – and long overdue – face-lift.

The location of the Littlewoods outlets is the second floor of Gostinyi Dvor. There could scarcely be a better site in all of St Petersburg owing to its favoured position on the Nevsky Prospekt, the city's most famous boulevard, and its historical importance. Gostinyi Dvor is a triangular structure with 100-metre-long colonnades on two tiers. While shabby inside and out, renovation work should transform its peeling yellow stucco and ornate architecture to their former glory.

There is another locational feature, though it may not be quite appropriate to call this an advantage. In the immediate environs of Gostinyi Dvor is one of St Petersburg's leading money-changing districts. Thus, prospective customers, armed with roubles, can do the tour of the black marketeers and try to get the best rate for the two most popular hard currencies, the US dollar and the German mark. However, Gostinyi Dvor has now installed an exchange kiosk near the Littlewoods store which more and more customers appear to be using. This is proving to be a very positive development: it is helping to marginalise black-market activity, while educating consumers about personal finance decision-making.

Staff and management structure

Littlewoods' operations in Russia are controlled by a governing board consisting of directors representing the three joint-venture partners (that is, Littlewoods, Gostinyi Dvor and Mayak). The chairman of the governing board is Mr Malcolm Landau, chairman of the governing body of the joint-venture company (Littlewoods Trading) and an executive director of the Littlewoods Organisation. The board meets about eight times a year: in April 1993 it met for the first time in the UK. The key function of the governing board is to establish policy and formulate strategy.

Responsibility for day-to-day operations falls on the shoulders of the general director. His main task is to implement the business strategy laid down by the governing board (whose meetings he attends in a non-executive capacity) and to co-ordinate the activities of the St Petersburg-based management team. Below the general director the key management posts are: store operations, financial control and personnel.

A merchandising/marketing manager is about to be appointed. Only the personnel manager is a Russian; the rest are all of UK nationality. The other key Russian appointment, and it is a part-time one, is the company secretary, who is a professor of law at the University of St Petersburg. His advice is frequently sought on fiscal and taxation matters, and he is invited to attend meetings of the governing board in a non-executive capacity.

All in all the joint venture employs some 120 staff, of whom 14 are Russian sales staff attached to the rouble store and 16 work in the hard currency store. Each store has its own sales staff supervisor. Behind the scenes there is an extensive storage area, managed by a supervisor with twenty years' experience with Gostinyi Dvor and seven assistants.

Staff recruitment and training

There is a relatively high turnover of sales staff, for which three main explanations are offered: marriage, children, and the resumption of education. Nevertheless, there is considerable loyalty to Littlewoods among Russians working for the Littlewoods stores. Staff are attracted by advertisements on television and newspapers and by hearsay from staff already working for Littlewoods. The starting salary for sales staff (in December 1992) is 7,000 roubles (approx. $40 per month plus a hard currency premium of $25.00). There are problems with the taxation of hard currency earnings and a solution may be to offer staff a discount on hard currency items. Either way, these are good wages for Russians: more than that earned by a qualified engineer.

The main attraction for working for Littlewoods is the hard currency bonus. This helps to explain why some of the staff are overeducated for their work. For example, the data input operator has a PhD in chemistry. It is assumed, too, that some of the more qualified and entrepreneurially minded staff are learning about western ways of management and business organisation in order to set up their own companies.

Littlewoods offers all staff a two-day induction programme, comprising an introduction to the company, preparation of merchandise, rotation of food, customer service and understanding how the sophisticated electronic tills operate (no match, of course, for the lowly abacuses which still remain throughout all shops in Russia as the main engines of calculation!).

One problem that Littlewoods experienced was inducing their shop assistants to approach customers (that is, perfect strangers) and ask them if they wanted any assistance. Russians appear to be curiously bashful in this respect: which may explain, in part, why the cultural equivalent of 'service with a smile' has all too often been 'service with a scowl'. But even a little training can be a dangerous thing. There was an instance of one of the sales assistants telling a customer to get lost (to put it mildly) when this person declined to make a purchase after inspecting five items.

Supplier relationships

Hard currency merchandise in the St Petersburg store is selected by Littlewoods buyers in the UK. Three Russian buyers purchase items for rouble sales, the main points of sourcing being Germany, Estonia and South Korea. Otherwise, the policy is to try to purchase as much as possible from Russian manufacturers. Here Littlewoods is steadily exerting its own disciplines and controls to secure the required standards of quality, service and delivery. In return, the Russian supplier can expect repeat business.

When Littlewoods entered the market, the supplier was very much king. The UK retailer encountered the problem of not always receiving what they thought they had ordered from their Russian suppliers. When buyers visited a manufacturer, they were likely to be shown the best items which were in effect 'unorderable'; articles ordered would arrive in colours other than those specified; if you ordered 50 items, you might receive between 30 and 60. If a particular item sold well (a popular line in anoraks is a case in point), the supplier might simply say that no more were available.

This state of affairs meant that Littlewoods not only had limited control over its supply channels in Russia, but it also affected the timing of launches and the effectiveness of promotions, while adding uncertainty to sales forecasting. However, with the Littlewoods' policy of supplier development, the situation has changed quite markedly. Malcolm Landau cites several reasons for the transformation of supplier attitudes.

First, the company's supplier development policy was deliberately evolved as a kind of education process, aimed at creating close relationships with those firms that 'learn best'. Second, many of the suppliers had become privatised enterprises and were beginning to recognise the disciplines of the market-place. Third, and connected to this, the suppliers were acquiring new skills. For example, once they had abandoned crude forms of income/expenditure accounting, improved financial management took its place with an enhanced appreciation of costs and pricing.

Product policy, sales and buyer behaviour

Altogether Littlewoods offer some 2,000 product lines, including foods, in the hard currency shop (all food, incidentally, is available in the rouble shop). The company is also promoting Index, its catalogue service, offering consumer electrical goods, furniture, gifts and toys. Although a similar service is provided by a Finnish concern and a German one, this form of purchase is highly unusual in Russia, and Littlewoods is unique in requiring a 25 per cent deposit from Russian customers – a further example of how the UK firm is in effect educating Russian consumers.

Russian customers appear to be highly discriminating. They assume a far higher standard of quality in foreign goods from certain countries. Products from former socialist countries as well as some South East Asian countries

(Taiwan, Malaysia and India) are hard to sell. An otherwise beautifully made blouse, purchased by a customer for $32.00 (a bargain price by western standards) was promptly returned to the store when it was discovered that it had been imported from Romania.

Up to now consumer marketing research has only been conducted on a limited basis; the tendency is to ask supervisors about customer tastes and reactions. The market is as yet unsophisticated in consumer terms. In the words of Malcolm Landau: 'Setting up a highly successful selling operation in St Petersburg has been a form of marketing research in its own: we are continually learning new things about the business environment and customer tastes. We must respond more quickly than we could conduct research and analyse the results.' Landau calls this 'test-marketing on the ground'.

Thus there is no clear-cut profile of the average Russian consumer as far as Littlewoods is concerned, but the clientele has changed. 'The rough element and good-looking ladies', who frequented the store in the early days, have become less noticeable, partly because hard currency is gradually becoming accessible to wider classes of Russians. Nor should it be assumed that Russians can only afford to pay paltry amounts of hard currency. Reebok trainers come with a price-tag of $170.00 a pair, and sales have exceeded the expectations of both the manufacturer and Littlewoods. Similarly there is no problem in selling men's suits at $300, a sign of a growing class of *nouveaux riches*.

First results

Littlewoods are not publicly disclosing the figures for their business in St Petersburg, but its turnover for 1992 has been put at $4m. based on the totality of both hard currency and rouble operations. Indeed the company has been able to declare a dividend showing a small profit for the first full year of operation.

So far the venture appears to have succeeded despite the intractability of Russia's economic and political problems. It is estimated that there are around 300–400 hard currency purchases and 500–600 roubles purchases per day. However, these daily averages should be understood in terms of, first, the big shopping days, Thursday and Saturday; second, the introduction of a 'happy hour': the reduction of prices by 10 per cent on selected items is a constant source of mystification to Russian customers; and third, the general business climate.

However, the most significant indicator not only of Littlewoods' success, but, more tellingly, of its confidence in the Russian market has been the launch of another retailing joint venture in St Petersburg in April 1993. Under this arrangement Littlewoods has taken a 70 per cent stake in a recently privatised supermarket, called Dieta, whose employees hold the balance of the equity. The supermarket, located in a dormitory district in the vicinity of St Petersburg airport, represents exactly the kind of business development opportunity that

Littlewoods was seeking.

The new store, which has access to a large dormitory population with heavy customer flow, occupies double the floor-space of the Littlewoods' store in Gostinyi Dvor. The provision of a well-stocked supermarket in the suburbs is almost unheard-of in Russia. It is then no exaggeration to describe Littlewoods as retailing pioneers in Russia.

The general business climate

As for the general business climate, the Littlewoods joint ventures are exposed to three critical factors outside their control: changes in the cost of living and exchange rates; the nature of the prevailing system of tax and duty (for example, in September 1991 taxes on clothing and foodstuffs rose overnight from 5 to 15 per cent and from 10 to 20 per cent respectively); and the threat of economic and political collapse.

However, it is not the Littlewoods' policy to look upon these factors as threats to future business. Instead, it sees them as elements which are creating in Russia, to quote Landau again, 'an exciting and fast-moving consumer market'. Every day, he comments, there is some new change which impacts upon the Littlewoods business: legislation, purchasing power, consumer taste and the exercise of choice. It is a constant challenge to keep up with the rate of change.

As Russia slowly but surely develops its market economy, Littlewoods can be expected not only to take up more locations in the Russian market, but to implement an already identified strategic aim: that of 'bringing western retailing methods to an increasing number of Russian people' (Littlewoods press release, October 1991). But in this process no one should overlook, let alone underestimate, the remarkable efforts that Littlewoods has been making to educate employees, suppliers and customers. In other words, the company is attempting to break the old mind-sets about the inferior status of consumers and their needs (Holden, 1992) and to evolve a systematic approach, with adequate resource back-up, to changing Russian attitudes and thinking.

It would be folly to deny the scale and complexity of this task. The fact that Littlewoods identified this issue so rapidly and 'fixed' it in their strategic plan so centrally is a significant learning point – not only for other western retailers, but any other concern seeking to take up a position in the Russian market.

Acknowledgements

The author is indebted to Mr Malcolm Landau, chairman of Littlewoods Trading, and Sarah Collins, store manager of Littlewoods in St Petersburg, for providing much of the detailed information contained in this study.

References and further reading

The Daily Telegraph (1991), 'Littlewoods looks to the rouble', 2 October.

Holden, N. J. (1992), 'The painful evolution of consumer orientation and marketing awareness in the USSR 1953 – 1991', Manchester School of Management Working Papers, 1992, p.37.

Littlewoods News (1991), 'Challenge in Russia', October.

Littlewoods Press Release (1991), 'Littlewoods to open in St Petersburg', October.

Littlewoods News Release (1993), 'Littlewoods opens third shop in Russia', February.

Pylyayev, M. I. (1889/1990), *Staryi Peterburg* (Old Petersburg), SP 'IKPA', Moskva.

Reuter Textline (1991), 3 October.

Salisbury, H. (1969), *The 900 Days: The Siege of Leningrad*, Pan Books, London.

Sunday Times (1991), 'Littlewoods goes Russian', 16 June.

Vityazeva, V. and V. Kirikov (1986), *Leningrad – Putyevoditel* (Guide to Leningrad), Lenizdat, Leningrad.

Times (1993), 'Training trainers for Yeltsin', 18 March.

Part Five

RETAIL LOCATION

In 'Location techniques', Sophia Bowlby and David Foot provide a working example of the major evaluation techniques, including measures of potential, trade area analysis, regression and a gravity model. The importance of micro site factors, often more difficult to quantify, is also demonstrated.

The growing importance of geodemographic databases in decision making on location is illustrated by David Bennison and Ian Clarke in 'Network effectiveness: marketing locations work better'. The case shows a systematic approach to catchment area analysis and reflects problems typically faced by retailers.

In most countries, local and government planning policies have greatly influenced and constrained location decisions, as Ross Davies demonstrates in 'Retail planning policy'. Through the analysis of a recent planning policy guidance note, the issues of in-town versus out-of-town retailing can be debated.

Location techniques

Sophia Bowlby and David Foot
University of Reading

Context

There have been significant changes in retail location over the last 30 years. Population has decentralised and car use has increased. As a result there have been numerous developments of suburban centres, out-of-town centres, retail warehouse parks and regional shopping centres (Howard and Davies, 1988; RTPI, 1988; Schiller 1986). The town centre has also been the focus of much change and redevelopment. Town centres are increasingly specialising in clothes and other comparison goods, many sold from purpose-built covered centres (Dawson, 1988). Another important change has been the growth of large multiple retailers, with outlets throughout the country. Multiple retailers expanded rapidly during the 1980s, both through mergers and takeovers and through organic growth (Wrigley, 1987). This process of territorial expansion, as well as the creation of new store formats, has been vital to retailers' ability to remain profitable and attract investment from the City.

As a consequence of these changes, large retailers have had to take an increasing number of decisions about where to site new outlets and how to rationalise their existing portfolio of stores.

The importance of site location

Regardless of how adept the retailer may be, if an outlet trades from a poor site, the company will not realise its full potential. But while most retailers have developed expertise in selling their products, they know much less about site location. As a result, a number of retailers and consultancy companies have developed and implemented a range of techniques for evaluating sites. A simple introduction to the range of such techniques and appropriate applications is given in Bowlby *et al.* (1984a,b, 1985a,b). More detailed discussion of techniques and applications is given in Davies and Rogers (1984) and Wrigley (1988). Two of these techniques will be used in the case study.

Locational techniques

There are a number of analytical techniques which can help retailers make locational decisions. However, the way in which the techniques are applied will vary with the characteristics of the retailer's business: the analysis will not be the same for outlets selling different types of goods, and will be very different for out-of-town stores and town centre shops.

The retailer looks for a catchment population which will generate sufficient expenditure to make the outlet profitable. Competition from other retailers and sometimes also from the retailer's own existing outlets has to be considered carefully. Some retailers, such as large food retailers, look for sites well away from competitors. Conversely, comparison goods retailers, such as fashion retailers, choose to locate in centres with a number of competitors so that the shopping centre as a whole will attract customers.

In order to carry out site location analysis, quantitative data is required. Some companies have a great deal of information, others have very little. The main techniques used by retailers are as follows:

1. *Potential measures.* The potential of a shopping centre is analysed in terms of population, consumer expenditure, competition and accessibility within a certain catchment area. A retail company will look for towns with high population and consumer expenditure on their products and low competition.
2. *Trade area analysis.* A group of existing stores, similar to the proposed new store, is used to develop a model of the relationship between the characteristics of the surrounding area and sales attracted to the site. Total potential sales in a catchment area are estimated. Then penetration rates are estimated to determine the proportion of these sales attracted to the retailer's store. The results of studying existing stores are then used to estimate the potential of the new site.
3. *Regression analysis.* Existing stores, similar to the proposed new store, are used to estimate an equation relating variations in sales to a set of variables, such as population, competition, store size and store characteristics. The equation is then used to estimate sales at a new site.
4. *The gravity model.* An equation is estimated expressing shopping trips in an area in terms of consumer expenditure, store size and travel times to the store and to competitors' stores. For example, such a model could be developed for 1991 and then used to estimate changes in sales throughout the area when a new store is built.
5. *Micro site factors.* These are local site factors which influence sales, such as the environmental quality of the store, car access and store visibility. They are frequently difficult to quantify.

Siting a new superstore

The problem

A site in South Reading with potential for developing a superstore is being offered for sale. A food retail company, already operating many out-of-town superstores and hypermarkets, is interested in purchasing the site. The company requires a full analysis of a store's potential viability before making a decision. You have been commissioned to write a report and make a recommendation about the development of a superstore on the site. Suitable methods of analysis using both the *trade area* approach and the *regression* method are explained below. We start by describing the site and our definition of the catchment area.

The site

The site is at Junction 11 of the M4 Motorway at the southern edge of the Reading urban area (see Figure 17.1). The A33, Reading to Basingstoke main road, passes the site and crosses the M4 at this junction. At present the site belongs to Berkshire County Council and is used as a motorway maintenance depot, but this could be moved to another site. The site is large enough to build a superstore with ground level parking for 2000 cars.

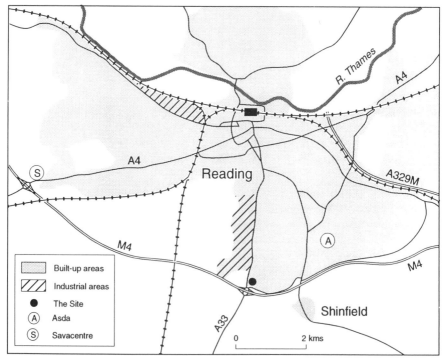

Fig. 17.1 Site location

Table 17.1 Residential population within the site catchment area

Travel time from site (minutes)	Resident population 1991 (cumulative)
Within 10 minutes	76,652
Within 20 minutes	300,851
Within 30 minutes	625,776

Note: Travel times are theoretical car travel times calculated using a 1 : 50000 OS map. Different speeds are assumed for different types of road, plus a three-minute trip-end time to park the car at the superstore. Speeds assumed are: Motorways 60mph; A roads (dual carriageway) 50mph; A roads (2-way) 40mph; country roads 30mph; urban roads 20mph; Reading town centre 15mph.

It is a highly accessible site, but Junction 11 does become congested during peak hours: 8.00 a.m. to 9.15 a.m. and 16.30 p.m. to 18.00 p.m. While busy at other times, it does not, then, pose a traffic problem. However, Berkshire County Council has a plan to build a by-pass to the west of Junction 11, which would effectively divert A33 traffic away from Junction 11.

The resident population within certain travel times of the site at non-peak hours have been calculated (see Table 17.1) and mapped (see Figure 17.2). The shape of these catchment areas is greatly influenced by speeds on different types of roads. To the east and west is the M4, to the south the A33, but to the north is Reading town centre and slow-moving traffic.

Competition within 30 minutes drive time is shown in Table 17.2, which divides the competition into three categories according to store size: hyper-market, superstore and mini-superstore. The closest hypermarkets are Asda to

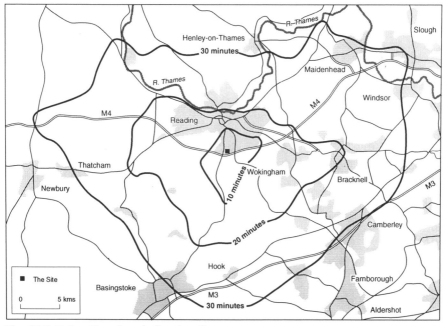

Fig. 17.2 Drive-time bands for the site

Table 17.2 Competition: other large food outlets within the site catchment area

Travel time (minutes)	Hypermarkets	Superstores	Mini-superstores
0–9.9	1	0	0
10–19.9	1	5	6
20–29.9	1	4	4

Type of store	Size range net floorspace	Average net floorspace
Mini-superstores	1,000–1,999m^2	1,500m^2
Superstores	2,000–4,999m^2	3,500m^2
Hypermarkets	5,000m^2+	6,500m^2

the east in Lower Earley (6 minutes) and Savacentre at the next motorway junction to the west (12 minutes). One of the superstores in the 10 to 19.9 minute time band is owned by the same food retail company that is considering the new site.

The reason for the low number of outlets between 20 and 29.9-minutes drive time is the spacing of urban settlements in this area: there are several large towns just beyond 30 minutes travel time from the site. These towns – Slough, Windsor, Farnborough, Aldershot, Basingstoke and Newbury – all have large food outlets that will serve some of the population living within the new site's catchment area.

Financial analysis

The food retailing company looking at this site already operates a large number of out-of-town superstores. They have considerable information about all the financial aspects of developing and operating superstores. The company can therefore estimate quite accurately the costs involved in developing this site, in terms of purchasing the site, building the store and all the running costs.

The company requires a certain level of profit from any new development. When this financial calculation was carried out for the site in South Reading, it was estimated that the superstore needed to attract sales of £326,000 per week at 1991 prices to make it a viable proposition. Superstores of this size expect about 80 per cent of total sales to be on food. Therefore the objective of the whole site location exercise is to determine if consumer expenditure at, or preferably above, this level is likely to be attracted to a new superstore on this site.

Preliminary site analysis

Before undertaking a detailed locational analysis, it is always useful to carry out a general study of the area to gain a good understanding of the problems. Much of this initial analysis will be map work and the site can be studied at two levels. Firstly, a detailed study of the site and the area close-by (see Figure 17.1), looking at the road system, urban development and the location of other large food outlets. Secondly, a more general look at the whole area (see Figure 17.2) using the 1 : 50000 OS maps, particularly number 175, but also numbers 174, 185 and 186, again looking at the location of urban development in relation to the site, the road system, other outlets and any physical barriers to traffic movement. This preliminary analysis will give the researcher a 'feel' for the problem. Where possible, a visit to the site and to competitors' stores can be helpful.

Trade area analysis

This method of analysis looks at the characteristics of the area surrounding the site in order to estimate retail sales. The population size within each of the three travel bands in 1991 are shown in Table 17.1. The Family Expenditure Survey provides estimates of the per capita consumer expenditure for 1991 in Britain. The estimates for supermarket sales are £15.28 per person/per week for food and £17.12 per week/per person for non-food. The total consumer expenditure in the three travel bands can be estimated by multiplying the population by the per capita expenditure.

The next question is how much of the total estimated expenditure can be attracted to the new superstore. As stated before, the food retail company operates a number of out-of-town superstores. They have carried out a customer survey at 25 of the superstores which are in similar location to the South Reading site. Survey data from this *analogue group* of 25 outlets provides information about average relationships between a superstore's characteristics and the surrounding area. In particular, average penetration rates can be determined: for each of the three travel bands, Table 17.3 shows the average percentage of food and non-food expenditure captured by the 25 analogue stores. The percentage of sales attracted to a store decreases with distance away from the store. Expenditure attracted to the new site can be calculated by using these average penetration rates. All these calculations can be set out on the worksheet (see Table 17.4), to give total estimated sales for the new site.

So far no mention has been made of competing stores. Each of the 25 analogue superstores will clearly face a different level of competition. Thus the percentage penetration rates allow for an *average level* of competition in each of the travel bands. The competing stores in the three travel bands for the South Reading site are shown in Table 17.2.

A measure of the intensity of competition in an area is the amount of store floorspace per head of the local population, thus indicating how well an area

Table 17.3 Average penetration rates for the 25 analogue superstores (the percentage of total expenditure attracted to a store for the three travel bands)

Travel time (minutes)	Food (%)	Non-food[1] (%)
0–9.9	9.42	1.71
10–19.9	4.24	0.81
20–29.9	1.19	0.21

Note: [1] Non-food sales in superstores includes alcoholic drink, tobacco, some household durables and clothes.

is served. In this instance, only food stores with over 2,000m^2 are effectively viewed as competition.

The total hypermarket and superstore floorspace can be calculated by using average sizes for these outlets. This information can be set out in Table 17.5, and the floorspace per person in food stores over 2,000m^2 in size in each travel band can be calculated.

The national figure for floorspace of food stores of over 2,000m^2 in size per head of population is rapidly increasing as more and more stores are built.

Table 17.4 Trade area analysis worksheet

Turnover required to make store viable:
    Total   =
    Food sales   =
    Non-food sales =

Food sales

Catchment	1991 population	Weekly potential sales	Market share to new site
0–9.9 mins.			
10–19.9 mins.			
20–29.9 mins.			
Totals			

Non-food sales

Catchment	1991 population	Weekly potential sales	Market share to new site
0–9.9 mins.			
10–19.9 mins.			
20–29.9 mins.			
Totals			

Total estimated sales for new store (food and non-food sales) =

Table 17.5 Competition worksheet

Catchment	1991 population	1991 competition (m²)[1]	Floorspace m² per head
0–9.9 mins.			
10–19.9 mins.			
20–29.9 mins.			
Totals			
Including new site 0–9.9 mins.			
Totals (0–29.9 mins)			

Note: [1] Hypermarkets and Superstores.

Fifteen years ago it was extremely low, but by 1991, the value was 0.055m² per head for the UK as a whole, and 0.064m² per head for the outer south-east of England (the south-east excluding London). These are *average* values and thus some areas, usually rural ones, have lower values, and others, usually urban or suburban areas, have much higher values. The average for the trade areas within 30-minutes drive time of the 25 analogue stores is 0.083 m² per head. There must be a saturation point when the population cannot support any more large food stores, but it is not known what this is. The analyst must clearly look carefully at competing stores in relation to the new site.

Regression analysis

Another form of locational analysis is to use the analogue stores to form a regression equation. Here, retail sales in the 25 analogue stores is the dependent variable. Variations in sales are explained by a series of independent variables, such as population and competition in the catchment area, size of store and store characteristics. With just 25 observations, only a small number

Table 17.6 Regression equation for the 25 analogue stores

Variables:	Y	=	retail sales
	P	=	population within 20-minutes drive time of superstore.
	C	=	competition, defined as the floorspace of all stores over 1,000m² within 20-minutes drive time of the site measured in square metres.
	Y	=	$186{,}835 + 0.7822\,P - 1.1381\,C$
			$(t = 3.4) \quad (t = 2.1)$
			Coefficient of determination $r^2 = 0.88$

Note: All 25 analogue superstores are of similar size and in similar out-of-town locations.

Table 17.7 Regression worksheet

Population within 20 minutes	(	$) \times 0.7822$ =	
Competition within 20 minutes	(	$) \times -1.1381$ =	
Constant		=	£186,835
Total estimated sales		=	

of independent variables can be included: Table 17.6 shows the best equation based on the 25 analogue stores. In the equation, sales are explained by a large constant factor, together with population within 20-minutes drive time – a positive influence on sales – and competition from stores over 1,000m² within 20-minutes drive time – a negative influence on sales. Both population and competition are significant variables, as shown by the *t* values in Table 17.6. The coefficient of determination (r^2) is 0.88, showing that differences in sales between the 25 superstores are highly associated with the level of population and competition at each outlet.

This equation can be used to estimate sales at the new site using the worksheet in Table 17.7. Population within 20 minutes is given in Table 17.1. Competition from stores of over 1,000m² within 20 minutes can be estimated from Table 17.2, by assuming average sizes for the three types of store. The total sales estimate can then be compared with the trade area estimate and with the sale required to make the superstore viable.

The report and recommendations

A report of about 2,000 words, plus maps and tables, needs to be written to explain your recommendations. This can follow the procedure of investigation outlined above. Thus the report should include:

- A brief description of the project.
- The results of a preliminary analysis including some maps.
- The results of the trade area analysis (see Table 17.4). Compare the results with the financial target.
- The results of the analysis of the level of competition in the catchment area.
- The results of the regression analysis (see Tables 17.6 and 17.7). Again, compare the results with the financial target and with the trade area results.
- Any other relevant points, such as the socioeconomic characteristics of the population and micro-site factors.
- Make a recommendation to the retail company. Should they purchase the site and develop a superstore, or is the site not viable?

Stop press

A planning application has just been submitted to develop a food superstore, 1½ miles north of the site, on the A33 towards Reading. It is about half-way between the site and Reading town centre. How do you think this will affect your analysis, and will it change your recommendation?

References and further reading

Bowlby, S. R., M. Breheny and D. Foot (1984a), 'Store location: problems and methods. 1: Is locating a viable store becoming more difficult?', *Retail and Distribution Management*, **12**(5) 31–3.

Bowlby, S. R., M. Breheny and D. Foot (1984b), 'Store location: problems and methods. 2: Expanding into new geographical areas', *Retail and Distribution Management*, **12**(6), 41–6.

Bowlby, S. R., M. Breheny and D. Foot (1985a), 'Store location: problems and methods. 3: Choosing the right site', *Retail and Distribution Management*, **13**(1), 44–8.

Bowlby, S. R., M. Breheny and D. Foot (1985b), 'Store location: problems and methods. 4: Are existing stores in good locations?', *Retail and Distribution Management*, **13**(2), 40–4.

Davies, R. L. and D. Rogers (eds) (1984), *Store Location and Store Assessment Research*, John Wiley, Chichester.

Dawson, J. A. (1988), 'Futures for the high street', *The Geographical Journal*, **154**(1), 1–22.

Howard, E. B. and R. L. Davies (1988), *Change in the Retail Environment*, Longman, Harlow.

RTPI (Royal Town Planning Institute) (1988), *Planning for Shopping into the 21st Century*, RTPI, London.

Schiller, R. K. (1986), 'Retail decentralisation: the coming of the third wave', *The Planner*, **72**, 7.

Wrigley, N. (1987), 'The concentration of capital in UK grocery retailing', *Environment and Planning A*, **19**, 1283–8.

Wrigley, N. (ed) (1988), *Store Choice, Store Location and Market Analysis*, Routledge, London.

Network effectiveness
Making locations work better[1]

David Bennison and Ian Clarke
Manchester Metropolitan University

Context

Quenchers plc, a national chain of off-licences, originated 25 years ago as the off-licence trade division of a small Droitwich brewery. During its first ten years Quenchers built a network of 34 shops in the West Midlands, but in 1978 the company was taken over by one of the brewing conglomerates, which acquired it primarily for its tied estate. The brewery was closed immediately and the site sold to a property developer. The off-licence division was put up for sale, at which point Bill Corfield, the managing director of the division, led a management buy-out; he has remained managing director and chairman ever since. An accountant by training, he is a dynamic, entrepreneurial individual, who led a programme of sustained expansion to build up the branch network from the original 34 shops to 453 by the end of 1992.

The shops are now spread throughout mainland UK - the most northerly outlet in Inverness, the most southerly in Penzance. The expansion has mainly been through a programme of continuous acquisition of independent and small regional companies, although new units have been developed, most notably in places where acquisition was particularly problematical. Most of the store portfolio is located in classic town centre and suburban district centre locations, with the branches typically having net sales areas of about 500 sq. ft.

The expansion has historically been largely financed out of profit growth, resulting from tight controls on the business and economies of scale achieved in both buying and distribution. Organisationally, the company remains under the strong personal control and authority of Bill Corfield. Known in the company as 'The Bill' – by some with affection, and by others with fear – he prides himself on knowing the names of all his store managers, and always makes a point of dropping in unannounced on branches when in their vicinity. He has personally involved himself with every acquisition, not only through close scrutiny of the financial accounts, but also by visiting the outlets. 'Parking close by for six cars on

---

[1] This case is based on a fictitious company, Quenchers, and any resemblance to a real company or individuals is entirely unintended and coincidental.

the street, and a takeaway within 50 yards' has been his basic rule of thumb for site evaluation since the early days. Although the Property Department used some simple checklists to assess each site at the time of acquisition (noting such details as size of frontage, and the proximity of parking and competitors), there was no system in place for keeping them up to date, and the information was not actually used by anyone.

Within the past three years Quenchers' profits have begun to decline: return on capital invested has fallen from 13 per cent in 1988 to 6 per cent in 1992. In particular, volume trade in a static market has been hit hard by the growth of competition from superstores. This problem has been accentuated by considerable competition from the growing number of discount supermarkets, which have been responsible for raising consumers' price perceptions considerably over the last two years. Thus Quenchers' stores have been losing bulk sales and are under pressure to reduce their profit margins further. Since the control systems in the company are already very sophisticated there is little prospect of achieving any further substantial productivity gains through them – a fact which is beginning to raise concern among the company's major institutional investors.

Direct national competitors, particularly Thresher, Oddbins and Victoria Wine, have done much to identify their market positioning and formulate strategic plans. Both Thresher and Oddbins have focused on the more affluent market segments, whereas Victoria Wine has preferred to retain a broader appeal in order to exploit scale economies from its branch network, which is larger than those of the other two chains.

The scenario

The problem

The latest six-monthly sales figures have confirmed fears that the company shows no signs of improving its lacklustre performance. A summary break-down has also shown that there are some increasingly sharp regional dispari-ties. In particular, Bill Corfield has noted that shops in the Greater Manchester area – once one of the best regions – are now significantly underperforming the average sales returns on space for the company as a whole. As three of the stores had been acquired only recently, within the past eighteen months, he decided that he needed to visit the area to see if he could find out what the problem was. He asked Steve Robinson to accompany him. Steve is the marketing director for Quenchers, based in the head office at Droitwich. He has been in the post for two years, having originally joined the company eight years ago as an area manager for East Anglia.

Two of the three new stores are in Manchester city centre – one in York Street, near the Town Hall, and the other on London Road, between Piccadilly railway station and the main shopping area. These stores were, in fact, both performing well in excess of their predicted sales. However, the third, at Wythenshawe, was at least 25 per cent below forecast. Bill Corfield also decided that they should drop in on Quenchers stores in Fallowfield, Didsbury and Heaton Moor – suburbs of widely differing character – to see if they could get a better feel for what was going on. He also wanted to take the opportunity to visit his daughter and young grandson, who were living in Chorlton-cum-Hardy.

Before setting out, Steve got the Property Department to send him the checklist of site features of the stores they proposed to visit. He thought he might be able to update and add to them as they went to see each branch.

The visit

As Bill and Steve walked around Manchester city centre, they were impressed by the changes that had taken place in the year since they had last been there. There was the new Metrolink tram system, and extensive programmes of refurbishment and renovation had made further significant progress. 'Maybe the Olympics here aren't quite such a daft idea,' commented Bill. They noticed too that the Safeway store in the Market Place shopping precinct had been completely refitted – 'Rather like the new Tesco Metro concept,' observed Steve.

As soon as they had visited the two Quenchers shops they had come to see, congratulated the managers on their performance and added some details to their checklists, they went off to Chorlton before visiting the other four. There is no branch of Quenchers in Chorlton and Bill knew that his daughter went to Victoria Wine if she wanted anything from an off-licence, since it was the one nearest to her home. He was therefore a little surprised when, during the course of their chat over lunch, she mentioned that she had started going to the local Threshers instead. 'They've changed it,' she said. 'It's now called Threshers Food & Drink, and they've turned half of the shop over to food – things like milk, bread and cornflakes. It's very handy if I run out of anything, and I might as well just buy my drink when I'm there. Actually, you know, it makes you feel less self-conscious about buying alcohol if you're getting some other things as well. I reckon I'm buying more!'

Both Bill and Steve knew, of course, that Threshers had been developing different fascias and merchandising techniques, but they had not actually seen one of the new Food & Drink stores. So, before going off to Fallowfield, they dropped by. 'I'm not sure,' said Bill as they came out. 'Over half the space is given over to food, and they've only got one side with beer, wine and spirits. How do you think the cigarette and drink sales will be holding up?' They continued their discussion as they drove on to Fallowfield. On the way they passed a couple of large poster hoardings advertising the Asda Dales store in Longsight. Steve pointed them out to Bill, saying it was yet another example of the grocers differentiating themselves – this was Asda's first attempt at following Gateway's example of refitting some stores as discount operations.

Visits to the four other Quenchers stores took up the rest of the afternoon, and proved frustratingly inconclusive. On the way home down the M6, Bill and Steve reviewed their day. The chairman was clearly worried that there was no obvious explanation for why some stores were performing so much better than others. The conversation came back to Threshers' approach, and then to what Safeway, Tesco, Asda and Gateway were doing. He knew that a number of the largest grocers had set up specialised site assessment functions, and some at least seemed to be reaping the benefits from a careful, logical approach to store development. He was also conscious that the large brewers such as Allied and Whitbread had been segmenting and developing their pubs to fit their localities. 'Yes, maybe that could offer us a way forward,' he mused. 'We can't afford any more advertising or promotions, and we're squeezing our suppliers and distribution so hard the pips are squeaking. But are we squeezing all we can out of our sites? Could we make our locations work better for us? What say you look into it, Steve?'

The next day

As soon as he got into the office the next morning, Steve Robinson asked his secretary to clear his diary for the next three days, and began to think how he could approach the problem the chairman had given him.

The company generates a vast array of EPOS-based data, but beyond basic operational applications, relatively little use is made of it. Steve decided to focus on the group of 25 stores in the Manchester area and asked Computer Services for data from them. Sales, sizes, number of customers, average spend, and percentage sales participation by product category for each branch were provided (see Table 18.1). He also put together the various items from the checklists he had updated for the six stores visited in Manchester (see Table 18.2).

From the store performance data, he plotted some graphs to look for relationships in an attempt to find an explanation. While he was able to tease some things out of the data, he quickly became aware that he did not have the technical expertise to explore the information fully, and neither did anyone else in the company. Closer scrutiny of the site features of the stores they'd visited also suggested one or two things to him, but again nothing that was at all conclusive. He went home that night contemplating what options were open to him to meet Bill Corfield's request.

A way forward

The following morning Steve was back in his office, leafing through some magazine cuttings he had been collecting. He reread one from *Retail Week* (2 October 1992) about Threshers, which finished by noting that the marketing director expected database activity to be 'cranked up' quite considerably in the near future. There was also another article in his cuttings file about the growth and application of databases in retailing. Steve wondered if this might be the way forward, and asked his secretary to get the number of CCN

Table 18.1 Store performances

BRANCH	TURNOVER WEEKLY	£/LF¹	SIZE (LF)	WEEKLY CUSTOMER COUNT	AV SPEND	INDEX²	SALES PARTICIPATIONS						
							SPIRITS	WHITE WINE	RED WINE	FORTIF. WINE	BEER	LAGER	TOBACCO
A ROCHDALE	11000	23.4	470	1692	6.5	81	9.5	1.5	1.5	0.5	3.5	2.0	81.5
B BURY	10500	30.0	350	2100	5.0	62	18.0	7.0	4.0	2.5	6.0	3.5	59.0
C BOLTON	12500	24.0	520	2907	4.3	54	22.0	6.0	4.0	1.0	4.0	3.0	60.0
D MIDDLETON	13000	30.2	430	1529	8.5	106	13.0	4.0	3.0	1.0	5.0	2.0	72.0
E WALKDEN	11200	28.7	390	1418	7.9	99	18.0	3.0	3.0	0.5	4.0	2.5	69.0
F PRESTWICH	13100	52.4	250	1424	9.2	115	16.0	5.5	4.0	3.5	6.0	5.0	60.0
G OLDHAM	16100	29.8	540	4128	3.9	49	14.5	4.0	2.0	1.0	4.5	3.0	71.0
H SALFORD	12300	45.6	270	2795	4.4	55	22.0	4.0	2.5	1.5	2.0	1.5	76.5
I ASHTON-U-LYNE	11600	29.7	390	4142	2.8	35	18.0	4.0	1.5	1.0	3.0	1.0	71.5
J YORK ST	23500	56.0	420	2350	10.0	125	25.0	7.0	8.0	1.5	3.0	2.0	53.5
K PICCADILLY	13500	62.8	215	2700	5.0	62	16.0	9.0	7.5	0.5	3.5	7.5	56.0
L MOSS SIDE	5000	15.9	315	2381	2.1	26	12.5	3.5	1.5	2.0	11.0	8.0	60.0
M STRETFORD	6200	14.8	420	2000	3.1	39	12.5	5.0	3.5	1.5	6.0	2.5	69.0
N HYDE	8600	29.2	295	1791	4.8	60	12.0	4.0	2.0	1.0	4.0	2.0	75.0
O SALE	15600	46.6	335	1300	12.0	150	14.0	4.0	4.0	2.5	3.5	5.0	77.0
P DIDSBURY	9000	33.3	270	720	12.5	156	8.0	9.0	11.0	3.0	3.5	6.0	59.5
Q HEATON MOOR	16050	53.5	300	1070	15.0	187	11.0	8.0	7.0	2.0	4.0	5.5	62.5
R FALLOWFIELD	4500	25.0	180	1800	2.5	31	5.0	5.0	4.0	1.0	8.0	7.0	70.0
S WYTHENSHAWE	3500	29.2	120	1944	1.8	23	4.0	2.0	1.0	2.0	5.0	1.0	85.0
T ALTRINCHAM	18500	52.9	350	1370	13.5	169	16.0	3.5	3.5	1.5	3.0	4.5	68.0
U HAZEL GROVE	15000	36.6	410	1316	11.4	142	11.0	4.0	4.0	1.0	3.0	2.0	75.0
V HANDFORTH	19000	52.8	360	1218	15.6	195	23.0	5.0	7.0	3.0	3.0	5.0	54.0
W BRAMHALL	8700	58.0	150	713	12.2	153	14.0	3.0	2.5	2.0	6.0	7.5	65.0
X WILMSLOW	12500	36.8	340	1470	8.5	106	17.0	11.0	10.0	1.0	4.5	6.5	65.0
Y ALDERLEY EDGE	21000	60.0	350	2100	17.5	219	18.0	12.0	13.0	1.5	5.5	5.0	45.0
AVERAGE	12458	38.3	337.6	1899.1	8.0	100.0	14.9	5.4	4.6	4.6	4.6	5.0	65.8
NAT. AV	1348		340	1920	9.4								

Note: ¹ LF = linear footage; ² Index: average spend compared to all stores.

Table 18.2 Locational details of selected stores

	Central York St	Man. Picca- dilly	Store Didsbury	Heaton Moor	Fallow- field	Wythen- shawe
Performance data						
Weekly sales (actual) (£)	23,500	13,500	9,000	16,050	4,500	2,800
Predicted forecast (£)	16,450	12,150	8,550	13,640	5,000	3,500
Error[1]	+30%	+10%	+5%	+15%	−11%	−25%
Customer data						
Number customers p.w.	2,350	2,700	720	1,070	1,800	1,944
Average spend	£10.00	£5.00	£12.50	£15.00	£2.50	£1.44
Competition						
Presence of key competitors[2]	2	–	–	1	–	2
Marks & Spencer[3]	1	–	–	–	–	–
Major superstore[4]	–	–	1	–	–	1
Location						
Peak point pedestrian flow[5]	150,000	150,000	30,000	25,000	15,000	12,000
Location flow[6]	70,000	60,000	24,100	25,100	13,500	11,400
Location as % peak[7]	47%	40%	97%	100%	90%	95%
Type[8]						
Major central shopping street	1	–	–	–	–	–
In town centre	–	–	1	1	1	–
Edge of centre	–	1	–	–	–	–
Shopping centre	–	–	–	–	–	1
Proximity to traffic generators[9]						
Bus station	1	1	–	–	–	–
Rail station	–	1	–	–	–	–
Cinema	1	–	–	–	–	–
Major car park	1	–	–	–	–	–
Store characteristics						
Visibility[10]	N	N	Y	Y	N	Y
Frontage[11]	5.0m	4.0m	3.0m	3.5m	2.0m	2.0m

Notes: [1] Error is weekly sales measured against predicted forecast: $((\text{Actual}-\text{Forecast})/\text{Actual}) * 100$.

[2] Score 1 for any one of the following within 200 metres:

- Thresher
- Peter Dominic/Bottoms Up
- Wine Lodge
- Wine Rack
- Augustus Barnet
- Cellar 5/Drew
- Galleons
- Victoria Wine
- Unwins

[3] Within 300 metres.

Marketing, which according to the article was a major supplier of retail databases in the UK.

As he was discussing his request for some information about CCN's services, the analyst he had been put through to mentioned that they were holding one of their regular Retail Planning Conferences in London the following week. These one-day events allowed CCN personnel to explain and demonstrate the latest developments in their systems, and existing users to describe their applications and experiences. Steve immediately reserved a place for himself.

At the conference, Steve was impressed by the nature of the software and databases on display. He found it surprising that they were being used by such a wide range of different companies – from large grocers and mail order to banks, insurance companies and some of the newly privatised utilities. Over coffee and then lunch, he outlined Quenchers' problem to a couple of CCN analysts. They offered some advice and agreed to supply Steve with some sample data covering the Manchester area (see Exhibit 18.1) from their databases.

The data and maps from CCN arrived in Droitwich within the week. The company provided examples of two databases:

1. *The MOSAIC residential classification,* which is widely used for market profiling and segmentation. CCN sent data on the number and proportion of households which fell into each of the ten MOSAIC groups for Greater Manchester as a whole (taken to represent the city centre catchment area), and for the local centre catchment areas around Fallowfield, Heaton Moor, Didsbury, and Wythenshawe (see Table 18.3). Maps showing the relative distribution of three of the main groups were also provided (see Exhibits 18.2, 18.3 and 18.4).

2. *Indicator,* a database of sales and consumption of on- and off-licence drinks. CCN provided estimates of total off-licence expenditure for Greater Manchester as a whole (for the city centre stores), and for the four local catchment areas (see Table 18.3). They also sent maps showing the relative distribution within Greater Manchester of drinkers of beer and lager; spirits; and wine, cider and perry (Exhibits 18.5, 18.6 and 18.7).

---

[4] Score 1 for modern conforming superstore of J. Sainsbury, Tesco, Asda, Safeway, Morrisons within 1 kilometre.

[5] Point in town centre where pedestrian count is at its highest.

[6] Pedestrian count close to the store.

[7] Location pedestrian count as percentage peak.

[8] Nature of store location as classified by 4 categories of site.

[9] Score 1 for any of listed facilities within 500 yards.

[10] Visibility of the store from the peak pedestrian count point in the town centre.

[11] Width of store display frontage (metres).

Table 18.3 CCN data

	City centre	Didsbury	Fallow-field	Heaton Moor	Wythen-shawe
Mosaic groups (% households)					
1. Prosperous pensioners	3.1	8.5	8.9	15.5	1.0
2. Older couples in leafy suburbs	6.3	17.8	6.7	16.4	2.7
3. Families in inter-war semis	9.3	12.6	4.0	16.4	1.2
4. Older communities	15.3	8.6	8.7	9.1	2.2
5. Singles and flat dwellers	8.9	26.1	47.0	22.2	0.6
6. Disadvantaged council tenants	13.2	6.2	10.0	3.1	57.8
7. Older council tenants	9.3	2.4	3.6	1.6	12.6
8. Go-getting council tenants	10.1	3.9	5.0	0.5	20.4
9. Young families and mortgages	18.2	12.6	5.9	13.3	1.5
10. Country dwellers	5.9	0.7	0.1	1.9	0.0
Indicator Off-licence annual total spend (£)	102,481,946	630,974	769,925	1,503,695	1,453,434

Steve eagerly opened the package from CCN and began to examine both the data and the maps. He also got out the data he had already collated (see Tables 18.1 and 18.2). He had found the insights from his own company data only of limited value because they did not seem able to give him a good fix on the importance of geographical/locational influences on store performance. The information from CCN looked as though it could provide the solution he was looking for, and he eagerly began to work on it.

Case study questions

1. *What are the advantages and disadvantages of the approach to location decision making traditionally used in Quenchers? Why had a more analytical and systematic approach not been adopted?*

2. *Examine the internal Quenchers data on the Manchester stores (see Tables 18.1, 18.2). What relationships, if any, can be discerned between store performance, sales contributions, and location from this information?*

3. *Examine the information supplied by CCN Marketing (see Table 18.3, and Exhibits 18.2 to 18.7). How does this add to an understanding of the reasons for differential branch performance?*

4. *In the light of the preceding analysis, assess how the branch network could be made more effective by making locations 'work better'.*

Acknowledgements

We would like to thank CCN Marketing for providing data and maps, and, in particular, Nick Evans and Martin Davies for all their help and advice. We are also indebted to our colleagues John Pal, Ian Kell and Steve Greenland for their comments and assistance.

Exhibit 18.1 CCN Marketing: Quenchers location planning project

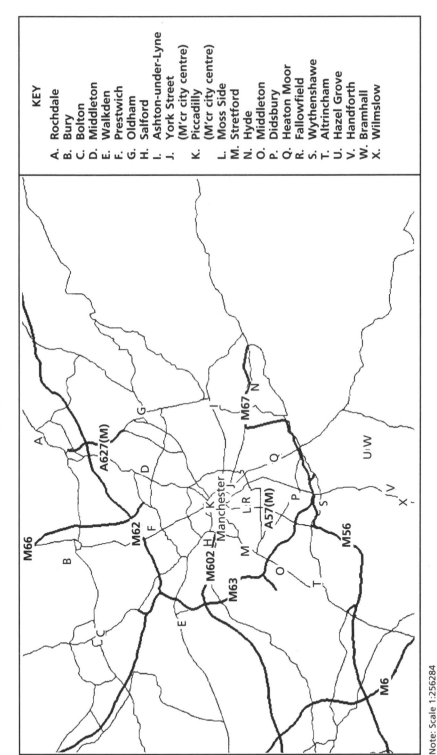

KEY

A. Rochdale
B. Bury
C. Bolton
D. Middleton
E. Walkden
F. Prestwich
G. Oldham
H. Salford
I. Ashton-under-Lyne
J. York Street
   (M'cr city centre)
K. Piccadilly
   (M'cr city centre)
L. Moss Side
M. Stretford
N. Hyde
O. Middleton
P. Didsbury
Q. Heaton Moor
R. Fallowfield
S. Wythenshawe
T. Altrincham
U. Hazel Grove
V. Handforth
W. Bramhall
X. Wilmslow

Note: Scale 1:256284

Source: © CCN Marketing 1992, © Post Office 1992, © Automobile Association 1992

Exhibit 18.2 Penetration of L2s – older couples in leafy suburbs – within Greater Manchester

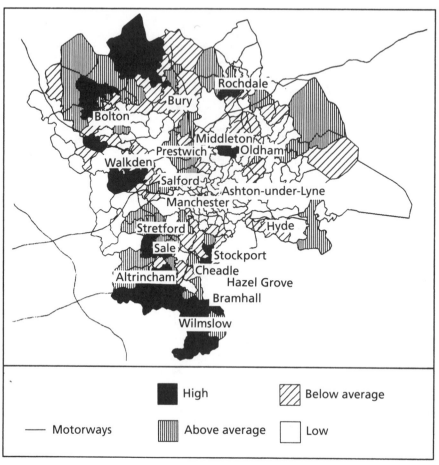

Source: CCN Marketing – Macromap

Exhibit 18.3 Penetration of L5s – singles and flat dwellers – within Greater Manchester

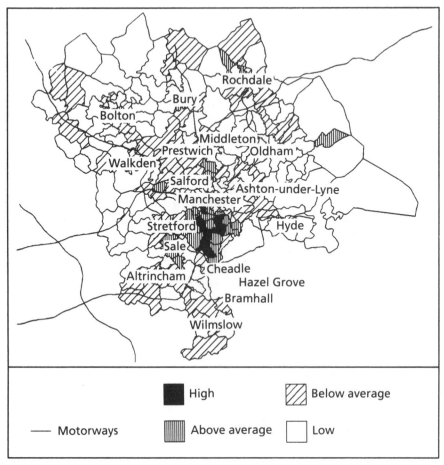

Source: CCN Marketing – Macromap

Exhibit 18.4 Penetration of L6s – disadvantaged council tenants – within Greater Manchester

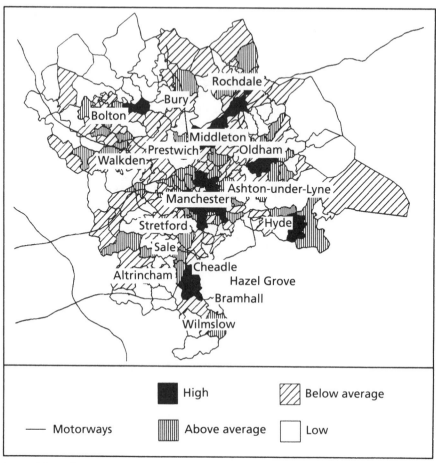

Source: CCN Marketing – Macromap

Exhibit 18.5 Penetration of beer and lager drinkers within Greater Manchester

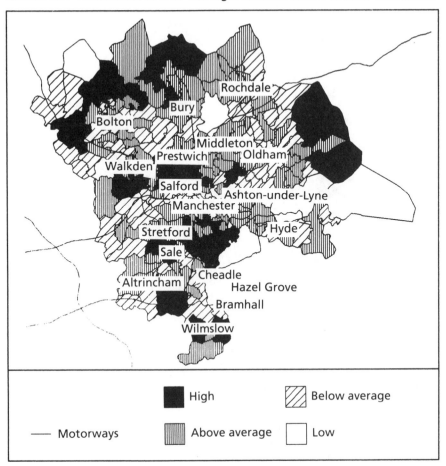

Source: CCN Marketing – Macromap

Exhibit 18.6 Penetration of spirits drinkers within Greater Manchester

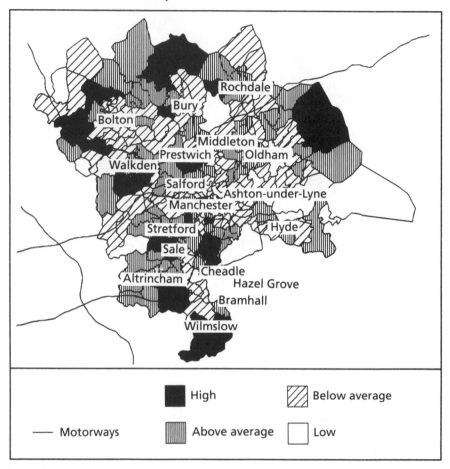

Source: CCN Marketing – Macromap

Exhibit 18.7 Penetration of wines/cider and perry drinkers within Greater Manchester

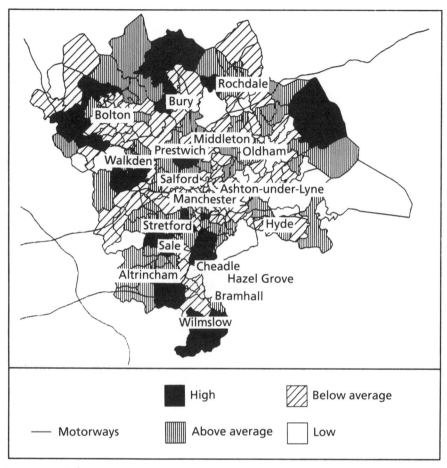

Source: CCN Marketing – Macromap

Retail planning policy

Ross Davies
Templeton College, Oxford

Context

This case concerns the application of town and country planning policies towards the retail industry and consumer requirements in shopping provisions. Emphasis is given to some new Department of the Environment guide-lines, published to assist local authorities in the formulation of the retail and shopping component of their Development Plans. Retail planning procedures are somewhat different in Scotland and Northern Ireland to those in England and Wales; but the tenor of policy tends to be the same, especially on the key issue of how much new retail development should be allowed 'out-of-town', as distinct from 'in-town'.

The case study does not seek to challenge the reader to consider the rights or wrongs or fairness of retail planning policy. The policy exists, although subject to interpretation by local authorities. What follows is an account of policy, how it has changed over recent decades, similarities and differences to policies pursued in continental Europe and the US, and finally, how policy seeks to balance the interests of various groups in society, sometimes in competition and conflict. The study is, therefore, a learning exercise to raise questions about how retail planning policy can impact on a company's business development programme and the performance of its existing shops and to encourage managers to consider how the planning system provides a framework for their own strategic thinking and decision making in the longer term.

The responsibilities of retail planning

Retail planning policy at the national level has never commanded the attention and debate typically surrounding policies on housing, transport, agriculture or manufacturing. The policy, however, as in the case of these other sectors, is rooted in land-use allocation. The starting premise is to ask: how can shops and shopping centres be best located geographically such that they meet the needs of the retail industry, and at the same time, the shopping requirements of all sections of the population? Such a generalisation, of course, immediately pits two concepts against each other: providing locations that will enhance the *efficiency* of the retail industry and locations that will prove *equitable* for all types of consumers. The conundrum is made more complicated when other factors are brought into the equation: how much protection should be given to retail land uses already in being and how much scope should be given to new developers to locate where they want? How much importance should be attached to historical retailing legacies and how much encouragement given to new retailing innovations? Should planning policy discriminate in favour of small shops and those consumers with limited accessibility, such as the elderly and infirm?

Such questions form the underlying bases of the retail planning policy determined by government. The policy, however, is no longer enshrouded in legislation, as policies in housing and transport still tend to be. The policy is advocated and disseminated to local authorities in a series of Guidance Notes. It is then up to the local authorities to interpret the policy in their Development Plans in the light of their local circumstances and according to local views. The local authorities, however, cannot complete transgress against the advice contained within the Guidance Notes. The Department of the Environment retains legally enforceable powers to approve or reject Development Plans, as well as to 'call in' controversial local proposals.

It is inevitable that retail planning policy, at both the national and local levels, becomes coloured by the political climate of the day. Under the Thatcher Government, for example, retail planning policy was almost abdicated as the new culture of enterprise took hold. During the existence of the socialist-dominated Greater London Council in the first half of the 1980s, it proved extremely difficult for retailers to get permission to build large stores in free-standing locations, against a policy that effectively discriminated against big business in favour of the independent shopkeeper and the poorer consumer. Such extreme positions in policy formulation are unlikely to be found in the 1990s. The new 'caring' approach of the present Government, and the ideal of its Citizen's Charter, are already to be sensed in the latest DoE Planning Policy Guidance Note (a revised PPG6: Town Centres and Retail Development, 1993). This begins, under the heading of Government Policy:

1. The Government's objectives are:
    - to ensure the availability of a wide range of shopping opportunities to which people have easy access;
    - to encourage town centres (including primary and secondary centres) to play a full part in the life of the community; and
    - to see that full use is made of the advantages of town centre locations for new development.

2. In-town and out-of-town retail development each has its own distinctive role to play. The Government believes that these roles can complement each other. Town centres can offer the range, quality and convenience of services and activities that are attractive to the local population, to visitors and investors. . . . Out-of-town retail developments also offer opportunities that consumers want in a different form, but their scale, type and location should not be such as to trigger a long term decline of those town and neighbourhood centres which would otherwise serve the community well. At a more local level, district centres, smaller parades, and

individual shops in rural areas each make a particular contribution to serving the public.

The pendulum of retail planning policy

The reference in the above statement to town centres, district centres, neighbourhood centres and smaller parades harks back to the way in which retail land use was organised within urban areas during the 1960s and 1970s. Within the dual system of Structure Plans (strategic plans produced by the counties) and Local Plans (physical plans produced by districts), a hierarchy of centres was designated and virtually all new development was expected to be accommodated within it (see Figure 19.1). While there was growing pressure from retailers and developers to build 'out-of-town', the major wave of decentralisation did not occur until the 1980s.

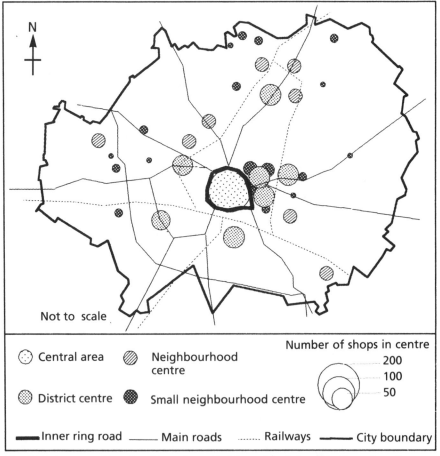

N

Not to scale

			Number of shops in centre
⊙ Central area	⊘ Neighbourhood centre		200
			100
⊛ District centre	● Small neighbourhood centre		50

━━ Inner ring road ──── Main roads ⋯⋯ Railways ━━ City boundary

Fig. 19.1 Coventry Planning Department's hierarchical classification of centres, 1961.

Retail planning in the 1970s

During the heyday of Structure Plans and Local Plans, the DoE assisted the local authorities in maintaining hierarchies of shopping centres by issuing two Guidance Notes: Development Control Policy Note 13 (DoE, 1977), which stated that proposals for large new food stores in free-standing positions should be resisted, and DCPN 14 (DoE, 1978), which said the same about the new, specialist, bulky-goods stores or retail warehouses. When retailers and developers had such proposals turned down by local authorities and went to Appeal, the DoE generally sided with the stipulations encapsulated in the Structure Plans and Local Plans. The prevailing retail planning policy of the decade, therefore, was to preserve a traditional land use arrangement predicated on the principles that a hierarchy of shopping centres had served the community well in the past and any significant amount of decentralisation would undermine its effectiveness in the future.

The policy proved to be contentious and stimulated a serious debate over the likely adverse effects of new outlying development on the existing retail environment. Several studies of impact were undertaken, particularly of the new food superstores, with some of these studies funded by the DoE itself (Scottish Office, 1977). Generally speaking, the impact studies, investigating the consequences of a significant shift of trade away from traditional centres on a scale sufficient to seriously undermine them, proved to be inconclusive. As criticism mounted towards the end of the decade over the strictures of planning policy, an increasing number of large out-of-town stores were being granted permission. However, of the 85 new shopping centres of more than 200,000 sq.ft built in the 1970s, all were located in existing town or city centres, with the few exceptions, such as Brent Cross, established as strategic foci of new and growing communities.

Retail planning in the 1980s

Retail planning policy did not change abruptly in the early years of the 1980s. Rather, a series of events occurred which cumulatively began to erode the authority and effectiveness of Structure Plans and Local Plans. First came the cancellation of the 1981 Census of Distribution, which made it difficult for local authority planners to monitor and research retail trends and developments in detail. Next came the creation of Enterprise Zones and Urban Development Corporations which enabled retail development to take place on an *ad hoc* basis within the inner areas of several cities without reference to a formal plan. Then there was the abolition of the Metropolitan Counties, which meant the loss of strategic planning towards retail development in all of the main areas of population concentration in Britain.

Other events followed to undermine the effectiveness of Structure Plans in the shire counties, not least a huge increase in the number of Appeals, the majority of which the DoE was by now supporting. At mid-decade, the DCPNs

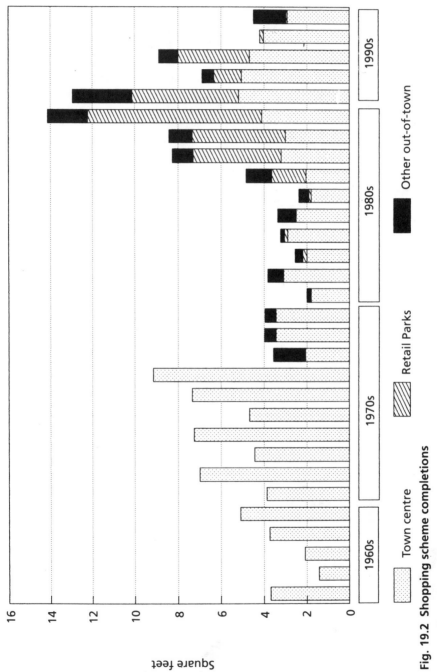

Fig. 19.2 Shopping scheme completions

Source: Hillier Parker.

13 and 14 seemed hardly worth the paper they were printed on; and the Government came in for a new round of criticism, but this time that planning policy had virtually ceased to exist (Davies, 1986). In a belated attempt to clarify its position, the Government issued a new document in January 1988, called Planning Policy Guidance 6 (PPG6): A Guidance Note on Major Retail Development (DoE, 1988). What the new Note did, however, was not to articulate a new strategic approach within which the burgeoning decentralisation process might be managed, but rather it signalled that, under the banner of Thatcherism, planning would be development (rather than planning) led.

Already, however, the vacuum in planning policy had encouraged a huge tide of out-of-town development proposals (see Figure 19.2). It came in all forms and guises: the proliferation of food superstores and retail warehouses; the introduction of American-style regional shopping centres; the formation of a new centre concept, unique to Britain, called the Retail Park or Retail Warehouse Park. The number of food superstores opened during each decade grew from 186 in the 1970s to 629 in the 1980s; in the case of the DIY shed operations, from 100 to 1,020; for the new retail parks, there were none in 1980 and more than 250 ten years later. It was the proposals, in the second half of the decade, for out-of-town regional shopping centres, however, which proved to be most controversial. Fuelled by the dramatic upsurge in consumer spending, there existed in 1987 no less than 42 proposals for these mega-schemes (Reynolds, 1987).

However, by the end of the decade the DoE became concerned that speculative development might be out of control, and many retail companies also feared the impact of the proposed regional centres on their outlets in existing centres. This led to a clamp-down on the number of planning permissions granted; of the 42 original proposals, only four had been built and opened by the end of the decade: the Metro Centre in Gateshead; Merry Hill Centre in Dudley; Meadowhall Centre in Sheffield; and Lakeside Centre in Thurrock. Several proposals were refused at Public Inquiries; many others failed to materialise because of a lack of investment support. A few remain as schemes 'in the pipeline', set back from realisation for the present by the effects of the 1990s recession.

Retail planning in the 1990s

The new out-of-town regional shopping centres of the late 1980s ushered in yet another round of impact studies. This time, however, they produced more compelling evidence that town and city centres were being seriously affected in terms of trade diversion and a polarisation in shopping behaviour (see Figure 19.3) (Oxford Institute, 1992). The cumulative effect of so much general decentralisation was such that many town and city centres were beginning to show clear signs of physical decline. The severity of the early 1990s recession compounded these problems; large numbers of retail companies rationalising their portfolios of stores were causing high incidences of vacant premises in

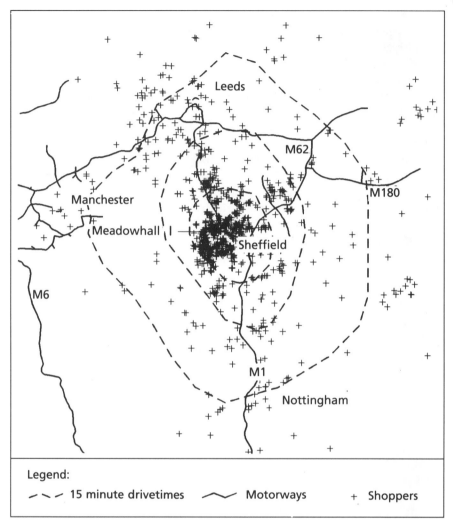

Fig. 19.3 Meadowhill Catchment Area: customer survey, October 1990

Source: OXIRM 11.90

all parts of the traditional retail environment.

The retail industry itself joined the clamour of local authority planning departments pressing for the return of responsibility in retail planning policy. The Oxford Retail Group in particular, comprising a dozen or so retailers, developers, funding institutions and agencies, established a dialogue with the DoE to argue for a revision of PPG6 (Oxford Retail Group, 1989). With the advent of the Major Government and a changed political mood towards greater sympathy for the environment, the DoE did finally change its stance, publishing a revised Guidance Note in spring 1993 (DoE, 1993). As suggested by its title 'Town Centres and Major Retail Development', the new Note signalled that the new thrust of retail planning should lie in rejuvenating traditional town and city centres. This would be achieved by encouraging new investment in these traditional areas, upgrading their physical appearance and introducing town-centre management practices.

The new Guidance, however, does not suggest a return to the restrictive position of retail planning policy of the 1970s. Instead, the emphasis is on achieving a 'balance' between the needs of town and city centres and further pressures for out-of-town development. In its summary, the Note states:

> The main changes of policy are:
> – to set retail development clearly in the context of town centre vitality and viability, while continuing to encourage competition between different types of shopping provision;
> – to elaborate the concepts of vitality and viability, introduced in the previous version of PPG6;
> – to stress an appropriate balance between in-town and out-of-town facilities;
> – to emphasise the role of the town centre in development patterns that minimise the need to travel and promote choice of public transport to help keep down CO_2 emissions;
> – to encourage planning authorities to be realistic in planning for the future of town centres; and
> – to indicate the role that good management of town centres can play in promoting vitality and viability.

Other key tenets of the new policy are given in Table 19.1.

How effective the new policy ultimately proves to be in reality during the next few years will be contingent, of course, on the extent to which it is followed in the local authority Development Plans.

Table 19.1 Further key features of the revised PPG6

- Clearer understanding of the retail industry and retail property market than shown in the original PPG6.

- The development plan process is the key catalyst for improvements to, and investment in, town centres.

- Food superstores in free-standing positions are now commonly accepted by local authorities and appropriate sites should be identified in Development Plans.

- 'Regional out-of-town shopping centres (however) . . . should normally be allowed only where they would fulfil an important retail need, taking full account of all likely impacts.'

- The assessment of impact of large out-of-town development should embrace their social and environmental effects as well as economic effects.

- 'Local authorities should *balance* the need to make the best use of existing retail facilities and the opportunities offered by possible new retail developments.'

Comparisons with retail planning in other countries

Ostensibly, the new policy brings the UK much more in line with the planning policies of other European countries, a position in marked contrast to that prevailing over the last two decades. During the 1970s, when Britain sought to resist decentralisation, France, Belgium and West Germany seemed to welcome and encourage it. France and Belgium, in particular, saw the introduction of large numbers of hypermarkets, whereas West Germany experienced the development of several out-of-town shopping centres. However, in each of these countries adverse reactions to these developments led to new legislation towards the end of the decade, which severely curtailed out-of-town development throughout the 1980s (Davies, 1979). The Scandinavian and Mediterranean countries had consistently opposed the decentralisation process throughout both decades, although large-store development has been made possible in Spain in recent years and the planning restrictions in Sweden are presently being lifted.

One consequence of the stricter planning policies of continental European countries is that their town and city centres are generally in better economic and physical condition than those in the UK. France, the Benelux countries and Germany in particular have invested considerably more in improving their traditional environments, as can be seen by the quality of pedestrianisation schemes, the provision of car parking and the ease of access for all kinds of vehicles. A possible downside to the effects of stricter planning controls has been the more limited choice in shopping facilities that continental consumers can enjoy compared to those in Britain. Certainly, the distinctively British retail park is a type of centre not readily found outside this country.

The convergence of planning policies across Europe may be further encouraged in future by much of the thinking and discussion now going on within the European Commission. DGXI, for example, the Directorate concerned with the urban environment, has already published a Green Paper which advocates control of the decentralisation process (Commission of the European Communities, 1990). Aimed foremost at a reduction of pollution levels, the Paper argues that reduced pollution can only be achieved if there is less use of cars and greater investment in public transport systems. Public transport systems seem to work best when they are focused on town and city centres. In any event, towns and cities contain important historical legacies which ought to be protected. Hence sprawl, whether of housing, industry or other land uses, should be resisted.

Comparisons of past British retail planning policy, particularly that of the 1980s, have also been made with circumstances in the US (Davies, 1988). Such comparisons, in truth, are difficult to make, since the American planning system is based on a series of zoning ordinances, enforced by county courts. There is usually little evidence of retail planning policy as such within the zoning maps; commercial land use is mainly allocated after the needs of transport and housing have been met. What prompted the comparisons, however, was the emergence in the UK of proposals for out-of-town regional shopping centres.

Concern was expressed that, if many were allowed, the 'doughnut' effect witnessed in so many American cities would be replicated in the UK – that is, that the town or city centre would die with a succession of suburban shopping centres. Of course, such concern can easily be exaggerated, but there is no doubt that in the second half of the 1980s the lack of an effective UK retail planning policy generated a pace and scale of retail development not unlike that in the US.

Conclusion

During the last 25 years, retail planning policy has swung from a restrictive stance to one of openness and, most recently, to a compromise: what has been called in the new PPG6 a 'balance' in retail planning. Critics of the document might say that it contains something for everyone, but this is in essence what planning has to do. It has to reconcile the interests of divided pressure groups; to meet the requirements of large and small businesses; to ensure that all sections of the population have adequate access to shopping facilities; and to weigh the benefits of development in the short term against the legacies they will leave in the long term.

The political mood of the country in the 1990s is one which favours a more cautious, sensitive approach in planning. The experience of the recession, too, has by itself slowed down the development process considerably, such that we are not likely to see, outside of food retailing, much more dramatic change to the retail environment for some time to come. Consumers too have become increasingly conscious of the environment, not simply in its urban manifestation, but also on issues pertaining to health, safety, packaging and pollution. Retail planning, for this decade, seems to have found its appropriate form.

References and further reading

Commission of the European Communities (1990), *A Green Paper on the Urban Environment*, Eur. 12902, Commission of the European Communities, Brussels.

Davies, R. L. (ed.) (1979), *Retail Planning in the European Community*, Saxon House, Farnborough.

Davies, R. L. (1986), 'Retail planning in disarray', *The Planner*, July, 20–22.

Davies, R. L. (ed.) (1988), 'Planning for retail change: international comparisons', *Built Environment*, **14**(1), 5–62.

Department of the Environment and Welsh Office (1977), 'Large new stores', *Development Control Policy Note 13*, HMSO, London.

Department of the Environment and Welsh Office (1978), 'Warehouses: cash and carry etc.', *Development Control Policy Note 14*, HMSO, London.

Department of the Environment and Welsh Office (1988), 'Major retail development', *Planning Policy Guidance Note 6* (PPG6), HMSO, London.

Department of the Environment and Welsh Office (1993), 'Town centres and major retail development', *Planning Policy Guidance Note 6* (PPG6), HMSO, London.

Oxford Institute of Retail Management and Building Design Partnership (1992), *The Effects of Major Out-of-Town Retail Development*, HMSO, London.

Oxford Retail Group (1989), *Planning for Major Retail Development*, Templeton College, Oxford.

Reynolds, J., 'The pressure for new centres', in Oxford Institute of Retail Management (1987), *The New Regional Shopping Centre Phenomenon*, Research Paper A11, Templeton College, Oxford.

Scottish Office (1977), *The Impact of Large Retail Outlets on Patterns of Retailing: A Synthesis of Research Results in Great Britain*, Scottish Office, Edinburgh.

Part Six

MERCHANDISE MANAGEMENT

Leslie de Chernatony sets out a systematic approach to buying decisions in 'Matching the brand's strength against the retailer's power'. Of value both to suppliers and to retailers, this case illustrates approaches to negotiation and the value of the relationship approach.

In 'Carrefour: development of the retailer brand', Luca Pellegrini focuses specifically upon own brand decisions. By tracing development over time, the case illustrates how this company has used a variety of formats in response to changing competitive conditions.

A comprehensive account of in-store merchandising is provided by Francis Buttle in the case 'Jaeger Ladies'. The elements and effectiveness of merchandising strategy are analysed, attention also being given to the differences between free-standing stores and shops within shops (concessions).

Switching to the grocery sector, 'Better Buy Superstores plc' by Nitin Sanghavi provides the opportunity to plan and evaluate a store's layout. In particular, attention is given to the allocation of space to various product categories within the store.

Matching the brand's strength against the retailer's power

Leslie de Chernatony
City University Business School

Context

The consultant's presentation

'So, in conclusion, ladies and gentlemen, if the Ecovert chain of grocery stores is to achieve its goal of increasing its share of the UK grocery retailing market from 8 per cent to 11 per cent over the next 3 years, and thereby become the third biggest retailer, we've identified several areas which you need to work on. As we explained during this presentation, consumer research showed that you are perceived as offering limited brand choice within the major product fields, you are slow to stock new lines and your prices are not particularly attractive. My colleagues have indicated how we can work with you over the next few months to identify efficiency gains. This will mainly come from your logistics systems. It should reduce your operating costs and, in turn, help you reposition your lines as good value for money. Clearly this will need communicating to the market.

We have checked against retail audit data consumers' perceptions about limited brand choice and being slow to stock new lines. In many product fields you stocked the brand leader, but your number two brands tended not to be the national number two brands. Also, when tracking which grocery retailers took new brands, you always lagged behind the other major multiples,' said John Wise, senior consultant at Retail Strategy.

'Excuse me,' said Peter Store, managing director of Ecovert, 'I fail to see why we, as the third biggest grocery retailing chain, should act as a charity for new grocery brands. You've rightly identified that profitability per square foot is low, then you say we should cut back shelf space on successful brands to try out unknown brands! We negotiate hard with our suppliers and I'm not prepared to take the risk of new, untried brands. Let's see what they do through other retailers and when we are more confident about their potential, then we'll take them – at the right terms.'

'But, that's part of your problem,' continued John Wise. 'When we spoke to a sample of your suppliers, they all spoke about your buyers' aggressive purchasing demands. Often they felt that you negotiate with unreasonable objectives, delaying decisions by unnecessarily claiming a need to talk with others. To be blunt, they didn't relish the thought of pitching for new business with you and we sensed that on new business they were placing an unusually low priority on pushing new brands through you. Change is needed.'

'You're right,' said David Home, marketing director of Ecovert. 'I felt this just over a year ago when I joined Ecovert. I sensed that our negotiating stance is too rigid and we continually expect better terms. If we don't watch it, this consumer perception of being a laggard rather than a leader will worsen, as we make our suppliers even less interested in pitching with new business.'

The fuse of the firework had successfully been lit and a heated debate started. The chairman, Michael Dell, stopped the arguments until a later date and asked John Wise to continue.

The debate about merchandising and negotiations

Some time later, an executive committee meeting was held at which the consultant's report was discussed. Many of the recommendations were accepted, but a lot of time was spent arguing about stocking new brands. Eventually, it was agreed that, provided suppliers could show a strong business plan, backed by thorough market research, Ecovert would be more receptive to new grocery brands.

What took much longer to resolve was the style of negotiations. Several further meetings resulted, with a variety of policy papers being circulated. Finally it was agreed that negotiations would be preceded by more analysis, so that a more appropriate style could be employed. David Home was made responsible for developing an analysis procedure to help the buyers.

Marketing director's approach to negotiations

Just over a week later, David Home started thinking about the problem. All too often, he thought to himself, Ecovert buyers make the assumption that they are in the most powerful position and then go out with the same, hard negotiating stance. Why don't we start to look at negotiations from the point of view of the seller, he thought? If Ecovert starts to anticipate the seller's view of the situation this may help structure a more conducive negotiations environment.

As he thought about the rep's perception of the situation, he started to wonder how suppliers prioritised their marketing activity behind new brands targeted at different retailers. He remembered de Chernatony and McDonald's (1992) book, *Creating Powerful Brands*, and, getting his copy, he browsed through the chapter on retailer issues in branding. The brand strength–retailer attractiveness matrix struck him as a neat technique which might help.

The following day he was able to start applying these ideas. Andrew Glass, Oral Hygiene's buyer, called. He had been approached by Oral Bright, one of their toothpaste suppliers, about a new brand of toothpaste, Wonder White. 'I'm lukewarm on this concept,' explained Andrew Glass, 'sure, they are an up and coming company, but their current brand, Cavity Stop, is still less than two years old and retail audit data shows it's the fourth most popular toothpaste. I think they may well be taking sales away from Cavity Stop by launching Wonder White.'

David Home smiled to himself when he heard this comment. 'Have they an attractive business plan? What market research has been undertaken?'

Andrew took him through what he saw as being an overly optimistic business plan, along with their considerable amount of consumer research. Oral Bright planned strong promotional support, with a consumer leaflet drop followed by TV and radio advertising. Trade support included an end of aisle gondola to display the brand.

After going through the proposals David and Andrew finally agreed that if Oral Bright did back the brand as they proposed to, it looked quite attractive. They met the next morning to discuss how Andrew should negotiate.

The strengths of Wonder White

'When you meet with the national account manager from Oral Bright, you've got to think about his perception as to where the power lies,' said David. 'A successful gamekeeper was no doubt once a poacher! The first thing we've got to consider is the strength of the new brand. A winning brand is built through an understanding of critical success factors. Strong brands match these factors well. So, what are the key factors, essential to you, when you decide whether to list a new brand of toothpaste?'

'Well, in order of importance,' replied Andrew, 'it's first and foremost the profit we can make. Next it's whether the brand has a unique product advantage. Then I look at the match between the image of the brand and our image. I'd then look at the support we could expect. Finally I'd look at the supplier's commitment to customer service.'

'Fine,' replied David. 'My next question is much easier. I want to know the importance of each of these factors. You've ranked them, now let's start to put a weighting against them, remembering that these five weighting factors have to add up to one. What we have to assume is that these five factors would be used by our competitors, with roughly the same weightings.'

Together they discussed the five factors and eventually agreed the weightings as profitability 0.35, unique product advantage 0.25, image match 0.2, retailer support 0.15 and customer service 0.05.

'Now,' continued David, 'Oral Bright will no doubt be planning to do pitches amongst our competitors. We've got to find a basis for assessing the strength of Wonder White through our stores and those of our competitors. I suggest we look at each of the five factors and rate how well the brand meets our needs, then those of our competitors. We'll score using a 10-point scale with 10 standing for very good and 1 for very bad. I know it's subjective. Let's start by looking at our stores.'

'The profit levels are OK,' replied Andrew. 'I'd score this at 5. Compared

Table 20.1 Wonder White's strengths through each retailer

Retailer	Critical success factor				
	Profitability	Product advantage	Image match	Retailer support	Customer service
Ecovert	5	10	10	5	5
Deliplus	10	5	1	1	5
Shoprite	1	10	5	5	5
Grand Stores	10	10	10	5	5
Multijoy	5	5	1	1	1
Tratelle	1	5	1	5	5

with the other brands of toothpaste we stock, we don't have one that offers total protection against tooth decay. So on unique product advantage, it's 10. Their high-quality image matches well with ours, so I'd score the brand at 10. The level of retail support is adequate, so I'd score it at 5. The level of customer service we've had in the past is OK, so I'd score this at 5.'

'Now, put yourself in the shoes of Grand Stores, the number one grocery chain. Let's use the same scoring procedure to see how well Wonder White fits their needs.'

Eventually, David and Andrew produced the information in Table 20.1, showing how well they thought the brand matched each retailer's needs. For each retailer, individually, they multiplied each critical success factor score by its weighting. The resulting five figures were then aggregated for each retailer, giving a score of between 1 and 10 to indicate the strength of Wonder White in that particular retailer. Andrew plotted these scores for the six retailers on a horizontal axis which he called Wonder White's strength.

The attractiveness of each retailer for Wonder White

'Our next task is to put ourselves inside Oral Bright and consider how attractive we are to them,' David announced. 'Then we've got to think how attractive our competitors are to them. From your considerable contact with suppliers, what factors, in your view, characterise an attractive retailer?'

'Now you are getting difficult,' retorted Andrew. 'Well, I suppose my first concern would be likely annual sales volume. Next, it would be retailer loyalty – I'd certainly not like to keep on doing new presentations because of an "on-off" relationship. Then it would be the likelihood of the retailer demanding special terms. Finally, I'd look at their geographical coverage. Don't tell me, just as before, you now want me to estimate the weighting importance for each of these "attractiveness factors".'

Andrew's final view about the weighting of the attractiveness factors was annual sales volume 0.35, retailer loyalty 0.30, likelihood of demanding special terms 0.25 and geographical coverage 0.10.

Table 20.2 Estimated retailer attractiveness

	Attractiveness factor			
Retailer	Sales volume	Loyalty	Demand special terms	Geographical coverage
Ecovert	10	1	1	5
Deliplus	5	5	5	10
Shoprite	1	10	5	1
Grand Stores	10	10	10	5
Multijoy	10	10	1	5
Tratelle	1	1	10	1

'Right, we are nearly there,' said David. 'Put yourself in Oral Bright's shoes and score us, then each of our competitors on the attractiveness factors. Again use a 10-point scale, with 10 as very good and 1 as very bad.'

'You don't ask much,' replied Andrew. 'OK, lets start with us. In terms of annual sales volume we have the right shopper profile and a high level of traffic. I'd score this at 10. As regards loyalty, our record is bad; if I can get a better deal with a different supplier I'll switch. On loyalty we'd be around 1. For likelihood of demanding special terms, they must know that I always push hard and so, as we're not good on this factor, I'd score us at 1. Our geographical coverage is strong in the South, but thins out in the North, so I'd score this at 5.'

Repeating the exercise for their competitors, they arrived at the information in Table 20.2. For each retailer, individually, they multiplied each of the attractiveness factors by their weightings. The resulting four figures were then aggregated for each retailer, giving a score between 1 and 10, indicating the attractiveness of each retailer. On a vertical axis, called retailer attractiveness, Andrew plotted each retailer's position.

The negotiations strategy

'So, Andrew, we can start to talk about your negotiating style from the matrix you can draw,' announced David. 'On the horizontal axis we have Wonder White's strength through each of the named retailers and on the vertical axis we have the attractiveness of each retailer. Plot the co-ordinates for Wonder White through each retailer. Once you've finished plotting, draw a vertical line half-way across the brand strength axis and a horizontal line half-way up the retailer attractiveness axis.'

Case study question

What negotiating style should Andrew Glass adopt?

References and further reading

de Chernatony, L. and M. B. H. McDonald (1992), *Creating Powerful Brands*, Oxford, Butterworth-Heinemann.

Carrefour
Development of the retailer brand

Luca Pellegrini
Università Bocconi, Milan

Context
Carrefour

Carrefour is one of the largest food retail companies in France. Founded in 1960 by Marcel Fournier and Louis Defforey and quoted on the Paris stock exchange since 1970, by the end of 1991 the company operated 491 stores and employed 40,000 people. In 1991, after two major acquisitions, those of Montlaur and Euromarché (the latter also a leading food retailer), total sales reached FFr 100.4 billion, almost 70 per cent of which were in France. The hypermarket is Carrefour's typical store format, one which it did in fact 'invent' in 1963 on opening its first hypermarket at Sainte-Geneviève-des-Bois, near Paris. The company is also active in food discounting in France with 199 stores trading under the Ed name.

Since the 1970s Carrefour has tried to export the hypermarket formula overseas. Although not all these attempts have been successful, it currently operates 34 hypermarkets in Spain, 24 in Brazil, four in both Argentina and Taiwan, plus a further one in the US. The main achievement outside France has thus been in Spain, where Carrefour is a leading retailer. Openings are progressing in Italy, where further substantial investment is expected.

Besides its own stores in the food sector, Carrefour has diversified by acquiring minority holdings in a number of companies trading in other retail sectors. These include 22 per cent of Comptoirs Modernes (supermarkets, in France), 30 per cent of But (furniture, in France), 45 per cent of Média Concorde (electrical appliances, in France), 29 per cent of Castorama (DIY, in France and Italy), 18 per cent of both Office Depot and Costco (office supplies and furniture, and warehouse stores respectively, in the US) and 30 per cent of Carpet-Land (carpets and floor coverings, in Belgium, France and the Netherlands).

Carrefour and own brands: prelude

Carrefour grew rapidly after its first hypermarket opened in 1963. The impact of its new retail formula was considerable and, although soon copied by other firms, the scope for new stores was vast. During the company's first ten years its main goal was therefore growth and to capture local markets before their competitors moved in (Burt, 1986). To this end, a number of new stores were opened through franchise contracts. Local autonomy at store level was preferred to centralisation, which granted considerable freedom to store managers in sourcing, pricing, promotion and several other organisational decisions (Toussaint, 1984).

The motives leading to the development of an own-brand policy can be traced to the mid-1970s, when food retailing in France saw a number of important changes. These can be summarised as follows:

- In 1973 the French Government enacted the so-called Loi Royer, an important statute which aimed to slow down the growth of large stores (defined as stores of more than 1,000 or 1,500 sq.m., depending on the size of the municipality). The law successfully obstructed many plans for new hypermarkets.
- By 1975 there were already 287 hypermarkets in France. The hypermarket formula introduced only 12 years earlier was now present in most large local markets. Carrefour, with its 37 stores, had to face rivals of similar size in an increasingly competitive environment.
- The impact of hypermarkets as aggressive price discounters was diminishing. The supermarkets, which had also developed rapidly in France after the war and numbered 2,620 by 1975, had narrowed the price differential between super and hypermarkets to 5–6 per cent. Two retailers, Leclerc and Intermarché, were particularly fierce competitors, as their positioning was, and has remained to this day, based on a very aggressive discount policy.

Thus intensifying competition, slower growth for the foreseeable future, a weaker position in terms of price advantages and the realisation of the commodity-like character of the service provided by hypermarkets, led Carrefour to look for ways both to relaunch its aggressive pricing and to give a more distinctive character to its stores. The answer was own brands.

Case study question

Why introduce own brands?

The 'produits libres'

Private labels were not unknown at the time in France. Supermarket chains in particular, such as Casino, were already offering a large selection of goods, either under their own trade name or using other labels they controlled. In fact, own brands already played an important role in maintaining profitability and, at the same time, enabled supermarkets to discount and match hypermarkets on prices of major manufacturers' brands.

This was one of the reasons why Carrefour did not want simply to introduce a line of products under its own name. This had been done before; the company now desired something more innovative. It wanted to use own brands to stress to its customers the effort the company was making to provide lower prices without compromising on product quality. Besides, Carrefour wanted it understood that this effort was part of a more general policy. The company saw itself as acting on behalf of its customers in the market: obtaining the best value for money for them and guaranteeing the quality of the products supplied.

Launching Carrefour's line of own brands was to be the occasion to make a more general statement of these goals and the company's mission; advertising and in-store promotion was to play an essential role in the launch.

Etienne Thil, the Carrefour executive in charge of own-brand marketing, gave the following account of events leading up to the launch of 'produits libres' (Thil and Baroux, 1983). To help him devise the communication strategy for the new line of private labels, he went to Jacques Séguéla (later to become one of French advertising's most famous names). With their team, they identified the two most notable characteristics of Carrefour's own brands: the common name they were to share and the advertising campaign which would accompany their launch.

The name, 'produits libres' (free products), was a bold and open attack upon leading manufacturers' brands; the adjective 'libre' communicated that the range was free of both the manufacturers' brands and many of the costs associated with them (marketing costs, commercialisation costs, advertising costs). One of the campaigns devised (but eventually not used) stressed this point: 'Voici les produits libres. Sans nom. Aussi bon. Moins chers' (without a name (a brand), but, nevertheless, of the same quality and cheaper). In fact all fifty products were to be called by the name of the commodity itself (seed-oil, soap, shampoo, yogurt, etc.) and identified by a common packaging: white with a red and blue band. No other name was to appear, even the name of the company was only included to say 'proposé par Carrefour': the band with the company's colours was enough.

The attack upon manufacturers' brands was underlined by the advertising campaign and the ensuing public uproar. The massive campaign, costing the unprecedented sum of FFr 30m., was based on a very simple slogan, 'Produits libres: aussi bon, moins chers' and used the imagery of a seagull flying in a blue sky to symbolise freedom. The reaction of the press gave the event wide coverage, and the public debate about the significance of such a move by a retailer, seen as a way of poaching into the preserve of manufacturers, made the campaign even more prominent and successful.

'Produits libres' were launched 1 April, 1976: All Fools' Day!

Case study questions

Carrefour chose a peculiar way to introduce its own brand products. What were the reasons behind their unusual approach? What are the main features of the different types of own brands? What are the elements of the underlying policies that they stress?

'Produits libres': success and decline

Success

The 'produits libres' were an unqualified success. During the first year of their existence their average market shares in the product categories offered reached 40 per cent in terms of sales. One year after their launch they accounted for 13.6 per cent of grocery sales, 4.3 per cent of fresh food sales, 3.9 per cent of textiles sales and 5 per cent in total overall. The success was such that the number of products was increased from 50 to 100 by the end of 1976.

As they had to guarantee large volumes of sales, the 50 products originally chosen were all common items, presented in just one specification – the one corresponding to the standard version of each product (for example, natural yogurt). The price differential with respect to comparable branded goods varied, depending on the product involved – for simple commodity-like products between 10 and 15 per cent, around 20 per cent for more complex goods, and up to 30–40 per cent for items with strong brand loyalty like shampoo and lacquer.

The success of 'produits libres' led most competitors to follow Carrefour by launching their own such type of private labels. The leading French trade magazine, *LSA*, started to refer to these ranges as 'produits drapeaux' (flag products), as they were often identified by the colour of the company proposing them (*LSA*, 1978).

Promodès was the first to follow: in July, three months after Carrefour, it launched 90 'produits Continent' (the trading name of the company). Other large French food retailers waited just a little longer: Mammouth ('produits familiaux'), Euromarché ('produits oranges') and Radar ('produits R') until 1977; Difra ('produits blancs') and Cora ('produits simples') until 1978; Disco ('10 sur 10') until 1979 (*LSA*, 1979). The two exceptions were Leclerc and Intermarché: they argued that to remain faithful to their discount policy they had to concentrate on manufacturers' brands, the ones, they said, that consumers were really looking for (though they did introduce some private labels under names that did not reveal the identity of the company). Leclerc, in particular, openly sided with manufacturers and went as far as buying a page in the daily *Le Monde* on which to argue strongly against Carrefour's initiative.

The 'produits libres' also spread abroad: to Germany, Belgium, Sweden and the UK. But the most notable development of Carrefour's idea was in the US. There, a supermarket chain by the name of Jewel was looking for a way to fight back following an attack upon its home market by Aldi, the name epitomising German hard discounting. Jewel revised the concept of 'produits libres' and introduced what later became known as 'generics': products in many ways similar to the 'produits drapeaux' but of lower quality (McEnally and Hawes, 1984; McGoldrick, 1984; Harris and Strang, 1985). From the US, generics became widespread, also appearing in France a few years later in 1980.

...and decline

But the initial euphoric response to 'produits drapeaux' did not last very long. The central role of the advertising campaign during the launch of 'produits libres' was certainly a very important factor in their success, but it was to become a weakness in the longer run. Such a scale of advertising expenditure could not be sustained and the general publicity inevitably faded as the 'produits drapeaux' became accepted as just another component of retail assortments. In the absence of other actions to strengthen the line of products offered as 'produits libres' their novelty could not last: consumers were losing interest. Besides, while Carrefour and other retailers stayed still, manufacturers continued their efforts to communicate to consumers and build up brand loyalty, devising new ways to serve them better with new products. 'Produit libres', providing just the standard version of a given good, could not resist this pressure for long. By the beginning of the 1980s their impact was lost and their sales started to decline.

Carrefour, as with most other retailers, did little to counteract this decline. In the early 1980s the number of 'produits libres' was still only 105, their packaging was unchanged; the only notable addition to the original basket of private label goods being a line of textile products (called Tex) in 1982. But Tex was hardly an unconventional move, failing to arouse any of the commotion reminiscent of 1976.

However, Carrefour did continue to build up its leadership in terms of communicating with its customers. Its advertising was imaginative; a magazine, *Le Journal Carrefour*, published in 1980 was distributed free to its customers; and its own retail card, the 'Carte Pass', was launched a year later as a way to strengthen store loyalty. But no further action took place on the own brands front.

Reasons for inaction

Why did it happen? Why did such a promising beginning not lead to attempts to revitalise the 'produits libres'? The answer can be found on considering the implications of own brands on retailers' organisations and on the way they see their mission. Launching, as Carrefour did, a limited line of simple, commodity-like products does not pose serious problems. The candidates are obvious: items guaranteeing a high volume of sales will obtain efficiency in logistics and in space allocation; products that are simple to specify, so that quality can be easily controlled; goods with no shortage of production know-how, so that producers can be easily found (Morris, 1979). Exactly the characteristics of 'produits libres'.

But to advance further demands a complete change of attitude. It means entering narrower market segments, proposing different specifications of the same good to serve different consumer targets. To do this a detailed knowledge of consumption patterns in many different product categories is needed.

And this is just a prerequisite. Once the desired products are selected, detailed specifications must be provided to the manufacturers. Product quality must be rigorously and continuously tested to ensure that the name of the chain and all the products sold with it are not damaged by a single defective product. To be able to perform these functions the retailer must have in-house knowledge of an increasing number of diverse products: it needs numerous experts in specialist fields. It must build up a department devoted to the development and control of own brands.

Even if the retailer is prepared to invest the resources needed to acquire knowledge usually specific to manufacturers, the investment must be accompanied by a radical change of attitude. The retailer has to be willing and able to modify its role: from an economic agent moving goods across space, to an interpreter of consumer needs. It was probably this new attitude which Carrefour lacked in the early 1980s. This would have gone against the grain of conventional retailing wisdom, not least in relation to hypermarkets and especially in a country like France: French hypermarkets were thought to be large, cold and impersonal stores, which customers visited infrequently. These are not characteristics conducive to developing the store loyalty essential to successfully supplying a large assortment of own brands. Their mission was thought to be discounting. Moreover the entire retail system was under constant pressure to keep prices as low as possible from the aggressive pricing practised by Leclerc and Intermarché, companies which, thanks to this policy, were fast gaining market share. Further costly development of own brands would have been an intolerable risk at a time when the main rivals insisted on fierce price competition. Neither was it clear whether consumers were prepared to shift their franchise permanently from well-known brands to own labels in an increasingly wide range of products.

Case study question

Why did Leclerc and Intermarché resist adopting own brands, considering them to be incompatible with their discount positioning?

Towards own brands proper

Generics: a short-lived experiment

Once more, it was increasing competition and the need to stress its distinctive character which led Carrefour to revitalise its private labels. The first initiative was taken in 1983 with the introduction, next to the existing 'produits libres', of a line of generics called 'premiers prix'. It was a reaction to what other retailers had already done. In 1980, for the first time in France, the Co-operative Movement introduced a line of generics in its stores and was followed two years later by many other retailers. Carrefour was therefore one of the last to adjust. However, it soon became clear that the co-existence of 'produits libres' and generics was problematic. Although generics were of lower quality, it was difficult to secure the different positioning of the two lines of products in consumers' minds. The results of research concerning their perceived positioning left Carrefour in no doubt: they were perceived as essentially the same. In general, by the mid-1980s 'produits drapeaux' and generics alike entered a phase of sharp decline and some retailers, notably Euromarché, decided to move to own brands 'proper', abandoning all other types of private labels.

The right time to relaunch private labels had come for Carrefour too. By the mid-1980s Carrefour's efforts to give special character to its stores, to induce more frequent visits by providing a wide selection of fresh products, and to improve the dialogue with its customers (*Le Journal Carrefour*, the 'Carte Pass') had quite transformed customers' perceptions of its hypermarkets.

Again, the company was looking for a way to distinguish itself from its competitors – at a time when they had almost reverted to the traditional approach of using their trade name for their own brands. Carrefour did not want to give up the search for something different. It was looking for a way to repeat the success of ten years earlier, when the 'produits libres' had turned the launch of a new line of private labels into a significant occasion to reinforce ties with its customers.

The result arrived in 1986 with yet another innovation by Carrefour: the 'produits concertés'.

Produits concertés

The 'produits concertés' were conventional own brands in that they carried the name of the company, but they were introduced in the stores under a dramatically different procedure (*LSA*, 1986). The 100 products to be labelled 'concertés' underwent a thorough process of selection and testing: 250 manufacturers were contacted to provide samples; 5,000 product analyses were conducted; 500 panels of consumers were employed to test them. Then, once the products had been selected, Carrefour asked its customers to pass judgement on them, promising that only those receiving the approval of at least 80 per cent would find a permanent place on store shelves. As one would expect, the rate of approval by the 66,000 customers involved in the test was very high, just short of 100 per cent, so that all but one product gained a label saying 'ce produit a reçu l'accord des clients de Carrefour'. For the second time, Carrefour had succeeded in making own brands an important occasion to interact with customers and build store loyalty.

By the end of 1986 the 'produits concertés' numbered 150, accounting for 12 per cent of Carrefour's grocery and fresh food sales (to which the 20 per cent share of the Tex label in textiles has to be added). As with the launch of 'produits libres', an advertising campaign was conceived to support the new own-brand initiative. The claim of the new campaign, 'Jour après jour Carrefour invente Carrefour' conveyed an idea of inventiveness, of awareness of consumer needs and of readiness to change in accordance with their wishes. This message has remained an enduring feature of Carrefour's customer communication. The association being built around the company's name were tied less and less to the usual themes of retailers' advertising, prices and assortments. As with manufacturers' brands, the name Carrefour was to be associated with a specific life-style, an attitude to shopping and consumption that the company summarised in its 1988 claim 'Avec Carrefour je suis positive'.

Follow the British!

The relaunch of own brands was also different in other respects to the time of 'produits libres'. What changed, besides the name, was the back-up that the policy received. Unlike before, when the lack of know-how made it impossible to increase the number of goods offered under the company name, now there was a department in charge of own labels and widening consumer choice. At the beginning of the 1990s it already employed 23 full-time specialists, operating in close unison with manufacturers and a number of laboratories in order to control and certify the quality of own brands (*LSA*, 1987; *LSA*, 1990a). Their duty was to look after the products on sale, propose new ones and to test and develop them with manufacturers – which were now seen not just as suppliers, but as partners in a long-term venture. Carrefour provides the direct contact with consumers; manufacturers must provide production expertise and quality. Quality has become a company preoccupation. It wants own brands to be comparable to the equivalent products by leading manufacturers, meaning both intrinsic quality and carefully designed packaging (*LSA*, 1990b).

The direction taken by Carrefour is clear. It is going to follow the way of retailers such as Marks & Spencer, Sainsbury and Tesco in the UK and Migros in Switzerland (Davies *et al.*, 1986; de Chernatony, 1989). The choice of products under the retailer name is no longer limited to simple, standardised goods. Since both store loyalty and retailer credibility are now stronger, a state precipitated in part by the own brands themselves, it is now possible to offer more sophisticated goods and even those that confer status (for example, the selection of Carrefour's wines, its champagne and cognac). Besides which, own brands have become an instrument to respond to issues increasingly valued by consumers, such as caring for the environment or information about the characteristics and ingredients of products. Through own brands the retailer expresses its autonomy from manufacturers, taking upon itself the responsibility for selecting goods on behalf of its customers and subsequently guaranteeing them with its name.

Carrefour's customers seem to recognise the effort made on own brands. In 1991, research was conducted to ascertain how customers perceived the efforts made by 14 large French retail chains with respect to three different kinds of products: leading manufacturers' brands, low-priced manufacturers' brands and own brands (see Table 21.1). Carrefour came second with respect to own brands (after Casino, a leader in this field in France), tenth with respect to low-priced manufacturers' brands and eleventh with respect to leading manufac-

Table 21.1 Customer research
Customer perceptions of the efforts made by 14 major French retailers with respect to:

> A – leading manufacturers' brands;
> B – low-priced manufacturers' brands;
> C – own brands.

Company	A (%)[1]	B (%)[1]	C (%)[1]
Casino	18	6	72
Carrefour	17	12	68
Cora	26	6	60
Aldi	8	20	59
Hyper U	22	13	53
Monoprix	21	14	49
Euromarché	29	15	48
Mammouth	32	13	47
Continent	29	13	46
Prisunic	28	11	43
Lidl	9	39	34
Intermarché	27	33	30
Leclerc	31	36	25
Auchan	44	28	22

Note: [1] More than one answer possible.

Source: *LSA*, n. 1265, 11 July 1991, 42.

turers' brands. Significantly, the effort towards own brands is perceived even more strongly by Carrefour's non-customers; when they were asked Carrefour came first (Baroux, 1991).

Carrefour's achievements in the development of own brands have been remarkable, even more so considering the store format of the company, the hypermarket. Hypermarkets attract customers from a very large market area and can not be targeted to narrow segments of consumers, like, say, local supermarkets. It is thus more difficult to develop close ties and store loyalty, conditions which are essential for own brands. Carrefour overcame these difficulties, with repercussions extending far beyond its own stores: a measure of their success is that the diffusion of own brands in hypermarkets is now on a par with the level in supermarkets (see Table 21.2) (*LSA*, 1991). Furthermore, own brands have helped Carrefour to differentiate its positioning from rivals. The brand property of its stores is based on an attitude to shopping and consumption that stresses freedom of choice, participation and dialogue. Own brands and the manner in which they have been communicated to customers have undoubtably been instrumental to this achievement.

Table 21.2 Private labels in France: market shares, 1990

Product categories	Super[1] (%)	Hyper (%)	Total (%)
Cleaning products	21.6	22.3	21.7
Bakeries	18.2	19.7	18.8
Preserves	21.1	18.7	21.8
Confectionery	10.5	16.3	14.1
Dairy products	27.8	25.4	24.1
Other groceries	19.8	17.7	19.4
Soft drinks	30.6	22.7	25.3
Fresh products	21.3	22.2	22.0
Hygiene and beauty	21.9	22.2	22.1
Wine and spirits	14.9	15.3	14.8

Note: [1] Supermarkets of more than 800 sq. m.

Source: *LSA*, n. 1253, 18 April 1991.

Case study questions

How can own brands of a quality similar to that of corresponding branded products cost less yet still give a higher margin to the retailer?

Why may branded products, leaders in their market segment, be unprofitable to retailers? Is there a relationship between this fact and the launch of own brands?

Are there substantial differences between the properties of manufacturers' and retailers' brands? Could the concept of brand equity (Aaker, 1991) be applied to own brands?

Libre Service Actualité (LSA)

Libre Service Actualité (*LSA*) has been an essential source in reconstructing Carrefour's own-brands development. Besides the articles quoted in full, more detailed information concerning 'produits drapeaux' and 'produits concertés' (products offered, merchandising decisions, sales, etc.) can be obtained from a number of other articles which appeared in *LSA*. Among them, the following are particularly useful:

- *LSA*, n.688, 3 November 1978, 157–60;
- *LSA*, n.710, 20 April 1979, 20–2;
- *LSA*, n.882, 25 March 1983, 172–3;
- *LSA*, n.918,27 January 1984, 100–8;
- *LSA*, n.938,15 June 1984, 34–8;
- *LSA*, n.1014, 21 February 1986, 75–99;
- *LSA*, n,1257, 16 May 1991, 96–8;
- *LSA*, n.1273, 10 November 1991, 46–8.

References and further reading

Aaker, D. A. (1991), *Managing Brand Equity*, The Free Press, New York.

Baroux, C. (1991), 'La perception des marques et des enseignes', *LSA*, n. 1265, 11 July 1991, 40–50.

Burt, S. (1986), 'The Carrefour Group: the first 25 years', *International Journal of Retailing*, 7(3), 54–78.

Davies, K., C. T. Gilligan and C. J. Sutton (1986), 'The development of own label: product strategies in grocery and DIY retailing in the United Kingdom', *International Journal of Retailing*, 1(1), 6–19.

de Chernatony, L. (1989), 'The impact of the changed balance of power from manufacturer to retailer in the UK packaged groceries market', in L. Pellegrini and S.K. Reddy (eds), *Retail and Marketing Channels*, Routledge, London, 258–73.

Harris, B. F. and R. A. Strang (1985), 'Marketing strategies in the age of generics', *Journal of Marketing*, 49(4), 70–81.

LSA (1978), 'Pourquoi les produits drapeaux?, n. 676, 30 June 1978, 85–102.

LSA (1979), 'Produits drapeaux, un phénomène européen', n. 724, 7 October 1979, 95–9.

LSA (1986), 'Carrefour lance les produits "concertés", n. 1014, 1 February 1986, 13–14.

LSA (1987), 'Marques des distributeurs: un souci permanent d'excellence', n. 1075, 19 June 1987, 55-7.

LSA (1990a), 'Certificat pour marque de distributeurs', n. 1227, 18 November 1990, 86–90.

LSA (1990b), 'Le design de marques de distributeurs. A vos marques!', n. 1236/37, 20/27 December 1990, 92–4

LSA (1991), 'Marques propres: jusqu'où monteront-elles?', n. 1253, 18 April 1991, 30–42.

McEnally, M. R. and J. M. Hawes (1984), 'The market for generic brand grocery products: a review and extension', *Journal of Marketing*, 48(1), 75–83.

McGoldrick, P. (1984), 'Grocery generics: an extension of the private label concept', *European Journal of Marketing*, 18(1), 5–24.

Morris, D. (1979), 'The strategy of own brands', *European Journal of Marketing*, 13(2), 59–78.

Thil, E. and C. Baroux (1983), *Un pavé dans la marque*, Flammarion, Paris.

Toussaint, J.- C. (1984), *La politique générale de l'entreprise. Un cas concret: Carrefour*, Chotard et Associées, Paris.

Jaeger Ladies

Francis Buttle
Manchester Business School

Context

A meeting was convened in June 1992 to discuss merchandising strategy. Present were John Ball (retail director, Jaeger), Ken Jackson (director of personnel, Jaeger), Mick Webber (head of Visual Merchandising department, Jaeger), Doug Duffin (total quality co-ordinator, Jaeger) and Cyril O'Dell (representing the Retail Stores Development department, Jaeger).

Ball called the meeting to order. 'There is one item on the agenda. Merchandising strategy for 1993 and beyond. Several related issues are up for discussion. Do we want to have a common merchandising strategy across all our stores, both free-standers and shop-in-shops? Whether or not we decide to go ahead with a common strategy we face the problem of deciding how merchandising decisions should be made. In particular, what should be the input from customers, branches, areas and head office? Third, if we do decide on a common strategy, how should we implement it? Should what is possible in the concessions drive what we do in the free-standers, or should what we want to do in free-standers determine what we try to do in concessions? It is clear that many concession managers don't believe a single strategy for the entire chain is feasible. I've just received a fax from one. I quote: "A lot of the concessions just cannot do what Head Office wants. And if we try to then our hosts come down on us like a ton of bricks."'

Background

Jaeger was founded in 1884 when Lewis Tomalin opened his first Jaeger shop in London. Tomalin had translated the book 'Health Culture' by a German professor, Dr Gustav Jaeger of the University of Stuttgart. Dr Jaeger claimed that people would be much healthier if they dressed in clothes made entirely of animal fibres, principally wool. Tomalin obtained permission to manufacture and distribute merchandise under the banner 'Dr Jaeger's Sanitary Woollen System'. By 1900 there were 20 shops retailing clothing made from cashmere, alpaca, angora and camel hair. Cotton and silk commodities were not marketed. Lewis Tomalin's grandson, Humphrey, realised that the Sanitary Woollen System was losing its consumer appeal, and, about 1920, set about converting Jaeger into a fashion house.

Maurice Gilbert, trained by Gordon Selfridge, joined Jaeger in 1929 with a view to rejuvenating the company. His strategy was to retain the animal fibre emphasis but update the styling which he dubbed 'absolutely awful'.

Jaeger today

In 1967, Jaeger was acquired by Coats Patons. By 1986, Coats Patons had evolved, through additional acquisitions and divestments, into Coats Viyella plc. Coats Viyella (CV) is organised into 6 divisions: threads, yarns and fabrics, precision engineering, fashion retail, homewares, and clothing.

Fiona Harrison, chief executive of Fashion Retail, is responsible for the profit performance of three operating companies – Jaeger Ladies, Jaeger Man and Viyella Ladies. In sum, these three companies accounted for 7.8 per cent of CV's turnover in 1991. Jaeger Ladies operates 146 retail outlets in the UK, of which 89 are shop-in-shop concessions. The balance are free-standing stores.

In 1991, CV generated sales revenues of £1947.5 million, a gross profit of £575.6 million and operating profits (after distribution costs, administrative expenses and exceptional items) of £126.4 million. 1990 equivalents were £1825.5 million, £560.2 million and £106 million. Exhibit 22.1 (see below) details Fashion Retail division's 1990 and 1991 performance. During the recessionary years of the late 1980s, early 1990s, the division's focus had been on reducing costs, improving its information technology capability, and improving product and service.

Jaeger is a vertically integrated company which designs, manufactures, distributes and retails its own branded products. It employs about 3,000 people throughout the UK, of whom around 800 work in Jaeger Ladies shops. Jaeger's management, as well as other managements in CV, are expected to abide by CV's Statement of Values. Developed in 1990 by the newly appointed group chief executive, Neville Bain, these values are designed to give direction to strategic decision making. Extracts appear in Exhibit 22.2 (see below).

Jaeger stores

Jaeger Ladies operates 57 free-standing branches as well as shop-in-shop concessions in the UK. Jaeger Ladies has outlets from Aberdeen to Truro and Belfast to York. Head office is in Broadwick Street, London, not far from the flagship store in Regent Street. Approximately 37 per cent of Jaeger Ladies' turnover in 1991 was from concessions. Other Jaeger Ladies data appear in Exhibit 22.1.

Jaeger Ladies stores are located in the big cities (e.g. Edinburgh, Manchester), smaller cities and towns (e.g. Exeter. Newbury), tourist areas (e.g. Bath, Stratford) and some popular retirement communities (e.g. Southport). Concessions are located in department stores run by House of Fraser (e.g. Guildford's Army and Navy, Cheltenham's Cavendish House, Cardiff's Howells), John Lewis Partnership (e.g. Windsor's Caleys, Norwich's Bonds,

Southsea's Knight and Lea) and other chains. Independent department stores such as Denners (Yeovil), Hoopers (Torquay) and Camp Hopson (Newbury) also host Jaeger concessions. Of the concessions, 83 are in branches of the department store multiples.

Principal competitors of Jaeger Ladies are Alexon, Aquascutum, Mondi and Windsmoor.

Concessions are typically much smaller than the free-standing shop, having on average about 625 sq.ft of floor space, but ranging from 200 to 1200 sq.ft (see data in Exhibit 22.1). One or two concessions have more square footage than some of the smaller free-standers.

Free-standers differ from concessions in many ways. Free-standers have one or two points of customer entry; concessions tend to be open to customers from all part of the surrounding store. Free-standers have higher staffing levels, more ranges and more stock within ranges. They tend to be better equipped with sales fixtures. All free-standers have TVs, VCRs (which play Jaeger videos), fitting rooms, settees or armchairs, coffee tables, coffee-machines, music, china, newspapers, magazines and children's toy boxes. Not only does the 'look' of the host store hamper the introduction of such amenities to concessions, but so does the lack of space and the trading practices of some host store managements. One large London department store, for instance, will not permit Jaeger to supply coffee, chairs or newspapers to customers. The concession manager was told in no uncertain terms: 'We don't want people sitting down reading newspapers.'

Restrictions sometimes apply to signage and colours. No concession has music in-store. Coffee service can be particularly problematic in department stores having their own restaurant operations. Some hosts will not allow Jaeger concessions to accept Jaeger's own Customer Account card. Other stores' accounting systems are not able to accommodate Jaeger's returns policy. When a Jaeger customer returns a garment to one particular host store's customer service desk, the store has no means of transferring the return from its own accounting system to Jaeger's.

Some department store concessions are located next to children's clothing departments, others next to downmarket merchandise. Some shop-in-shops are located away from the principal in-store traffic arteries. The best locations, at the top of an escalator or near an entrance, are often unavailable. Sometimes, department store corporate colour schemes clash with the fashion colours that Jaeger Ladies introduces seasonally.

Jaeger's nine area managers will often attempt to negotiate improved customer service provision with host store management. It is often more productive to speak with local store management than to negotiate with the host store's head office. Negotiations with department stores' head offices are conducted by Jaeger Ladies' retail director and the retail managing director. Concession managers are encouraged to use their initiative to improve the service they give customers. Duffin, Jaeger's TQM co-ordinator, observed, 'With concessions we try to be as flexible as possible and not to be too prescriptive.'

With the exception of John Lewis Partnership concessions, all shop-in-shops are staffed by Jaeger employees.

Jaeger Ladies' customers

Jaeger Ladies merchandise has a reputation for high quality and excellent design. Merchandise is designed for the affluent, fashion-conscious, 35-years-and-over woman. Jaeger's goal is to meet the needs of their customers' social and professional wardrobes. Changing demographics will swell the number of over-35s in coming years and Jaeger wants to be positioned to take advantage of this opportunity. Management believes their excellent service and outstanding customer care are keys to winning and keeping customers.

Customers who patronise free-standing stores differ from those in concessionary stores. Free-standing customers enter the shop with an intention or willingness to buy Jaeger products. Most Jaeger executives agree with Ball's observation, 'These customers are Jaeger types; they know and they wear our merchandise'. Ball also contends that many customers in concessions enter the host store for reasons other than shopping at Jaeger.

Management also suspects that there may be some significant differences between the shopping behaviour of men and women. According to retail folklore, women tend to spend longer in the store, handle and try on more items prior to making their choice, seek more advice and help from sales staff, expect more fitting-room attention and are less likely to use window and internal displays to determine their purchases. That said, not all Jaeger customers shop in the same way: Regent Street, London, customers tend to want fast service, whereas shoppers at, say, the Bristol store prefer a more leisurely pace.

Marketing goals

Obtaining and retaining customers through customer satisfaction is a primary marketing objective. Jaeger executives have recently begun to use the Jaeger Customer Account card database to obtain insight into customer retention. The key indicator is purchasing activity over periods of 6 months, 12 months and longer.

By 1994, customer satisfaction information will be available at branch level as customer comment cards are currently being introduced. Head office has also conducted mystery shopper and customer complaint-handling research. In a 1992 follow-up survey of customers who had previously complained (70 per cent response rate), Jaeger found that the vast majority of customers were 'satisfied' or 'very satisfied' with the way their complaint had been handled.

Jaeger merchandise

Jaeger Ladies launch two main collections a year: spring/summer and autumn/winter. Each comprises several ranges. Rather than introducing an entire collection at the beginning of each season, Jaeger's policy is to release merchandise gradually to the stores as the season progresses. The emphasis is still upon natural fibre. A selection of products and prices from the autumn/winter 1992 brochure appears in Exhibit 22.3.

Merchandising at Jaeger

Merchandising staff occupy a whole floor at the Broadwick Street head office. There are three areas of merchandising activity:

1. The merchandising/buying office which controls the acquisition of merchandise and its distribution to branches.
2. A visual merchandising (VM) department responsible for window and in-store display.
3. A retail stores development (RSD) department which is responsible for setting up and equipping new branches, in addition to refurbishing existing stores.

Stock levels are determined by branch sales. The more a branch sells, the more stock it will receive, in terms of both breadth and depth. The Regent Street store stocks everything that every other branch has, and more. The Glasgow, Edinburgh and Manchester branches are on the next tier, having somewhat less stock. The smallest concessions stock very few ranges with little depth within each range. All branches are linked to a computer/telephone system which enables store staff to find the nearest location of an item, should it not be in stock when a customer requests it. A request is entered into the system, which searches the stock records of the nearest three branches. This enables a staff member in, say, the Army and Navy concession in Guildford to tell a customer, 'Sorry, Madam, we don't have it in stock, but the High Street branch does. I'll bring it over if you like.' Where branches are not close together, Jaeger employs its own delivery people to pick up and drop off items. Logistically, it is sometimes necessary to arrange a special delivery service; at other times it fits with the driver's normal schedule.

Mick Webber is head of Visual Merchandising (VM). His merchandising goal is to make shopping at Jaeger such a pleasant experience that the customer is motivated to return often to the store: 'It's all about service, comfort and style.'

There are eight merchandising areas around the UK, in addition to London. Each area has its own merchandising staff. Their responsibility is to visit each store every two weeks to install window and in-store displays. Most of their efforts are directed at dressing windows in free-standers. One or two windows may be merchandised. The merchandisers work in collaboration with store managers to find a theme which emphasises new, fast-selling or specially promoted merchandise. Jaeger's policy is to change displays as new merchandise is introduced to the store. Having merchandised the window, the merchandiser then attends to the display fixtures next to the window, so that they complement the window and stimulate purchase. Webber commented: 'The window gets them interested; the adjacent fixtures sell the merchandise.'

Unlike some fashion stores Jaeger does not merchandise all its in-store floor space. 'There is plenty of space to walk around the store without hindrance. Our customers don't like to be hemmed in. Jaeger is not like a supermarket where people push past you! Space is all important,' was Webber's comment. Jaeger prefers to display just three or four sizes of an item from a range. Displaying a single item suggests that the store does not carry sufficient stock, whereas more than five items occupies too much space.

Webber divides Jaeger merchandise into four classes: evening wear, business wear, occasion wear (for example, weddings) and casual wear. Not all stores carry these four classes in equal proportion. 'Cheltenham,' observed Webber, 'has very little by way of casual wear. Our customers in that town buy Jaeger for evening wear.' Each area merchandiser tries to find natural divisions in the display area of each store, within which a single class of merchandise can be displayed. Boundaries between classes of merchandise may be marked by walls, alcoves, different floor coverings (for example, carpet at the front and wood at the rear), or different elevations. The goal of grouping similar merchandise together is to make it easier for shoppers to find the class of garment they want.

Colour flow within each class of merchandise is a dominant consideration in merchandising most large stores' interior fixtures. Webber likes to generate full-store shopping by placing warm colours at the back of the store to draw shoppers in. Thus colours are sequenced to lead shoppers to the back of the store. 'Merchandising by colour alone seems to infuriate a lot of our shoppers,' noted Webber. 'That's why we colour co-ordinate our merchandising within each class of clothing. On the other hand, some stores are so small that we find it difficult to accomplish. In a small store we don't define the areas as much. Instead we go by colour alone or by weight of the garment.'

Each store features one or more 'dress-out' areas. These are elevated display spaces, often lit, in which mannequins are dressed out in a set of clothing (known as an 'option') which is displayed on adjacent fixtures. The rest of the shop is merchandised to draw shoppers' attention to other options. 'In the dress-out areas, we display what is possible; the merchandising of the rest of the store suggests other permutations.' Jaeger's own range of accessories are merchandised close to the colour to which they relate.

Jaeger designs its own display fixtures in-house, but has them manufactured by outside contractors. There are fifteen different standard units. Each has its own low voltage, adjustable lighting. Most can be modified to meet local structural conditions and in-store traffic flows. The VM department has developed a *Standard Merchandising Procedures Manual*, which defines for branch and area staff the preferred location for each fixture and the preferred practices for merchandising the garments upon it. The fixtures are designed both to respond to and to influence in-store traffic flows (see example in Exhibit 22.4). In its recommendations for merchandising the fixtures, the *Manual* takes account of 'eye space' and 'reach space'. Eye space is space into which customers can not easily physically reach (above eye level, below knee level). This is reserved for visual, rather than tactile appeals to shoppers. Spaces which can easily be reached are reserved for promoting the tactile appeal of merchandise.

Webber makes very little use of point-of-sale (POS) print material. 'There should only be one showcard in the window and I like it to be something which has been featured in magazine advertising. Too much material detracts from the atmosphere of the store and draws the eye away from the merchandise. When we do use POS it is for a specific purpose. For example, we do use POS to encourage customers to open accounts.'

The merchandising task in concessions differs from that in free-standers. In concessions, many people use the Jaeger floor space as a route to some other department. They may be attracted to the merchandise and even handle it, but rarely do they buy. Often they do not replace items where they found them. Consequently, displays 'must be less fussy. They need to withstand frequent shopper interference. Service by the sales staff becomes more important when shoppers cannot easily find what they want.'

Only 5 per cent of concessions, mostly in the smaller chains, allocate Jaeger a permanent window display space. Jaeger's own merchandising staff build these displays. Some hosts rotate window displays and give Jaeger notice that it will have use of the space for a defined future period, normally one week. Then, Jaeger's merchandisers will attempt to dress the window in a way compatible with the free-standers. In other host stores, Jaeger's product may be used in window displays but the items and theme are selected by the host store's staff. An additional problem is that Jaeger merchandise may be mixed with other brands in these displays. Often, shoppers do not know that it is Jaeger merchandise featured. Concession managers are encouraged to negotiate window display space.

Many concessions refuse to allow the full expression of the Jaeger corporate colours in-store: black, white and natural wood. Others refuse the use of signage, and of Jaeger's own fixtures. Instead, these shop-in-shop managers must use whatever the host store provides.

Jaeger's store managers are encouraged to liaise with specialist departments at Broadwick Street, including Visual Merchandising. VM employs specialists who, on more than one occasion, have commented that 'the branches do an amateurish job when left to their own devices'. Webber expresses the head office view when he says that liaison should take place whenever possible. 'Particularly,' Duffin added, 'if the branch is doing something with brochures or window displays.' Branch management can call head office staff to discuss their ideas. According to Duffin, 'If there is a big change round in the branch, if there is a large cost involved, £2,000 or more, or if it is something the customer will see, then the area manager needs to become involved. Sometimes this can conflict with Jaeger's commitment to branch and area "ownership" of customer service initiatives.'

Recently, the Retail Stores Development (RSD) department completely refitted the Kensington branch. Branch management was allowed considerable input to some aspects of the refit: customer seating, coffee machines and tables, and fitting-room considerations, for example. The RSD department has developed a standard kit for branch refits. This kit is reviewed every six months. Webber feels that his Visual Merchandising department should have a much closer working relationship with RSD. 'I see things more visually than RSD. Our corporate colours are visually well suited to our display needs, because they do not drain colour away from the garments. RSD has sometimes used unnecessarily distracting colours. RSD sometimes give me badly configured spaces to work with. Instead of RSD installing their standard kit regardless of configuration, I would prefer us to look at the space and find out what it can offer us. The best store would be one where the display space is designed first and the building constructed around it!'

The TQM initiative

In September 1989, the Fashion Retail Division introduced a total quality management (TQM) initiative that management felt was in keeping with the company's tradition of high-quality materials, tailoring, design, customer service and corporate integrity. TQM was defined as: 'The efficient and effective use of all available resources, both internal and external, to achieve optimum levels of customer satisfaction with the quality of our products and all associated customer service provisions.' Total Quality was intended to become a permanent feature of the division's way of doing business. The strategy for building TQM was devised by a steering committee of six people including the division's retail director, John Ball, and group director of personnel, Ken Jackson. Jackson became TQM champion, allocating 50 per cent of his time to the project.

Several principles guided the TQM initiative, as the following extracts from the Divisional TQM strategy document show:

1. TQM is a long-term commitment, not a quick fix.
2. Senior management fully supports TQM.
3. There will be an open-door policy on employees' input with absolute confidence assured.
4. Foster team work by encouraging initiatives which are cross-functional and multi-disciplinary.
5. Successful initiatives should be made known throughout the Group.
6. Project teams and Quality Improvement teams should take ownership of their initiatives.
7. All business units should be working on at least one major project.
8. Managers should be trained in TQM principles and techniques.

The steering committee opposed the imposition of any single TQM model on Jaeger Ladies and other business units in the Division, feeling it was better that they should develop their own approach.

The Jaeger Ladies' TQM initiatives were in turn driven by a steering committee within the business unit. Jaeger Ladies' own approach to TQM was based on empowering individuals and groups to pursue their own initiatives, with a view to developing a fund of hands-on experience to share across the entire business unit. Rather than taking a strictly top-down approach, Jaeger opted to empower the lower levels of the organisation. Their brief was to pursue service excellence.

To set the TQM initiative moving, Jaeger Ladies' steering committee set up a number of major projects and quality improvement initiatives.

The first of these projects examined the company's relationships with its cloth suppliers. The second project focused on the quality of retail customer service (QRCS). Other projects focused on the company's policy and procedures on customer merchandise returns, the Jaeger customer account card, BS5750 systems being installed in factories and on internal customer–supplier relationships within Jaeger.

Quality improvement initiatives were more modest endeavours. The Division's steering committee suggested several: staff training in product knowledge, customer service training, range planning, sales budgeting, and customer service guarantees. The Jaeger Ladies' steering committee in turn invited staff to develop their own quality improvement initiatives. Several of these are detailed in Exhibit 22.5.

The Quality of Retail Customer Service (QRCS) project

The QRCS project was described as follows:

> The development and implementation of a new approach to identifying and defining from the customer's view point the most important and valued aspects of customer service at the retail point of sale. Thereafter, to introduce a method of monitoring regularly the levels of service actually being achieved by our branches in order to generate action plans for a process of continuous improvement.

The project team invested in research. Three populations were investigated. Loyal customers were surveyed to find out what they felt was important for excellent customer service. Potential customers were surveyed to find out their perceptions of Jaeger and their understanding of excellent service. Finally customer-contact staff, branch managers and head office personnel were surveyed to find out their definition of, and opinions on, excellent service. Respondents were asked to check a number of items on a five-point Likert scale ranging from very unimportant to very important.

In their report to the steering committee the QRCS project team noted: 'The results were extremely surprising. Firstly, the things we, as a business, felt were important for customers were at best seen to be fairly relevant (such as window and interior displays) and at worst totally irrelevant (such as display-ing methods of payment in windows.' Exhibit 22.6 contains further details. The project team's report stressed: 'It is the warm, human contact, not the displays, systems or "look" that are most important.'

When Jaeger's own employees were surveyed, it was revealed that the factors they thought important were not always the factors that customers, either loyals or potentials, thought were important. Questionnaire analysis found that branch managers placed more importance than loyal Jaeger cus-tomers upon:

- 'Window displays are eye-catching and encourage you into the branch.'
- 'Interior displays are attractive and appealing.'
- 'You are greeted immediately upon entering the branch.'

Area managers/head office personnel placed more importance than loyal Jaeger customers upon:

- 'Window displays are eye-catching and encourage you into the branch.'
- 'Interior displays are attractive and appealing.'
- 'There is a standard procedure for dealing with customer complaints.'

Loyal Jaeger customers placed more importance than branch managers, area managers and head office personnel upon:

- 'Assistants give you their honest opinion regarding your selection of garments.'
- 'You are invited to special customer events.'
- 'You can reserve garments.'
- 'The manager is available to assist you when required.'
- 'Staff serve one customer at a time.'
- 'Staff are wearing a representation of the stock available.'

Mystery shopping

During October 1991, mystery shopper research was undertaken. Rather than use an external market research agency, Jaeger executives opted to manage the project in-house. Fifty-eight mystery shoppers, demographically matched to the Jaeger Lady profile, were recruited to visit stores across the UK. After a formal briefing, pilot research was done in the London branches. After modifying the research design, a bench-mark study involving nearly three hundred visits to Jaeger Ladies shops was conducted over a one-month period. The objectives were to 'gain a global measure of service performance levels across the UK', and 'to identify the key areas needing particular emphasis for improvement as well as the more global picture of improvement opportunities'.

Each mystery shopper was expected to enter about five stores, make one or more purchases in each store and then complete a 26-item questionnaire, covering the topics listed in Exhibit 22.7. By way of financial incentive for participating in the research, the shoppers received a 33 per cent discount on any purchased merchandise. In addition to making purchases, the shoppers were set other tasks, for example, applying for a Jaeger Customer Account and returning some merchandise. Most questionnaire items required a response on a three- or four-point rating scale. A sample of the results appears in Exhibit 22.8. In addition to analysing the questionnaire data, Duffin and Jackson met with mystery shoppers in regional debriefings around the UK. As Duffin commented: 'These debriefs really give you the heart and soul of the results.' In these sessions, mystery shoppers described window displays and interior displays as being 'not very exciting, but not very boring either', 'no better than the competition', 'not very inspiring', and 'a little bit clinical'.

Today, mystery shopping activity is an on-going component of Jaeger's efforts to monitor customer satisfaction.

Quality Improvement Initiatives (QIIs)

As is clear from Exhibit 22.6, many branch- or area-initiated QIIs were undertaken in 1990 and 1991. The Jaeger Ladies business unit is organised into geographic regions. In early 1990, Jackson and Duffin visited each of these regions to attend the monthly meetings of branch managers, advise them on the TQM development and invite them to develop their own initiatives at the area level. Each area took ownership of two or three as their personal projects for a six-month period. In February 1991 at the annual Ladieswear conference, each area presented its own recommendations for improving performance.

Some QIIs seemed particularly relevant to the merchandising decisions facing Ball and his committee:

Ticketing

Ticket information was clear, but the information on the tickets was not what customers required. Neither was the positioning of the ticket on the merchandise easy to locate. Ticket location decisions were made by warehouse staff at Kings Lynn. They tended to do what was easy from their own operational perspective.

Fitting rooms

Fitting rooms were found to be too small for customers to try on clothes in comfort and privacy. There were insufficient numbers of hooks for clothes. The stool was inappropriate, having a rounded surface from which clothing easily slipped to the floor. Mirrors did not allow customers to examine their appearance from the rear. Several customers had commented that the rooms must have been designed by a 'male midget'.

In-store music

In 1990, some employees were bringing in their own tapes to play in the stores' music systems. Their tastes were not always sympathetic to those of Jaeger's customers. Neither was the music endorsed by the company particularly appealing to customers. A music project group surveyed 3,000 customers, revealing the music likes and dislikes of customers on a regional and, in some cases, branch level. A music company, Candy Rock, has been contracted by the area initiative group to supply music matched to area/store preferences. Tapes played on Saturdays tend to be more up-beat than tapes played mid-week. The area group also ensure that music systems are properly maintained by external contractors.

Brochures

Like most fashion companies, Jaeger had asked its advertising agency to create and produce its seasonal brochures. These are distributed in-store and sent direct to all account customers. Prior to the project, customer and staff input to brochure design had not been conscientiously sought. The agency now included three classes of merchandise in a high-quality full-colour product printed on heavy paper stock: items available generally across branches; different parts of the season's range (formal, weekend, businesswear); and special 'aspirational' items that were available only in one or two stores. In 1991 the initiative also resulted in Jaeger developing a video to display each season's new items. Customers can watch it in-store or take it home.

Provision for children and husbands

Very often Jaeger Ladies' customers shop in the company of their husbands or children. Their attitudes and actions can curtail what might otherwise be a pleasant shopping experience for the woman and a productive transaction for Jaeger. Action was needed to keep all accompanying persons entering a Jaeger branch occupied and content. It was not uncommon for some Jaeger shoppers to spend up to three hours in the store.

Carrier bags

The QII team examining carrier bags found that the 1989 models were unsuitable. The accessory bag, knitwear bag and coat bag were all too small. Furthermore they could not be stood upright on a flat surface, and customers felt the handles unappealingly masculine and too angular. They were not comfortable to hold and could not be slipped over the forearm when customers wanted to use their hands for other purposes.

Wrapping

Jaeger has long offered customers a Christmas wrapping service. The QII team found customers wanted this service year-round. Wrapping paper had been supplied on large rolls. Now customers wanted individual sheets and staff wanted smaller rolls. The team suggested that paper be colour co-ordinated to seasonal themes.

In February 1992, the Jaeger TQM steering committee launched an initiative inviting branches to contribute ideas for quality improvement. Ideas collected at branch level are disseminated through branch and area meetings. In addition, a newsletter is produced at London head office, summarising all suggestions for quality improvement. As a result, a large number of improvements have been introduced at branch level. Head office tends to endorse and recommend some items as suitable for chain-wide adoption.

The future

As Jaeger moved into 1993, the TQM programme is attempting to promote a corporate culture focused on producing 'customer delight', not merely 'customer satisfaction'. Jaeger management wants the shopping experience at Jaeger Ladies to be so delightful that it produces not just good word-of-mouth, but a truly emphatic and enthusiastic endorsement of the Jaeger experience.

Exhibit 22.1 Fashion retail division, 1991, 1990 (£m.)

	1991	1990
Turnover	150.8	144.7
Operating profit	1.9[1]	9.5
Net assets	57.9	72.8
Employees at year end	4,635	4,944

Jaeger Ladies (figures from 1991)

	Free-standers	Concessions
Turnover per sq. ft	£425	£424
Contribution to Jaeger Ladies' total turnover[2]	56%	37%
Average retail transaction	£118	unknown
Average floor space (sq. ft)	1,391	625

Note: [1] Much of the fall in operating profit between 1990 and 1991 is due to exceptional, non-recurrent expenses being incurred. Gross profit percentage was the same in 1991 as in 1990.

[2] Total does not add to 100 per cent, because 7 per cent of Jaeger's sales were through clearance shops.

Exhibit 22.2 CV's statement of values

- *Competitive ability.* We must be competitive in the market place, today and tomorrow, maintaining our products' edge and identity against the competition. We compete on quality, service and value.
- *Quality, service and value.* The key characteristics we must aim for in every respect of the Group's activities are quality, service and value. Our products sell on this premise and the best way to cement partnerships with customers is by adding value in this way. We need to deliver value for money through manufacturing excellence coupled with appropriate commercially focused research. Our policy is to focus on quality in all that we do: quality products for our consumers, and quality service to our customers.
- *Taking advantage of change.* Change is constant in markets, in ideas, in people, and in technology. We therefore need to have decisive leadership and fast management reaction to secure maximum advantage from such changes.
- *Committed people.* Committed people are key to our Group's success. People must know what is required of them and should be given help to meet those expectations. Our standards should be demanding and this will require appropriate rewards.
- *Clear objectives.* Our Group must have clarity of purpose to compete effectively. Its strategy must be clearly communicated and the objectives which flow from the strategy, both corporate and individual, must be understood. Objectives must be attainable and their achievement should stretch the abilities of those for whom they are set. Managers must build their competence to improve their chances of complete success. Each manager will be held accountable for the attainment of his or her objectives.

▶

- *Simple organisation.* We must concentrate on the key tasks of the business and all decisions should be taken as close as possible to the point of impact. The organisation should reflect the market and customer focus of the business, with as few layers as possible.
- *Openness.* An openness of style in involvement of people in decisions that affect them is of the greatest importance. It requires management trust and an ability to listen, ability to weigh-up and decide.
- *Responsibilities.* Our group recognises its responsibilities to our shareholders, employees, customers, suppliers, governments and society. It will seek to keep its responsibilities to them in balance.

Exhibit 22.3 A selection from the autumn/winter 1992 collection

Item	Price (£)
Botany wool roll-neck sweater	59
Wool twill trousers	109
Wool blouson jacket	125
Wool and cashmere skirt	89
Silk shirt	129
Printed silk chiffon scarf	49
Leather skirt	199
Wool, cashmere and angora coat	349
Cotton mix, 3/4 raincoat	229
Cotton check shirt	75
Jaeger jeans	65
Wool gloves	7

Exhibit 22.4 Extract from the Standard Merchandising Procedures Manual

Use of fixtures

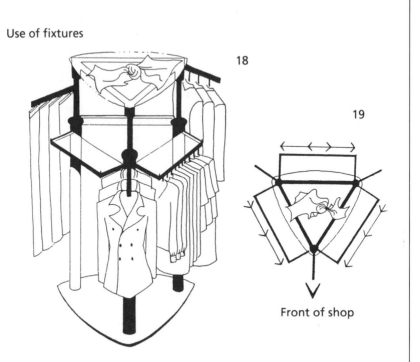

18

19

Front of shop

Tower units

Tower units are a perfect way of highlighting capsule collections or new merchandise. They are also useful for hanging printed fabrics which need separating.

The rails should be forward facing, with the centre arm facing the customer as she enters the shop or department. This arm should be simply dressed with jackets, coats or dresses (not skirts).

The merchandise on the adjoining rails should also face to the front. The merchandise on the third rail of the triangle can be arranged to face either way (see Sketch 19).

The centre glass shelf should be very simply dressed with a single accessory. The narrow glass shelves above the rails should be kept completely clear.

Exhibit 22.5 Customer service excellence: the loyal customer's view (combined loyal/potential customers' opinions ranked in parentheses)

Rank order		Relative importance	Factor
1	(1)	15	Staff friendly and approachable.
2 =	(2 =)	11	Service is consistent on every visit.
2 =	(2 =)	11	Assistants give you their honest opinion regarding your selection of garments.
4	(4)	11	You can reserve garments.
5	(7)	10	Staff can quickly locate any stock requested.
6		10	Staff provide helpful advice while you are trying on garments.
7 =		10	Staff serve one customer at a time.
7 =	(5)	9	Staff are not always waiting to pounce on you.
9		9	All enquiries/requests are dealt with quickly and efficiently within the timescale promised.
10		8	The manager is available to assist you when required.
11		8	Staff are aware of current fashion trends and are able to discuss them with you.
12	(10)	8	Fitting rooms are of a high standard.
13		8	You are greeted immediately upon entering the branch.
14 =		7	Interior displays are attractive and appealing.
14 =		7	The full range of colours/sizes available in a branch is on display to facilitate self-service.
16 =	(6)	7	Window displays are eye-catching and encourage you into the branch.
16 =		7	Alterations advice is available.
18	(9)	6	The branch looks well stocked.
19		6	Merchandise which is advertised is always in stock.
20		6	Staff are aware of all advertised lines.

Notes: Ranked (8) for combined loyal/potential customers was 'Merchandise in windows is clearly priced'. This factor is not in the loyal customers' top twenty. The column headed 'relative importance' indicates the relative contribution of each factor to excellent service. 'Friendly and approachable staff' (ranked # 1) is rated 50 per cent more important than 'staff can quickly locate any stock requested' (ranked #5).

Exhibit 22.6 Jaeger Ladies Quality Improvement Initiatives (QIIs)

1. Ticketing	9. Special order book
2. Fitting rooms	10. Packaging
3. In-store music	11. Wrapping
4. Dry-cleaning	12. Alterations
5. Staff room visuals	13. Telephone service
6. Brochures	14. Carrier bags
7. Provision for husbands	15. Receipt wallets
8. Provision for children	16. Customer profiling

Exhibit 22.7 Mystery shopping question topic list

- External appearance of branch.
- Merchandise pricing in window display.
- Greeting upon entry.
- Staff approachability.
- Staff availability to help.
- Manager availability.
- Is the manager recognisable?
- Number of customers served simultaneously by one staff member.
- Efficiency/promptness of enquiry handling.
- Branch stock levels.
- Staff awareness of fashion trends.
- Speed of stock location.
- Staff awareness of advertised lines.
- Helpfulness of staff advice.
- Honesty of staff advice.
- Standard of fitting room.
- Availability of advertised stock.
- Colour/size availability.
- Selection within size.
- Availability of alterations advice.
- Availability of garment reservation.
- Eye-catching quality of window displays.
- Eye-catching quality of interior displays.
- Speed of till transaction.
- Comparability of service in other Jaeger branches.
- Consistency of service compared to other branches.

Note: These topic areas were selected from an original list of 180 customer service variables. The original list was shown to 160 loyal Jaeger customers, 140 potential Jaeger customers (aged over 35, affluent, social class A or B) and retail staff, who were all asked to select the top 20 factors and place them in rank order. The 26 factors listed here were felt to be most significant indicators of excellent customer service.

Exhibit 22.8 Samples of results from 1991 mystery shopping research

1. Thirty-three per cent of customers were greeted on entry or shortly after entry to the branch.
2. Sixty-five per cent of customers found advice while trying on garments to be either non-existent or very limited.
3. Seventy-five per cent of merchandise returns were handled well.
4. On three visits staff did not know how to action a refund.
5. Window displays were thought to be rather dull and unattractive.
6. Interior displays were generally regarded as quite dull. This was a particular problem in concessions.
7. Ninety-five per cent thought the merchandise in window displays was clearly priced.
8. On 76 visits the garment that customers wanted to buy was not in stock. Of these, 27 items were in the popular sizes 10, 12 and 14. Seventy-one shoppers purchased *exactly* what they had wanted prior to entering the branch. Free-standers are thought to be better stocked than concessions.
9. The standard of fitting rooms was 'fairly high' although many problems were identified: too few hooks (62 visits), too small (53), better mirrors needed (23), poor lighting (11), poor privacy (6).
10. On 25 occasions when an item was not available in a customer's size, no attempt was made to source the item from other Jaeger outlets.
11. Staff were generally very quick at locating requested stock. Concessions performed less well than free-standers.
12. The standard of Jaeger service tended to be very consistent across branches.
13. The exterior appearance of the branches was rather bland, being neither welcoming, nor unwelcoming.

Better Buy Superstores plc

Understanding merchandising and space management in food retailing

Nitin Sanghavi
Manchester Business School

Context

Having recently been appointed as 'Marketing Director–Superstores' at Better Buy Superstores, Peter Jones was now scrutinising the monthly return figures for each store. Charged with the task of improving these sobering figures, he wondered what should be done about the poor performance of a number of outlets. The Bury superstore was a good case in point; its figures showed a substantial shortfall from the level of sales required to meet company profitability targets, with particularly poor figures in non-food sales. However, he had only limited funds with which to redesign and refit, together with the shortest possible 'pay-back' period in which to recoup them.

Background

Better Buy Superstores plc was one of the leading supermarket and superstore operators. With 90 supermarkets (averaging 15,000 sq. ft selling space) and 60 superstores (each with over 25,000 sq. ft selling space), in 1991 the group turnover reached £1,400 million. Profitability, however, was low at only 2.3 per cent of turnover. This compared with the industry leader, Sainsbury, which achieved a margin of some 7 per cent of turnover.

Based in Birmingham, most Better Buy stores were located in the Midlands and north-west of England. The company was endeavouring to extend its operations into the south, but competition for new superstore sites was fierce against the market leaders, Sainsbury and Tesco. Better Buy had been successful in obtaining a number of sites, however, and saw superstores as the key element of its future development strategy. In comparison with its main competitors, Better Buy management was notably concerned with its ability to successfully merchandise various product ranges. Thus the Bury superstore typified the company's problem, performing relatively badly both overall and in certain product areas. It clearly warranted further attention.

Bury superstore

Located at the end of the high street, the Better Buy superstore in Bury had two entrances/exits. The first of these was from the high street and the other from the car park, situated to the right rear of the store. The net sales area was approximately 40,000 sq. ft, of which around 60 per cent was allocated to food and 40 per cent to non-food: a ratio determined by Better Buy policy.

Better Buy had purchased the store from the Pioneer Society in 1990, which had used it as a department store. The store layout following its conversion to a superstore is shown in Figure 23.1. The non-food department was placed adjacent to the high street entrance, and a turnstile entrance into the non-food departments was provided. However, it was estimated that 80 per cent of customers used the car park entrance.

The store was not carpeted and lighting was provided by standard neon fittings throughout. A range of sales promotion activities were in evidence at the superstore. Display equipment was normally high, free-standing gondola units, which were also used for fruit and vegetables. There were no front presentation fittings for textiles and clothing. An in-store bakery produced freshly baked bread and pastries.

Over the period from October 1992 to January 1993, the store's average weekly turnover was approximately £128,600, of which around £26,700 was non-food. Personnel and 'other' expenses were running at 5.9 per cent and 10.7 per cent of turnover respectively. Details of various product groups and their

Table 23.1 Better Buy superstore – Bury. Section – Food

Subsection department	Average weekly turnover (£)	Weekly net sales (£)	Approx sq. ft	Sales participation (%)	Space participation (%)	Average margins (%)
Grocery	42,714	40,032	11,187	42.39	47.46	11
Butchery	13,303	13,303	1,056	14.09	4.48	23
Toiletries	5,457	4,644	262	4.92	1.11	21
Provisions	13,825	12,825	4,487	13.58	19.04	22
Delicatessen	3,858	3,283	1,358	3.48	5.76	24
Wines/Spirits	10,094	8,591	3,390	9.10	14.38	10
Tobacco/ Cigarettes	3,598	3,062	161	3.24	0.68	6
Fruit & Veg	7,417	7,167	1,268	7.59	5.38	21
Bakery	1,522	1,522	402	1.61	1.71	20
Food total	101,788	94,429	23,571	100.0	100.0	17.55

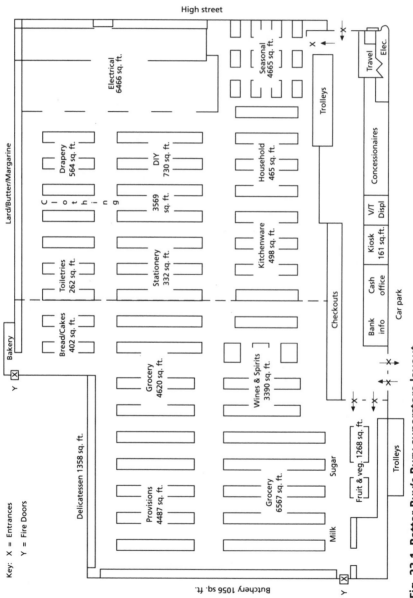

Fig. 23.1 Better Buy's Bury superstore layout

Table 23.2 Better Buy superstore – Bury. Section – Non-food

Subsection department	Average weekly turnover (£)	Weekly net sales (£)	Approx sq. ft	Sales participation (%)	Space participation (%)	Average margins (%)
Drapery	1,672	1,439	564	6.27	3.26	30
Electrical	7,053	6,003	6,466	26.18	37.40	18.5
Stationery	1,411	1,201	332	5.24	1.92	31
Clothing	5,116	4,504	3,569	19.64	20.64	29
Seasonal	4,169	3,548	4,665	15.47	26.98	29
DIY	1,660	1,413	730	6.16	4.23	28
Kitchenware	2,937	2,500	498	10.90	2.88	29
Household	2,732	2,325	465	10.14	2.69	31
Non-food total	26,750	22,933	17,289	100.00	100.00	28.18

subsections, together with their sales and square footage breakdowns, are shown in Tables 23.1 and 23.2. The sales/expenses analysis is given in Table 23.3. The profit (loss) analysis based on the present turnover is given in Table 23.4. The estimated costs involved in re-equipping and fitting-out the store are indicated in Table 23.5.

In February 1993 Bury superstore was trading unprofitably. Moreover, Morrisons – a large regional food operator – was planning to open a large superstore only half a mile away within the next few months. Peter Jones wanted to achieve profitability within a relatively short period of time. He looked at the pricing structure, which he found to be quite favourable against the competition, and he had already undertaken various marketing initiatives such as local advertising, money-off coupons, special promotions and introducing different brands, including own labels, into various product ranges. He also undertook several cost-cutting measures, converting more full-time staff into part-time, reducing the number of 'baggers' at the checkouts, obtaining better discounts and extended payment terms from local suppliers, and so on.

In addition to the above measures, Peter Jones realised that the space productivity of the store would have to be improved. To do this he would need to examine and assess merchandising aspects of the store, especially the store layout and space planning for the various departments. Keen to put forward recommendations to the board for approval to improve space productivity, he was, however, unsure as to how he should proceed and what information would be required to improve space productivity over the short, medium and long term.

Table 23.3 Better Buy superstore – Bury

Department	Weekly turnover (£)	Weekly net sales (ex. VAT) (£)	Profit £	Profit % participation	Personnel expenses £	Personnel expenses % participation	Other expenses* £	Other expenses* % participation	Total square feet	Sales per square foot
Food										
Grocery	42,714	40,032	4,404	20.98	1,490	19.60	3,770	27.38	11,187	3.58
Butchery	13,303	13,303	3,060	14.58	1,320	17.36	356	2.58	1,056	12.60
Provisions	13,825	12,825	2,821	13.44	985	12.96	1,512	10.98	4,487	2.86
Delicatessen	3,858	3,283	788	3.75	328	4.32	458	3.33	1,358	2.42
Wines /Spirits	10,094	8,591	859	4.09	258	3.39	1,142	8.29	3,390	2.53
Cigarettes/Tobacco	3,598	3,062	184	0.88	153	2.01	54	0.39	161	19.02
Fruit & Veg	7,417	7,167	1,505	7.17	430	5.66	427	3.10	1,268	5.65
Bakery	1,522	1,522	305	1.45	183	2.41	136	0.99	402	3.78
Toiletries	5,457	4,644	975	4.64	418	5.50	88	0.64	262	17.73
Non-food										
Drapery	1,672	1,439	432	2.06	173	2.28	190	1.38	564	2.55
Clothing	5,116	4,504	1,306	6.22	450	5.92	1,203	8.74	3,569	1.26
Electrical	7,053	6,003	1,111	5.29	420	5.53	2,179	15.82	6,466	0.93
Stationery	1,411	1,201	372	1.77	132	1.73	112	0.81	332	3.62
Seasonal	4,169	3,548	1,029	4.90	248	3.26	1,572	11.42	4,665	0.76
DIY	1,660	1,413	395	1.88	180	2.36	246	1.79	730	1.94
Kitchenware	2,937	2,500	725	3.46	225	2.96	168	1.22	498	5.02
Household	2,732	2,325	721	3.44	209	2.75	157	1.14	465	5.00
Total	128,538	117,362	20,992	100.00	7,602	100.00	13,770	100.00	40,860	

*Other expenses allocated on the basis of space occupied (1 sq. ft = 33.7 pence)

Table 23.4 Better Buy superstore – Bury

Sales/Profit (Loss) analysis (actual – based on present turnover)

Net sales area	= 40860 sq. ft approx.	
	Food	23,571 sq. ft approx (sales) £4.00 per sq. ft (58%)
	Non-food	17,289 sq. ft approx (sales) £1.33 per sq. ft (42%)
Average weekly turnover (gross)	= Food Non-food Total	£101,788 (79%) 26,750 (21%) £128,538
Net weekly sales (exclu. VAT)	= Food Non-food Total	£94,429 22,933 £117,362
Estimated margins of net sales	= Food Non-food	15.78% 26.56%
Estimated gross profit per week	= Food Non-food Total	£14,901 6,091 £20,992 (16.33%)
Estimated expenses per week	= Personnel Other expenses Total	£7,602 (5.91%) 13,770 (10.71%) £21,372
Net profit (loss) per week	= Gross profit less expenses Net (loss) = 0.3% of turnover	£20,992 21,372 (£380) per week

Case study questions

1. *What actions should Peter Jones take to improve space productivity at the Better Buy superstore in Bury, in the short, medium and long term?*

2. *How should he evaluate current sales/space performance of the Bury store? Does he require any additional information? If so, what kind and why?*

3. *Should he make any changes to the store layout? Where?*

4. *How should he evaluate the performance of various departments within the Bury store?*

Table 23.5 Superstore cabinet fixtures/fitting out costs

Non-food

Fixtures

1. Free standing 6 ft high gondolas – heavy duty metal type fixtures with peg-board backing, base, plus three shelves included – cost of £600 per metre (approx.)
2. Hooks to go on peg-boards – assorted sizes – £150 per metre (approx.)
3. Zig-zag rails to hang clothes – 1 metre length – £90 per rail (approx.)
4. Shelf-dividers, front risers, shelf backers, A4, A3 ticket holders – all in assorted sizes, combined cost £80 per metre (approx.)
5. Wire baskets – 1 metre length – £140 each (approx.). Small wire baskets 2 ft length – £60 each (approx.).

Fitting out costs

1. Fitting out cost for the above fixture £50 per metre (approx.)

Food

1. *New chiller unit* – for dairy, butter, fruit, vegetables, chilled meats etc.
   £850   per metre – for cabinet
   £1,050   per metre – fitting out costs (including plant, electrical work, installation)
   ——
   £1,900   per metre – total cost

2. *New freezer unit* – for frozen foods
   £1,500   per metre – for cabinet
   £1,050   per metre – fitting out cost as above
   ——
   £2,550   per metre – total cost

3. *Grocery fixtures* – free standing 6 ft high gondolas, heavy duty metal type fixtures with peg-board backing, base plus shelves included
   £500   per metre – fixtures
   £50   per metre – fitting out charge
   ——
   £550   per metre – total cost

4. *Bakery fixtures*
   (a)   Metal racks/wicker basket type fixtures
            £410   per metre approx. for fixtures
   (b)   Serve-over type cabinets with storage drawers etc.
            £720   per metre – fixtures (including equipment)
            £140   per metre – fitting out cost
            ——
            £860   per metre – total cost

5. *Wines and Spirits* – new wooden fixtures with racks, baskets etc.
   £500   per metre – fixtures
   £90   per metre – fitting out costs
   ——
   £590   per metre – total cost

6. *Re-cladding existing chiller/freezer unit*
   Assuming the unit is in reasonable condition
   £70   per metre – re-cladding cost
   £1,090   per metre – fitting out costs (labour costs higher than when putting in a
            new unit)
   ——
   £1,160   per metre – total cost

Note: All figures are approximate – based on average heavy duty metal type fixtures with standard accessories included in price, e.g. base plus three shelves etc.

   All prices are exclusive of VAT.

   Prices are based on the requirement of an average size superstore, e.g. 35,000 sq. ft.

References and further reading

Mason, J. B. and M. L. Mayer (1990), *Modern Retailing: Theory and Practice*, Business Publications, Plano, Texas.

Davidson, W. R., P. J. Sweeney and R. W. Stampfl (1990), *Retailing Management*, John Wiley, New York.

Part Seven

COMMUNICATING WITH CUSTOMERS

The use of sales promotion and sponsorship are explained by Malcolm Hughes, who describes 'How the Boots Company reached a precise market target using music'. The case shows how this well established and traditional retail company appealed to a young and volatile market segment by sponsoring a pop group's UK tour.

Communication of a different sort is the focus of 'Marks & Spencer Financial Services – where do they go from here?' In this case, Steve Worthington demonstrates the benefits of a successful store card strategy, drawing comparisons with the activities of Sears Roebuck in the US.

Staying with the theme of retail financial services, 'The marketing of place' draws attention to the important role of the designed environment. Steven Greenland's case illustrates the many, often conflicting, elements and objectives of retail design and refurbishment programmes.

Communicating with customers – sales promotion

How the Boots Company reached a precise market target using music

Malcolm Hughes
Watermill Consultants

Context

The Boots Company is undoubtedly one of the best known and respected trading names in the UK, having undergone a complete repositioning from 'cash chemist' of the 1950s to modern multi-department store of the 1990s. But despite having absorbed a number of other businesses on the way, notably Timothy Whites in the retail sector, Boots has still managed to retain its essentially local feel.

Yet Boots has changed out of all recognition since Jesse Boot was collecting herbs for remedies. It now sells a wide range of music products (both recordings and equipment), photographic goods, food and confectionery. Clearly, the wider the range of merchandise offered, the more comprehensive the spread of competing retailers: many of which will have established reputations as specialists in their respective territories.

Boots recognised that in the fight for target markets it must adopt contemporary promotion practices. But Boots also has another problem. In the fiercely competitive market for teenage cosmetics, it needs to be consonant with the tastes and aspirations of young women in the 13–17 age group. This is a highly esoteric area, riddled with subtle shifts of fashion and bombarded with specialist magazines, each saturated with advertising for products focused on this volatile group. How could a large and respected drug store chain identify with this shifting army without seeming embarrassingly out of its depth; 'trendy' in the worst senses of BBC 'yoof' programming and hence alienating its mission?

Pop music as a sales promotion device

There is a vast, global market for products linked to popular music – that is, merchandise which is not the music itself, but associated with the groups themselves – books, posters, print items of all kinds, clothing and sponsored products such as drinks, foods, toys and videos. Those who manage relationships in this area are true 'thin ice' operators, finely tuned to shifting tastes and fashions.

It was into this minefield that Boots decided to venture to promote the relaunch of its range of '17' branded cosmetics by sponsoring the promotion of a pop group tour of the UK.

The relaunch of '17' cosmetics, one of the largest branded ranges of cosmetics ever created by a retail chain, was itself very demanding of fashion judgements. Girls in the 13–17 age bracket are notoriously aware of tiny changes of image; but the link with a stylish pop music group could give the relaunch the extra spin needed to lift the product range out of the ordinary in a competitive market.

The market planners at Boots then ran into several problems at the same time. Pop music events are arranged months, even years ahead, mainly because of the shortage of suitable sites and venues for large audiences in the UK. Who could forecast which group, which music, would be fashionable at that distance? The company could find itself promoting a pop group out of favour at that time. Secondly, popular music is an international interest. If a group becomes 'hot' it may embark on a worldwide tour to capitalise on its ephemeral fame. There would be little purpose in a joint promotion with a pop group who might be in Japan during the relaunch. Further, the pop world is notorious for unacceptable behaviour – unacceptable to adult authority that is – and the association of a cosmetic product for young women with drugs and violence, for example, could destroy the brand image, perhaps terminally. Lastly, the pop music business cannot be described as the accountant's favourite industry: its attitude towards costs and validating expenditure is flippant, its adherence to budgets is legendary by its absence.

The author of this case study spent a memorable summer vacation from university as a 'roadie' (a driver/loader) for a 'supergroup's' European leg of a world tour. To describe the proceedings as 'an expensive nightmare' cannot begin to do justice to the meaning of the words.

The problem

You are asked to assume the role of the marketing manager of the Boots '17' range of teenage cosmetics and to write a working outline for an internal planning meeting to address the following objectives:

- How would you select a pop group to sponsor, given the problems outlined above?
- Since Boots are a national retailer, how would you ensure full UK coverage for the promotion?
- What benefits would you require in return for your investment and how would you measure and assess your return in a form that would be

understandable to the senior management of Boots?

- Give a detailed plan of how you would run a pop concert to maximise the '17' brand presence, including pre-show publicity, concert events, post-venue exploitation and any other mechanisms that you feel are appropriate and acceptable.
- How would you seek to involve and enthuse Boots staff at all levels and areas in the promotional activity?
- What systems would you put in place to cope with the need for disaster limitation (e.g. the arrest of the lead singer on a criminal charge)?
- How would you maximise the public relations benefits of the promotion?
- Describe your planning and control priorities as the promotion proceeds, giving particular attention to expenditure restraint.
- Set out a plan for the deployment of your own marketing staff as the events proceed and outline the logistics of such an operation.

The solutions

The first action that the Boots Company took was to hire the services of a specialist promotional advisor (West Nally), who made a study of the market relationships between the 13–17 segment and those pop groups which were beginning to 'emerge' as particularly appealing to this segment. The trick was to avoid those groups which were already established such as Wham! or Duran Duran and hence too expensive and unavailable, and to pick a group just starting to rouse popular interest, which also had the right 'clean' image for Boots to associate with.

West Nally recommended 'King', a middle-of-the-road group who had enjoyed one hit record and seemed likely to grow in popularity with the key market. The group were not associated with unacceptable behaviour and reflected well in the music and general media. The group were also commercially astute enough to see that a sponsored promotion with Boots would enhance their appeal with the record buying and concert gong public. They were also not unacceptable to the parents of the 13–17 age group – clear influences in this market.

A national tour was planned for the winter concert season, taking in around a dozen venues from Aberdeen to St Austell, with two concerts planned for Nottingham so that the Boots manufacturing and head office staff could attend. The Boots Company, like all large businesses, employs many young women in various roles as well as the parents of the same age group, so this utilisation of the promotion was significant.

An extensive programme of public relations activity was carried out to gain coverage in the music and feature press aimed at this age group. Details of the tour and of Boots' involvement were also carried by local and national adult press, national and local radio and on music television programmes. So successful was this pre-tour publicity that no additional paid advertising was judged to be required.

All the tour venues were heavily '17' branded with the usual items of clothing, hats, posters and other publicity material about 'King'. The '17' symbol and logo was widely visible and coupons were distributed at the concerts to stimulate store visits and brand purchasing after the event.

All 1,000 stores of the Boots network displayed bold point-of-purchase material featuring 'King' and the relaunched range of cosmetics during the period running up to the tour. This material also gave details of a competition over the same period (pre-Christmas), the prizes being '17' product packs and free tickets to the concert – with a chance to meet the band in person!

Special efforts were made at the Nottingham venue to introduce the band to as many staff as possible, efforts which were supported by a 'tour' of the head office and local store visits. A small team of Boots and West Nally marketing staff, including a marketing accountant, a merchandiser and a public relations executive, travelled with the tour at all times so that problems could be resolved on the spot without constantly referring to head office.

The results

From Boots' point of view, the 'King' sales promotion was a cost-effective success. There were a number of reasons for this verdict, some quantitative and some qualitative:

- On the numbers side, there was a near 20 per cent increase in brand volume sales across the range. This was higher than forecast for the basic relaunch pack on the evidence of previous experience and constituted a record improvement for the product.
- The concert series was a significant success with all venues sold out and additional concerts being required in several of the towns and cities.
- Over 7,000 teenage girls entered the competition for free seats and cosmetics. In comparison with other brand competitions this was again judged to be a very good level of response given the highly competitive nature of the market and the target audience.
- There was a strong positive feedback in letters and through the branches from the target market and parents with respect to the relevance and acceptability of the promotion.
- There was a good level of staff support and enthusiasm, particularly in the younger age groups who enjoyed the idea of their employer becoming more youth orientated and 'trendy'.
- The concert series passed off without any serious incidents and the publicity surrounding the tour was wholly beneficial. It also turned out that the tour found 'King' at the peak of popularity–identified as a future 'supergroup' and much sought after; this was an unexpected and welcome bonus.
- The final costs of around £200,000 were well within budget and the financial aspects of the promotion were well controlled throughout by the tour team.

Conclusions

The success of the Boots/King promotion depended on a substantial amount of give and take on each side as the two cultures sought to work together for mutual benefit. The appointment of the specialist agency West Nally was clearly a key ingredient in forming this essential bridge between the two sides.

Great care was taken in the planning phase ensuring that all the elements of the promotion were in place, that the relationships between Boots and King were comfortable, that staff and branches were closely involved. Care was also taken at all levels to ensure that the interests of the many parties present were taken into account – the brand publicists, agents, record companies, venue staff and management, promoters, security, authorities, and so forth, all had to be dealt with and their rights safeguarded since their opposition could bring the proceedings to a standstill.

The mobile management team proved invaluable in representing the sponsors' interests and in solving the hundreds of small daily problems which are inherent in a tour of this kind. In the event, everyone behaved well, nobody was arrested and the tour passed without difficulties. There was a degree of risk, however, as there is with all third-party sales promotion and it is easy to imagine the sigh of relief from all concerned as the lights finally went out at the last venue!

It is possible, without too much exaggeration, to trace the line from the first successful pop sales sponsorship through to the global impact of Band Aid five years later.

Marks & Spencer Financial Services
Where do they go from here?

Steve Worthington
Manchester Business School

Context

This case examines why the pre-eminent retailers in the UK and the US have diversified their operations into retailing financial services and raises the question of whether this has been a good long-term strategic decision. There are many similarities between Marks & Spencer and Sears Roebuck. Both were founded in the mid-1880s (1884 and 1886 respectively), both have large market shares in the products that they trade in, both represent 'value' to the consumer and both have sought to widen and deepen their customer franchise by moving into the provision of financial services. There are also, of course, many differences, particularly reflected in the different 'cultures' of their respective countries of origin. These differences need to be considered in determining which direction their future strategy should take.

Marks & Spencer

The largest clothing retailer in the UK, Marks & Spencer has 17 per cent of the domestic market. It also has around 4 per cent of the retail food business and thus manages to combine a mass market clothing operation with an upmarket convenience food operation. This combination, of being a dominant retailer in one market and an upmarket niche player in another, may help to explain why Marks & Spencer has had mixed success in their attempts to develop new markets in other countries. It also provides a backdrop to the decision to move into financial services, as this both offers new products to their existing customers, as well as providing for diversification into new markets.

In the early 1980s Marks & Spencer realised that its customers were increasingly interested in paying for their purchases by plastic card, instead of the existing payment mechanisms of cash or cheque. Worthington (1992) describes the evolution of the various means of payment and of consumer attitudes to the taking of credit. Until then, Marks & Spencer had maintained a firm policy against accepting credit cards, issued by the major card associations such as Visa and Mastercard, and charge cards, issued by American Express and Diners Club. The main reason for this was that Marks & Spencer did not want to become involved in the expensive arena of merchant service charges: fees which the retailer pays the credit and charge card organisations to compensate them partially for the costs involved in issuing and administering the cards. However, Marks & Spencer had seen a lot of other retailers moving into the plastic card market and had noted the benefits of a store card. These included the strengthening of the relationship between the store and the consumer and the prospect of additional lines of profit through the sale of related financial services to the store card holders. For a wider discussion of the advantages of store cards see Worthington (1986) and Burke (1989).

Along with other retailers, Marks & Spencer had developed budget accounts for their customers to enable them to have access to credit in order to spend in their stores. With a corporate culture that is both cautious and wary of relying on outsiders, it was no surprise that Marks & Spencer then trialed a plastic store card in Scotland, nor that in 1985 they formed St Michael Financial Services to take over the running of the budget accounts from Citibank and to take over the Scottish trial from North West Securities. The new company was to launch a retail card throughout the UK, to be known as the Chargecard, and in 1988 its name was changed to Marks & Spencer Financial Services, a wholly owned subsidiary of Marks & Spencer plc, with its managing director now a main board director of the parent company.

The Chargecard

The Marks & Spencer Chargecard now has over 2.5 million account customers and over three million plastic cards in circulation, making it the largest individual store card in the UK. The growth of the Marks & Spencer card programme has been accompanied by heavy investment in both methods and technology. Marks & Spencer is regarded as a pioneer in the use of credit-scoring techniques and in the rapidity of its response to Chargecard applications and customer enquiries. Each of the 50 largest stores has an instant-credit service facility, where an application can be keyed in, credit-checked and credit-scored on the spot. If an application is accepted, an account number can be generated immediately by the store's system, a credit limit can be established and the customer can begin using the credit there and then. The whole process can take as little as five minutes and the actual plastic card will be delivered to the customer within 10 days. An interesting feature of Marks & Spencer's security system is that the card must be taken to a Marks & Spencer store to be validated before use. This is intended to prevent the interception of cards in the post and their subsequent fraudulent use.

Because Marks & Spencer still decline to accept other credit or charge cards, it has also been able to develop point-of-sale software for the Chargecard without having to worry about the wider needs of the industry. This has resulted in a very strong authorisation process at the point of sale, with numerous controls to prevent cardholders spending over their credit limit, or those in payment arrears from using their cards for delinquent spending. However, the system is still sensitive enough not to inconvenience the vast majority of customers by needless authorisation calls.

To promote the card Marks & Spencer rely largely on in-store promotions within its *circa* 300 UK stores. This consists of take-one leaflets, reminder adverts and the occasional blitz campaign where, for example, employees hand out leaflets to customers as they walk through the doors of the store. Incentives to acquire a Chargecard are often based around prize competitions and the fact that Chargecard holders are entitled to free copies of the quarterly Marks & Spencer magazine, as well as invitations to sale previews and fashion evenings.

Marks & Spencer Financial Services has its headquarters in Chester and employs around 560 full-time staff, who perform all the functions associated with a credit card operation such as marketing, insurance, processing of payments and debt recovery. There are financial services desks in most stores, but while employees can help customers to fill in application forms, they are not authorised to discuss details of accounts or to give financial advice. All this is done from Chester and in this way it is felt that Marks & Spencer can maintain its reputation for service, quality and value, as well as fulfil its compliance obligations. The decision to keep the card operation in-house was strongly influenced by this perceived need to exercise close control over customer relations and by the company's continuing reluctance to pay merchant service charges. Had Marks & Spencer co-branded their card with an established card issuer or card association (for example, Visa), it would have lost both income through having to pay the merchant service charges and control at the point of sale. However, by offering their own facility, they help maintain their traditions of service, quality and value. Besides the saving on merchant service charges, there is also a saving on the handling and processing of cash and cheques when the Chargecard is used and, of course, profit to be earned on the credit taken on the card.

So far Marks & Spencer has resisted any temptation to enter the wider credit card business by, for example, allowing its card to be used beyond its own stores or by offering its processing expertise and capacity to other credit card companies. The Chargecard now generates around 18.5 per cent of the group's annual turnover and customer balances (that is, the total amount of outstanding credit being taken) were £365 million at the end of 1992. The first year's loss for the Chargecard of £10 million had become a profit of just over £5 million by 1988/89 and was just under £16 million for 1991/92. Projections of profitability for future years are extremely healthy. Of the 2.5 million cardholder accounts, 12 per cent are thought to be dormant, with no activity on the card for the last six months. At any particular time about a third show a nil balance in that they have not been used, another third show a balance upon which the cardholder is paying interest, while the remaining third show a balance but this is paid off in full at the end of each account period, thereby avoiding any interest payment.

Other financial services

The card base has been effectively used to cross-sell other financial services to Chargecard holders, such as personal loans, personal equity plans (PEPs) and unit trusts. The personal loan programme was launched to cardholders in 1988 and extended to all customers in 1989, although Chargecard holders receive preferential discount rates on loans they take out. Marks & Spencer can offer their personal loans at lower rates than the high street banks and building societies because the loans go to customers the group already knows well. Indeed, most of the 100,000 loans outstanding have been made to Marks & Spencer cardholders.

The company also has two unit trusts with a total of 75,000 investors: the £110 million Investment Portfolio launched in 1988 and the £58 million UK Selection launched in late 1989 to take advantage of the market for personal equity plans (PEPs). About 70 per cent of the UK Selection unit holders are PEP investors and this product was targeted specifically at those with an above average level of income, very much the classic Marks & Spencer customer.

The operation of the two unit trusts is innovative, in that what the financial services division has done is to apply the well-proven Marks & Spencer retailer–supplier relationship to unit trusts. Here the investment managers of the funds are not in-house, but instead the money is placed in the hands of a number of outside specialists whose performance is then rigorously monitored. These specialists are then in exactly the same position as any other supplier to Marks & Spencer; they provide goods that are subsequently branded with the Marks & Spencer name, and if they do not deliver the required value, they risk losing the business. The unit trusts were marketed on the basis that their aim was a good, steady performance rather than a roller-coaster ride: a longer-term growth approach that seems to suit both Marks & Spencer and their unit trust investors.

The move into other financial services from the Chargecard base can be seen both in tactical and strategic terms. Tactically, it enables the company to take advantage of the database it holds on existing card customers to, for example, avoid promoting loans to those already struggling with large debt on their Chargecard. Conversely it enables Marks & Spencer to better evaluate their customer base. Being safe in the knowledge that the majority of their Chargecard holders are in the higher socioeconomic groups (ABC1s) and that a large proportion of account holders clear their balances monthly, allows Marks & Spencer confidently to target saving products such as PEPs and unit trusts at the appropriate customers. There are also beneficial spin-offs for their mainstream retailing activities, as for instance, the Chargecard database can be used to analyse how far customers are prepared to travel to visit an out-of-town Marks & Spencer store and to remind customers that they can use their Chargecard to have food and drink delivered to their home, friends or family.

Strategically, the move into loans and savings products enables Marks & Spencer to further diversify its operations and to take advantage of its impeccable triple A credit rating, which allows it to borrow at the cheapest rate on the money markets. Furthermore Marks & Spencer can position itself as a respected provider of financial services, so that if required, it could expand these activities and become a major player in this market, directly competing with the traditional banks and building societies. Bliss (1988) discusses the potential for retailers in these markets.

Marks & Spencer is the only triple A-rated retailer in the world, which gives it a higher rating than most UK banks and all but a handful of financial institutions worldwide. For the year ending 31 March 1992, the company's financial activities, which includes treasury, insurance and financial services, contributed £23 million to the overall profit of £638.7 million. The company's expansion into North America and continental Europe will provide opportunities to widen the market for its financial services, as is already the case in Spain where a Chargecard has been launched for use in the growing network of Marks & Spencer stores there. Given the company's expansion plans, this could become a European-wide facility by the end of the decade. Such a development would truly pose a threat to the existing card issuers, but it would be following a route already taken by Sears Roebuck in the US.

Sears Roebuck

From its early days Sears Roebuck & Company (Sears) has been associated with mainsteam American retailing. By the end of the 1970s it seemed quite natural that the company that had founded the first mail-order sales catalogue should extend its concept of 'one-stop shopping' into financial services. The logic of the era had been corporate diversification, and it appeared to make sense to expand the activities of the then world's largest retailer into the retailing of financial services such as insurance, property, stockbroking and credit. Sears had first begun to offer credit to farm families in 1911 and had been providing mortgages for its customers in California since 1960, through Sears Savings Bank. Sears had already acquired Allstate Insurance in 1931, and the deregulation of the American financial services industry in the early 1980s encouraged Sears to further invest here, by purchasing the Wall Street stockbroker Dean Witter and the real estate agency Coldwell Banker in 1981.

The Discover card

Sears already had a store card, the SearsCharge, which by the early 1990s had approximately 45 million active cards and accounted for 65 per cent of Sears' sales. In 1986, Sears decided to go further into the credit card market, by launching the Discover credit card as a rival to the existing credit and charge card networks of Visa, Mastercard and American Express. The start-up cost was estimated at $1 billion but the card achieved profitability within three years. The Discover card can be used in a wide variety of both competing and non-competing retail outlets, as well as in the Sears stores. By 1992 it was accepted by over 1 million outlets in the retailing and service trades and there were some 41.2 million American consumers holding a Discover card. The card had been readily accepted by other retailers because the service charges made by Sears are lower than those charged by the other card networks. Customers had been attracted to the card by the absence of any annual fee and an annual rebate equivalent to 1 per cent of the value of all purchases made with the Discover card. Indeed with the reputation of Sears behind it, the Discover card had become a serious competitor to the existing credit and charge cards in America and part of the portfolio of financial services offered by Sears to its customers. Worthington (1988) describes the launch of the Discover card in the context of the power relationship between retailers and banks.

Bottom-line pressures from Sears Roebuck had, however, forced the Discover card to charge a higher-than-industry-average interest rate to those who chose to borrow on the card. In a country such as the US, where consumers tend to hold a number of credit and/or charge cards, this had resulted in a lower usage rate of the Discover card. This would be a double blow for the Discover card, for as Sears is both the issuer and acquirer for the card, it stands to lose money both from lower outstanding interest-bearing balances and from lower merchant discount volume, as consumers use the Discover card less in non-Sears retail outlets. The income streams available to a credit card operator are: as an issuer, interest paid on the balance outstanding on the card; an annual fee if this is charged; and as an acquirer, a percentage of each sale made using the card, paid by the merchant to the organisation that collects and handles those payments made on that card. Sometimes called the merchant discount fee, it is also known as the merchant service charge and obviously the more the Discover card is used and the greater the value of the goods and services bought on that card, then the larger the return from the merchant service charge to Sears. Also, the more Sears' cards are used in their own retail outlets, the less the merchant service charges they have to pay to others.

Other financial services

Sears had attempted to integrate the retailing of financial services with its traditional retail products and distribution channels, leading commentators to describe Sears as a retailer of 'socks and stocks'. Over 300 in-store financial centres were established, dealing in both stocks and real estate, as well as a combination of in-store and free-standing offices of Allstate Insurance. In early 1989 Sears changed the character of their in-store financial centres, from being manned by staff from Dean Witter and Coldwell Banker to being unmanned desks. Help was given to potential customers in the form of leaflets and free telephone lines were installed, linked to nearby offices of the two organisations. Sears decided upon this realignment of its financial services operation on realising that a retail store does not necessarily provide the correct ambience for trading in stocks and shares or real estate.

The in-store centres are, of course, only one method of product distribution for Sears Financial Services. There are also some 3,000 traditional offices run by the various financial subsidiaries and much effort is put into co-ordinated direct mail programmes via the regular monthly statement mailings to Sears credit card holders. The subsidiaries have also made increasing use of the Sears catalogues to promote their services.

Deconglomeration

However, in the autumn of 1992, having spent $38 billion in the last decade assembling the Sears Financial Network, the giant retail chain finally admitted defeat in its 'socks and stocks' strategy. By the end of 1993 Sears will have dismantled its financial services empire and refocused on its core businesses. Sears plan to sell off Coldwell Banker, Dean Witter (including the Discover credit card division) and 20 per cent of Allstate Insurance. This deconglomeration will move more than $20 billion in debt off Sears' balance sheet, while the equity sale will raise about $3 billion.

The irony is that it has been the financial services divisions that have kept Sears core merchandising business afloat in recent years, providing more than two-thirds of the company's $1.6 billion profit in 1991. What failed to materialise were the much-vaunted 'synergies' of a retailer selling financial services alongside their traditional goods and services. As recently as May 1992, Sears was still defending its dream of providing for all the retail needs of middle-class Americans, extending the nineteenth-century principle of the mail order catalogue and the twentieth-century department store into merchandising concepts such as cable TV shopping channels and diversifications into financial services.

Thanks to the success of the financial services subsidiaries – Dean Witter is America's third largest retail brokerage and Allstate now the world's second largest property and casualty insurer – Sears was able to avoid the need to deconglomerate itself. However, Sears shareholders finally revolted when they saw the company slip from dominance of the suburban Middle America market to third place behind the discounters Wal-Mart and K-Mart. Apparently distracted by its financial services business, Sears managed to squander its legendary heritage, missing out on the opportunity to capitalise on a century-old reputation for value, at a time when 'value' is a key point of competitive advantage in a turbulent marketplace.

The problem

Given this background information on the two retailers, how would you further develop Marks & Spencer's interests in financial services?

Case study questions

1. *Would you follow the Sears Roebuck example and move Marks & Spencer further into the provision of mainstream financial services such as insurance?*

2. *Would you follow the Sears Roebuck Discover card example and make the Marks & Spencer Chargecard a rival to the existing Visa, Mastercard, American Express and Diners Club card networks in either the UK or throughout Europe?*

3. *Would you seek to co-brand the Marks & Spencer Chargecard with one of the above existing card networks?*

4. *Would you start to accept other credit cards as a means of payment in Marks & Spencer stores?*

5. *Would you start to accept debit cards as a means of payment in Marks & Spencer stores?*

6. *If you did choose to accept other plastic cards as a means of payment, would you join in with other retailers if they sought to establish an alternative merchant acquirer network for all the card transactions that occurred in their stores?*

References and further reading

Bliss, M. (1988), 'The impact of retailers on financial services', *Long Range Planning*, **21**(1), 55–8.

Burke, T. (1989), 'Retailer plastic: own label credit cards – a new competitive weapon in the high street', Working Paper No.38, Westminster University, London.

Worthington, S. (1986), 'Retailer credit cards and direct marketing: a question of synergy', *Journal of Marketing Management*, **2**(2), 125–31.

Worthington, S. (1988), 'Credit cards in the United Kingdom: where the power lies in the battle between the banks and the retailers', *Journal of Marketing Management*, **4**(1), 66–70.

Worthington, S. (1992), 'Plastic cards and consumer credit', *International Journal of Retail and Distribution Management*, **20**(7), 3–9.

CASE **26**

The marketing of place

Environment design and refurbishment management in a retail service delivery setting[1]

Steven Greenland
Manchester School of Management

Context

Janet England is a new manager in the Premises Function, which oversees the branch network of United Kingdom Bank (UKB), a large supplier of financial services. In recent years the industry's major players have been reconsidering their branch distribution strategies and started rationalising their networks in an attempt to make them more efficient and profitable. This process has not only involved reducing the actual number of branches, but most institutions have also opted for more open-planned, facilitative, 'user-friendly' and retail-orientated outlet designs. Such designs devote a greater proportion of space to the customer and employ a broad range of retail marketing and merchandising techniques. The branch personnel are also encouraged and trained to be financial services retailers rather than transaction processors. These developments have been necessitated by numerous factors relating to the dynamic nature of the financial services market, and include:

- The increased use of ATMs (automated teller machines).
- The continued miniaturisation of technologies, which has freed branch space for other activities.
- Banks having to compete more directly with building societies and their friendlier image.
- The need for greater efficiency with increased industry competition in a period of economic hardship.
- Merger/acquisition activity producing confused corporate identities across some networks.

[1] This is a 'synthetic' case drawing upon numerous real life cases, and any resemblance to specific companies or individuals is purely coincidental. The case was prepared with the assistance of funding from the Financial Services Research Centre, UMIST.

- The rapid growth in the size of financial service product ranges on offer.
- The removal of processing and enquiry functions out of the branch to centralised locations, which has provided considerable cost savings and allowed more branch staff and space to be devoted to selling activities.
- The increasing sophistication of the financial consumer, who has become more aware of the offerings of different institutions.

UKB has been reluctant to increase expenditure on its network and has been slow to embark upon the process of rationalisation. As a result, its network is inefficiently large and its branch styles have become outdated, being characterised by:

- Low profile frontages with small windows.
- Drab exterior signs.
- Narrow entrances.
- Small customer areas.
- Lack of internal signs.
- All counters behind extensive bandit screens (usually bullet-proof glass or plastic).
- Large visible 'back-office' areas.
- Limited use of automated banking services.
- Formal interview room in the 'back-office' area.
- Inefficient lay-out configurations.
- An orientation towards traditional banking practices rather than an emphasis being placed upon customer service.
- Lack of conformity with the rest of the network, in terms of uniform colour schemes, signs, lay-outs, etc.
- Lack of retail merchandising techniques, such as effective display and promotional techniques, and in-store traffic flow controls.

Through 'tracking' studies, UKB has become aware that the strength of its corporate image has been in gradual decline over the past eighteen months. Also, research based on a sample of its key branches indicates that the bank has not been generating the same level of new accounts being opened as it has in the past. This time period has coincided with its main rivals undertaking substantial rationalisation and refurbishment programmes. UKB's top level management have realised that the situation might partly be improved if the branch network presents a more attractive, friendly and uniform appearance, in terms of design and lay-out. However, changes made to the network could be extremely expensive. Nevertheless, refurbishment is a necessary ongoing expenditure and the substantial costs involved could be offset to a degree through the sale of excess outlets. Economies of scale in branch design, refurbishment tasks and network management should also be experienced through the centralisation of these functions. As a result UKB has formed a central Premises Function at their head office, responsible for the management of the entire branch network.

The project

Janet England, a specialist in both retail design and staff and customer management, was recently 'poached' from a consultancy to apply some of her expertise to UKB's branch network. The tasks she has been given are:

1. Produce a design brief for the frontage and interior banking hall of UKB's branches, detailing the desired design objectives (that is, for that area of the bank seen by the customer).
2. Apply this brief to an actual site and produce a lay-out blueprint of the frontage and banking hall area, the components of which should be accountable, well reasoned and fulfil the specific design objectives. (The site selected for this purpose was recently acquired from a fast-food chain for a branch relocation. The branch requiring the relocation is a medium-sized outlet currently located some 500 metres away, used mainly for personal financial services. Further details are given below.)
3. Anticipate possible negative staff and customer reactions to the relocation. How might the process be managed to minimise any adverse effects on morale and satisfaction levels?
4. Would monitoring/measuring the success of the management of the planned relocation and the extent to which the design objectives have been fulfilled be a worthwhile exercise?
5. Where possible, indicate appropriate methods for accurately assessing the above factors, detailing any potential problems that may arise.

Site details

The new site is amongst a row of modern high street shops. It occupies the first two floors of a three-storey, south-facing building; the third floor being leased by the adjacent retailer (see Figure 26.1). The inside of the unit is rectangular in shape and has a 20m frontage, which includes three steps. It is on the town's main shopping thoroughfare, with the pedestrian traffic flowing in a predominantly east to west direction. The interior is approximately 30m long, with a ceiling height of 6m, and it has one central support column in the centre of the room.[1] The ground floor is to comprise the customer banking hall area with the first floor being used for processing activities and staff facilities. Up to a maximum of eight members of staff may be allocated to the ground floor, meaning that at least two members of staff from the old site will no longer be required; however, it is hoped that this reduction will occur through natural wastage rather than by enforced redundancies. In the previous branch, staff roles were more account and processing driven, whereas in the new branch they will have more of a retail orientation and will be expected to help in the active promotion of products.

---

[1] The approx 20 × 30m rectangular unit can easily be scaled down to be drawn on A4 paper or graph paper.

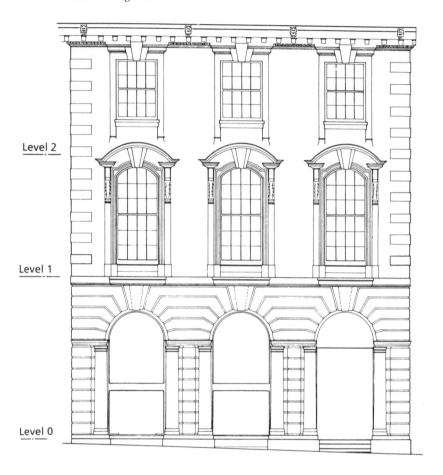

Level 2

Level 1

Level 0

Fig. 26.1 The front elevation of the new branch site

Note: UKB has obtained planning permission to alter the frontage on the ground floor only.

The design brief

A limited design brief, detailing some of the more basic design objectives, has been given to Janet as a starting point. These state that the new branch design should incorporate the following objectives:

- Provide an ergonomically sound environment with an appropriate balance between branch/service functions.
- Positively influence the organisation's corporate image.
- Incorporate effective retail merchandising techniques.
- Have a positive effect upon sales and levels of user satisfaction.
- Prevent robbery/fraud.

Table 26.1 Branch attributes ranked in order of importance

Rank	Branch attribute	Mean
1.	Pleasant staff	8.19
2.	Fast moving queues	8.17
3.	All desks open when busy	8.15
4.	Branch clean and tidy	7.74
5.	Efficient branch lay-out	7.60
6.	Working ATM	7.58
7.	Organised queuing system	7.44
8.	One or more exterior ATM	7.21
9.	Branch being located near other facilities	7.17
10.	Efficient branch atmosphere	7.14
11.	All pens working	7.10
12.	Ample writing surfaces	6.95
13.	Adequate lighting	6.84
14.	Privacy at information desks	6.80
15.	Comfortable air conditioning	6.77
16.	Private interview rooms	6.76
17.	Spacious customer areas	6.71
18.	Comfortable air temperature	6.66
19.	Easily visible time and date	6.60
20.	Function of counters clearly labelled	6.50
21.	Reception/information desk	6.36
22.	Pleasantly smelling branch	6.35
23.	Current interest rates clearly displayed	6.33
24.	All the withdrawal/deposit slip trays full	6.32
25.	Branch located near home	6.31
26.	Sign/light to indicate when cashier free	6.27
27.	Nearby parking facilities	6.10
28.	Adequate seating	6.00
29.	Few other customers in the branch	5.83
30.	Tasteful branch decor	5.76
31.	Branch being quiet	5.74
32.	Rubbish bins	5.61
33.	Attractive stationery	5.39
34.	Easily accessible interior ATM	5.21
35.	Promotional information near queue line	5.11
36.	Deposit letter-box	4.97
37.	Visible TV security cameras	4.92
38.	Plush furnishings	4.75
39.	Wide entrance	4.73
40.	Eye-catching exterior sign	4.70
41.	Attractive staff uniform	4.65
42.	Counters for different functions	4.50
43.	Imaginative promotional literature	4.38
44.	Cashiers name displayed on till or badge	4.32
45.	Cashiers behind screen/glass	4.21
46.	Video screen giving service information	4.14

Table 26.1 (continued)

47.	Live plants/floral displays	4.07
48.	Automatic doors	3.87
49.	Impressive building	3.64
50.	Able to see office are behind counter	3.50
51.	Employee tree with staff names/positions	3.34
52.	Soft background noise	3.16
53.	Large windowed frontage	3.10

Note: The table is based upon a survey conducted by the Financial Services Research Centre, UMIST. It displays the mean levels of importance attached to various branch attributes, ranked in order of importance. Mean scores are based upon a 1–9 importance scale where: 1 = not important; 9 = extremely important. This brief needs to be expanded in order to explain clearly the various design objectives in full. After all, there is little or no hope of producing an effective design without a comprehensive and well-thought-out design brief.

Janet has also been told to pay particular attention to the management of the relocation, as discussions with other banks revealed that branch relocation and refurbishment can lead to account closures and both customer and staff dissatisfaction if not properly handled.

Importance of branch attributes

To assist the new premises manager, Janet also has access to a piece of UKB research revealing the importance consumers attach to the various attributes of a bank branch. The data were generated by a questionnaire survey administered to a sample of approximately 500 consumers from various banks, in their homes. Table 26.1 displays the branch attributes ranked in order of their perceived importance. The mean ratings are based upon a 1 to 9 importance scale. Janet has examined the table and believes it to provide a useful audit of the branch environment, as well as showing some interesting attitudinal information. However, she is aware of the difficulties involved in attempting to examine the effects of design and environment on individuals. These stem mainly from two facts:

1. Environment effects are transitory. People are only aware of the influence of the retail environment when they are actually in that setting.
2. As many effects occur at or below the level of consciousness, individuals may not actually be fully aware of the influence of specific design features.

Some of the results in the table seem questionable to Janet. For instance, the large glass frontage is ranked as the least important of all the elements. However, some of her previous qualitative work, which utilised in-depth questioning techniques and was performed inside shopping retail outlets, revealed that windows were actually a significant contributor to the overall ambience and utility of a design, affecting lighting levels as well as allowing users to see in and out of the branch.

Case study questions and points for discussion

1.   *Compared with the other elements of the marketing mix, how important is the retail/service delivery setting?*

2.   *How should the retail/service delivery setting satisfy both the needs of the consumers and of the staff?*

3.   *In preparing the design brief, how would you strike the balance between over- and under-specification of its objectives?*

4.   *Perform the five tasks given to Janet England, the new Premises Function manager.*

Part Eight

OPERATIONAL ISSUES

In 'Laura Ashley: the logistics challenge', Helen Peck and Martin Christopher depict the national and international growth of this company. The case demonstrates how logistics systems must not only keep pace with business growth, they must be seen as a key component of business and marketing strategy.

'Harrisons plc' by John Fernie analyses a superstore chain, within which the logistical system no longer fitted the scale and marketing strategies of the company. The case focuses upon the pros and cons of a centralised distribution system, in terms of efficiency, customer service and increased buying/bargaining power.

In 'Seven-Eleven Japan Co. Ltd', the focus shifts to the role of technology and information in modern retailing. With this case, Leigh Sparks also provides a basis for the analysis of the convenience store format, comparing the American and the Japanese approaches.

Laura Ashley
The logistics challenge[1]

Helen Peck and Martin Christopher
Cranfield School of Management

Context
State of the company, 1990

In February 1990, the retail and manufacturing group Laura Ashley plc announced end of year losses of £4.7m., on a turnover of £296m. The announcement came as a complete shock to the financial institutions of the City of London which, though growing accustomed to increasingly lacklustre forecasts from Laura Ashley, had nevertheless expected results which were broadly in line with profit forecasts issued only a month earlier.

Laura Ashley had been one of the retail stars of the 1980s. But, like so many other speciality retail success stories of that decade, it appeared to be crumpling under the strain of high interest rates and deepening recession. Difficult trading conditions across several key markets, crippling interest payments and order processing problems were cited in the 1990 annual report as the causes of the company's difficulties. Press commentary was more circumspect, remarking on how the company seemed to have lost its way since the untimely death of its eponymous founder, Laura Ashley.

Days later, the banks were called in following a breach of the company's loan covenant. Refinancing was eventually arranged after protracted negotiations, subject to stringent conditions. The banks demanded a reduction in the company's £89m. debt and improvement in operations. In particular something had to be done about the company's appalling logistics performance. At the year end the company had £105m. tied up in stock, yet still could not deliver to the shops on time. Distribution problems were particularly acute in North America, where that year's autumn/winter clothes collection had arrived approximately three months late, resulting in immediate mark-downs.

[1] This case was prepared as a basis for class discussion and not as an illustration of good or bad management practices.

Early development of the business

In the summer of 1953, Bernard and Laura Ashley chanced upon some attractive hand-printed head scarves during a holiday in Italy. The young couple were convinced that, after a little experimentation, they could produce something similar themselves. Back home in the kitchen of their London flat the experiment commenced. With an initial investment of £10, a batch of 20 scarves was produced. These were sold to the Oxford Street branch of John Lewis. Encouraged by the early success of the head scarves, the whim became an obsession. Laura designed a range of tea towels and other kitchen accessories which found a ready market through department stores, wholesalers and craft shops.

In time Laura's husband Bernard left his job in the City and became the driving force behind the development of the business. He used his engineering skills to adapt second-hand machinery for production and took responsibility for the fabric printing, and selling the goods. Meanwhile Laura worked on new designs, finding inspiration in old patchwork quilts, books and magazines.

In 1960, the Ashley's left their flood-damaged warehouse in Kent and moved the business to a disused railway station in the village of Carno, Powys, in Laura's native Wales. The business was principally a textile design and printing operation, but it acquired a retail sideline in 1965 when it opened a small sales outlet in Mid-Wales. Three years later the first Laura Ashley shop in London opened in a quiet part of Kensington. The move into fashion was equally haphazard – and just as fortuitous – it followed the success of 'Basic Dress 1', a simple above-the-knee housedress. The housedress was the forerunner of the famous floral frocks, long white nightdresses and Edwardian-style pin-tuck blouses. Laura Ashley's countrified and quintessentially English designs invariably conjured up rose-tinted and rose-printed folk memories of bygone days. The 'Laura Ashley look' soon acquired a loyal following in London and the home counties, as well as interest from overseas. Laura understood the value of nostalgia. Her cloths were designed not for real country people, but for city dwellers who craved a romanticised version of a rural idyll.

By 1970 the number of shops had grown to three, and turnover of the business was approaching £1m. The dedicated staff of the Carno factory often worked long into the night to make delivery to shops by the following day. In those early days 'distribution' often meant overnight dashes to London with a car-load of stock.

In 1972, the Ashleys started exporting to continental Europe and the first overseas shop opened in Geneva. The business was growing rapidly and the Ashleys realised that they needed professional management support if plans for further expansion were to be realised. By 1974 Bernard Ashley was looking westward over the Atlantic. Peter Revers, who had joined the company two years earlier, was dispatched to America with instructions to set up a transatlantic division. Peter Revers' mission quickly bore fruit following the opening of a combined retail store and US office in San Francisco. In the same year

Bernard recruited John James, an accountant with overseas experience at Unilever, to fill the post of financial controller. In 1976 John James was promoted to joint managing director, allowing Bernard Ashley to turn his attention to development of the business overseas.

By 1977 the company had a total of 12 shops; one in the US, six in the UK and five scattered throughout Holland, West Germany, Switzerland and France. A second fabric and wallpaper printing factory was acquired in Helmond, Holland, to meet the growing demand and to supply the European market.

By 1980, the business was becoming too large to manage as a homogeneous unit, so the company was split into six integrated divisions. There were initially three retail divisions – the UK, North America and continental Europe – supported by Design Services, the Production Division, which was responsible for all aspects of production, transport and logistics; and Group Services, which dealt with all the company's financial management, accounting, corporate planning, legal and information technology requirements. A fourth retail division was later added to manage the company's expansion in the Pacific.

The business went on from strength to strength, fuelled by the beginning of a retail boom in the British market. By the end of 1984 the Ashleys themselves had become tax exiles. Turnover was set to reach £96.4m., and the business was opening one new store per week somewhere in the world. At this point the company was ready to invest in a substantial increase in its production capabilities. In December of that year, a long-awaited decision regarding the location of an important new 130,000 sq. ft textile and wallpaper factory was finally made. The new site would become the centre of the group's international activities, and further expansion of production and distribution facilities would also occur in close proximity to the new plant. Carno's infrastructure simply could not cope with the necessary increase in demand for electricity and effluent disposal. The alternatives were a nearby site in Newtown, or one close to the European Division's existing factory and distribution site at Helmond. Despite generous financial incentives from the Dutch government, the Ashleys eventually opted to keep the business in Wales, once an adequate (though more modest) offer of funding was secured from the Mid-Wales Development Authority. In the event expansion also went ahead at the Dutch site, raising its production capacity by approximately 30 per cent.

The opening of a shop in Tokyo's prestigious Ginza district, in February 1985, gave the Ashleys a toe-hold in Japan, following the signing of a joint-venture agreement with Japanese partners, the Aeon Group. Under the terms of the contract, clothing and home furnishings for this and other planned Japanese outlets would be made up locally from fabrics supplied from Wales. The company had been slowly building its presence in Australia through a joint-venture agreement. In July 1985 full control of the Australian business was acquired and the Australian market was targeted for more rapid development.

Flotation and the death of Laura Ashley

All was going well and the business was poised for even greater things. In the summer of 1985 an official announcement confirmed rumours of a public flotation. The offer was expected to raise around £23m. to fund the next round of business development. A majority holding – approximately 72 per cent of the stock – would remain under the direct control of the family. Of the shares in the offer, around £1.2m. worth were to be made available to Laura Ashley staff at no cost to the employees themselves. Employees were also given preferential rights to apply for additional shares in the offer.

The fairy-tale story came to an abrupt end on the night of the 8 September 1985. Laura fell down the stairs and was fatally injured. The family had been celebrating Laura's 60th birthday. She died of her injuries a week later. The untimely death of Laura Ashley was a serious blow for the company and a personal tragedy for her family and many employees. Through the years the company had retained the culture of a close family business. The opening of the new flagship store in London's Oxford Circus was postponed for the funeral.

Bankers suggested that the flotation should be aborted, but were persuaded by other members of the management team that Laura's death was inconsequential to the day-to-day running of the business. The flotation went ahead. The business was valued at £270m., and the share issue was oversubscribed 34 times. The Ashleys had reduced their direct involvement in the day-to-day running of the business to some extent the previous year. Bernard Ashley scaled down his involvement much further following the death of his wife.

Post-flotation retailing

During 1986 the expansion of the retail empire continued apace. The company already had 108 shops in the UK. The signing of an agreement to open shops-within-shops in Sainsbury's Home Base chain of DIY stores also assured Ashley's of a presence in mushrooming edge-of-town shopping developments. In continental Europe retail coverage remained patchy, but a new flagship store opened in rue St Honoré in Paris. In America and the Pacific, the company was on the verge of realising its ambitions to have a Laura Ashley store in every large city in Australia, and in every city with a population of over one million in the US. The North American division had opened its 106th American store and was making significant in-roads into Canada. The division, led by Peter Revers, was contributing about half of the company's overall pre-tax profits.

The Laura Ashley look was consistent throughout the world, but brand positioning differed between the home and overseas markets. In the UK, Laura Ashley was a moderately priced purveyor of rustic charm to the urban middle classes. In the US it was seen as an exclusive designer label. The difference was reflected in the margins which were as high as 18–20 per cent in North America, almost double those in the UK.

Retail order management

A specially designed electronic point-of-sale (EPOS) system had been installed in the UK shops in 1984, at a cost of around £500,000. The system fed point-of-sale information back to the company's headquarters in Mid-Wales. Similar systems were installed in the US and continental Europe during the following year. Each retail division was allowed the freedom to develop its own system provided that development proceeded at a relatively consistent pace throughout the organisation. An order processing system, designed to the company's own specification, linked to the EPOS systems. Theoretically at least, it allowed a shop in Dallas to receive goods within a week of receipt of order, roughly the same timescale as for a shop in Tunbridge Wells or Glasgow.

The EPOS system notified Carno that an item had been sold, triggering an automatic replenishment order. An optimum stock level for each store was calculated each season at headquarters. The aim was to maintain consistent stock levels in all stores. If shortages of any item occurred, then the system automatically gave priority to full replenishment at the larger stores.

Supply of materials – in-bound logistics

In-bound stock was shipped by sea, and then by road to Carno. Raw material, mostly cotton greige cloth, had historically been sourced from India and Pakistan. As cloth of a superior quality became available in China, the company switched its principal source of supply to China. The introduction of legislation in 1984, limiting the import of cloth of Chinese origin into the US forced the company to find alternative suppliers once again. By January 1985 the company was purchasing approximately 10.4 million metres of cloth per year from the countries shown in Table 27.1.

The usual policy was to hold approximately four weeks stock in Carno. Over the years the range of fabrics used by the group had gradually widened; clothing made from linen, taffeta, tweeds, gabardines and wool/cotton mixes also featured in the collections. In the years immediately following flotation, the use of colour-woven fabric increased significantly, particularly wool/cotton

Table 27.1 Sources of materials (cloth)

Country	%
West Germany	31
Columbia	27
China	20
Thailand	8
Others	14

Source: Laura Ashley Flotation Offer Document 1985.

mixes. By 1986 it accounted for around 12 per cent (by value) of the fabric used by the company. As the proportion of colour-woven fabric increased the company abandoned its policy of single sourcing the cloth and established additional sources of supply. In fact the company made sure that all materials, from dye stuffs to paper, were no longer single sourced. The move to dual or multiple sourcing was felt to be beneficial to the group because 'it would not suffer any significant disruption in production if a single supplier were unable to meet the Group's orders'.

Production and manufacturing facilities

In 1985, the business owned two fabric and wallpaper production plants, one at Carno and one in Helmond, processing 5.5m. and 4.3m. metres of fabric and 8.5m. and 7.5m. metres of wallpaper respectively. Around 20 per cent of wallpaper was produced outside the group, either because of fluctuating demand or because the group had neither the capacity nor the technology to produce some of the more sophisticated designs and surfaces. Helmond tended to concentrate on furnishing fabrics, with a making-up facility on the same site, supplying home-furnishing items for the continental European market. The group had two other factories in the UK devoted to making up items in the home furnishing range, one specialising in accessories like cushions, the second working on bespoke items like made-to-measure curtains and blinds.

Garments were cut out at the Carno site and then supplied to one of eight garment making-up plants located within an 80-mile radius of Carno. The garment factories employed around 1,200 people in Wales, with another 180 employed at a plant in Dublin, Ireland, which made up cloths for export. Fabric, complete with 'lay-plans', was also supplied to a third-party manufacturer in Kentucky. The complex Laura Ashley signature blouses and dresses with their intricate-smocking labour-intensive pin-tuck details were produced by the relatively slow 'make-through' process, by which one person made the whole garment. The system was more costly to operate than a sectioned approach, but worked well for complex designs. Quality was good and the system was highly flexible, and could rapidly accommodate changes in demand. From the mid-1980s the group started experimenting with other manufacturing systems, establishing high-productivity units at two of its plants. Under the new process, each worker completed only one stage of the making-up process; the work was less interesting for the machinist, but enabled simple garments to be produced in large numbers.

Production planning

Two fashion collections were produced each year – spring/summer and autumn/winter – usually incorporating around 125 items (chosen from hundreds of samples), and often made up in a choice of colours or fabrics. In addition there were the children's and bridal ranges. When deciding which of the many samples should be included in a new collection, some input from store managers and market reaction had always been taken into account, but in Laura's time the final selection process remained distinctly unscientific, based largely on Mrs Ashley's own discretion. Sometimes there were mistakes, but her instincts were reliable enough to transform the business from cottage industry into one of the few truly international retail brands. She understood that there tended to be a time lag in taste and fashion between London and the provinces, and intervened on many occasions to stop initially slow-selling items from being dropped from the product range.

Design of the collections started some 18 months ahead of launch. Home furnishing is a less seasonal and slightly less fickle business than fashion, so only one collection was produced each year. A substantial proportion of the range was new each year, but best-selling lines were likely to be retained for a number of seasons. A separate and exclusive 'Decorator Collection' range of furnishings was also produced for interior designers. Gradually the soft-furnishing collection was expanded to incorporate upholstered furniture and a complementary array of paint, tiles and bedlinen.

The group's production/manufacturing capabilities were organised to produce relatively short runs of goods in a wide range of styles and colours. In 1985 the group or its subcontractors produced 85 per cent (by value) of the goods sold in Laura Ashley shops. The company's policy was to maintain production capacity at a level slightly below that of peak demand, thereby allowing the company to maximise productivity within its own manufacturing facilities, and guaranteeing security of employment for its own factory workers. To meet periodic peaks in demand, additional capacity could be found with other manufacturers.

Knitwear was produced by third-party suppliers. Complementary but peripheral items, such as ceramic tiles and paint, were produced outside the group to Laura Ashley designs and specifications. In addition, the group produced a range of perfume through its own Swiss-based subsidiary and a selection of decorating books from 1981.

For its core products, long-term production planning and short-term planning of production runs were responsibilities of the production planning director, who would be advised by merchandisers from the Retail Divisions. Demand for clothing was usually calculated around 16 months in advance, with six-month production forecasts derived from the demand forecasts. These production forecasts were revised on a monthly basis, to enable production to be concentrated on best-selling lines.

Out-bound logistics

Finished goods were handled through two large warehouses in the UK, one for home furnishings in Carno (30,000 sq. ft) and one in nearby Newtown (34,000 sq. ft) for clothing. On completion of the new distribution centre in Newtown, all out-bound activity was transferred to the new site. The Carno facility was then used for storage of production cloth. A third, much smaller, warehouse at Greenford, Middlesex, was used to distribute clothes and furnishings to London shops. Goods were delivered to the UK shops in the company's own lorries. Overseas, a 13,000 sq. ft warehouse in Helmond handled goods for continental Europe, from where they were distributed by the company's own fleet or by third-party carriers. Clothing for the US was dispatched weekly direct to the shops by airfreight. Home furnishings were sent by sea to a 60,000 sq. ft warehouse in Mahwah, New Jersey, and distributed from there, again using third-party carriers.

Expansion in manufacturing and logistics facilities, 1986–87

By 1986 garments manufactured by the group in Mid-Wales accounted for 10 per cent of all UK garments exported to the US. Still more capacity was needed. The company had more or less exhausted the supply of labour in the Carno area, so two new garment-sewing factories were sited in Wrexham and in Gresford, North Wales. A Kentucky-based garment manufacturer, which had been operating almost as a dedicated supplier to Laura Ashley, was also acquired. The US production facilities were expanded significantly over the next three years. In 1986, the combined output of the company's production facilities in Holland, the UK, Eire and the US had reached 13.7m. metres of fabric, 2.4 million garments and 2.3 million rolls of wallpaper.

The following year the Newtown factory came on stream. It added a further 5m. metres of fabric and 10m. metres of wallpaper production capacity. By now the Production Division was taking on some third-party work to utilise capacity.

The Newtown distribution facilities were extended further to increase warehousing from 105,000 sq. ft to 130,000 sq. ft, and enlarge the existing mail-order facilities. The company had been involved in mail order for many years, accounting for roughly 5 per cent of business through the early 1980s. The rapid growth in retail business reduced this proportion to around 3 per cent in 1986 but, in absolute terms, mail-order business was still growing. Newtown was processing approximately 12,000 orders per month, about half of which were pre-paid orders taken in the shops for made-to-measure curtains, blinds, loose covers and furniture. In Japan, Laura Ashley made history by introducing garment and home furnishing mail-order catalogues for the local market. The catalogues, using the local language, were believed to be the first of their kind ever produced in Japan.

Acquisition of other brands

By 1986 the company employed over 7,000 people and owned or leased 362 retail outlets in 13 countries on four continents. The company was also supplying a number of franchise and third-party outlets in other countries where the company had no shops of its own.

Flushed with the success of building its global retailing activities, the business went on a shopping spree of its own. During a two-year period, the company acquired the facilities of some of its existing suppliers and a number of other small niche brands. Bryant of Scotland (a knitwear manufacturer) and Sandringham Leather Goods were the first two brands to be added to the portfolio. Approximately 40 per cent of their output was immediately taken by Laura Ashley's retailing division. Penhaligon's, a perfume manufacturer with five shops in London, was acquired in 1987. Meanwhile in the US it bought Willis & Greiger, a traditional outdoor clothing specialist, best known for supplying a flying suit to Charles Lindbergh (worn when he crossed the Atlantic in the 'Spirit of St. Louis') and flying jackets for the US airforce during the Second World War. Willis & Greiger had retail and wholesale operations in America.

Changing direction of design

Two years after Laura Ashley's death, radical changes had occurred in the product design and selection processes. Gone were the selection sessions where collections would be chosen from hundreds of designs. In order to eliminate waste and cut costs, the number of sample garments made up was halved. The core products themselves were changing as accountants sought to cut costs by reducing the number of tucks and pleats and volume of fabric in each dress. The distinctive Laura Ashley look was gradually eroding. In the shops, racks of long flowing skirts were replaced with short straight ones which lent themselves more easily to volume manufacturing techniques.

The spring 1987 collection demonstrated a new and more catholic design philosophy; the collection included Caribbean prints, striped shorts and polka dot dresses. The management felt that the new design strategy and further extension of product lines demonstrated that the company itself was maturing and adopting a suitably sophisticated approach to a fiercely competitive retail environment. Laura Ashley products increasingly echoed the designs in every other high street multiple. Almost unnoticed, its traditional customers melted away. Sales per square foot were already in decline but were as yet undetected, masked by the overall increase in retail space.

Other cost-cutting programmes were introduced in an attempt to cut manufacturing costs. Sectionalised working was introduced in all factories and the work rate was increased. There was growing pressure from new management to close some of the Welsh factories and buy in more goods from overseas suppliers. Wage rates in Britain and a strong pound made external sourcing ever more attractive.

Decline

Amid rising concern for the financial well-being of the business, John James took over from Bernard Ashley as chief executive in 1988. He had been trying to persuade Bernard Ashley to close some of the factories and source externally, but to no avail. Bernard refused point blank to discuss the proposal. The matter became a point of friction between Bernard Ashley and other members of the management team. A major reorganisation of the business followed. The group was now operating a number of SBUs rather than on a divisional basis. The new structure allowed greater autonomy for the operating divisions, freeing them if they wished to source a higher proportion of their products externally.

Meanwhile, the Production Division was neatly dismembered. Half became Brand Management, a profit centre charged with design, image protection, sourcing and supply with a strengthened buying organisation. The rest became Laura Ashley Industries which was in turn subdivided into Apparel (garment manufacturing), Print (textile and wallpaper) and Soft Sewn (soft furnishings manufacture and distribution). Accounting and financial systems were put in place in advance to support each of the new units.

Investment continued in the factories in a bid to improve efficiency. 'Fast Track', a rapid response throughput garment-manufacturing system, was installed in the Newtown garment factory at a cost of £670,000. The system circulated garments above the heads of the workers, where they remained until the machinist was ready to work on them. It eliminated the need for workers to lift and move bundles of garments between workstations, reducing manufacturing time per garment quite substantially. A computerised cutting room was also installed in the Carno factory.

The downside of the new manufacturing systems was that the finishing on more complex designs had to be contracted out to third parties, with inevitable impact on logistics and margins.

On the retail front – in keeping with the mood of the times – Laura Ashley became a 'life-style concept' with the launch of two new retail ventures. 'Mother and Child' shops were opened as stand-alone shops or in-store boutiques, offering an upmarket selection of matching mother and baby wear, and children's clothing. A co-ordinated range of nursery furniture and furnishings completed the package. The second concept was 'Laura Ashley Home', introduced first in the US in November 1988 and then in the UK and Europe in early 1989. Laura Ashley Home stores were opened in slightly less prominent city-centre locations. They contained a vastly widened product range which included wooden cabinet furniture, and a selection of glass, lighting and tableware.

In the UK, a new 50,000 sq. ft distribution centre was set up in Milton Keynes, to support the UK launch of Laura Ashley Home venture and to provide a reliable home delivery service for items of furniture. In Holland, distribution activities moved to new larger premises at Veldhoven Airport, Eindhoven.

By now though, the retail boom of the 1980s had run its course; but the programme of shop openings continued in the hope that the slowdown was a temporary pause. Profits for the group had peaked in 1987, but measures had been taken to reverse the long-term decline in sales per square foot of retail space. However, turnover and group profitability were still running in opposite directions. In the UK and Europe, sales from 1989 crept upwards, but margins were looking increasingly sickly. Rising interest rates had frozen the housing market, tipping furnishing sales into a dramatic decline. To add to the woes, delivery was becoming more and more erratic.

Undaunted, the company continued to explore new ways to restore its fortunes. Two new ranges of clothes, 'Michelangelo' (women's) and 'Sandringham' (men's), were produced for trade shows early in the year. These expeditions into the wholesale clothing market offered an opportunity to utilise some of the group's excess manufacturing capacity, but were later felt to be diversionary, so were abandoned. A franchise agreement was also signed with the Stinu Corporation of America, trading under the retail brand 'Units'. Units specialised in retailing block-colour women's separates. The contract gave Laura Ashley the exclusive right to operate Units shops in the UK.

Meanwhile, the North American division was increasingly going its own way. It had acquired Revman Industries Inc., a company which specialised in making and selling upmarket bedlinen in the US. The licence to produce Laura Ashley bedlinen – America's leading brand of designer bedding – passed to Revman with the acquisition. Revman added it to a portfolio of licences on other leading designer bedlinen products already held by the company. A range of occasional furniture was also being produced under licence by Baker Inc., a well-known American furniture manufacturer. In a bid to increase market penetration further, the exclusive Laura Ashley occasional furniture and fabrics ranges were both being sold in department stores as well as Laura Ashley's own shops.

Sales in the US, like the UK, rose by 7 per cent, but adverse currency movements seriously damaged the division's profitability. Prices could no longer be raised to counteract a strengthening pound and the weakening dollar. The North American division had been plagued with delivery problems too. Shipments of garments and furnishing fabrics should have arrived weekly by air, but late processing at the factories meant that shipments missed the weekly flight. Rather than putting the goods on the next available flight, freight forwarders often held the consignment over to the following week so they could consolidate the loads. Service to the West Coast 'Ocean Stores' was particularly poor; replenishment cycles that used to take around 10–15 days gradually lengthened to 39 days from factory to shop. As their performance deteriorated, they sank lower and lower in priority of delivery, eventually receiving shipments of garments by sea. Exasperated sales assistants did what they could to remedy the situation. They attempted to fill customers' orders by chasing goods from other parts of the country, by working their way down an alphabetical telephone list of all the American stores. The late arrival of the autumn/winter clothes collection had been the final straw.

Management shake out

To meet the conditions of refinancing, the company embarked on a programme of debt reduction and disposal of peripheral brands. A personal request from Bernard Ashley secured a £45m. cash injection from the group's Japanese partners in August 1990. In return the Aeon Group received a 15 per cent stake in Laura Ashley, an extra 10 per cent stake in the existing joint venture and a 47.5 per cent stake in Revman Industries. John James resigned his post only days after the transaction. Mike Smith, director of the UK retailing division, and an accountant by training, took over from James as caretaker until a new chief executive could be found.

Once John James had gone, Bernard Ashley was finally persuaded, with great regret, to dispose of nine of the company's twelve factories. A total of six Welsh sewing factories and the factories in Dublin, Helmond and Kentucky were to be sold, closed, or transferred to the Carno and Newtown sites. The move reduced the 8,000 strong workforce worldwide by 1,500. A rationalisation of the design studios followed soon afterwards. Peter Revers, head of the North American division, stood down in the following November.

With immediate debt problems alleviated, the management team quickly turned its attention to remedying some of the problems of sourcing and supply. The group was currently sourcing about 70 per cent of its home furnishings in-house. The management, determined to retain control of its fabric design and printing, agreed that the figure should remain roughly the same. As for garments and other product ranges, they decided that the proportion of bought-in products would increase from the existing 45 per cent to 85 per cent, with almost immediate effect. The out-sourced items would come from a host of new suppliers in the Far East (mostly Hong Kong) and Eastern Europe. Laura Ashley sold well over three million garments a year through its stores, and the move offered a possible saving of up to £2 for each garment sourced externally.

New management appointed

A new chief executive was finally appointed in July 1991. The new man was Jim Maxmin, an energetic American, who had previously been chief executive of Volvo Concessionaires and more recently director of World Retailing at Thorn EMI. Bernard Ashley had already agreed to become a non-executive director of the business on the appointment of a new CEO, and Mike Smith left to pursue opportunities elsewhere.

Logistics was now top of the agenda for Maxmin and a new management team. Some of the logistics and service problems had latterly been addressed by the old management team. Shops were no longer stocking heavy items like tiles if customers could not drive to the shops and no delivery service was available, but much remained to be done.

An examination of the group's logistics operation revealed a disjointed and tangled web. There was a sizeable in-house distribution department operating large warehouses in Newtown, Milton Keynes, Eindhoven and Mahwah, using a total of ten largely unconnected management information systems. This was before the Japanese subsidiary's two warehouses in Osaka and Tokyo were added into the equation. The group used no less than eight principal linehaul carriers, and a multitude of other transport suppliers, to serve over 540 stores in 28 countries. The warehouses were holding over 55,000 lines of inventory (though only around 15,000 were current stock), ranging from 35m. rolls of fabric, through to hand-made wedding gowns, bottles of perfume, wooden wardrobes and tins of emulsion paint – only 5 per cent of lines were common to all stores.

Delivery systems were hopelessly clogged, with overall stock availability at around 80 per cent. Separate stockholdings existed for each division, sometimes within the same facility. The result was that when a store in Dusseldorf experienced a stock-out on an expensive bedspread, it was told that the item was unavailable, even though over 500 of them belonging to the UK division were sitting in the same warehouse.

There appeared to be problems with the order processing system too. A sale recorded by the EPOS system would automatically trigger a replenishment order. The system was programmed to give automatic priority for replenishment of the larger stores, but made no account for the speed at which goods sold, or the urgency of the order. Large London shops would be replenished on a daily basis, whether the stock was selling quickly or not, but a small regional store which sold its entire allocation of an item within a day, might be left for weeks with a total stock-out. The system was also flawed in that it did not distinguish between real sales and goods redirected to other stores. In the UK alone, the company was spending a small fortune by handing out £25 vouchers to placate frustrated customers whose orders stubbornly refused to arrive.

It also turned out that the move towards 'cheap sourcing' had involved hidden costs. Supply routes had become contorted as goods manufactured in Hong Kong or China were transported to Wales and then on to the US or back to the Pacific. Other difficulties had also arisen. By placing orders piecemeal with a multitude of overseas suppliers, securing additional supplies to meet unforeseen demand became difficult. Laura Ashley's orders were not reliable enough, or of sufficiently high volume or high value to command flexibility or priority customer status from suppliers.

There were quota problems too, particularly for the US. For goods imported from the Far East to Europe, a quota could be acquired in advance and the goods 'drip-fed' into the market. The US was more of a gamble; American legislation demanded that goods had to be shipped immediately *en bloc* to quota. This meant that either a large slice of the quota could be acquired early on, and goods shipped in bulk against it; or quota could be acquired in small chunks at periodic intervals. The snag with the latter was that so many other businesses wished to import from the Far East that quota might not be available for subsequent shipments. Competition for quota to import from the Far East was so intense that attempted violations were not uncommon. A succession of violations by Far Eastern clothing manufacturers (unconnected to Laura Ashley) had put the US customs on their guard. The result was that in-bound shipments originating in the UK were cleared very quickly through customs, but similar shipments from the Far East were likely to experience long delays.

The task of putting Laura Ashley's logistics in order looked formidable; nevertheless Maxmin was convinced that in the increasingly tough global marketplace it was essential to have a responsive, yet low-cost logistics system. He also knew that decisions would have to be taken quickly, particularly if Laura Ashley was to match the performance of retail competitors like Benetton or The Limited in the US.

Case study question

What actions should the company take to develop logistics systems to cope with the increasingly tough global marketplace?

Background data

Tables 27.2–27.7 below give background data on the development and expansion of the Laura Ashley operation on a worldwide basis.

Table 27.2 Growth of retail operations: number of retail outlets

	United Kingdom[1]	Europe	North America	Far East	Australia	Total
1968	1	–	–	–	–	1
1970	3	–	–	–	–	3
1977	6	5	1	–	–	12
1980	25	34	11	–	1	71
1981[2]	29	35	15	–	1	80
1982	39	39	28	–	1	107
1983	55	42	43	–	1	141
1984	72	43	55	–	1	171
1985	87	47	84	1	12	231
1986	109	53	113	2	15	292
1987	140	61	137	5	19	362
1988	157	66	167	12	25	427
1989	171	75	185	24	25	480
1990[3]	182	95	213	41	24	555

Notes: [1] Includes Republic of Ireland; [2] Includes Homebase outlets;
[3] Includes franchises opened 1986–1990.

Source: Laura Ashley, Offer Document 1985 and Annual Reports 1986–1991.

Table 27.3 Geographic spread, January 1991: retail outlets worldwide

European Division		*North American Division*	
Austria	2	Canada	11
Belgium	4	Mexico	1
Denmark	1	US	201
Finland	1		
France	26		
Germany	16	*Pacific Basin*	
Greece	3	Australia[1]	24
Holland	8	Hong Kong	1
Iceland	1	Japan	37
Ireland	2	Korea	1
Italy	8	Malaysia	1
Middle East	2	Singapore	1
Norway	2		
Portugal	1		
Spain	12	Total	555
Sweden	3		
Switzerland	5		
UK	180		

Note: [1] Fabric is also distributed in New Zealand and sold through independent retailers.
Source: Laura Ashley Annual Report 1991.

Table 27.4 Turnover by region (£m.)

Year	British Isles	North America	Europe	Pacific and others	Total
1984/85	39.7	13.4	40.1	3.2	96.4
1985/86	56.4	56.2	16.1	2.8	131.5
1986/87	78.4	66.5	21.6	4.4	170.9
1987/88	95.0	74.8	24.8	6.9	201.5
1988/89	125.9	90.2	28.5	7.8	252.4
1989/90	142.6	117.2	28.6	8.2	296.6
1990/91	143.5	136.2	40.7	7.1	327.5

Table 27.5 Retail space by region (000 sq. ft)

Year	British Isles	North America	Europe	Pacific and others	Total
1985/86	155.6	115.6	72.7	13.1	357.0
1986/87	233.1	161.2	77.5	20.3	492.1
1987/88	302.7	197.7	95.4	34.0	629.8
1988/89	344.2	235.6	100.7	57.0	737.5
1989/90	393.7	255.6	99.0	68.1	816.4

Source: Laura Ashley Annual Reports.

Table 27.6 Stock levels as percentage of sales, 1980–1990 (£000)

	Dec. 1980	Dec. 1981	Dec. 1982	Jan. 1984	Jan. 1985	Jan. 1986	Jan. 1987	Jan. 1988	Jan. 1989	Jan. 1990	Jan. 1991
Sales	25,393	34,153	44,556	66,701	96,448	131,513	170,892	201,477	252,431	296,608	327,533
Stock	7,225	8,880	10,652	17,053	22,732	35,603	45,521	66,824	75,790	104,804	64,642
Sales (%)	28.4	26.0	23.9	25.6	23.6	27.0	26.6	33.2	30.0	35.3	19.7

Source: Laura Ashley Annual Reports.

Table 27.7 Sales per square foot for total operation

	Sales (£m.)	PBIT[1] (£m.)	Sq. ft (000)	Sales/sq. ft (£)
1984	96.4	14.1	259.9	370.9
1985/6	131.5	18.0	357.0	368.3
1986/7	170.9	22.5	492.1	347.2
1987/8	201.5	23.1	629.8	319.9
1988/9	252.4	20.3	737.5	342.2
1989/90	296.6	(4.7)	816.4	363.3
1990/91	327.5	(6.7)	n/a	n/a

Note: [1] Profit before interest and tax.
Source: Laura Ashley Annual Reports.

Harrisons plc

John Fernie
Dundee Institute of Technology

Context

The Harrisons chain of superstores is a major force in grocery retailing in Great Britain. In 1989/90 it had sales of £3.55 billion, and profits before interest and tax of £180 million. Its market share of the packaged grocery market was 8 per cent, a figure which has remained relatively stable throughout the 1980s.

Harrisons' success has been largely achieved through organic growth. In 1965, Fred Harrison, a butcher from Rotherham in South Yorkshire, bought five grocery shops in the Sheffield area. He converted these shops to 'large' supermarkets with an average selling space of 13,000 square feet. From the initial success of these stores, Harrison began to build even bigger outlets, converting buildings such as mills and cinemas to his 'superstore' concept. Along with other enterprising Yorkshire grocers, he pioneered this concept and quickly widened his product

Table 28.1 Geographical distribution of Harrisons' stores

Region	1965–69	1970–74	1975–79	1980–84	1985–89	1990[2]	Total
Scotland	–	1	6	1	2	1	11
North	7	2	2	–	2	1	14
Yorkshire/Humberside	9	8	1	3	1	2	24
North-west	4	6	6	3	1	1	21
East Midlands	1	1	–	1	1	–	4
West Midlands	–	3	2	2	1	–	8
Wales	–	1	2	2	1	–	6
East Anglia	–	–	–	1	1	–	2
South-west	–	–	2	3	3	1	9
South-east	–	–	3	8	8	4	23
Total	21	22	24	24	21	10	122
Average gross space (000 sq. ft)[1]	50.5	52.2	55.0	69.0	85.0		60.2
Average selling space (000 sq. ft)[1]	27.5	32.6	36.5	42.0	43.0		36.9

Note: [1] Includes extensions subsequently built; [2] under construction.

range to include non-foods. By the early 1970s Harrisons was well established in the north of England and having 'test marketed' the concept, the company now sought purpose-built sites in new geographical areas (see Table 28.1). The 'ideal' sites were those of 60,000 square feet gross, 45,000 square feet net, with adequate car parking spaces (one space per 60 square feet of selling space) on the same level as the store.

In 1974 Harrisons became a public limited company. The company was popular with the City: its freshness and innovation was changing the nature of the grocery market. Moreover, the company's liquidity position was strong and it had been able to self-finance new store development.

The late 1970s was a period of expansion and phenomenal growth, to the extent that it was one of the fastest growing companies in Britain from 1977–79. Within a decade it had come from nowhere to capture around 8 per cent of the grocery market. Its marketing policy was clearly defined: it stocked a wide range of branded goods, sold at the most competitive prices at edge-of-town superstore sites.

Strategy

The 1980s witnessed a change in the marketing environment. Low inflation placed pressure on margins and Harrisons began to face intense competition from traditional grocery 'majors' embarking upon multi-million pound store development projects. The superstore was now an established concept. Tables 28.2 and 28.3 show the main operators of the largest retail outlets in Britain (superstores have a sales area of over 25,000 square feet, large supermarkets 10–25,000 square feet). Responding to these pressures, Harrisons reviewed its marketing strategy in 1985/86. Emphasis shifted away from a pricing strategy on branded goods to the more financially lucrative value-added Harrisons' brands in newly designed stores. Advertising was dramatically increased to stress the 2,000 own-brand lines in conventional product areas such as biscuits, tinned vegetables, cakes, cereals and soft drinks. Harrisons had eliminated the slow-moving, less popular brand lines to accommodate the Harrisons label. Additionally, electronic point-of-sale (EPOS) technology was introduced to a number of stores prior to incorporating a full system by 1989. Initially, EPOS was used to monitor supplier performance.

New project

By 1988/89, this new strategy was beginning to show results. In particular, the popularity of the own-label products led the company to introduce Harrisons' brands into the chilled and frozen foods sector. Harrisons recognised that these changes in marketing strategy would have significant implications for buying and distribution in the company. Until this time, the senior management team at Harrisons had only a small team of buyers and the sales director had responsibility for distribution. In 1989 Harrisons began to recruit specialists in these areas, but as an interim measure it recruited Fearney Consultants to advise on a distribution strategy.

Table 28.2 Superstore openings by region (as at 1 February 1990)

Operator	Scotland	North	Yorkshire and Humberside	North-west	East Midlands	West Midlands	Wales	East Anglia	South-west	South-east	Total
Asda	23	16	18	32	12	16	9	4	11	37	178
Gateway	4	5	1	3	4	2	1	2	1	2	25
Normans	–	–	–	–	–	–	–	–	4	3	7
Wm. Low	4	–	–	–	–	–	–	–	–	–	4
Wm. Morrisons	–	5	17	8	5	1	–	–	–	–	36
Safeway	2	6	5	4	1	4	2	1	4	14	43
Savacentre	1	1	–	–	–	1	–	–	–	4	7
J. Sainsbury	–	3	10	7	8	15	3	8	9	49	112
Tesco	8	2	10	13	15	18	13	6	18	57	160
Co-ops	3	3	3	16	5	9	6	5	4	13	67
Independents	–	–	3	–	–	–	–	1	1	–	5
Total	45	41	67	83	50	66	34	27	52	179	644

Source: IGD Stores Database.

Table 28.3 Large supermarket operators by standard region (as at 1 February 1990)

Operator	Scotland	North	Yorkshire and Humberside	North-west	East Midlands	West Midlands	Wales	East Anglia	South-west	South-east	Total
Asda	1	1	7	1	–	–	–	–	1	–	11
Budgens	–	–	–	–	1	–	–	2	2	3	8
Gateway	34	10	9	11	21	21	17	10	30	58	221
J. Sainsbury	–	–	4	12	8	12	2	5	15	104	162
Normans	–	–	–	–	–	1	1	–	5	–	7
Safeway	49[1]	36	19	10	7	19	4	–	22	83	248
Tesco	7	3	13	11	7	7	7	6	12	48	121
Waitrose	–	–	–	–	2	4	–	4	5	58	73
Wm. Jackson	–	–	8	–	3	–	–	–	–	–	11
Wm. Low	20	3	4	–	–	–	–	–	–	–	27
Wm. Morrison	–	–	4	5	–	–	–	–	–	–	9
Co-ops	19	13	22	18	26	13	13	8	23	22	177
Independents	–	1	3	4	–	2	–	1	–	6	17
Total	130	67	93	72	75	79	44	36	115	382	1,093

Note: [1] Includes 2 in the Isles.
Source: IGD Research Services.

Harrisons receive 90 per cent of its grocery products directly from suppliers. For some product lines, such as wines and spirits, nominated carriers are used. It handles meat and product from its own warehouses, supplied by its own vehicles. Its meat plant/warehouse in Rotherham is 125,000 sq. ft and serves all 122 stores. Its four produce warehouses range in size from 25,000 sq. ft in Cambuslang to 75,000 sq. ft in Leeds (the other two sites, both 50,000 sq. ft, are located at Manchester and Cirencester). In total, Harrisons has a vehicle fleet of 206, all of which are refrigerated. The Rotherham-based fleet is relatively new and all vehicles are of maximum legal weight with 40-foot articulated units. The product fleet is older and mainly comprises 14-tonne rigid vehicles many of which are also used for third-party distribution. The bulk of the direct delivery products (except perishables) work on 7–10 day lead times and, compared with most of its competitors, Harrisons hold considerable amounts of stock at each store (see Table 28.1). Moreover many store managers have complained about unreliability of deliveries and 'back-door' congestion at their stores.

Project brief

As the consultant in charge of this project, you are asked to:

1. Advise Harrisons on the pros and cons of a centralised distribution strategy compared to its current policy.
2. Assuming that a centralisation strategy is adopted, propose a new depot network and discuss the various options available to Harrisons in the operation of this network.
3. From your proposed network in (2) above, discuss the implications of your new distribution strategy upon store warehouse operations and the back-up administrative/information systems required.

Tables 28.4 to 28.8 below give further background information on other multiple grocery retailers.

Table 28.4 Percentage of groceries through centralised distribution by volume

Retailer	1986	1987	1988	1989	1990	1991
Argyll: Safeway	80					
Presto	40–60	70	80	85	90	93.5
Asda	10	20	20	50	80	83
CRS	40–60	40–60	40–60	80	80	80
CWS	40–60	40-60	40–60	70	70	70
Gateway	40–60	40–60	40–60	50	80	88
Kwik Save	80	80	80	80	80	80
Wm. Low	50	50	60	70	80	85
Wm. Morrison	50	50	50	70	90	90
J. Sainsbury	80	80	80	85	90	92
Tesco	40–60	40–60	70	70	90	97
Waitrose	80	80	80	80	80	90

Source: IGD Research Services.

Table 28.5 Profile of stores and depot characteristics, 1991

Operator	Number of stores	Average selling space of store (000 sq. ft)	Number of depots	Size range (000 sq. ft)	Number of composites
J. Sainsbury	303	22.9	21	64–440	7
Tesco	389	25.2	18	110–350	8
Safeway[3]	500	14.4	14	20–510	4
Asda[4]	296	43.5	8[1]	180–370	6
Gateway	727	9.2	27	5–245	0
Kwik Save	720	6.5	11	90–250[2]	0
Iceland	519	4.1	6	45–195[2]	0
Wm. Low	63	12.2	3	120–220	0
CRS	472	5.4	20	15–180[2]	0

Notes:
[1] Does not include transhipment depot.
[2] Does not include depots where chilled or frozen produce is consolidated by contractors.
[3] The Safeway figure includes Safeway and Presto but not Lo-Cost. The 310 Safeway stores have an average size of 19,300 sq. ft compared with the 190 Presto stores' average of 6,300 sq. ft.
[4] Prior to the purchase of 61 Gateway superstores in 1989, Asda had 129 stores with selling space of 4,762,000 sq. ft.

Table 28.6 Properties of an average-sized depot by operator, 1991

Operator	Size (sq. ft)	Number of pallet locations	Number of lines handled	Number of cases distributed per week	Peak Christmas week	
					Number of lines handled	Number of cases distributed
CRS	80,000	3,200	4,200	125,000	–	–
CWS	100,000	6,000	5,500	110,000	5,500	132,000
Gateway	165,000	12,102	5,000	221,846	–	–
Grandways	125,000	12,000	6,800	175,000	7,500	250,000
Iceland	89,000	5,300–11,000	1,800	125,000–500,000	2,000	190,000–620,000
Kwik Save	130,000	8,000	650	400,000	–	–
Littlewoods	108,000	8,750	3,000	250,000	3,300	320,000
Wm. Low	220,000	16,000	6,000	220,000	6,500	340,000
Normans	35,000	3,000	2,400	60,000	3,500	90,000
Superwarehouses						
Safeway	290,000	20,000	5,500	550,000	6,000	660,000
J. Sainsbury	180,000	12,500	2,800	400,000	–	–
Tesco	–	–	–	–	–	–

Source: IGD Research Services.

Table 28.7 Properties of a Tesco's composite and grocery depot, 1991

	Composite	Grocery
Average size of depot (sq. ft)	250,000	280,000
Number of pallet locations	14,300	19,600
Number of lines handled per week	5,000	4,500
Number of cases handled per week	578,000	607,000
Peak Christmas week		
Number of lines handled	5,100	4,540
Number of cases distributed	890,000	900,000

Source: IGD Research Services.

Table 28.8 Total warehousing space by operator (000 sq. ft), 1991[1]

Tesco	4,320
J. Sainsbury	4,000
Safeway	3,210
Asda	2,452
Gateway	2,000
Kwik Save	1,116
Iceland	455

Note: [1] Includes non-foods.

Seven-Eleven Japan Co. Ltd
From licensee to owner in eighteen years

Leigh Sparks
University of Stirling

'Seven days a week, we open at seven. And seven days a week, we're open till 11. We've got soup to nuts and that's why we sing, 7-Eleven's got everything.'
(1949 American television advertising jingle)

Context

In 1973, Ito-Yokado Co. Ltd signed an agreement with The Southland Corporation to license the development of the 7-Eleven convenience-store chain throughout Japan. At the time The Southland Corporation was a major retail force focusing on convenience stores. This licensing was an international spatial exploitation of the 7-Eleven concept. In 1991, Ito-Yokado Co. Ltd, together with its subsidiary company, Seven-Eleven Japan Co. Ltd, purchased 70 per cent of The Southland Corporation and removed it from Chapter 11 bankruptcy. In eighteen years the licensee had developed from a non-existent operation to controlling and effectively owning the entire business. Everything for 7-Eleven now includes Japanese owners!

This case examines the operational practices which have made Seven-Eleven Japan a formidable retailer and invites consideration of two general issues: what role can technology play in a retail business; and how can Seven-Eleven Japan best revitalise The Southland Corporation?

The Southland Corporation

In 1927, an employee of The Southland Ice Company answered the requests of his customers by selling bread, milk and eggs from the steps of his ice dock. With that simple idea – giving customers what they want, when they want it – 'Uncle' Johnny Green began a 60-year tradition of customer service and innovation that remains a driving force of Southland. (The Southland Corporation 1986 Annual Report)

One of those 'innovations', the 7-Eleven convenience store format, began in 1946 when all Southland's units converted to a convenience approach and longer operating hours. Introduced in Texas, The Southland Corporation expanded convenience stores in the 1950s and 1960s across the US, although initially in the South. The approach was refined during this time, most notably through the addition of 24-hour opening in 1963. In an international move, the concept was licensed to Japan in 1973. Subsequently licences have been granted in over 20 countries. On the back of the continued expansion of the concept, Southland began to look at new opportunities. Encouraged by petrol sales at the stores (added increasingly from 1976) Southland purchased Citgo Petroleum Corporation in 1983. By this stage, petrol was the largest single product group in the stores (approximately 22 per cent of sales). Other retail acquisitions also occurred during the 1970s and 1980s, outside convenience stores. In 1987 affiliates of the Thompson Company acquired The Southland Corporation in a leveraged buy-out (LBO) and the company announced its desire to concentrate on its convenience retailing business. Divestitures of non 7-Eleven businesses occurred and even some convenience stores were closed or sold. Following the LBO, the business did not grow sufficiently rapidly to support its debt requirements (estimated at $3.6bn in 1990) and in 1990 Chapter 11 bankruptcy was filed. Ito-Yokado Co. Ltd and Seven-Eleven Japan Co. Ltd moved in to take over the business.

7-Eleven's convenience stores are extended-hour retail stores, emphasising convenience to the customer and providing groceries, take-out foods and beverages, gasoline (petrol) and other items. Operations are influenced favourably by warm weather, as a large part of the product mix consists of items consumed during leisure-time. Competition has increased from oil companies, drug stores and extended hours supermarkets. The company aims to build the customer base in addition to increasing the number and frequency of purchases through competitive pricing, extending branded food service programmes and extra customer services. Generally, the stores are open every day of the year for 24 hours and are located in neighbourhood areas, on main roads, in shopping centres, or on other sites where they are easily accessible and have parking facilities for quick in-and-out shopping.

There are many possible explanations for the demise of The Southland Corporation, among which an unfortunately timed and overly optimistic leveraged buy-out has pride of place. However, it can be argued that the retail concept itself had not been maintained. Ito-Yokado themselves make the comment:

> (The) conclusion reached was that convenience stores in the United States have strayed from their original mission of providing shoppers with convenience. By emphasizing volume-selling at discount prices, the stores had to limit their product mix. Consequently they have failed to respond to changes in customer needs. Four priorities that emerged . . . are the need to discontinue discount retailing, to create a merchandise mix reflecting customer needs, to maintain proper inventory levels and to place greater emphasis on quality and freshness control. (Ito-Yokado Annual Report 1992)

You might be forgiven for believing that convenience stores would be doing, or at least attempting to do, all of these things, and particularly a convenience store chain of over 7,000 stores in the US and Canada. However, this is not the case, nor has the problem been restricted to 7-Eleven. Other large chains such as Circle K and National Convenience Stores have also experienced difficulties. To understand how convenience stores might be operated with customers in mind it is possible to look to the 7-Eleven franchise in Japan.

Seven-Eleven Japan Co. Ltd – development

Seven-Eleven Japan Co. Ltd obtained the rights to the 7-Eleven name in Japan in a deal with The Southland Corporation in 1973. Seven-Eleven Japan Co. Ltd, set up for the purpose of the deal, is a majority-owned subsidiary of Ito-Yokado Co. Ltd. Ito-Yokado itself runs a large variety of retail chains, including superstores and supermarkets, department, discount and speciality stores and restaurants. In market capitalisation terms Seven-Eleven Japan are Japan's leading food retailer. In less than 18 years of operation a chain of over 5,000 convenience stores has been developed. By the end of financial year 1993 (February) there were 5,106 stores in the chain, sales had reached 1,195 billion Yen and the company was recognised as a pioneer in convenience store operations. Table 29.1 provides some of the broad milestones in this progress. The comparative development of the Japanese chain in store numbers can be gauged from Figure 29.1.

Convenience stores in Japan account for approximately 2 per cent of the retail sector sales. Large chains dominate the market with the top three (Seven-Eleven, Daiei Convenience Systems and Family Mart (Seiyu)) accounting for over half the market, and Seven-Eleven itself being the market leader with approximately a one-third share. While store numbers are not vastly greater than its main competitors, the sales and especially the profitability of Seven-Eleven overshadows the performance of their competitors.

Table 29.1 Seven-Eleven Japan Co. Ltd – important milestones

1973 (Nov.)	Seven-Eleven Japan Co. Ltd founded.
1974 (May)	First 7-Eleven store opened in Tokyo.
1979 (Oct.)	Tokyo Stock Exchange Listing.
1980 (Nov.)	1,000th store opened.
1984 (Feb.)	2,000th store opened.
1987 (April)	3,000th store opened.
1989 (Dec.)	First internationalisation (58 Hawaii stores bought from The Southland Corporation).
1990 (June)	4,000th store opened.
1991 (March)	With parent Ito-Yokado bought 70 per cent of The Southland Corporation.
1992 (Dec.)	5,000th store opened.

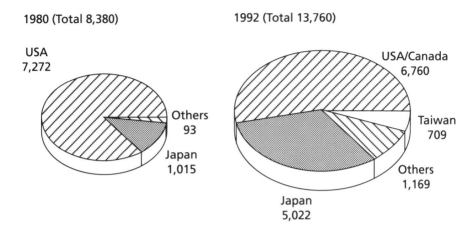

Fig. 29.1 Seven-Eleven stores worldwide

Unlike The Southland Corporation, Seven-Eleven Japan is based almost entirely on franchisees who manage themselves independently. Seven-Eleven supports the franchisees by providing management advice, point-of-sale (PoS) systems, utility cost sharing and a minimum guaranteed annual gross profit, and strives to raise the productivity and profits of franchised stores. Franchise commission calculations are based on an individual store's gross margin, with royalties being 45 per cent of gross profit. To ensure efficiency and stability, the store expansion policy is based upon a market dominance strategy which is built around clusters of 50 or 60 stores. Through such local saturation and clustering, Seven-Eleven gains a high-density market presence and thus raises distribution and advertising efficiency, improves brand awareness, raises system efficiency and the efficiency of franchisee support, and prevents competitors from entering into their local areas. Thus despite such a large number of stores, Seven-Eleven Japan is still present in only 21 of Japan's 47 prefectures. Figure 29.2 and 29.3 present details of the growth of stores and sales in the company in the recent past.

Seven-Eleven Japan Co. Ltd – operations

Seven-Eleven Japan's mission emphasises the need to keep up with and respond to changing customer needs, which themselves reflect the growing impact of social and environmental movements. Customers have been seen as the key element of the retail operation: 'It is not enough to look at the business from the viewpoint of a retailer. You must look at it from the consumer's viewpoint,' is an oft-reported refrain. This focus on consumer needs is developed particularly through the strategic use of information and information management. By utilising data and information throughout the business and beyond, quick responses are given to changing consumer needs. Such responses are, it is argued, more accurate, relevant and timely. In particular the

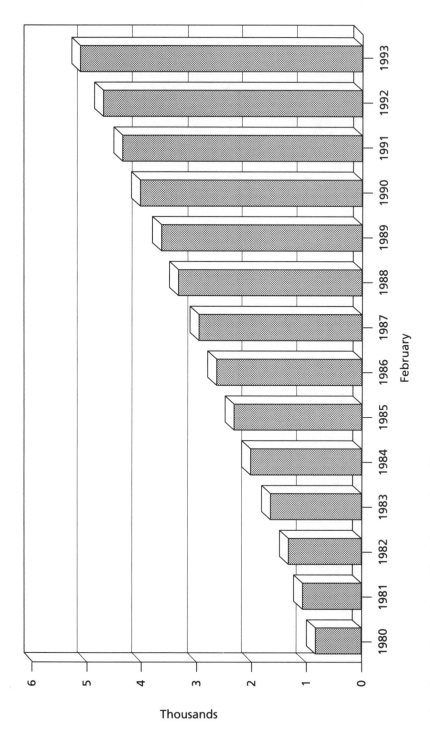

Fig. 29.2 Seven-Eleven Japan Co. Ltd – number of stores

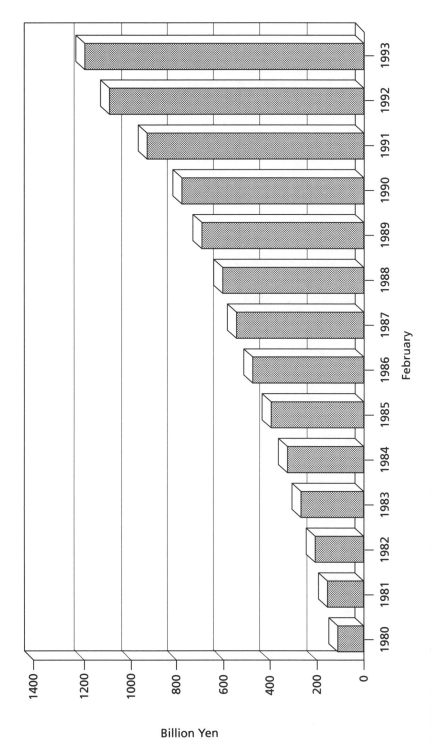

Fig. 29.3 Seven-Eleven Japan Co. Ltd – net sales

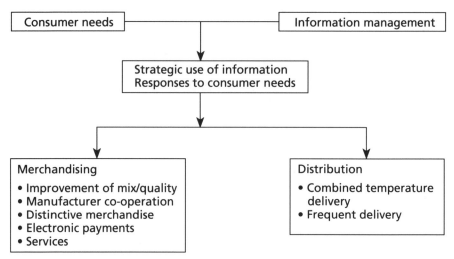

Fig. 29.4 Seven-Eleven Japan Co. Ltd – merchandising strategy

responses have focused on merchandising and distribution. The approach is laid out schematically in Figure 29.4. Figure 29.5 provides details of the information systems that are at the heart of this approach.

The data and the system

Fundamentally the business is driven by the capture and then widespread use of disaggregated data. Once the data have been identified and captured and the system built to use the data, then business changes become possible, either to improve the system or better to meet customer demands.

Such is the scale of the business that over 1.65 billion customer visits occurred in fiscal year 1993. This is more than 13 times the Japanese population. From these visits some 7.0 billion items of PoS data were collected on customers' age and sex, sales volume of all products, what products sold out and how product sales patterns are changing. This PoS data capture system is linked to the company's electronic ordering systems, merchandising and design systems and a full EDI network linking retail outlets, head office, distribution centres and dedicated and independent manufacturers/wholesalers. The level of data collected allows item-by-item inventory control and the identification of sales patterns by the time of the day, week, month, or any other time period required.

The system outlined above and shown in Figure 29.5 has been developed over time as the company and its needs have grown. Computer processing was introduced in 1975 and the beginnings of on-line network development occurred in 1979. The PoS data capture system commenced operation in 1982 and was integrated with the merchandising system in 1985. Since 1987 a total system has been in place, with elements being replaced, enhanced, or up-graded as more advanced, up-to-date technology becomes available. The data

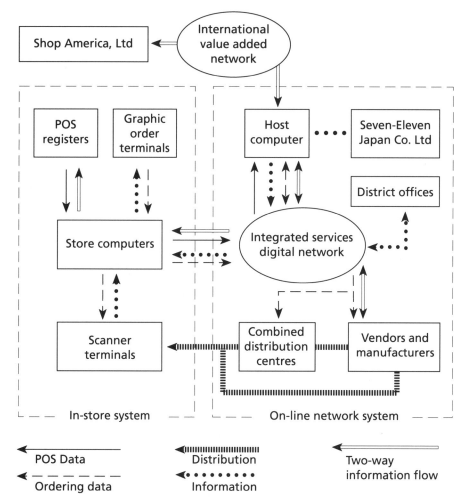

Fig. 29.5 Seven-Eleven Japan Co. Ltd – information systems

capture and network capabilities allow item-by-item movement by time of day and type of purchaser to be utilised throughout the company. This basic building block allows store staff to make scientifically based ordering decisions, head office staff to make chain-wide merchandising and distribution policies, and producer staff to assess demand and make up realistic production and distribution plans.

The basic components of Seven-Eleven Japan's information system have been developed in-house. They include a PoS cash register, a store computer, a graphic order terminal (GOT) and a scanner terminal. PoS cash registers speed up the checkout operation and record data such as time of purchase and type of customer. Such information is processed by Seven-Eleven Japan's host computer and returned to the store computer, where it can be accessed and used. The store computer can be used to place orders, display sales and store information, evaluate store product assortments, and functions generally as a

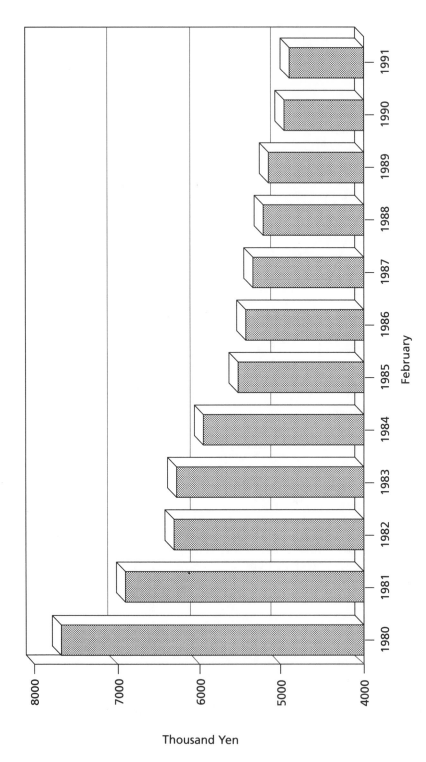

Fig. 29.6 Seven-Eleven Japan Co. Ltd – average per store inventory

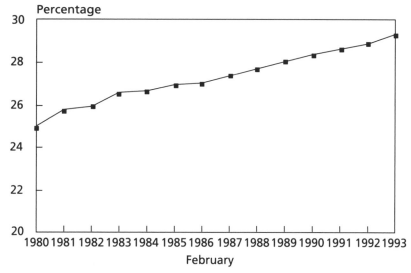

Fig. 29.7 Seven-Eleven Japan Co. Ltd – gross profit margin

management information system. The GOT is a notebook-sized portable computer providing product information and advice to store employees as they check shelves for items that need reordering. Able to read bar codes, the scanner terminal further simplifies ordering and taking inventory of shipments received. These components within the company are linked and integrated via an Integrated Services Digital Network (ISDN) which Seven-Eleven Japan claim is the largest of its kind in the world. This investment has vastly increased the volume and speed of data transmission.

The use of information technology in the company has had a number of effects. Fundamentally, there has been a large reduction in inventory (by 50 per cent

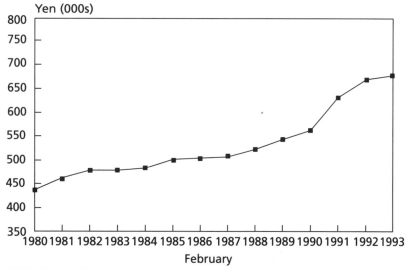

Fig. 29.8 Seven-Eleven Japan Co. Ltd – average per store daily sales

in the 1980s) and an increase in gross profit margins (from 25 to 28 per cent in the 1980s). Figures 29.6 and 29.7 show this. Not solely related to information technology but clearly linked to the way in which the stores meet customer needs, the average daily sales per store have risen over the 1980s and dramatically in the 1990s (see Figure 29.8).

Merchandising systems

The item-by-item data capture provides the basis for a sophisticated merchandising system. The merchandising innovations began with inventory paring and item-by-item control. Fine-tuning product line-ups is the basis of product consolidation, which involves the replacement of slow-moving products with fast-moving ones in demand. The result is a reduction of opportunity loss owing to sold-out products and an increase in customer loyalty. Replenishment of product lines can be made to maximise the sales of certain products at certain times of the day and night. For example, prepared dishes might have three purchase peaks in a 24-hour period (for example, at 07.00–09.00, 13.00–15.00 and 17.00–23.00), with deliveries timed accordingly to ensure availability, an appropriate product mix, freshness and quality (for example, at 03.00, 11.00 and19.00). The merchandise mix can thereby be adjusted by the dimensions of breadth, location and time. The results of the various time periods in terms of sales and wastage can be seen on screen in the stores. Information is available both numerically and visually, and on a next-day basis across the company.

The information usage is aimed at keeping product line-ups current by putting the customer at the centre of all operations. The data analysis enables slow-selling products to be eliminated and replaced by faster selling lines. In any one year it is estimated that approximately 50 to 65 per cent of the lines are replaced. In the soft drinks market, for example, there is little price or product differentiation among the 4,000 lines on the market. Seven-Eleven Japan have identified the most important 70–80 of these (that is, 2 per cent of the total available), from which each store makes its own stocking decisions using a process they term 'product consolidation'. Product consolidation is based on item-by-item control using information from head office and ordering advice from field consultants. Purchasers (that is, stores) make hypotheses about what will sell, confirming their accuracy through analysing these items' sales results. Hypothesising, ordering, verifying and continuous repetition of this process focuses the store on successful products. The smaller range and lower inventories are constantly refined to meet consumer demands and increase sales.

The provision of information is not only limited to within the company, but can involve manufacturers too. The benefit of the supply of information electronically to manufacturers in this fashion is an increase in co-operation and a reduction in total system costs. The rapid provision of accurate, detailed data allows informed production decisions to be made. For some products,

Seven-Eleven Japan has gone further and entered dedicated production agreements involving new site developments for production. Particularly in the field of delicatessen, prepared dishes and filled buns, such developments allow the product range to be tailored to the market and also to be dedicated and differentiated from the competition. The unique nature of the products again enhances the operation at store level, having the additional advantage of being high margin as well. At the same time Seven-Eleven Japan have gone further with some suppliers and taken on the risk themselves by agreeing not to return unsold items. This reliance on the system breeds confidence in the system, both in the company and the manufacturers.

With an information network already in place, Seven-Eleven Japan looked for ways to exploit their investment, particularly if it could improve convenience. In 1987, the electronic payment of electricity and gas bills through the stores and the computer network began. This had the merit of providing an enhanced service to existing customers and also attracting new potential customers to the stores. The company made no charge for the service, instead holding on to the money for a number of days and placing it on deposit. The earning of interest in this way is seen as a solution to the system payment issue. Subsequently the service has been expanded to allow payment of, for example, life assurance premiums, television fees and telephone bills. In fiscal year 1993, 8.2 million such electronic payments were made using the system compared to 5.5 million in the previous year.

In addition to electronic payments, other service provisions have been expanded to meet consumer needs. Photocopying, fast film processing, telephone card vending machines and accepting pre-paid cards as a method of payment in the stores, have all enhanced the physical service provision. It is also possible to use the electronic network to ensure the delivery of gift-packaged fresh flowers and individually customised lunch boxes. Such product personalisation is a reflection of a commitment to meet changing customer needs.

The most recent new use of the network to date is the provision of a service called Shop America. This catalogue service provides products from overseas to the Japanese market at a large discount, using both the stores and the network for customers to place orders. Such merchandise can only be ordered at 7-Eleven stores. The service had 300,000 subscribers by February 1992.

Distribution systems

Electronic data dissemination enables the faster understanding of activities across a more widespread spatial area. The corollary of this, however, is that the provision of 'better' data places a sterner requirement on physical movement. The Seven-Eleven Japan distribution system has therefore had to alter as the information and technology revolution was introduced.

When Seven-Eleven Japan began, it had to grapple with the existing distribution system in Japan, which was characterised by many vehicle journeys and multiple layers in the distribution channel. In the conventional system

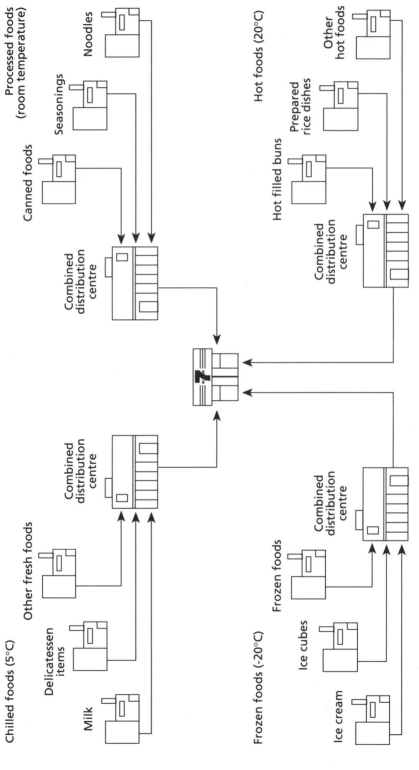

Fig. 29.9 Seven-Eleven Japan Co. Ltd – distribution systems

only one supplier's goods are carried at a time on delivery vehicles and there are many layers in the channel. To change this a combined small-lot delivery system, incorporating different suppliers' products, delivered on the same delivery vehicle, was developed. From 1976, the company began to develop the combined delivery system allowing consolidation of products before delivery to stores. From the mid-1980s this has involved temperature-controlled combined delivery and subsequently the strategic development of a dedicated distribution operation. To improve the freshness of perishable foods, as well as to improve efficiency, deliveries now combine products from different suppliers in a system which separates products by temperature rather than by producer or wholesaler (see Figure 29.9). In such a way, product freshness is enhanced and the store location pattern around centres ensures prompt yet frequent delivery if required. Deliveries per store per day are claimed to have fallen from 70 in 1974 to 11 in 1992. The aim, however, is to minimise deliveries by maximising the content of each through use of the merchandising system.

Seven-Eleven Japan Co. Ltd – the role of technology

Outlined and examined above is a retail system which has taken twenty years to reach its present state; a system showing classic elements of Japanese incremental improvement. The company's profit and sales growth was facilitated by a long-term technology strategy and the recognition of the importance of information in the business. This information imperative has been used to improve the merchandise mix and quality at both store and company levels. It also drives other elements of the business internally such as distribution, as well as externally, in areas such as manufacturer relations. In addition, the technological infrastructure has been used to enhance the retail product and service offer in terms of electronic payments, service additions and Shop America. The prerequisite to all this, however, is an understanding and awareness of how to enhance service and meet changing customer needs, together with and an appreciation of how these can be better achieved through business information systems. It is also necessary to note that the information is disseminated via a human resources policy which requires a basis of a cascading system of regular staff meetings.

The Southland Corporation – reprise

The purchase of The Southland Corporation by Seven-Eleven Japan Co. Ltd raises a number of possibilities and issues. Foremost amongst these is the opportunity for 7-Eleven in the US and elsewhere to be 'Japanised'. Already discussions are underway, but it must be recognised that solutions must come as much from America as from Japan. Given the sizes of the companies and the need for high-quality performance, this combined approach is a fundamental issue. To assist in discussion of this issue some further comparisons are made in Tables 29.2 and 29.3.

Table 29.2 Store level comparisons

	The Southland Corporation	Seven-Eleven Japan
Average floorspace (sq. ft)	2,600	1,060
Approximate number of lines	2,000	3,000
Average inventory (Yen million)	14.0	4.5
Average daily sales (Yen million)	0.5	0.6

Table 29.3 Product mix comparisons (percentage of sales)

(a)	Seven-Eleven Japan 1992	
	Processed food	40
	Non-food	24
	Fast food	21
	Fresh food	15
(b)	7-Eleven Southland 1990	
	Gasoline	22
	Tobacco	18
	Beer/wine	10
	Soft drinks	10
	Food service	9
	Groceries	8
	Non-foods	6
	Dairy products	5
	Candy	4
	Baked goods	4
	Health/beauty aids	2
	Customer services	2

Sources

This case has been prepared from a wide variety of source material. This includes:

Annual Reports	Ito-Yokado Co. Ltd
	Seven-Eleven Japan Co. Ltd.
	The Southland Corporation (including Form 10–K).
Brokers report	Kleinwort Benson International Inc.
Newspaper clippings	

Acknowledgements

The author wishes to thank and acknowledge the following: Professor John A. Dawson, for his initial work on Seven-Eleven Japan; Dr Roy Larke and Professor Ian Gow, for Japanese material and translation; Mr A. Tanae, for rapid provision of reports by Ito-Yokado and Seven-Eleven Japan; and various student cohorts in Stirling and Singapore, for telling me when I was confusing rather than helping understanding.

Part Nine

PEOPLE AND RETAILING

In 'Adding value through the human resource function', Mick Marchington highlights the role and major strategic importance of HRM within retailing organisations. Specifically, the case considers personnel management effectiveness, programmes for graduate trainees and the management of employee relations.

The issues and techniques of coping with organisational change are the focus of 'Management restructuring: effects on the workforce' by Adelina Broadbridge. Faced with an excessive hierarchy of management and supervisory levels, a variety store manager tackles the task of implementing a flatter, more flexible structure.

The management of change within the organisation and at store levels is also the main focus of 'Managing the Babyhouse', by Alan Mitton. The case introduces individual appraisals, reminding us that store managers must manage people and personalities, not simply holders of job titles.

Adding value through the human resource function
The case of food retailing

Mick Marchington
Manchester School of Management

Context

Over the course of the past decade food retailing came to be recognised as a major industry, both in Britain and abroad. Its market leaders now rank among the largest companies in the UK not only in financial terms, but also with respect to the number of people they employ. Much of this success has been built upon rapid advances in information technology, food hygiene, marketing, physical distribution and, of course, customer service. Accordingly, it is hardly surprising that much of the literature – especially for the student market – tends to focus upon these sorts of issues. Retailing texts devoting more than a chapter to human resource considerations are something of a rarity. Even then, these contributions have tended to come from staff at specialist retailing research centres whose disciplinary roots are outside of the personnel and industrial relations field (Johnson, 1987; Jones, 1989). More recently, there have been some articles written by people from the Human Resource Management (HRM) area, but this literature is still at an early stage of development (Ogbonna and Wilkinson, 1988, 1990; Marchington and Harrison, 1991).

This lack of analysis of human resource issues is surprising given the importance of people to food retailing companies, to the extent that high levels of customer service are reliant on relatively low-status employees. The importance of 'moments of truth' (Carlzon, 1987), whereby customers interact with staff for little more than a few seconds at a time, is just as relevant to supermarkets as it is to airlines. Unlike their counterparts in manufacturing, these staff are the principal point of contact between the company and its customers, the main gatekeepers of the corporate image. As such, it might be expected that HRM or employee relations would have been a central concern of academic analysis in food retailing, and that the problematic nature of management–employee relations would have been investigated in greater depth; after all, there are several indicators of the problem – for example, high levels of labour turnover, a pool of poor-quality recruits and low degrees of commitment from staff.

Unfortunately, in the literature, human resource considerations tend to be treated in a relatively simplistic, superficial and unitarist manner, with solutions being presented as if they were unproblematic. It is assumed that problems can be overcome by prescribing more technical training, more elaborate and glossy communications devices or increasingly sophisticated selection techniques; in other words, it is anticipated that a little bit of managerial tinkering with the machinery can rectify things. Clearly, each of these is important in its own right, but there is also a need to consider the problematic nature of management–employee relations and the fact that labour is different to any other resource at the employer's disposal.

This introduction sets the backcloth to the case study which follows. It aims to examine the contribution that human resource practitioners can make to the successful operation of a company to help it to achieve the overall goal of 'high levels of customer service'. The case itself is synthetic, constructed from the experiences of three leading food retailers in Britain (J. Sainsbury, Tesco and Safeway). Although the three have much in common – in particular, at the time of writing, their commitment to high-quality products and services – there are also differences, not least in relation to a number of human resource practices and management styles. The use of a synthetic case therefore increases the learning potential from the exercise, in that we can draw upon all three to suggest alternative solutions.

For the purposes of the case, we will regard human resource management as those strategies and practices which the company (and in particular the personnel function) adopts in order to ensure the most effective use of labour. As such, it includes policies regarding recruitment and selection, induction, communications and involvement, training and development, employee relations and disciplinary control. The focus is not just on the more visible work performed by personnel and training managers in stores, but on the more strategic and long-term contributions which are made at corporate headquarters or at regional/district level; this means that the human resource function also contributes to organisational design and management development, and to the creation of an appropriate quality culture throughout the company. These contributions are not particularly apparent to many observers, but without them it is unlikely that firms would be as successful. This highlights a final point before setting out the case study in more detail; it is extremely difficult to measure the contribution made by the human resource (HR) function in any organisation, a factor which has undoubtedly led to problems in personnel's continuing search for legitimacy within management. This ought to be borne in mind throughout the remainder of the case study.

The changing context of food retailing

Food retailing is an extremely competitive sector of the British economy, which comprises not just the well-known leading superstores but also a mass of small (often family-owned) shops across the country. The market share held by the latter has been declining for many years, with the top six or seven companies now accounting for about two-thirds of all food and drinks sales in Britain. Among these larger companies, the market has become increasingly polarised between those which sell on the basis of cheap prices and no frills, and those which compete via a policy of high quality and width of choice. By the early 1990s, the market leaders were increasingly drawn from this latter segment, with the three companies referred to in this case all being firmly located in the quality/choice segment. The market leaders have all experienced continued growth over the last decade and, in contrast to most other parts of British industry and indeed many other parts of retailing, profits have remained healthy during the recession. Over the late 1980s and early 1990s, the quality-end of the market has enjoyed a period of almost unprecedented success, but with the intervention of companies such as Aldi and Netto this may be open to more direct challenge by the end of the century.

There has also been an overall growth in the number and size of stores in recent years, such that many of the newer stores occupy more than 25,000 square feet and employ several hundred staff. A high proportion of the staff employed work part-time, at certain times of the year the number of temporary staff increases dramatically, and the workforce as a whole is relatively young; although there are exceptions to these general trends of course. The majority of staff employed are women, the vast proportion of which are on the lower grades: in common with most industries the ratio of men to women increases the further one goes up the hierarchy. The opening hours of these food retailers have increased substantially to the point where 75 or 80 hours per week (including seven hours on Sundays) is now relatively common. Most of the leading companies also employ staff in the evening or at night (for example, shelf-filling, warehousing, cleaning) and some occupations (for example, bakers and butchers) start work several hours before the shops are actually open to customers. In short, the leading food retailers are now large employment units in their own right, employing more people than many factories and operating for more hours as well – especially during the early 1990s.

Business strategy and human resource management

The synthetic retailer will be named Superco, and indeed, with some few adjustments it could be any of the three high-quality leaders in the industry. The company employs 75,000 staff across Britain, both at the headquarters in the south-east and in its 250 stores located around the country. Superco now has a national coverage, having expanded from its southern base, although there are still parts of the country where stores are less likely to be found. It is organised into regions and districts, with each district containing approximately 15 stores. In addition, the company has a number of warehouses, each located in a strategic position to ensure maximum speed of response for deliveries to individual stores. The vast bulk of products are held at these large warehouses, with deliveries being made to each store several times each day. It is company policy not to carry much in the way of stock, even of items with a longer shelf life.

Superco's mission statement demonstrates its commitment to market leadership through the provision of high-quality customer service, partnerships with suppliers and participation in the local community. A copy of the mission statement is given to each new employee during the induction programme, with extra copies available should anyone need one. The importance of this mission statement is made clear to staff by a statement from the chief executive in the booklet which introduces them to the company. In relation to employees, the ethos is one of 'resourceful humans', that is developing and involving staff to ensure that they possess the skills and abilities needed to achieve competitive advantage. Reference is made to training opportunities (both on and off the job), to the welfare of staff, to their participation and involvement in teams, and to high pay and benefits at work. In brief, it states: 'We value our people. We will create an atmosphere in which our people can develop their talents and contribute as part of an energetic and enthusiastic team. We will invest in recruitment and training. We will reward them for achievement through the resourceful application of knowledge and skills.'

The HR function operates at four separate levels within the company (headquarters, region, district and store) and is headed by a main board director. This is seen to be important for two reasons: first, to ensure that he or she is able to contribute specialist knowledge and expertise in the personnel area and secondly, to promote awareness of the links between business strategy and human resource management. Increasingly, however, as with companies in other industries, the functional location of individuals is now less important than their contribution to the overall business.

Beneath the main board director are a number of other HR directors, each of whom has responsibility for a particular part of the business. This head office team are the architects behind the development of personnel policies which apply across the business as a whole, as well as playing a leading role in shaping the structure and culture of the company. Most recently, this has been apparent in the moves towards Total Quality Management, which the HR team took a leading role in introducing at board level and disseminating within the entire organisation. The human resource message is implicit throughout this initiative, which is aimed at creating a climate where continuous improvement becomes 'the way we do things around here'. Unlike some of the programmes which have focused solely on quality assurance and the achievement of BS5750/ISO9000, this is meant to be an overarching and ongoing process of cultural change which, over time, should become deeply embedded in the fabric of the organisation.

The corporate HR team is responsible (with the rest of the board) for creating and overseeing a set of core personnel policies which are meant to apply across Superco as a whole. These cover many of the routine aspects of employee resourcing, such as standard application forms and personnel specifications, induction programmes, remuneration and benefits packages, holiday entitlements, disciplinary and grievance procedures, offences for which an individual may be liable for summary dismissal, equal opportunities, personal appearance, pensions, profit sharing, and so on. In addition, the HR team is responsible for important employee relations issues such as the determination of pay and conditions for all staff, and for dealing with the relevant trade unions. All of these terms and conditions are laid out in a booklet for staff, which is distributed to new starters during their induction programme. This booklet, which needs to be read and 'signed-off' by each new employee, contains nearly 40 sections itemising company rules in specific areas. For example, in the section on disciplinary procedures, examples of serious misconduct which are stated are:

- persistent lateness or absenteeism;
- persistent work errors;
- rudeness to customers;
- smoking in unauthorised areas; and
- failure to carry out reasonable and lawful instructions.

Examples of more serious offences that render the employee liable for summary dismissal, including a number which are specifically directed at managers, are:

- theft, fraud, violent or abusive behaviour;
- breaking safety rules;
- malicious or deliberate discrimination (colour/creed/sex);
- abuse of authority; and
- being under the influence of drugs or drink while at work.

Management development

Given the continuing growth in the size of Superco over the last decade, the recruitment and development of managers has been a key activity for the HR function. Managers are selected by one of two routes; first, the company has been increasing its stock of graduates from all disciplines, although the recent development of courses in retailing and allied subjects has led to a greater supply of applicants with special interests in the area. Irrespective of their background, however, all new graduates embark upon a development programme which combines a mix of standard and dedicated placements; for example, someone who was keen to join the personnel function would receive the standard broad grounding in the business as a whole plus more detailed exposure to the work of the personnel function. The period spent as a graduate trainee varies depending upon the progress of the individual, but typically this would last for twelve to eighteen months. The second route into a management job is through Superco's internal promotion channels, whereby the company aims to develop (both on and off the job) individuals who express interest in career progression and who are shown to have the necessary capabilities in tests. The advantages of this route into management are that it reinforces the belief amongst staff that there is an open promotions policy, as well as tapping into a pool of highly competent labour. Through both routes, Superco is especially keen to provide opportunities for women who wish to advance.

The HR function at corporate headquarters has also led the development of courses and on-the-job training for executives and senior managers. The Senior Management Development Programme (SMDP) is designed to improve teamworking, ensure the cross-fertilisation of good ideas, enhance communications and enable these senior managers to perform to their full potential. These programmes consist of a series of modules over a one-year period, interspersed by individual and group projects back at the workplace. The principal subjects tackled include customer service, Total Quality Management, managing change and strategic planning. The SMDP is both designed and run by members of the HR function, but contributions are also invited from outside consultants as well as academics from leading management schools. The objective of the programme is simple: to ensure the preservation of high-quality customer service by continuously improving the performance of all managers.

The go-betweens: HRM at district and regional level

Given the number of staff employed by Superco and their geographical spread across Britain, it would be impossible for the personnel function at head office to offer advice on demand, or to oversee the detailed application of HR policies in the stores. For this reason, a number of years ago the company decided to set up a personnel presence at an intermediate level; there are now five regional personnel managers, each supported by a skeleton staff, who are responsible for ensuring consistency across the company as a whole. Different personnel problems and issues can arise in different parts of the country, especially in relation to trade union organisation and grievances, which should be addressed as they arise. Equally, the regional personnel managers are responsible for the development of managers within their patch and play an important role in their career progression – especially for new graduates and others who are on fast-track development packages. In addition, a regional presence is helpful for the district and store personnel managers who are in contact with each other on a regular basis, and for whom provision can be made for meetings to discuss key issues (such as disciplinary matters, new legal developments or personnel procedures, training packages) each month.

The tasks of the district personnel managers are much more practically orientated and involve contact with each store on a fortnightly basis at minimum. Clearly, if there is an important issue in a store, if a new store personnel manager has just been appointed, or a new store is about to be opened, the degree of contact can be much more frequent than this. Conversely, it is less necessary that the district personnel manager visits store which are run by experienced personnel professionals or are experiencing few problems. The primary input by the district level is to help out with disciplinary and recruitment difficulties, as well as to ensure that training is delivered in the right format at the requisite times. At all times, the need for consistency in policies is paramount to these intermediate levels, and of course for the company as a whole. This is especially important in the area of employee relations.

Employee relations

Superco has an agreement with USDAW (The Union of Shop Distributive and Allied Workers) which provides, in specified circumstances, for individual union members to be represented by the union in the event of a grievance or a disciplinary issue. In order to be eligible for representation, the union has to demonstrate that it has a substantial membership at the store involved, although no figure is quoted for this. Once it is agreed that the union should have these rights at a store, members are allowed to nominate a shop steward from within the branch to represent them should the need arise. This person would then be given time off with pay to undertake her/his union duties, although it is unlikely that these would take up more than a few hours each week. It is often difficult to find a willing recruit for the position of shop steward, and representing up to a hundred members is no easy task. Union membership across the company as a whole is less than 10 per cent of all staff. However, management in the stores are encouraged to co-operate with the union representatives and to lubricate relationships at the store – especially in those locations where unionism is more fully developed.

In addition, partly because of the desire among some staff to join a union, the company introduced a consultative committee structure at regional level in the mid-1980s. The purpose of these committees is to take an overview of issues which arise in separate stores and, should a common theme emerge, they would instigate a standard response rather than having each separate incident resolved on a one-off, *ad hoc* basis. Staff are represented on these committees by full-time union officials and relevant shop stewards once membership in a region exceeds 500 people, with the committees meeting every three to four months. Management is represented on these committees by store, district and regional line managers, plus representatives of the personnel function from both regional and head offices. Minutes are kept of the meetings, which are then passed to head office and acted upon as appropriate.

Pay and other working conditions are not subject to negotiation between management and trade union representatives, but instead are determined by management each year. This is an area in which the personnel/HR function plays a leading part, by both scanning the external environment for comparable cases, as well as estimating what the company can afford. Up until the late 1980s, a number of the larger firms were members of the Multiple Food Retailers' Employers Association (MFREA), and the rates negotiated there obviously had quite a strong influence over companies which were not members of the MFREA as well. Similarly, until its abolition in 1993, so did the pronouncements of the Wages Council for the industry because of its effect on the wages for the lowest paid employees in each company. The pay rates

Table 30.1 Selected pay rates/increases for 1992

Company/body	Date of award	Increase (%)	Range of weekly rates
Superco	April	4.6	£139–£161
Retail Co-op	May	4.2	£135–£148
Gateway	April	0.0	£120–£132
Wages Council	April	4.2	£120
Average figures	April	7.0	£305
(male manual)	April	6.1	£268
(female manual)	April	7.1	£170

of leading rivals is a significant factor in this exercise, and all the companies in this 'high quality' segment of the market pay great attention to the deals which other firms have offered (see, for example, Table 30.1); interestingly, within this group of employers, there is little difference in pay levels between those companies which negotiate with unions and those which do not. For further discussion of these points, readers are referred to Jackson, Leopold and Tuck (1992).

The personnel function at store level

While the head office team is responsible for creating a framework for all HR activities within the company (including issues concerned with cultural change and organisational design), these can never prescribe for every eventuality in the stores themselves. It is at this level that the contribution of personnel is most visible, and it is here that most of the activity tends to be of a tactical and fire-fighting nature – recruiting new staff, running induction programmes, dealing with absence and disciplinary problems, checking and updating staff records, ensuring the speedy dissemination of company information, and generally getting involved in the day-to-day activities of the store. The store personnel managers adopt a generalist and broad-based approach to their work. As we have already seen, they are assisted by the district personnel manager during routine or emergency visits, in particular on how to ensure that the company complies with all its obligations under employment law. In addition, the stores call upon teams of in-house specialists to help with customer care or technical skills training. The store personnel manager is part of the management team alongside the store manager and her or his three assistants. Personnel is seen very much as the store manager's right-hand person, being involved in most of the important activities that contribute to a high level of customer service.

The most serious personnel problems which confront the stores are in the areas of labour turnover/recruitment, absence and disciplinary control, and communications blockages. Labour turnover varies depending upon the location of the store, the state of the local labour market, and whether or not competitor stores are opening in the area. It is not unusual for figures of 50 per cent or more per annum, although many of these people leave within the first few months of joining the company; accordingly, there is also a high stability rate in many stores, and a fair proportion of staff with periods of service stretching back over five or more years. Labour turnover amongst the full-time staff and in specific jobs (for example, butchers and bakers) tends to be much lower, but the nature of customer demand necessitates the appointment of significant numbers of part-time workers. In an effort to reduce levels of labour turnover, Superco is now targeting its recruitment much more precisely than in the past, and it is also implementing other personnel policies to encourage greater employee identification with the aims of the company.

Unauthorised absence and disciplinary problems also cause serious headaches for Superco, as they do for any employer where a large proportion of employees have direct contact with customers. Much of the day-to-day firefighting work of the store personnel manager is concerned with trying to match the availability of staff with the requirements of the store. She or he is reliant upon pools of temporary, but qualified, labour to plug some of the gaps, as well as persuading other employees to work extra hours as appropriate. The use of disciplinary action for misconduct or a failure to comply with company standards is also part of the job, as is counselling poor performers or those with personal problems that are affecting their work.

Stores receive a considerable amount of information from head office, most of which is not directly relevant to the majority of staff. But, some issues do need to be communicated quickly to certain groups of staff – especially if these relate to products or services. Equally, there are certain messages which all staff need to know, either of a one-off nature or at regular time intervals. In both cases, the personnel manager needs to find the most effective mechanism for communicating this information quickly so that it reaches all concerned, does not lead to rumours, and is accurate; the options available for this include the line management chain, the use of the noticeboard near the canteen, special written messages posted around the store, or the use of formal communication events (such as team briefings on a regular monthly basis) during or after working hours. The latter may occasionally be combined with social events and teambuilding exercises, but in each case, a balance needs to be struck between cost and effectiveness.

Summary

The principal objective behind this case has been to examine the role of the HR function within a large, high-quality food retailing business. The issues to be addressed have included the structure of the personnel/HR function throughout the company (from head office to store level) and its contribution to the operation and success of the business. In particular, we have focused upon the role of human resources in attempting to shape the organisational culture, deal with problems which arise in the company, and ensure a consistent supply of appropriately qualified staff for each workplace. To some extent though there is a paradox between the grand designs formulated at corporate headquarters, which represent the view of 'people as our most important asset', and the mass of problems and difficulties which arise at the stores in attempting to satisfy the short-term requirement to maintain high levels of customer service. The key personnel issues which have been examined are human resource planning, recruitment, induction, training and development, performance manage-ment, employee relations, communications and welfare; in other words, the major activities which are reported in any personnel or human resource management textbook, or in any personnel manager's work. It is important not only to ensure that each of these discrete activities is discharged competently, but also that they are integrated with each other and contribute to the achievement of business goals. When people are involved, this is no easy task.

Case study questions and problems

1. *Outline the principal ways in which the personnel function can contribute to competitive advantage at Superco, and suggest ways in which this contribution could be improved.*

2. *What measures can be used to assess how the personnel function might 'add value' to the business? What are the limitations of these measures of personnel effective-ness?*

    You might find some of the following references useful for this: S Tyson and A. Fell, Evaluating the Personnel Function, *Stanley Thorne, 1992, Chapter 6; M. Armstrong,* Personnel and the Bottom Line, *Institute of Personnel Manage-ment, 1989, Chapters 7, 8 and 15; M. Marchington, A. Wilkinson and B. Dale, 'Who is really taking the lead on quality?',* Personnel Management, *April 1993.*

3. *Consider the roles that are occupied by the personnel function at Superco, and assess whether there are any differences between the practice of personnel manage-ment at head office, for the go-betweens, and at the stores.*

    In order to make this discussion more meaningful, students might like to read either J. Storey, Developments in the Management of Human Resources, *Blackwell, 1992, Chapter 6; S. Tyson and A. Fell,* Evaluating the Personnel Function, *Stanley Thorne, 1992, Chapter 2; or Marchington et al, 'Who is really taking the lead on quality?',* Personnel Management, *April 1993.*

4. *Critically review Superco's arrangements for managing employee relations, and consider whether or not this part of the company's activities could be improved. You might like to read M. Marchington and E. Harrison, 'Customers, competitors and choice; employee relations in food retailing',* Industrial Relations Journal, **22** *(4), 286–99, before addressing this question.*

5. *In the penultimate section of the case study (pp. 361–2), three major problems were presented which typically confront the store personnel manager; these are labour turnover/recruitment, absence and disciplinary control, and communicat-ions blockages. What measures would you suggest should be taken to deal with these? In each case, justify your solution in terms of costs and its impact on customer service.*

6.   *Superco prides itself on its programme for new graduate trainees (see pp. 358–9). Assuming that you had just started work for the company, provide a brief outline for a management development programme which would be appropriate for you, and state the reasons why this would be valuable. Before tackling this question, it might be worth visiting your local careers and appointments service to collect any information on graduate development programmes run by the large food retailers or other employers.*

References and further reading

Carlzon, J. (1987), *Moments of Truth*, Ballinger, Cambridge, Mass.

Jackson, M., J. Leopold and K. Tuck (1992), 'De-centralisation of collective bargaining: the case of the retail food industry', *Human Resource Management Journal*, **2**(2), 29–45.

Johnson, G. (ed.) (1987), *Business Strategy in Retailing*, Wiley, New York.

Jones, P. (ed.), (1989) *Management in Service Industries*, Pitman Publishing, London.

Marchington, M. and E. Harrison (1991), 'Customers, competitors and choice: employee relations in food retailing', *Industrial Relations Journal*, **22**(4), 286–299.

Ogbonna, E. and B. Wilkinson (1988), 'Corporate strategy and corporate culture: the management of change in the UK supermarket industry', *Personnel Review*, **17**(6), 10–14.

Ogbonna, E. and B. Wilkinson (1990), 'Corporate strategy and corporate culture: the view from the checkout', *Personnel Review*, **19**(4), 9–15.

Management restructuring
Effects on the workforce

Adelina Broadbridge
University of Stirling

Context

This case examines the effects of organisational restructure on a workforce. While the restructure described is based on a real situation, the case itself is fictional and the outcome described purely hypothetical. From it, the reader should be able to explore various key issues in human resource management. Of these, the case has the potential to explore areas such as communication, leadership, motivation, conflict, stress, team building and succession planning.

Hunters is a large variety store retailer, operating 100 stores throughout England and Wales. Organised into a number of regions for day-to-day operations, each has a regional manager responsible for the stores in that area. The board is responsible for the strategic and long-term operations of the company, organised through the headquarters of the firm in London.

Although each store within the company has its own performance targets to achieve, all stores work towards the mission of the company: 'to remain a leading retailer in the provision of family, clothing and household goods by offering our customers excellent value goods and services at all times'. The company places considerable emphasis on both the quality of its products and the service it offers to customers. Many of the products sold in the firm's stores are well-known brand names but certain products are sold under its own brand name. The company as a whole employs 11,500 staff, with each store having on average 100 staff.

The problem

Stephen Cunningham, store manager at the Manchester branch of Hunters Stores Limited, sat at his desk one afternoon in September, and wondered how to write a company report to head office on the effects of implementation of a new store structure in the company. His store had been selected, along with four others, to pilot the scheme. Head office wanted to know how the staff had reacted and adapted to the new store structure.

While Stephen could see the long-term advantages of the new organisational structure in terms of the business objectives, the implementation had caused much turbulence at store level. It had caused him endless problems. Prior to the new structure being implemented his staff had, in general, been hard working and had worked towards the objectives of the company. When the new structure was announced, however, they treated him with suspicion, and morale at all levels had generally suffered. Tension built up among certain members of staff, clearly affecting their performance and the level of customer service. His deputy manager, Jonathan Wright, seemed particularly stressed at the beginning and it had taken up much of Stephen's time trying to alleviate people's fears about their new roles.

The old structure

The old store structure followed a classical approach to organisational theory – with a pyramid structure of authority and control (see Figure 31.1). The store manager was at the apex of this structure; this was followed by senior, middle and junior managers, supervisors and, finally, general assistants. It was a bureaucratic form emphasising the distribution of power and responsibility within the store. A clear line of authority ran from Stephen Cunningham, the store manager, to the general assistants, resulting in six levels of control over general assistants.

The structure provided organisational control by ensuring a high degree of predictability in behaviour. Clear job descriptions were provided for all staff, outlining their relative levels of responsibility. Managers higher up in the structure co-ordinated the efforts of subordinates; the lower the manager's position in the hierarchy, the more specialised their duties, resulting in fewer responsibilities and opportunities for decision taking.

Each person in the organisational structure reported directly to his or her immediate superior. This system generally worked well, but caused problems if a particular grievance was aired. If a line manager was unable to resolve the grievance it might take time before Stephen heard about it. It would be passed through the chain of command, and inevitably, through the process the grievance was not communicated to Stephen in its original form. Some problems took a long time to resolve because of this, and depending on the nature of the grievance this could have wider implications on the staff and how they worked together to achieve the goals of the organisation.

The old store structure resulted in a rather top heavy management structure. A staff–management ratio of 25 : 70 meant high wage budgets at store level.

The store was structured along functional lines and followed a fairly simple structure. The senior management team co-ordinated the activities of six departments. Departmental managers were recruited to particular departments because of their interests and capabilities in certain areas. Targets were set at departmental level with all staff working towards those particular targets. Other staff were recruited to work for a particular department, and each of the six departments operated fairly autonomously within the store structure.

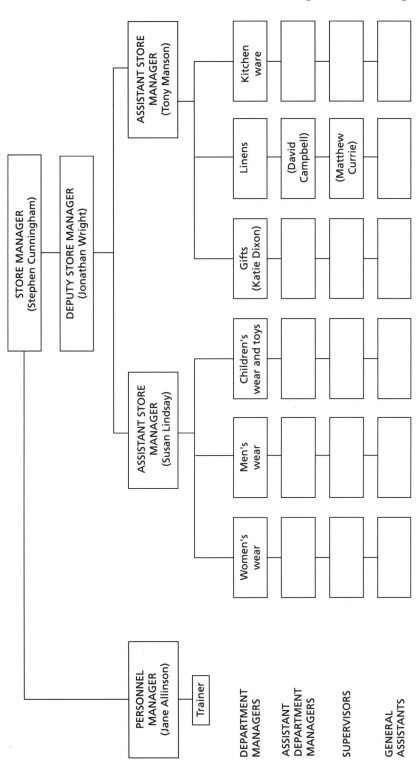

Fig. 31.1 Organisational chart – old management structure

The advantage of a departmentalised structure was the team effort which ensued. Staff understood their own department and merchandise very well. Every employee in each of the six departments had specific duties to meet the departmental goals. It did mean, however, that general assistants often performed routine tasks and had little opportunity to develop a range of skills. It also tended to focus staff attention on departmental as opposed to organisational objectives and reduced interdepartmental communication.

Stephen Cunningham had been the store manager at Manchester for three years. In his early thirties, he had progressed rapidly through the organisation after joining the company's graduate training scheme ten years previously. He was ultimately accountable for the successful running and cost effectiveness of the store. His role was to ensure that the store operated to achieve its overall targets and that his staff were fulfilling their roles. He was responsible for building up and maintaining team spirit and morale, while also identifying individual needs and satisfying them in a manner compatible with the needs of the task and the group. Stephen's role meant that he was involved in all the aspects of day-to-day operational management, including dealing with customer queries and complaints.

Where possible, Stephen tried to involve his deputy and assistant managers in a participative style of management. Rather than a 'tell and sell' approach, he tried to encourage consultation and allowed them some freedom, within limits, to make decisions on how to manage their staff in order to get specific tasks done. Each morning he would walk around the store with his deputy manager, Jonathan Wright, and discuss what needed to be accomplished that day. Jonathan would indicate any operational problems and Stephen would discuss the various options available with the relevant managers. Ultimately Stephen would decide on the solution, but it was not without involving the managers and listening to and encouraging their judgements of the situation.

Jonathan Wright, the deputy manager, understudied the store manager. He was involved in the whole range of operational aspects of store functions and ran the store in Stephen's absence. The assistant store managers, Tony Manson and Susan Lindsay, were each responsible for managing all the aspects of day-to-day operation of three departments. Their role was ultimately to ensure maximisation of sales within the three departments for which they held responsibility. They did this by guaranteeing that these departments were efficiently managed, and that merchandise was well presented, available and of excellent quality at all times. They assisted in the selection, training and development of staff to ensure that customer service levels were kept at an optimum.

The various department managers were involved in day-to-day operations and control of staff to meet the targets set to satisfy customer needs. Katie Dixon was the department manager of gifts; in her early twenties, she joined the company as a management trainee and had worked her way up through the store structure to become department head two years ago. She took pride in her work; her staff respected her and she spent a lot of time on the shop floor talking to customers, dealing with their queries and identifying their needs.

Recently, however, she had felt stilted in her position; she was an ambitious young woman and her line manager (Tony Manson) believed she had potential for further development.

Matthew Currie, 20, was the supervisor in the linen department. He was a fairly good worker and got on with the tasks asked of him, though he had no clear career aspirations. Quite happy in his current position, it allowed him some responsibilities such as supervising general assistants' work, scheduling lunch rotas, till rotas, and so on. He liaised with his department manager over stock control and ordering. He did, however, need to continually motivated to carry out his work, rarely taking the initiative to perform certain duties. David Campbell, his assistant departmental head, continually needed to follow up Matthew's work to make sure it had been done.

Rationale for change

The old structure had evolved over the years, but because of the way the business was changing, there was now less need for such a rigid hierarchical structure.

Over the past five years, the company had introduced new technologies including electronic point of sale, space management systems, automatic stock ordering systems, just-in-time distribution systems and electronic data interchange. Such systems had become far more centralised at head office, taking away many of the functional duties at store level. A new organisational structure was regarded as necessary to optimise the work of individuals with the needs of the business and meet the changes more effectively. The high staff–management ratio not only added to the high wage budget, but the new systems also meant that staff were now oversupervised. Staff lower down the hierarchy were not given enough scope to take responsibility for their own actions. Thus the previous hierarchical system was no longer compatible and had to make way for a new flatter pyramid, with fewer levels of management.

In such recessionary times, the company knew it was important to reduce costs, but striving for competitive advantage and customer care was also paramount. The company believed that competitive advantage could be gained by ensuring that the skills and attributes of staff were combined in an innovative fashion to increase their effectiveness. The company believed that real gains in product development, quality and effectiveness could be made by moving away from the traditional hierarchy. The new structure provided an opportunity to operate more flexibly, to remove internal interdepartmental barriers and to focus attention more strongly on achieving organisational rather than departmental goals.

New structure

The new store structure is illustrated in Figure 31.2. It was flatter management structure, consisting of just two levels (senior and middle management)

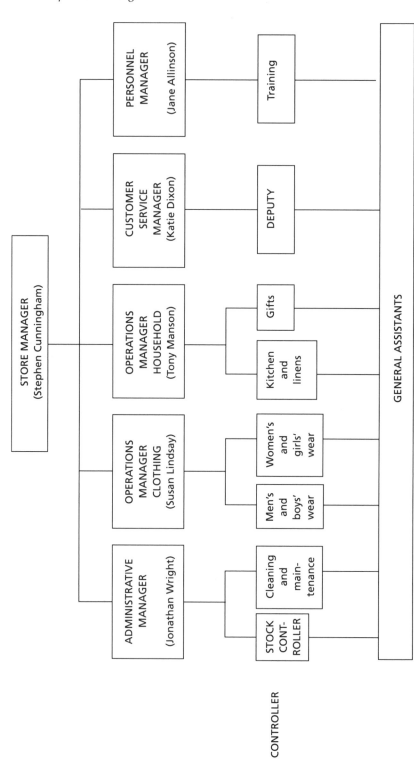

Fig. 31.2 Organisational chart – new management structure

between the store manager and general assistants. Thus it removed three superfluous layers of management.

Senior management team

The senior management team consisted of the following personnel:

Stephen Cunningham	Store Manager
Jonathan Wright	Administrative Manager
Jane Allinson	Personnel Manager
Susan Lindsay	Operations Manager – Clothing
Tony Manson	Operations Manager – Household
Katie Dixon	Customer Service Manager

The middle management team consisted of eight controllers who replaced the department managers, assistant department managers and supervisors. General assistants now reported directly to a controller, and the new structure allowed more communication between store manager and controller. The senior management team was organised so that each senior manager focused on particular 'issues', or areas, central to running a store. Thus each manager became a specialist, concentrating on one area, such as people, customers, administration and so on. They were totally accountable for that area, to ensure it was properly managed and to consider the strategic as well as day-to-day issues. So for example, Jane Allinson no longer only dealt with the day-to-day personnel issues of induction, training, on-the-job development, welfare issues and personal problems. Her new role included more of a strategic direction and took charge of the longer-term issues of store resources, motivation, career planning, as well as the training and development of the senior management team to ensure the store offered its customers the best possible service. Under the old structure, she had not been part of the senior management team, but now she was accountable as a member of the top team to provide ongoing feedback to the store manager. She contributed to the overall management of the store and was accountable for guaranteeing that staff issues were dealt with speedily, efficiently and fairly.

Relatively speaking, the duties of Tony Manson and Susan Lindsay did not change significantly. They still managed all aspects of the day-to-day operation of their respective areas and assisted in recruitment, training and development of staff so that the best level of service was provided at optimum cost. As members of the senior team they could be responsible for the store in the absence of the store manager and administrative manager.

Jonathan Wright (administrative manager) and Katie Dixon (customer service manager) experienced the greatest changes in their roles as a result of the restructuring.

Jonathan Wright found himself moving from the generalist position of deputising for the store manager, to that of a specialist responsible for all the store's administration. In this highly involved and important area of store operation, he was now accountable for the stock and the various administration systems in the store, which meant following specific routines. His new role involved accepting more responsibility than the previous role allowed.

Under the new structure Katie Dixon was promoted from departmental manager of gifts to customer service manager. Her role is to achieve a positive customer care service by ensuring that customers are treated with efficiency, courtesy and respect at all times. Any customer queries and/or grievances are dealt with by Katie. Well motivated for the post, she was already trying to develop her role strategically by setting up focus groups to talk to customers about their perceptions of the store. She plans to hold customer events and wants to try to foster community links by developing a PR role.

Middle management team

In terms of the overall store structure, most changes were evident at middle management level. The role of the new controllers was very similar to that of department manager under the old structure – that is, to control day-to-day operations according to set procedures, so that their area fully meets customer needs in terms of product quality, availability and presentation. They assist Jane Allinson in the recruitment, training and motivation of staff. They also provide the senior management team with appropriate paperwork for their area. However, problems arose because there were only eight controller positions to replace the 19 previous positions of departmental manager, assistant department manager, supervisors and trainers. The positions were originally open to applications from all staff in these posts. In practice, departmental managers were interviewed and appointed initially, but if any vacancies still existed, assistant department managers and supervisors were invited to apply. In the event, all the department heads became controllers (with the exception of Katie Dixon who was promoted to customer service manager), as did two assistant department managers.

Those assistant managers and supervisors not to be offered a controller position were offered voluntary redundancy or placed on protected salaries. Their role, however, was now that of general assistant.

The staff–management ratio was now 14 : 80.

Problems of communication and implementation

Stephen Cunningham was called into head office to be informed his store had been selected to pilot a new management structure that would strip away superfluous layers of management and make the remaining management staff accountable for specific areas of responsibility. A skeleton structure of the senior management team was outlined to him, but further details of the scheme were not available at that stage. For example, Stephen did not know how many controllers he would have, nor the job description of a controller or how it compared with the old structure. Head office were still completing the details, but anyway, it was not to take effect immediately. He was told that further details would be sent to him once they were finalised.

On returning to the store, Stephen called a meeting for his deputy manager, assistant store managers and department managers to brief them about the new structure. He told them all he knew, which was vague, as all job descriptions and accountabilities were to be devised at head office, but they understood that the new scheme would include just two tiers: a senior management team and controllers of general staff.

Talk of the new structure quickly filtered down to the general staff via the grapevine. Suddenly Stephen Cunningham was continually under pressure from the rest of his staff for further details about the changes and how it would affect their jobs. As he had no further information himself, he was unable to allay their fears. His staff found this very difficult to believe, causing them to become over suspicious of Stephen; this in turn fuelled further rumours and resentment. All this led to serious effects on the morale of the store staff. Everyone was worried about the future of their jobs. Even the general assistants were worried, as they wondered whether the new structure would mean redundancies at a general level.

Jonathan Wright, as deputy store manager, was confused about his new role as administrative manager. His new job description would not be available until nearer the implementation date, but he realised that his new store role would be a significant change. He enjoyed deputising for Stephen and saw it as good grounding for promotion to a store management position in the future. He perceived his new role as taking away the variety of functions of a deputy manager. At the same time, he understood that the new position would enable him to take control and be accountable for various operations. However, as the details were not finalised, he was also anxious about what the role would entail and whether he would be able to cope. His overall impression was that his new role would substantially downgrade his status. Instead of being 'the next in line' he would be one of a team of five, and where did that leave his chances of promotion?

The appointment of Katie Dixon in the new role of customer service manager also caused some resentment from the other members of staff. The rationale for creating this post was unclear to many staff. Although the emphasis was on customer care, the rest of the management team firmly believed this was the role of *all* staff, not just one person. Stephen Cunningham's and Jonathan Wright's previous roles meant that they had specific day-to-day responsibility to their customers, the importance of which they impressed upon all their staff through the company's mission. Stephen worried that the creation of this new post would impede a store approach to customer orientation.

Speculation was rife amongst departmental managers, assistant department managers and supervisors. As the number of controllers had yet to be finalised, these staff felt they were in open competition for fewer positions. Stephen found the departmental managers difficult to handle. They assumed Stephen knew more than he did about the new structure and generally did not believe him when he told them he had no further details. It took a long time before

Stephen regained his credibility with department managers. A job analysis for the position of controller was not complete, and assistant and department managers feared this would lead to their demotion. They perceived that their managerial status would be removed and feared that having fewer levels of control would be reflected in the salary structure of controllers. These rumours affected their work and commitment to the company. Previously, many departmental managers had worked very hard in their positions, often working perhaps a 45-hour week instead of the statutory 39 hours. With speculation about the new structure, many were no longer inclined to put in the extra hours and avoided planning future in-store events. Their general attitude to their work was 'do the bare minimum' and they felt they could no longer be proud of their position. Many spoke about taking voluntary redundancy if it were offered, because they could not cope with a loss of status.

The feeling among supervisors was mixed. Some were anxious they would become general assistants; others, including Matthew Currie, were hopeful of gaining a controller's position.

Morale of both management and the workforce was at an all-time low. Many managers complained they did not know where they stood in the new system, while the general staff were anxious for the future of their jobs. Intense speculation and uncertainty was evident throughout the store until further details were issued.

Further details of the scheme

The details of the new scheme were not made available to Stephen until a few weeks prior to implementation, which gave little time for him to consult all his staff and reassure them. In order not to foster any further rumours, and also because of time constraints, he held a mass meeting outlining the new structure (but not the rationale behind it). Posters outlining the new structure were also placed on departmental notice boards and in the rest rooms. During this time he and his senior management team had to interview all the prospective controllers, while also counselling and dealing with grievances from those assistant managers and supervisors not to be offered controller positions.

As the controller positions were similar to those of the old department managers, these staff adapted well to their new positions and many of their previous anxieties were alleviated, although they still perceived the role as a downgrading, owing to their change of title. The previous assistant department managers found the new role more difficult to adapt to as they had not received training in some areas (although on-the-job training was to be introduced). Their new management responsibilities, in addition to supervising general assistants, including training, appraisal, motivation, goal setting and communication as well as some detailed paperwork. Without training in specific areas, some controllers felt inadequate in their new roles, and lacked credibility. Some general staff found it difficult to accept these assistant departmental managers as controllers, while the controllers themselves experienced difficulties reporting directly to the senior management team.

As a result of the restructure, four assistant department managers and all six supervisors became general assistants. Although their previous salaries were protected, their morale was shattered. Matthew Currie felt particularly cheated. He had been keen to apply for a controller's position when he first heard about the new structure, but at the end of the day he was not even given the opportunity. His hopes were dashed when he heard that departmental managers would be selected for interview first. He officially heard about his relative position via a letter; Stephen had not spoken to him directly about it. All those in similar circumstances felt that a 'them and us' situation had developed within the store, that they had been given false hope and been kept in the dark too long before being told of their fate. This created conflict not only between these staff and the management, but also between the other general assistants: the sympathy they felt for their demoted colleagues causing a surge of resentment on their behalf. Some eventually left, unable to cope with the diminished responsibilities and status. Others, like Matthew, stayed but no longer felt committed to the company. Owing to the resultant conflict in the linen department, Matthew was eventually moved to menswear.

Six months after its introduction, things were beginning to settle down. With his senior management team taking accountability for various areas, Stephen was able to take a greater role in developing his management team. He was also able to think more strategically about the future of the store rather than be continually troubled with minor day-to-day operational problems. The senior management team and controllers were settling into their new roles. The general assistants were not overly affected by the change. If anything, the new structure had improved their communications with managers. Rigid departmental barriers had been broken down and they had more opportunity to change departments and learn more skills if they so desired. Nevertheless, morale had clearly been damaged, both prior to and during the implementation.

Stephen is now faced with drafting his management report to the board regarding the implementation of this new structure to all stores. What issues do you think he should highlight in his report? What recommendations could Stephen make to improve the process of introducing and implementing this new structure? Is it possible to introduce this new structure without demotivating staff?

Managing the Babyhouse

Alan Mitton
Manchester Metropolitan University

Context

Babyhouse Inc. is an international retailer of products for mothers and their babies. It has over 5,000 stores worldwide and sells a wide variety of products including maternity dresses, prams, buggies and pushchairs, nappies (diapers), cots, toys, footwear and baby clothes. It was founded 30 years ago when Mohammed Aziz, son of an Arab banker, bought Clark Stores. This ailing firm had 30 stores spread throughout the State of New York, selling mainly prams and pushchairs.

Growth and expansion

With the financial backing of his family, Aziz was quick to enlist outside help to revamp Clark Stores by extending its product range and breathing new life into its management. He changed the trading name to 'Babyhouse' and built up a new corporate image, offering everything for mother and her baby. All the stores became brighter and cleaner (almost clinical) and their merchandise was of good quality and well displayed. He also introduced a free catalogue which mothers or mothers-to-be could take home to help them choose their products.

The changes at Babyhouse worked well, although the ten-year baby boom which followed them would obviously have done little to hinder the company's remarkable success. Sales and profits soared. Soon Babyhouse expanded, both across the US and abroad (mainly into Europe).

The sell-out

At first, Aziz enjoyed the challenge of restoring an ailing company and all the buzz that surrounded the opening of new stores, especially those in foreign parts. However, he soon grew tired of all the problems that expansion brought him. He was continuously tied up in meetings to discuss problems, many of which he thought were trivial. These included bottlenecks in supply, faulty goods, distribution problems (goods dispatched to the wrong store), increasing competition, breakdowns with the computer and all the people problems (these drove him crazy – 'why can't they just get on with it?'). Facing potential divorce, enough was enough, and Aziz decided to quit and sell out while he was ahead.

Fortunately Aziz found a prospective buyer, a young man named Terry McLean, who had built up his own small chain of furniture discount stores in Britain, making the products himself. Terry was the 'talk' of the retail trades. He was frequently referred to as a self-made man with the 'magic touch'. While Terry was extremely interested in acquiring Babyhouse, unfortunately he could not afford to purchase it outright himself. Aziz helped him to borrow money to finance the acquisition. In fact, Aziz helped Terry to borrow much more money than Terry had imagined, or could afford.

The new era

Excited by the prospect of taking control of one of the world's leading retailers, Terry swiftly reorganised the management of Babyhouse. Unlike Aziz, who liked to do everything himself, Terry was a delegator: 'The only way to run a business is to get people to be responsible for their own affairs. Let them solve their own problems,' he said (and backed this up by introducing a share incentive scheme for all employees). He cut costs dramatically (mainly labour costs), built a new centralised distribution depot, bought a new centralised computer system and installed new electronic on-line tills in all the company's stores.

Although profit margins were maintained in the early years of Terry's reign, sales started to slide; so too did the share price of Babyhouse stock. Something needed to be done, and quickly. Having had a taste of acquisition, when he persuaded the directors of Babyhouse to buy his own company (FDS Ltd), Terry decided to pursue further growth by acquiring existing retailers. 'If we can't expand sales let's buy them!' he said.

Growth through acquisition

Over the next five years Babyhouse acquired many specialist retailers, both at home and abroad. Usually these were relatively small niche-market retailers in the women's clothing sector, but three years ago it also managed to gain control of one of Europe's leading department stores, Europa Home Furnishings. When Europa's share price was at an all-time low, Babyhouse managed to borrow yet even more money to make the acquisition. For Terry, this was the highlight of his career: 'You know they once refused to buy furniture from me when I started my own business. They wouldn't even give me an appointment with their buyer and now I own the company.'

The boardroom revolt

Despite the vast worldwide empire that Babyhouse controlled, all was not well. Sales were falling and the company was making substantial losses. Its share price plummeted. 'A carton of cream is more expensive than a share in Babyhouse,' one sales assistant grumbled to her friend on the shopfloor. 'Yes,' she replied, 'if you can afford to buy cream on the miserable wages they pay you here! Did you know we are not getting a pay increase this year? If they expect me to put more effort in, they have another think coming.'

The directors of Babyhouse were not happy either. It seemed that Terry was more interested in wheeling and dealing and living it up in the South of France than in attending to business. He frequently missed board meetings. 'The man's a maniac,' one director quietly whispered. 'The banks aren't too happy either,' commented another, 'they fear the company will default on its next repayment.' Dissatisfaction spread.

Before long Terry was ousted from the company and a new chairman, a director of its main banker, was appointed. This was followed by a senior management reshuffle and a large number of resignations at very senior levels.

More trouble in store

Changes were felt throughout the company; even the area and branch managers felt threatened, including the staff at branch 650.

Store 650 is one of the newest and largest of Babyhouse's mother and baby stores. Built in a prime retail location, it occupies three floors and comprises a stockroom, the main salesfloor (8,000 sq. ft) and a staffroom. It is staffed by a full-time manager, Ann Smalley, and nine part-timers (including two supervisors); but when it first opened six years ago there was a manager, an assistant manager, two departmental managers, a management trainee, two supervisors and 15 part-time members of staff. It was the show piece of the area.

At the moment, however, the store is well below its sales targets, as it has been for the last six months. Its poor financial performance has worsened still further by a high theft rate. Furthermore, staff are also kept extremely busy and their morale is very low.

Table 32.1 profiles each staff member, commenting upon their attitudes or behaviour at work. Figure 32.1 places each employee on an organisation chart. The results and criteria used during recent staff appraisals are summarised in Tables 32.2 and 32.3.

Ann, the store manager, has been with the company full-time since she left school. She is constantly telling staff to increase sales and to watch out for thieves. She worked as an assistant with Jane (now one of her supervisors) before being promoted two years ago to manager of branch 402 (2,500 sq. ft of selling space), 5 miles away in the next town. Ann was a highly ambitious and career-minded individual. She always had her mind set on becoming the manager of branch 650 and to help achieve this she had befriended both the

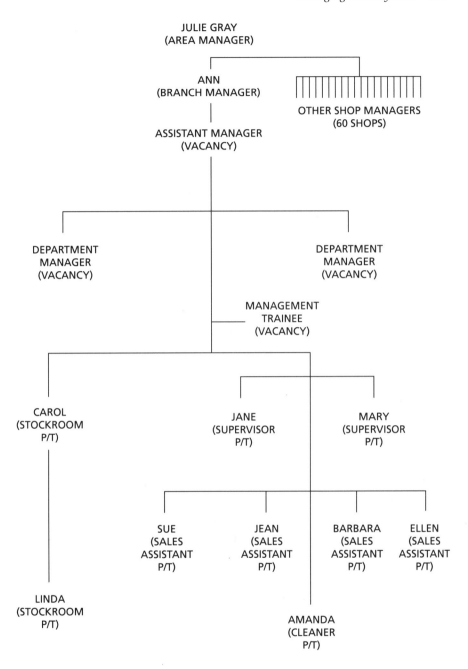

P/T = PART-TIME STAFF
(The above full-time positions have been vacant for over 2 years.)

Fig. 32.1 Organisational chart for branch 650, Babyhouse Inc.

Table 32.1 Staff profile at branch 650

Name	Position	Age	Years with company	Comments
Ann	Manager	28	12	Thinks she is doing better.
Jane	Supervisor (PT)	45	15	Feels she has to manage shop.
Mary	Supervisor (PT)	21	4	Plays up to Jane and Ann.
Sue	Sales Assistant	28	8	Likes talking to Ann.
Carol	Stockroom	45	12	Plays the system.
Linda	Stockroom	34	6	Ignores what's going on around.
Jean	Sales Assistant	17	0	Not all that interested.
Amanda	Cleaner	46	10	What a way to run a shop!
Barbara	Sales Assistant	19	2	Likes being on the till.
Ellen	Sales Assistant	23	1	Looking for another job.

area manager, Julie Gray, and the previous store manager.

Jane, formerly an office manager for a finance company (before having children), had looked forward to Ann's return as store manager but now sometimes wonders why. They had worked well together when they were both assistants, but now Jane complains that Ann:

- frequently tells you to do one thing, then either forgets about it, or tells you to do the opposite later;
- starts a job but never finishes it;
- is always going to meetings and leaving me in charge;

Table 32.2 Staff appraisals (branch 650)

Characteristics	Jane	Mary	Sue	Carol	Linda	Jean	Amanda	Barbara	Ellen
Self-control	A	A	A	A	B	C	A	C	C
Leadership	A	B	C	A	C	C	A	C	C
Attitude	A	B	C	A	C	C	A	B	C
Communication	B	B	B	B	C	C	C	B	C
Knowledge	B	B	B	C	A	C	C	C	C
Reliability	A	A	C	B	A	A	A	B	C
Organisation	B	B	C	B	C	C	B	C	C
Appearance	A	A	A	A	B	A	A	C	C
Responsibility	A	B	C	B	C	C	B	C	C

Note: See Table 32.3 for index to appraisal grades.

Table 32.3 Index to appraisal grades

Characteristics	Grade	Standard attained
Self-control		
Is full self-control maintained	A	Full control in all situations
In all situations?	B	Good control in most situations
Leadership		
Are leadership qualities displayed?	A	Outstanding leader, inspires confidence
	B	Some good leadership qualities
Attitude		
Are they enthusiastic/tactful with	A	Co-operative, enthusiastic, tactful
customers/colleagues?	B	Conscientious, pleasant manner
Communication		
Can they communicate well and	A	Highly articulate
convincingly?	B	Good powers of expression
Knowledge		
Have they a good knowledge of the	A	Excellent knowledge
merchandise and procedures?	B	Good knowledge
Reliability		
Are they reliable and efficient?	A	Very efficient and reliable
	B	Generally reliable and efficient
Organisation		
Have they the capacity to organise	A	Excellent organiser and trainer
and supervise?	B	Good organising ability
Appearance		
Are they neat and tidy and dressed	A	Excellent/well groomed
appropriately?	B	Favourable appearance
Responsibility		
Are they willing and able to accept	A	Accepts responsibility readily
responsibility?	B	Willing to accept responsibility

Note: Grade 'C' means 'below standard'.

- is completely disorganised and has little knowledge of the company's products and procedures;
- keeps disappearing upstairs to do 'her paperwork' (but it doesn't always get done);
- never backs me up when dealing firmly with the staff;
- never does anything about the shop being considerably understaffed; and
- spends all her time trying to look glamorous and keeps you back late at night (so her tea will be made when she gets home).

'You would be mad to accept a manager's job at Babyhouse!', said Jane. 'Being a part-time supervisor is bad enough. I like the work but I'm exhausted at the end of the day. I need at least two days off per week to recover.'

Mary, the other supervisor, like Jane was a part-time assistant when she joined the company. Mary has been trying to become a full-time supervisor even though she does like having days off during the week. She was trained by Jane and confides in her regularly; the pair work well together as a team when Ann is absent, although it must be said that none of them like going to meetings.

Sue used to be a full-time supervisor at the branch but left to have a baby. Her job was then split between Jane and Mary, thus creating two new supervisors, each working 20 hours per week plus overtime as required. She returned to the store later as a part-time sales assistant (working mainly on Saturdays), where she now has to take orders from Jane and Mary, which she does, albeit reluctantly.

Case study questions

1. *What demands has the expansion of Babyhouse placed on its managers and employees and how do you think they have reacted to them?*

2. *To what extent do you think the demise of Babyhouse has been responsible for low staff morale and motivation?*

3. *Ann realises that she has not been prepared well for the job of management. Despite the fact that she thinks she is doing well, in reality she is drowning. If it wasn't for Jane and Mary she knows that she could not continue. What advice can you give Ann to help her to become a better manager?*

4. *Ann is under constant pressure from Julie Gray to increase sales. She expects an increase of at least 25 per cent on last year's sales performance. Her own job is on the line. How can Ann increase sales? Incidentally, the person who took over from her as store manager in branch 402 (her former assistant manager) has just trebled sales, winning a holiday to Bermuda and a new car for her troubles!*

5. *How can the theft problem be resolved? (Apart from electronic tags there are no other security devices in the store.)*

6. *The personnel manager for Babyhouse Inc. wishes to change the staff appraisal scheme to provide management with a more informative picture of their staff so that they can better assess staff development and performance. Also, she recognises a need to relate appraisal to motivation and performance. As an outside consultant to the company you are asked to prepare a report to the personnel manager showing her how she should proceed.*

Index